Comparative Government–Industry Relations

GOVERNMENT–INDUSTRY RELATIONS

Volumes within this series incorporate original research into contemporary policy issues and policy-making processes in the UK, Western Europe, the United States, and South-East Asia.

Comparative
Government–Industry
Relations

Western Europe, the
United States, and Japan

EDITED BY

Stephen Wilks and Maurice Wright

CLARENDON PRESS · OXFORD

Oxford University Press, Walton Street, Oxford OX2 6DP
Oxford New York Toronto
Delhi Bombay Calcutta Madras Karachi
Petaling Jaya Singapore Hong Kong Tokyo
Nairobi Dar es Salaam Cape Town
Melbourne Auckland
and associated companies in
Berlin Ibadan

Oxford is a trade mark of Oxford University Press

Published in the United States
by Oxford University Press, New York

First published 1987
Reprinted 1989

British Library Cataloguing in Publication Data
Comparative government-industry relations:
Western Europe, United States and Japan.—
(Government industry relations; 1)
1. Industry and state
I. Wilks, S. R. M.   II. Wright, Maurice
III. Series
338.9   HD3611
ISBN 0–19–827493–9

Library of Congress Cataloging in Publication Data
Comparative government-industry relations.
1. Industry and state—Europe.   2. Industry and state—
United States.   3. Industry and state—Japan.
1. Wilks, Stephen.   II. Wright, Maurice.
HD3611.C63 1987   338.9   86-28631
ISBN 0–19–827493–9

Set by Colset Private Limited, Singapore
Printed and bound in
Great Britain by Biddles Ltd,
Guildford and King's Lynn

Preface

This volume is the first in a series of books and monographs to be published under the imprint of the Oxford University Press which will explore the relationships between government and industry in the United Kingdom and other major western industrialized countries. The series will include the work of scholars commissioned by the Economic and Social Research Council under its research programme on Government–Industry Relations, and also that of others working independently of that initiative both in the UK and abroad.

The intention of this first introductory volume is to collect a number of specially commissioned studies which reflect the current 'state of the art', but which at the same time comprise an internally coherent account of some important aspects of government–industry relations in the major OECD countries. It can be read at one or more of three levels. First, it can be taken as an exercise in comparative political economy which undertakes original and authoritative examination of specific aspects of industrial politics in West Germany, France, the UK, the USA, and Japan. The attention given to Anglo-German comparison is especially thorough and distinctive. Secondly, it can be read by a more specialist audience as a point of departure. It seeks to incorporate the most recent research on, and analysis of, government–industry relations, and can be regarded as a stock-taking of empirical and comparative approaches centred broadly on political science concerns. Thirdly, however, the inquiring researcher can find in the following chapters many implicit and explicit signposts for future research. For instance, the sectoral approach, the level of disaggregation, the ordering of empirical material, the original industry studies, and the attempts to apply and develop organizational and 'power-dependence' analytic approaches all provide pointers as to how research may (or may not) be fruitfully pursued. But, although the collection presents research findings, and suggests areas for future work, it might be more widely read as an accessible, free-standing review of countries, policies, and industries in a comparative context.

The mills of research initiatives, even highly proactive research initiatives, grind slowly and this volume appears exactly a decade after the appointment of an Exploratory Panel by the (then) SSRC Political Science and International Relations Committee with a brief to advise on research priorities in the field of central government. With a reassuring degree of prescience that Panel and a succeeding Working Party concluded that government–industry relations was an area of great importance, that it was under-researched, was researchable, and should be researched. That conclusion has, in our judgement, been amply justified, for reasons which we explore in the Introductory chapter.

The purpose of the ESRC's research initiative is to stimulate research in the field of government and industry relations so as to develop a better understanding of those relationships, and to contribute to the development of more rigorous theory. At the same time it is intended that the research will have practical benefits to practitioners in government and industry. The process of stimulation is now well advanced. As more ESRC research teams enter the field in the second part of the initiative, it is encouraging to note the increasing academic activity and interest displayed by scholars in the UK and other countries in the issues of government–industry relations. The progress of the initative is being followed closely in the US, Canada, and Australia, while several scholars from France and West Germany have been involved in different ways with the research of the contributors to this volume. In Japan a multi-disciplinary team of distinguished academics has been assembled to commission and supervise research complementary to the ESRC programme. Phase I of the research initiative began in the autumn of 1984 and was concerned with Anglo-German and Anglo-French comparative work. Phase II got underway in autumn 1986 and extended the comparison to Japan and the United States. Five of the chapters in this collection are based on work undertaken by research teams funded in the first phase. The other five chapters, written by distinguished authorities, reflect the concerns of Phase II, and provide a contemporary review of the countries and sectors on which research has just started.

The editors have been involved in this initiative from its inception: Maurice Wright as Chairman and Stephen Wilks as Research Co-ordinator of the managing ESRC Sub-Committee. It is unusual to express more than token thanks to the ESRC and its committees, but in this instance we have been extremely fortunate in our colleagues on the Government–Industry Relations Sub-Committee (and on our parent committee, Government and Law) who have provided interest, support, insight, and a much appreciated reliability. Our Secretary, Dr Tony Bruce, has in like fashion gone to unexpectedly generous lengths to provide material and administrative support. We would like to record our appreciation. A more formal acknowledgement is due to the ESRC for its generous support of a residential conference held at Trinity Hall, Cambridge, in December 1985. The conference provided an occasion for presenting papers by the contributors to this book, and, to our surprise and gratification, did what conferences should do but seldom achieve: the discussion and debate was sustained, extraordinarily constructive, and genuinely stimulating. We should also, therefore, thank our distinguished invited audience whose critical but sympathetic probing and reflections have helped translate the original papers into substantially improved chapters. Although it is a little unfair to pick out individuals, we are particularly grateful to overseas guests, including Gerd Junne of the University of Amsterdam and Michael Kreile of the Universtiy of Konstanz; to the industrialists, especially Sir Kenneth Corfield, Peter Cunliffe, Sir Arthur Knight, and Glyn England; to Civil Servants including John Barber and Tim Walker; and to academics, namely, Jack Hayward, Ronald Dore, Doug Pitt, Vincent Wright, Bob Bennett, and Dan Jones. In addition, of course, we are immensely grateful to our contributors who have patiently tolerated and responded to our requests for additions and revision with an impressive degree of professionalism. Finally, our thanks go to Jean Parry whose organizational and typing skills proved invaluable.

SW and MW
Liverpool and Manchester
May 1986

Contents

——————— *Notes on Contributors* ———————

COLIN APPLEBY is Principal Lecturer in Economics at Wolverhampton Polytechnic. He has recently spent two years on secondment to the Economic Development Unit of the West Midlands County Council. He researches and has published on issues of industrial restructuring.

JOHN BESSANT is Principal Lecturer (Research) at Brighton Polytechnic. He is qualified as a chemical engineer and his recent work has been concerned with innovation and microelectronics. His publications include, *Management and Manufacturing Innovation in W Germany and the UK*, with M. Grunt, (Anglo-German Foundation, 1986) and *Microelectronics and the Global Distribution of Income*, with H. Cole, (Frances Pinter, 1986).

RICHARD BOYD lectures in Far Eastern Politics at the School of Oriental and African Studies, University of London. He is working on a comparative study of the politics of the shipbuilding and steel industries in Japan and the UK. Previous research has been concerned with Japanese opposition parties and his book on the Japanese Communist Party is forthcoming from Cambridge University Press.

ALAN CAWSON lectures in Politics in the School of Social Sciences, University of Sussex. He is the author of *Corporatism and Welfare* (Heinemann, 1982), the editor of *Organised Interests and the State* (Sage, 1985), and has recently completed a book on corporatism and political theory.

WYN GRANT is Senior Lecturer in Politics at Warwick University where he specializes in the study of government–industry relations and economic and industrial policy. He is the author of *The Political Economy of Industrial Policy* (Butterworths, 1982), co-author, with D. Marsh, of *The CBI* (Hodder & Stoughton, 1977) and, with S. Nath, of *The Politics of Economic Policymaking* (Basil Blackwell, 1984), and the editor of *The Political Economy of Corporatism* (Macmillan, 1985).

KLAUS GREWLICH qualified as a lawyer and is Head of Division in the Planning Staff of the Foreign Office of the Federal Republic of Germany, Bonn. He has worked in the European Space Administration, in the cabinet of the OECD Secretary General, Paris, and at the European Commission, Brussels.

LEIGH HANCHER lectures in Law at the University of Warwick. She was Research Fellow at the European University Institute, Florence, from 1979–81. Her publications include, with T. Daintith, *Energy Strategy in Europe: The Legal Framework* (de Gruyter, 1986).

PETER HOLMES is Lecturer in Economics in the School of Social Sciences, University of Sussex. He is a specialist in French Economic Planning and has published, with S. Estrin, *French Planning in Theory and Practice* (Allen & Unwin, 1983).

MANLEY IRWIN is Professor of Economics at the Whittemore School of Business and Economics, University of New Hampshire. He has specialized in government regulation of business and industry and has acted as consultant to the US and Canadian Governments. His many publications in this field include *Telecommunications America: Markets Without Boundaries* (Greenwood, 1985).

KEITH MACMILLAN is Professor of Management Studies at Henley—The Management College. His books include *Business and Society* (Pelican, 1974) *Top Management* (Longmans, 1973) and *Education Welfare: Strategy and Structure* (Longmans, 1977). He is Editor of the *Journal of General Management* and has acted as consultant to international companies, the European Commission, and the Canadian Government.

WILLIAM PATERSON is Reader in Politics at Warwick University where he specializes in the study of politics and policy-making in the Federal Republic of Germany. His recent publications include *The West German Model* (Frank Cass, 1981) co-edited with G. Smith, and *The Future of Social Democracy* (OUP, 1986) co-edited with A. Thomas. He is co-author, with S. Bulmer, of *The Federal Republic and the European Community* (Allen & Unwin, 1986).

MATTHIAS RUETE was until recently visiting lecturer in German Law at the University of Warwick. He is currently working as a legal expert in the Health and Safety Division of the European Communities in Luxembourg.

ANNE STEVENS lectures in Politics in the School of Social Sciences, University of Sussex. She specializes in French politics and has researched and published on the French Bureaucracy and economic policy-making.

IAN TURNER is Research Fellow at Henley—The Management College. He has undertaken research in Britain and West Germany on the immediate post-war period and particularly on the history of the

Volkswagen works. He is currently engaged on research into government–industry relations in the pharmaceutical industry.

DAVID VOGEL is Professor of Business Administration at the University of California, Berkeley, where he specializes in business–government relations. He is the co-author of *Ethics and Profits: The Crisis of Confidence in American Business* (Simon & Schuster, 1976) and author of *Lobbying the Corporation: Citizen Challenges to Business Authority* (Basic Books, 1978) and *National Styles of Regulation: Environmental Policy in Great Britain and the United States* (Cornell UP, 1986). Since 1982 he has been Editor of the *California Management Review*.

TAKASHI WAKIYAMA is Professor and Director of the International Programme at the Graduate School for Policy Science, University of Saitama, Tokyo. He teaches and researches on the industrial and trade policy of Japan. Since March 1984 he has been on secondment from the Ministry of International Trade and Industry where he has worked as Head of the International Trade Research Division and of the Household Goods Division, and as Director-General of the General Affairs Department of MITI's Sapporo Office.

COLIN WHITSTON worked in industry before taking a degree at Ruskin College, Oxford. He has worked as Research Fellow in the Department of Politics, University of Warwick and is currently Research Fellow at the Warwick Industrial Relations Research Unit. He is conducting research into employee discipline and involvement and into trade unions and economic planning.

STEPHEN WILKS is Senior Lecturer in the Department of Political Theory and Institutions, University of Liverpool. He has researched on issues of industrial policy and industrial politics. His publications include *Industrial Policy and the Motor Industry* (Manchester UP, 1984) and, co-edited with K. Dyson, *Industrial Crisis* (Martin Robertson, 1983). He is a member of the ESRC's Government–Industry Relations Sub-Committee and is the Research Co-ordinator of the Committee.

MAURICE WRIGHT is Professor of Government at the University of Manchester. He is a specialist in the politics and administration of public expenditure, and his recent publications include *Public Spending Decisions* (Martin Robertson, 1980), which he edited, and *Big Government in Hard Times* (Martin Robertson, 1981), co-edited with C. Hood. He has taught, researched, and published on government and industry over many years, and is the Chairman of the ESRC's Government–Industry Relations Sub-Committee.

1

Introduction

Stephen Wilks and Maurice Wright

Government–Industry Relations is a subject much discussed and little investigated. It is also a very broad subject. The formulation 'government–industry relations' is generic and neutral in its connotations. This is quite deliberate. We are concerned with the whole range of interactions between the government, in its many manifestations, on the one hand, and industry, in all its complexity, on the other. Some aspects of the relationship may be hugely controversial and politically explosive: they may bring down governments and cause cabinet ministers to resign. Other aspects, such as government regulation of working conditions in shops and factories, may appear relatively trivial.

Perhaps the unifying theme underlying all study of government and industry in capitalist economies is an awareness of the ever-present tension between the two 'sides'. Easton's classic definition of politics as 'the authoritative allocation of values for a society'[1] can be contrasted with the logic of industry which represents 'the profitable allocation of values for a society'. If government is about 'who gets what, when and how'[2] so also is industry. But the distribution of benefits within society produced by the unrestricted operation of industry is unlikely to square with the choices selected by any given government. While industry is ruled by the logic of the market, government is ruled by the logic of the (democratic) political process.

Part of the fascination and the purpose of studying comparative GIR is to identify how different societies, at different times, evolve mechanisms to relieve tension and reach compromises. More germane still is the way in which societies appear to have identified and emphasized policy areas and issues in which the interests of government and those of industry coincide. Societies which have ostensibly managed to achieve increased investment, productivity, and growth, without squandering human and environmental resources, appear to have developed formulae and processes whose study is irresistible. The contrast is particularly acute for a British audience whose first reaction to government–industry relations is to anticipate a disaster area, and who are regularly exposed to instances where the interests of government and those of industry either collide, or exist in separate, unrelated, universes.

A broad dissatisfaction with the relations between government and industry has been a feature of British political economy for at least twenty-five years. Virtually every important facet of the relationship, from company financing and export credits to public ownership and public purchasing, has been the subject of commentary and criticism. There is by now a substantial body of literature on industrial problems[3] which more recently has focused on the question of industrial decline.[4] There have been many parliamentary and official reports, and numerous evaluations from leading industrialists and politicians.[5] It is our contention that within this literature there is only a very modest basis of consistent, sustained empirical research for many of the assertions and conclusions. This applies, it must be said, from the perspective of political science rather than economics. In seeking to understand and evolve theories to explain the mechanisms and outcomes of exchanges between government and industry, we are operating within a context of substantial ignorance. This may sound a surprising assertion but, with one or two notable exceptions, much of the writing on British government–industry relations is either intensely specialized or tremendously generalized. We have, for instance, no usable analysis of most of the key governmental actors. There is no book on the Department of Trade and Industry or the other major economic and industrial ministries,[6] while government agencies and business and union institutions have been very sketchily dealt with. The dissatisfaction with the present literature, and the research effort which underlies it, has been a driving force behind the ESRC research initiative. The direction of that initiative and the thrust of this book are discussed further below.

If dissatisfaction with the government–industry relationship has become congenital in Britain it has certainly been powerfully fuelled by foreign example. In the sixties the French model of indicative planning was, of course, extremely influential, while the experience of Italian public enterprise inspired a section of opinion in the Labour party. More recently, West Germany, the United States, and Japan (in roughly that order) have been held out as promising examples of how British institutions, processes, and goals might be adapted. Again, however, our understanding of how government–industry relations *really* works in France,

West Germany, and the USA is very patchy, while our general understanding of Japan is almost certainly still at the stage of caricature. In
extensive discussions held with industrialists and officials in 1979–80, on
behalf of the ESRC, there was an overwhelming expression of interest in
West Germany and Japan.[7] What might have been seen as desirable at the
end of the seventies has become essential in the second half of the
eighties. Our academic appreciation of the institutional basis and governmental contribution to Japanese industrial success is, again with some
honourable exceptions, dismally lacking.[8]

It would, of course, be interesting in its own right to know more about
individual countries, but if research on government–industry relations is
to be of any potential use to British policy or practitioner interests it must
be comparative. Only by systematically indentifying the ways in which
government–industry relations overseas differ from the UK practice, and
by advancing explanations for those differences, will any convincing or
useful lessons be extracted. But if comparison is a necessity it is also an
advantage. Rigorous, empirically based comparison can be an immensely
productive research method. It is also very demanding and very expensive. About half the chapters in this volume are internally comparative
including all the chapters that deal with Britain. We regard this as an
unusual and outstanding strength and one reason for this volume's claim
to originality.

The Subject-Matter of Government–Industry Relations

The subject-matter of government and industry is only partly described
by the term 'industrial policy'. With its connotation of industrial adaptation, it is too narrow, and as a 'summary term for the activities of government that are intended to develop or retrench various industries', it is
both tendentious and politically controversial.[9] There are, in practice, a
wide range of public policies—economic, social, and physical, as well as
industrial—which are intended by governments to affect in some way the
activities of those who own, finance, manage, and work in firms,
companies, and corporations. Such policies are concerned not just with
'development' and 'retrenchment', but also with location, product,
technology, market behaviour, health and safety, environmental protection, and so on. There are, of course, also the unintended or unwanted
consequences for industry of the impact of other public policies.

As a subject of academic inquiry, government and industry is not prescribed by tightly drawn boundaries. It crosses and recrosses the intellectual thresholds of several social science disciplines. The focus adopted in this book is, however, a distinctive one, reflecting a concern to explore questions which are central to political science, questions about the distribution and use of power, political control, and public accountability. Such questions have less immediacy for the economist, the sociologist, the lawyer, or the historian. But, as will be evident in the chapters that follow, these and other disciplines, with their own perspectives, modes of analysis, and paradigms, have a substantial contribution to make to an understanding of the complexity of the relationships between government and industry.

At the simplest level, the study of government and industry is concerned with the description of public and private organizations, their functions, personnel, and resources. Such an 'organizational map' is a necessary prerequisite for the more challenging task of analysing the relationships between those organizations; or, more strictly, between the key players within them. What do these organizations do? How do they do it and what are the physical and intellectual resources available to them? How do they relate to each other?

Relationships between government and industry are many, varied, and complex, and are conducted at different geographical and organizational levels. Those who contribute to these relationships are drawn from a wide range of governmental and quasi-governmental institutions and agencies; from individual firms, companies, and corporations, local, national, and transnational; some wholly private, some publicly owned, some neither clearly one nor the other. They are drawn also from associations representing the interests of groups of employers, employees, and consumers.

The relationships between key players are purposeful. They are established, sustained, displaced, and terminated to achieve for the players and groups concerned advantages consistent with their short- or long-term aims and objectives, and sometimes to deny to others similar advantages or benefits. Issues of public policy which are perceived by the key players to affect their interests provoke relationships. In seeking to influence the outcomes to those issues, key players interact. These interactions or linkages are the principal focus of the study of government and industry in the ESRC research initiative.[10] It aims to describe and explain what they are; how they have evolved, are maintained and change over time, are affected by dominant political, social, and economic cultures, and how they respond to changes in political ideology.

The relationships are relationships of mutual but asymmetric dependence. Each player's room for 'decisional manœuvre' on an issue is constrained by the material and intellectual resources available to him, appropriate to that issue and which he is prepared to use, and by those possessed by other players, who may perceive their own interests differently. Resources of money, legislative authority, information, and so on, are not equally distributed between the players, and the distribution may change over time. In their interactions—the process of exchanging resources— the players accept and normally observe both formal and informal 'rules of the game' which govern their conduct towards each other. These rules, too, may change over time by agreement between the players, or by the action of one or more actors with overwhelming resources. For example, central or state governments with a monopoly of legislative authority (resources) may act unilaterally to structure or restructure the rules governing the relationships.

Relationships take many different forms: between a firm and a part of a government agency; between a group of firms or a representative association and one or several different government agencies; between different groups of representative associations, individual firms, several government agencies, and so on. The structures of these relationships also vary: some are institutionalized, for example; some are formal arrangements but uninstitutionalized; others are informal and loosely structured. The precise form of the structure will be affected by such factors as the size, structure, and history of an individual industrial sector or sub-sector; by the type of product and market-characteristics; the strength and organization of representative groups; the political salience of the policy area or issue.

Structures may change over time; they also vary according to the type and saliency of the issue or event dealt with. Where such relationships are established and maintained for a discrete policy area, they may exhibit the characteristics of policy communities or networks of communication and influence similar to those which have been identified in other policy areas, such as education, housing, and health. In a policy area as large and as differentiated as 'industry', relations between government and industry are not conducted in one policy community or a single network of communication and influence, but several. Those communities or networks have different structures of relationships, characteristics, and personnel; their 'agendas' differ; and the political processes by which they interact also vary.

Not only are sectors and sub-sectors likely to differ: issues or problems common to two or more countries are likely to produce different structures of dependent relations. We discuss interdependence in the context of policy communities and networks at greater length in the concluding chapter.

Outline of the Book

The chapters in this book take broadly two approaches to the analysis and comparison of government–industry relations. First, there is the conventional approach of delineating national characteristics, including attitudes, strategies, policies, and consistencies in government–industry relations, so that national 'styles' can be compared. Clearly, this is the logical point of departure, both to bring a basic framework to the attention of a student or non-specialist audience, and to present some widely accepted generalizations to be confirmed or rejected by further study. Thus the first four chapters of the book present 'country studies' of, respectively, France, West Germany, Japan, and the United States. But the chapters on France, by Cawson, Holmes, and Stevens, and on West Germany, by Grant, Paterson, and Whitston, are, in fact, more ambitious and complex than simply country studies. They combine elements of national overview, empirical analysis of specific industries, and comparison with the UK. The chapters on Japan, by Boyd, and the United States, by Vogel, were written more intentionally as 'overviews' to present an up-to-date assessment of those countries to make wide comparison possible.

The following six chapters present, in the main, studies of industrial sectors. Again, the sectoral approach is fairly conventional and was selected by researchers and the editors as the best accessible way in which to 'cut into' the complexity of GIR and to begin to make comparison *within* as well as *between* countries. In some respects, the selection of industrial sectors is, in itself, unimportant. In terms of the overall undertaking, the important concern is to study government–industry relations in practice and in detail. This can be done in almost any industrial sector. Nevertheless, there is some deliberate degree of consistency in the choice of sector which allows comparison between sectors in one country and between countries in one sector. Hence we have concentrated on telecommunications in France (Chapter 2), in the USA (Chapter 10), and from a macro-European perspective (Chapter 11). There are similarly three chapters on chemicals and pharmaceuticals in Britain and West Germany

(Chapters 3, 6, 7). In addition, there is a study of a 'declining' sector in Chapter 8, which deals with the crisis-ridden foundries industry. The sectoral studies do not attempt to offer a comprehensive review of government–industry relations in each sector. For the highly disaggregated and detailed examination involved in useful empirical study that would be impractical. Indeed, the very concept of industrial 'sector' is a contested unit of analysis and, as outlined above, we could expect to find several policy networks within any one sector. The chapters thus take up the detail of issues, policies, or instruments, to derive and substantiate their analysis. Chapter 6, by Macmillan and Turner, considers the issue of cost-containment in pharmaceuticals and unravels the complex relationships involved in the introduction in Britain of the 'limited list', and the inactivity of German government faced with similar problems. The complementary analysis of pharmaceuticals in Chapter 7, by Hancher and Ruete, compares experience by reference to 'legal culture' rather than policy issues. In a distinctive combination of legal and organizational perspectives they take up the under-researched question of how different legal traditions affect the agenda, processes, and perhaps outcomes, of government–industry relations. In Chapter 8, Appleby and Bessant analyse a depressed sector which at first sight confirms diagnosis of British organizational failure and German organizational efficacy. They document the inability to mobilize government and industry in Britain to facilitate restructuring but they also reveal a capacity for initiative in the UK which is far less apparent in West Germany where the foundries industry tends to be ignored. Chapter 9 provides a provocative contrast to the preceding chapters by analysing one of the most remarked, apparently most effective, but also most mysterious of policy processes: the use of 'administrative guidance' in Japan. Wakiyama, a MITI official experienced as a practitioner of administrative guidance (writing in his private capacity), dispels some of the mystery, although European Civil Servants might still be taken aback by such an obvious method of pragmatically securing joint interests. Chapters 10 and 11 offer a decided contrast both with the empirical analysis of French telecommunications in Chapter 2 and with one another. Grewlich's discussion of European issues in telecommunications presents an important reminder that government–industry relations are not an exclusively national phenomenon and he argues the case for governmental initatives at the European level (again, writing in his private capacity). The reverse, free market, case is presented by Irwin's racy analysis of American telecommunications deregulation. The fascination of Irwin's discussion lies in the fluidity of traditional relationships and regulatory regimes. He demonstrates the rapidity with which the policy agenda of government–industry relations can change. The fundamentalist, liberal ideology that lies behind privatization was barely a whisper ten years ago, but has become a central part of the policy debate. Questions of regulation, deregulation, and re-regulation are now centre stage.

The concluding chapter does not attempt a systematic comparison, although it does draw out a number of significant points and arguments from earlier chapters. It concentrates on theoretical approaches to comparative analysis, emphasizes the importance of moving from national to sub-sector comparison, and offers some suggestions as to how that demanding task might be undertaken.

Notes

1. D. Easton, *A Framework for Political Analysis* (Eaglewood Cliffs, NJ: Prentice Hall, 1965).
2. H. Lasswell, *Politics: Who Gets What, When, How* (New York: Meridian, 1958).
3. For summaries and evaluations see D. Steel, 'Review Article: Government and Industry in Britain', *British Journal of Political Science*, 12 (1983), pp. 449–503; S. Young, *An Annotated Bibliography on Relations between Government and Industry in Britain 1960-82*, 2 vols. (London: ESRC, 1984).
4. See, for instance, S. Wilks, *Industrial Policy and the Motor Industry* (Manchester University Press, 1984), Ch. 1; D. Coates and J. Hillard (eds.), *The Economic Decline of Modern Britain* (Brighton: Wheatsheaf, 1986).
5. Particularly noteworthy, for its Report, for the range of evidence submitted, and for its impact is, House of Lords Select Committee on Overseas Trade, *Volume I—Report*; *Volume II—Oral Evidence*; *Volume III—Written Evidence*, 1268 pp. (London: HMSO, 1985).
6. With the exception of the Treasury, where the study by H. Heclo and A. Wildavsky, *The Private Government of Public Money*, 2nd edn. (London: Macmillan, 1981), illustrates the untapped potential.
7. See Report of an SSRC Working Party to the Research Board, Government and Industry Relations (SSRC, mimeo, 1981), Appendix II, 'Consultations with Practitioners'.
8. The major exception is the work of Ronald Dore, whose most recent publications include: *Flexible Rigidities: Structural Adjustment in Japan: 1970-1982* (London: Athlone, 1986); *Taking Japan Seriously: The British Economy in Confucian Perspective* (London: Athlone, 1986).

9. C. Johnson (ed.), *The Industrial Policy Debate* (San Francisco: Institute for Contemporary Studies, 1984), p. 7.

10. For an elaboration of the interorganizational, 'power-dependence' approach to analysing relationships, which provided an initial theoretical perspective for the projects funded under the initiative, see R. A. W. Rhodes, ' "Power Dependence". Theories of Central–Local Relations: a critical reassessment' in M. Goldsmith (ed.), *New Research in Central–Local Relations* (Aldershot: Gower, 1986) and the concluding chapter of this book.

2

The Interaction between Firms and the State in France: The Telecommunications and Consumer Electronics Sectors

Alan Cawson, Peter Holmes, and Anne Stevens

If we want to retain our identity as Frenchmen, in the context of Europe, of course, the state really must intervene. There comes a point when the state must take risks so that on the vast world economic scene, Frenchmen can get a small piece of the action.

Jacques Dondoux, Direction Générale des Télécommunications,
March 1986[1]

The French State and the French Economy

French government–industry relations operate within the context of a historical background that takes for granted a close relationship between government and industry, that accepts that the state should articulate historical priorities and expects that such priorities will continue to maintain an almost 'mercantilist' concern with French economic interests. Many French academic commentators and serving officials subscribe to a concept of the state as an enduring structure or system which gives order and sense to what would otherwise be societal chaos. They hold that the government of the day may make use of the state to implement its policies, and certainly may point it in a certain direction, but in the end the state should resist total domination by what may prove to be a transitory and partial regime and act in the interests of an ordered, permanent, general good.

Those who are influenced by this approach—and it is widespread amongst officials and probably also influences others who have passed through the same educational institutions—take it for granted that the state should act, not react. This notion also involves the idea that a common good is perceptible, and that if its pursuit involves making distinctions, discriminating, picking winners, then that is a necessary characteristic of the state. In France, at least since 1945, the state has been expected to play a major strategic role within society.

The rhetoric and ideology attached to the role of the state provides a vocabulary, a set of myths, and legitimizes the forms that the state's action takes. It does *not*, however, guarantee state dominance. The state is subject to many and varied constraints some of which are discussed below. Nor does a perception of the general interest really provide much guidance as to where, or indeed whether, to site a motorway or a nuclear power station. What the state actually does is far more likely to be what is politically prudent and achievable rather than what might by some abstract criterion be seen as desirable.[2]

The Main Actors in the System

In this section we analyse the range of actors involved in government–industry relations at the national level. It would be misleading to refer to the existence of a national 'industrial policy community' because, as we shall argue below, one of the main characteristics of the system is its fragmentation, often into a series of bilateral relationships between state agencies and firms. A single firm might deal with several state agencies with varying degrees of autonomy, and the relationship between the agencies might be marked by conflicting mandates and disputed hierarchies. There is no *single* government–industry relationship in France, but many.[3]

This observation should caution us against the view that the state is characterized by some kind of 'essential unity' such as is alleged in some Marxist theories which posit a role for 'the state' as instrument of class domination or guarantor of the accumulation process. We cannot speak of the state as *an* actor, and must recognize the role played by different kinds of actors within the state system. Unpacking what is meant by 'the state' involves examining its internal structure, as well as its external relationships with social groups, interest organizations, and firms. A disaggregated view, as afforded by sectoral analysis, can serve as a valuable corrective to the tendency to assume coherence between different parts of the state by derivation from an ideology of the role of the state as organizer and intervener in civil society.

The governmental side of relationships between government and industry is handled by a plethora of different actors. At various times both President and Prime Minister may be involved. In recent years, on the whole, the Prime Minister has overseen government–industry relations on a day-to-day basis, but the President has intervened decisively from time to time. For the period from 1958 to March 1986, when the President was supported by a majority in Parliament, it is important not to underestimate his potential power. For example, heads of nationalized companies were appointed in the Council of Ministers, which effectively meant by the President, for he chairs its meetings at which policy is reported and approved, presidential decisions are promulgated, and senior appointments announced and approved. The heads of nationalized industries thus tended to see themselves as responsible to the President and no one else, and go directly to him over major or sensitive matters. This meant that important decisions could be made in ways which involved only the President, the heads of the companies concerned, and possibly one or two advisers from the presidential staff at the Elysée. This appears to have been largely the case for the decision that Thomson's telecommunications activities should be taken over by the Compagnie Générale d'Electricité. Where the President lacks a majority in Parliament the role of the Prime Minister is likely to increase.

Parliament was much constrained by the 1958 constitutional provisions and has only very slowly come to make much use of the powers which it does possess. The areas in which parliament may legislate are specifically defined by the constitution. Very large areas of industrial policy thus require no explicit legislative backing. The short duration of parliamentary sessions, combined with the absence of an effective question time, and of adjournment debates and supply days, certainly weakens the parliamentary preoccupations of ministers as compared with their British counterparts.

Central ministries consist essentially of a number of divisions (*directions*), each under a *directeur*. These divisions tend to have an important sense of their own identity, reinforced by the fact that the extent of their responsibilities is laid down in a legal and public *arrêté*. Indeed, Hayward has described the Ministry of Finance as resembling a set of baronial fiefdoms.[4] Many officials, even at senior levels, may spend many years within one division. A hierarchy exists amongst divisions, a hierarchy that can have consequences, for prestige and standing are important in inter-divisional bargaining. At the apex of the hierarchy are the so-called *directions nobles*, especially perhaps the *direction du trésor* of the Finance Ministry.

The autonomy of the divisions is reinforced by the absence in French ministries of any person corresponding to the British permanent Civil Service head of the ministry (the permanent secretary). This means that French ministries are in effect confederations of divisions, with each *directeur* having equal access to the minister or his personal staff. It also means that *directeurs* may have a great deal of autonomy.

The personnel structure of the French Civil Service can be regarded as both fragmented and rigid. The fragmentation results from the *corps* structure, upon which is superimposed a more recent notion of categories. *Corps* group together officials of similar functions within a career structure. At the top of the pecking order are the so-called *grands corps*—notably the Council of State, the Court of Accounts, the Finance Inspectorate. These are distinguished by their small size, by their close camaraderie, and by the fact that the proper functions of the *corps* involve more the control of other officials than actual administrative work. In addition to the administrative *grands corps* the term *grands corps* is also applied, and similar status accorded, to two 'technical' *grands corps*—the *corps des mines* and the *corps des ponts et chaussées*. In their more specialized fields the armament engineers and the *corps des ingénieurs des télécommunications* are important and influential. All these technical *corps* recruit through the Ecole Polytechnique, in the latter case thence to the Ecole Nationale Supérieure des Postes et Télécommunications.

Suleiman[5] and Thoenig[6] have described the way in which these *corps* developed strategies to ensure their survival in key points within the administration. These strategies involve a claim to legitimacy based upon expertise. Suleiman's examination of this claim led him to the view that this expertise was of a very broad and general type, but that members of the *corps*, especially the Finance Inspectorate and the *corps des mines*, had nevertheless sustained over a long period an image which portrayed them as particularly well-fitted to be concerned with economic and industrial matters.

The *grand corps* have, moreover, ensured that wherever possible new sectors opening up come into the hands of members of the *corps*. For example, the *corps des mines* have ensured their position within the energy sector, including, as it has developed, atomic energy, making a fiefdom which largely escapes political control.

The Ministry of Finance plays a distinctive and important role in industrial policy. 'The Trésor has some claim to be the most important agent, as well as the coordinator, of industrial policy. In addition to supervising credit, it supervises the specialised financial intermediaries, such as the Caisse des Dépôts et Consignations and the Credit National, which give French industrial policy its peculiar effectiveness.' Diana Green's comment may overestimate the coherence of policy, but it illustrates the predominant role which many observers have accorded to the Trésor.[7] ʾ

It is customary to present the Planning Commission (Commissariat Général au Plan—CGP) as the element within the administration arguing for an overall and long-term perspective against the short-term financial logic of the Finance Ministry. This was apparently true in the 1960s, although the planners never had much power. The CGP once was responsible for monitoring the co-ordination of policy to industry, but in 1985 the Commissioner insisted that it was the job of the Prime Minister's office. Today the CGP should be seen as not much more than a place where substantive actors sometimes meet for non-substantive discussions. If anything, in the early 1980s the CGP tended to side with the Finance Ministry against the Industry Ministry in debates about industrial policy.

If the CGP is not the mouthpiece of any interest in particular, it seems widely acknowledged inside and outside the state system that the Industry Ministry is the lobby for business within the government. It is made up of essentially sectoral divisions, nominally linked in a 'Direction-générale de l'Industrie'. The ministry is liable to reorganization with every reshuffle. Since 1981 it has had five ministers and three structures. It is currently responsible for trade, posts, and telecommunications, having acquired and shed responsibility for research in the last two years. The Minister of Industry is seen as a low status minister, and his or her access to the President may be less than that of the heads of major firms. It is widely believed that Industry Minister Chevènement was forced to resign in 1983 by heads of nationalized industries, opposed to his interventions. Zinsou observes that in giving the Industry Ministry the key role in supervising the newly nationalized firms, the weakness of the supervisory agency was seen as an indication of the intention to preserve their autonomy.[8]

The relationship between state agencies and organized interests can reinforce the fragmentation arising from the vertical divisions in the administration that we have noted above. The close relationship which develops between certain groups and state agencies means that the agency may act as the client group's advocate, and the group may undertake certain quasi-official functions. Another device used by the government for handling state–group relationships is a policy of *contractualisation*—specific arrangements supposedly binding on both sides.

A feature of the French system which undoubtedly affects the relationship of the administration to external actors is *pantouflage*. This is movement by those who start their careers within the Civil Service out into nationalized or private industry, financial companies, or occasionally to trade associations, and sometimes back again. Such movement is especially a feature of the *corps des mines* and other officials of the Industry Ministry, and the Finance Inspectorate, although it is found elsewhere. In the 1970s, Birnbaum observed that 43 of the managing directors of the top 100 French companies had an administrative background.[9] There is virtually no way into administrative posts for those with industrial experience who have not started out in an administrative *corps*.

In theory, ministers can appoint anyone to the most senior posts in their own ministries and, in practice, they seek to ensure that the occupants of key posts match their own particular political orientation. In doing so, it is to those who also have the necessary Civil Service credentials that they mostly look.

As Suleiman has pointed out,[10] the well-devloped *esprit de corps* means that the *corps* themselves will take an interest in the careers of their members. Senior members, whether located within or outside the administration, often adopt a policy of *'renvoyer l'ascenseur'*—sending the lift back down—to the benefit of their juniors. A Civil Servant, so it has been alleged to us, may be influenced in his approach towards an enterprise by the fact that senior members of his *corps*, upon whom his career may depend, are to be found within that enterprise. Certainly, for many years, the acknowledged 'patron' of the *corps des mines* who was consulted, if informally, about appointments for the members of his *corps*, was located in the oil company Elf. The present 'patron' is the president of Gaz de France.

The pattern that emerges is one of closely interconnected, indeed interlocking élites: administrative, industrial, financial, and political. Indeed, the relatively limited nature of the industrial–financial–administrative élite in France, concentrated in Paris, means that contacts may exist and pressure be brought to bear without formal mechanisms for interest representation.[11] The trade unions are excluded from these élite mechanisms, and French governments have, over the last three decades, marginalized the unions. The extent to which there is interlinking, through common training and early career patterns, through common *corps* memberships, through family and marital connections, and through overlapping memberships of *conseils d'administration*, between the big industrial groups, the banks, and the administration, ought to be considered at least as much as any formal institutions. It is vital to recognize that this does not necessarily imply similar stances on any issue; but it may imply rather similar styles and language, and a degree of

intermixing far greater than that to be found, for example, between political and administrative milieux in Britain.

The Telecommunications Sector

A study of two industrial sectors in France enables us to consider in detail
the operation of government–industry relations within the general context set out above, and to draw from it some more general conclusions
about the role of the actors, and the structure of sectoral policy networks.
The telecommunications sector presents a number of distinctive features.
It is a sector in which the dominant actor, for most of the post-war period,
has been a division of a central ministry, the telecommunications division
(DGT) of the Ministry of Posts and Telecommunications (PTT). Its
power principally depends upon its position as purchaser of the output of
the sector and its ability to undertake and finance R. & D. Its role is
strengthened by its possession of internal and legitimated technical
competence and the autonomy it has been accorded *vis-à-vis* the rest of
the state system since 1970.

This autonomy has varied over the period studied, and the pattern of
government–industry relations has also varied with changing technical
and economic conditions in the industry. This section is chiefly concerned with the nature and effects of the forces pressing for change
during the 1970s, and the resulting shifts both of structures within the
industry and of relationships between the government and firms.

Telecommunications before the 1970s

As a result of political factors and the administrative and financial power
of the postal wing of the PTT Ministry, of which the telecommunications administration, the Direction Générale des Télécommunications
(DGT), was a subordinate part, telephone policy in France between the
wars concentrated on equipping rural areas with local networks rather
than building up urban and inter-urban networks. The network appears
to have been very badly run with a continuing lack of automation and
inter-urban links. At the end of the war the PTT Ministry set up the
Centre National des Études de Télécommunications (CNET). The
CNET, although nominally just a technical research centre, was given a
vast variety of tasks, for example price control on purchasing contracts.
In the post-war years, the PTT budget continued to be unified,

annualized, and very tightly and rigidly itemized under headings that made effective planning impossible. The Finance Ministry refused to let the DGT borrow freely, and telecommunications resources were used to subsidize the post. In the 1950s the state of the French network had been so bad that NATO feared it could not cope with essential military requirements and loaned the PTT more funds than the French government was willing to provide. In the late 1960s, it was commonly observed that half the population was waiting to have a phone installed, and the other half was waiting for the dialling tone. In 1967 a third of French telephones had no dials.

In 1970 a devastating critique of telecommunications policy was published by anonymous DGT officials. According to Dang Nguyen,[12] the authors in fact included both Gérard Théry, who became head of the DGT in 1974, and his successor in 1981, Jacques Dondoux. They argued that no one seemed to have made a major effort to raise the level of funding for investment.

The momentum for change arose from developments within the administration rather than from pressure from the firms who tended to adapt themselves to the situation. Until the 1970s market shares were not subject to competition. Between the wars ITT designed equipment that met the very idiosyncratic requirements of the French system. Through its two separate switching companies (CGCT and LMT) it provided different systems for rural and urban areas and, in return for a guaranteed share of the market, permitted its technology to be used by any other French firm. Only Ericsson's French subsidiary showed an interest and became the second supplier. The Compagnie Générale d'Électricité's affiliate CIT (later CIT-Alcatel) contented itself with a small share of the switching market and had an equity stake in Ericsson-France. Thomson had sold its interests in the 1920s and as late as 1969 agreed with CGE that it would keep out of telecommunications.

In the post-war years, CNET set the creation of a French technological capability as its priority. It concentrated on the development of new French technology which no one wanted to produce rather than on the expansion of the network. CNET put large sums of money into abortive co-operation with an unenthusiastic CGE which preferred to produce under licence, could not export its licensed technology, did not engage in R. & D., and, according to Ruges, used its telecommunications profits to finance other areas.[13]

ITT meanwhile was exporting significantly from France, and developing new products in France. To avoid major dependence on ITT,

the DGT decided in the 1950s that while the large cities would have
ITT's Pentaconta exchanges, rural areas would have Ericsson's CP400
system. CNET set up patent pools for switching and transmission, and
rigid market-sharing agreements designed to favour its preferred
suppliers, although to little avail.

1974–81: Forced change

Beginning in the late 1960s there was a series of changes within the state
system, resulting both from internal pressure within the PTT from the
growing *corps* of Ingénieurs des Télécommunications, and from external
political commitments. The DGT was given greater freedom to borrow,
and posts and telecommunications were separated within the ministry. In
1974 President Giscard appointed a new head of the DGT, Gérard
Théry, a member of the *corps* of Ingénieurs des Télécommunications.
Théry reduced the powers of the CNET and set up a separate Direction
des Affaires Industrielles et Internationales (DAII) to handle relations
with industry. The patent pools were abolished, as were the ordering
quotas. The President and the DGT announced a huge programme of
expansion of the network. In an unprecedented move, firms were invited
to bid for contracts and propose what technology they liked.

ITT's companies proposed two similar systems that its research centre
(Laboratoire Central des Télécommunications, LCT) had developed in
France with the aid of the CNET. CIT, the protégé of CNET, offered a
Japanese system. Ericsson offered its own system. Thomson was per-
suaded to join the bidding and offered a system designed by Canadian
Northern Electric. In the end the DGT, acting with the approval of the
President, decided to accept none of these bids. Instead, it announced
that it would adopt both ITT's Metaconta system and Ericsson's Axe:
but to be produced by Thomson in factories to be bought by Thomson
from Ericsson and ITT, who would receive royalties on export sales only.
ITT sold LMT to Thomson but retained CGCT, whose system was
being used and who were awarded 16 per cent of the market. The two
systems being used were 'space division' as opposed to the more powerful
digital 'time-division' systems, in which the new French E10 system in
fact had a world lead, although it was not quite ready for mass production
and needed further development for use as a subscriber exchange. The
CGE was told that it would be assigned the task of producing the next
generation of digital equipment, E10s, to be ordered in increasing

quantities from about 1978, but for the time being Thomson was victorious.

Many explanations of these decisions have been offered. The simplest is that Théry was rejecting outright the failed industrial strategy of the CNET and its luke-warm partner, the allegedly financially oriented CGE. The images of CGE and Thomson were then roughly the reverse of what they came to be in the early 1980s. Thomson-Brandt (as it was then known) was growing fast by acquisition, seemingly successfully, under its entrepreneurial founder, Paul Richard. The firm was an established military supplier. It also had links with the Giscard family; even after nationalization in 1982 a relative of Giscard was a top executive. With hindsight the political considerations underlying the decision to bring Thomson into telecommunications seem more significant than they may have done at the time.

Consequences of forced change

In fact, no sooner had Thomson got into telecommunications than things started going wrong. In 1977, the DGT changed strategy again, and decided to opt for a move to 100 per cent digital time-division technology as soon as possible. This restored a glow to the cheeks of CIT-CGE but left Thomson in trouble. To its surprise, it found in the files of LMT blueprints of its participation in the ITT digital switching programme, and decided to derive from it the MT20 system and complete it by 1980. This took far longer and cost far more than Thomson imagined, driving the whole group near to bankruptcy, and ultimately forcing it to hand over its telecommunications interests to CGE after nationalization.

ITT's CGCT was meanwhile left in the cold. The DGT offered it no prospect of a share of the new generation of digital equipment, and it had no other products of its own. ITT has told us that it had strong reasons to believe that its susbsidiary CGCT would be a major supplier of digital switching. When LMT was sold to Thomson, agreement was signed between ITT and the PTT Minister relating to the participation of CGCT in the digital switching programme for France. ITT offered S12 exchanges to the PTT with a guarantee on exports, but received no clear response from the government.[14] Accounts of this episode differ: French officials claim that ITT effectively ran CGCT into the ground, whereas ITT argues that the DGT was responsible for CGCT's problems by witholding orders from it. In the event, when Mitterrand's government nationalized the firm in 1982, it paid rather a high price for a firm in deep financial difficulty which has since proved a major employment headache.

In the late 1970s the DGT provided and regulated network services and acted as the supervisory ministry for the supply industry; its autonomy was considerably enhanced by its financial and technical control over the investment programme. It was liberated from the constraints of the Finance Ministry, and its head reported directly to the President. The DGT pressed Thomson and CGE to export by offering bonuses for export performance, hoping to cut costs by the realization of scale economies from exports. This could perhaps have been more easily achieved by the selection of one new system rather than four. The DGT itself was aware that its power rested on its control of an investment programme that rivalled the nuclear programme, and that its technical success in achieving saturation with telephone lines contained the seeds of its own destruction.

Telecommunications policy under Mitterrand

The policies of the Mitterrand government after 1981 strengthened the power of the supplier firms at the expense of the DGT. The government nationalized Thomson, CGE, and CGCT. Théry was dismissed and replaced by Jacques Dondoux, former head of the CNET. The placing of the PTT Ministry under the Industry Ministry in 1984–5 had little effect, however.

In various ways the DGT's power was constrained. It was obliged to sign a 'management charter' between itself and the government. A rival administration, Télédiffusion de France, was allowed to control direct broadcasting by satellite. In an attempt to gain better political as well as financial control of the DGT a Direction Générale de la Stratégie was created in late 1985 reporting directly to the PTT Minister. The Ministry of Finance's control over the DGT had already been enhanced when the Mitterrand government had made the politically contentious decision to allow DGT revenues to be tapped for central government purposes. The DGT had also been given financial as well as administrative resposibility for running parts of the *filière électronique* programme.

On the other hand, the DGT's power remains considerable. The telecommunications engineers remain an effective pressure group within the administration upon whose expertise both the Ministry of Finance and the Planning Commission are likely to rely for analyses of the sector. It has maintained its *télématique* programme, including its private law subsidiaries which are especially concerned with data transmission and other electronic services. It also got approval for most of its own cable plan, partly because when Théry was dismissed the DGT was able to field a 'reserve team' from within itself which was capable of securing allies within the new government, notably in the Ministry of Culture. It was also able to persuade the government of the potential benefits of its plans for the fibre optics industry.

Changes within the firms

Thomson had been virtually bankrupted by its entry into telecommunications, and before 1981 was never able to evolve a clear overall corporate strategy. It did not resist nationalization. The new chairman, Alain Gomez, made short-term profitability a clear priority, and was anxious to shed Thomson's telecommunications interests. The CGE, which had had considerable success with the E10 exchange, saw itself as *the* French telecommunications enterprise, and was keen to take over Thomson Telecommunications (but not its losses).

The political strategy of the CGE in the last ten years, above all since 1981, is impressive. Its exclusion from the key segments of the nuclear programme, when the pressurized water reactor was chosen, and the DGT's slight to it in 1975–6 were bitter blows. It was politically out of favour under Giscard. A. Boublil, subsequently Mitterrand's industrial adviser, wrote favourably of the CGE in 1977.[15] Its subsidiaries' successes with the E10 (not wholly its own) and the TGV (high-speed train) gave CGE immense industrial credibility in 1981. Although its chairman, Ambroise Roux, was an outspoken critic of nationalization, and left the firm, his management team remained, notably Roux's deputy, G. Pebereau, who has dominated CGE and CIT-Alcatel, as chief executive (*directeur-général*) since 1982, and chairman as well since 1984.

Much of Pebereau's power *vis-à-vis* the government derives from the fact that CGE has been consistently profitable. It has therefore not been a *demandeur* at the Trésor but has paid dividends. Alcatel is quoted on the stock exchange and both it and its parent can raise external funds. Although Alcatel is not 100 per cent owned by CGE, its strategy is determined by Pebereau as chairman and chief executive. He has managed to give the CGE the image of a coherent industrial corporation with a clear corporate strategy, which he has declared publicly would not alter if the the firm were denationalized. In 1983 the press reported warnings from the DGT about the dangers of a monopoly if CGE were allowed to take over Thomson Telecommunications.[16] But the heads of Thomson and CGE went directly to the President with arguments such as the need for economies of scale and they won. The technical side of the Industry Ministry was not consulted and one official even said that, under the policy of managerial autonomy for state enterprises, it was not proper for the government to express a view on such a merger.

Complex accounting arrangements meant that the state underwrote most of Thomson's losses within the new entity, which in 1985 became a single concern, Alcatel, under the direction of CGE. The merger has given rise to some difficulties but it would seem that CGE has more successfully integrated the web of firms that it took over from Thomson (including ex-ITT and Ericsson subsidiaries) than Thomson ever did.

CGE's own corporate strategy extends well beyond telecommunications where it is still heavily dependent on public switching, even as orders from the DGT itself fall. Although it has had a big share of the first generation of digital business, Alcatel is seeking foreign partners for future development. Pebereau's strategy was described by one Alcatel executive as seeking long-term techological co-operation with other European firms, but in the mean time co-operating with AT&T in certain fields, notably to get its E10 Five system sold in the US. Pebereau proposed that AT&T effectively take over CGCT and its share of the market. This firm had been promised that part of Thomson's MT20 business would be subcontracted to it (while Thomson itself had to close down plants because of over-capacity). Naturally the DGT is hostile to a move which would confirm Alcatel (with AT&T) as a monopoly supplier. The DGT would prefer to see CGCT linked with an outsider such as Ericsson or even with another present or former ITT subsidiary.

The Consumer Electronics Sector

Government–industry relations in French consumer electronics are dominated by the direct relationship between the state and Thomson, and to a much lesser degree between the state and Philips, which is seen as an alternative national champion, even though it tends to remain at arm's length. The dominant influence on the sector arises from international market factors and the way firms have chosen to respond to them. The Industry Ministry, which is responsible for supervising the industry, faces the firms from a relatively weak position. Unlike the DGT it possesses little technical or commercial expertise and has no procurement funds. It has in effect been 'captured' by Thomson. The Finance Ministry alone can exercise real leverage over Thomson, and it retains this power precisely because it has no industrial as opposed to financial objectives.

The firms have relations with government across a range of sectors, so that consumer electronics cannot be seen in isolation from the other activities of the firms. These relations tend to be highly personalized in informal contacts between the heads of firms and ministers, the Prime Minister, and the President. Relations are fragmented in the sense that firms deal with a number of ministries. At the same time the firms themselves are not monolithic, and their own internal divisions may have important external repercussions.

The role of the firms before 1981

The relatively limited impact of public policy in the sector in the 1960s was reflected in the essential identity of views between the 'national champion' (Thomson) and the state. With the 'passive protectionism' offered by the SECAM system,[17] Thomson pursued a strategy of growth by acquisition at a time when the promotion of mergers was the main interest of the state. By the early 1980s Thomson had eliminated all serious national competitors apart from Philips.

Thomson's biggest strength lay in military electronics. The biggest change in Thomson's structure took place in 1969 when the more consumer-oriented Thomson-Brandt, as it had become, took over the CSF company specializing in military and industrial electronics. A shareholding of less than 100 per cent was taken and the two firms were never properly integrated. After nationalization Thomson-CSF was only 51 per cent state-owned. A Finance Ministry official described Thomson as 'practically unmanageable' before 1981.

Thomson's strategy brought it into conflict with the state in the late 1970s when it began to buy up companies outside France and to establish production facilities and technical collaboration agreements in the Far East. The 'Asian strategy' was that of J. Fayard, head of Thomson's consumer electronics division, but it was opposed by A. Farnoux, head of the Videocolor subsidiary which made TV tubes (but not money) in Europe. Farnoux was eventually pushed out.

By 1981 Thomson had missed out on two generations of products after colour TV—the VCR and compact discs. It decided to invest in R. & D. for 8mm video equipment, but in the mean time top management sought closer co-operation with JVC, via the J3T deal in which Thomson, Thorn-EMI, Telefunken, and JVC would set up a joint operation in Europe. Thomson was allocated the (rather unpromising) video camera segment; this plan was opposed within the firm and some senior staff even resigned. Thomson had also begun to encounter difficulties with its staple product, colour TVs, where its growth had not led to a concentration or rationalization of production facilities. Multi-standard TV sets and cheap imports from Eastern Europe were undermining the protection offered by SECAM. Thomson was also coming under fire for its plans to make video discs (with TEAC) as well as its hi-fis in Asia.

Thomson shed several of its activities in the 1983 reshuffle with CGE. Consumer electronics became a larger share of Thomson's business and crucial as an outlet for its output of semi-conductors, a field assigned to it under the deal with CGE. Thomson, which throughout the 1970s had been a highly politicized firm and one of the most heavily subsidized, was putting short-term profitability first. Indeed, critics of the firm argue that it neglected consumer electronics R. & D. because investment in lobbying for arms contracts seemed more profitable.

Philips-France comprises a number of wholly owned companies operating under separate names. The TV subsidiary, la Radiotechnique, maintains brands of its own, and has some partly owned subsidiaries but its latest annual report announced that it was time to strengthen its 'links' with Philips. It had been involved in certain of the *plans composants* activities, but compared with Thomson maintains a low political profile and, as yet, does not seem to have exploited the enhanced esteem which the parent group now generally enjoys within the French state.

After nationalization

In principle nationalization might have been expected to enable the state to exert a degree of control, but in practice this has proved difficult. The government appointed a new chairman, Alain Gomez, and tried to persuade the firm to change its commercial strategy, and, amongst other things, to make more hi-fis in Europe and to seek a European partner. However the sponsoring Industry Ministry was weak. The government cannot override the commercial pressures which work against Thomson finding a European partner, and at the same time maintain its commitment to managerial autonomy for nationalized firms. The negotiation of a planning contract was awkward, not least because Thomson was dealing with at least three sponsoring agencies—the Ministries of

Industry and Defence and the DGT, which is concerned with micro-electronics as well as telecommunications. We know that Thomson fought hard to maximize subsidies and its own freedom of manœuvre. The planning contract was seen by the government as well as as by the firm to be a way of concentrating the firm's mind on its corporate strategy and guaranteeing its autonomy. Thomson executives admit they did not take the exercise very seriously. The Finance Ministry as usual refused budgetary commitments beyond one year, and the firm gave as few hostages to fortune as it could.

The firm continued to lobby for protection against Japan, directly to the Elysée. In this they had the loyal backing of the Industry Ministry. But the firm could not control the government. The Poitiers measures, which held up imports of Japanese (and other) VCRs, were (according to *Libération*)[18] imposed by the Finance Ministry in autumn 1982 because a heavy tax was to be imposed on VCRs from 1 January 1983 and the aim was to prevent a last rush of tax-free buyers. If true, this would explain the nature of the measures and their sudden removal, and the fact that the main victim of this measure was none other than Thomson—since most of the VCRs involved had been bought and paid for by Thomson from JVC. An alternative explanation, however, sees the main objective being to induce the Japanese to set up production facilities in France. In this version, the production side of Thomson was in favour of the move although it hit the importing branch of the firm.

The French government refused to allow the projected J3T deal, which would have given Thomson access to Japanese technology in video. It is not clear whether this refusal was implemented through the foreign exchange rules, or those for inward investment, or just political leverage. But the government has been very ambiguous about whether to beat or join the Japanese, and their intentions that Thomson should pursue a European alternative were frustrated by the outcome of the Thomson bid for Grundig, which resulted in Thomson's acquisition of Telefunken, and hence access to Japanese video technology through the J2T (JVC, Thorn-EMI, Telefunken) consortium.

The 'Grundig Affair'

Thomson offered in autumn 1982 to buy the 75.5 per cent share in his firm held by Max Grundig. It had to get the agreement of Philips who held the other 24.5 per cent (although legally Philips had to have 25 per cent to stop Thomson's purchase). Philips wanted to maintain Grundig's use of the V2000 system, which had 25 per cent of the German VCR market, and other supply links between the two firms. It apparently wanted some firmer assurances of commitment by Thomson-Grundig to the V2000 system. Gomez was willing to make some promises but, despite pressure from the French government, was very unwilling to sign any full-scale technical co-operation agreement with Philips before securing control of Grundig. Philips and Thomson had major technical disagreements. Gomez thought V2000 was doomed and the two firms had serious disputes over 8mm video standards. JVC had introduced Thomson to the international 8mm video standards group, and had backed Thomson's system for avoiding problems over PAL–SECAM incompatibility, but Philips strongly opposed Thomson on this. Some French observers feel that JVC was deliberately trying to slow down agreement on a new system to preserve its VHS market.

While Philips did not formally oppose the Grundig deal it apparently refused to sell its share to Thomson unless a wider deal was done, a deal which Thomson was not willing to contemplate. While Gomez was negotiating with Grundig (with the backing of Farnoux's supporters within Thomson) he encouraged Fayard to keep the lines open with JVC. Thomson also engaged in direct negotiations with Telefunken which Grundig proposed to take over and bring as part of its dowry to Thomson. The German Cartel Office made it clear that if Thomson took over Grundig *and* Telefunken its share of the German market would be unacceptably high, but many expected that Thomson-Grundig alone would be an acceptable merger, and were surprised when the Cartel Office vetoed it. Thomson reacted quickly. It did not appeal; instead it bought Telefunken and then signed a J2T deal with JVC, while Philips later took over Grundig.

Why did Thomson not appeal? Critics argue that Thomson never really wanted to buy Grundig. A somewhat more plausible interpretation is that Gomez was pursuing a double strategy: the Grundig deal would have been attractive if Philips had been willing to sell its shares, but otherwise J2T was preferred. The issue of Philips withdrawing from Grundig does not seem to have been invoked in the press during the negotiations, and indeed it has been claimed that Philips' share in Grundig was not discussed in the negotiations with Philips. Quatrepoint says only that 'sources close to the Cartel Office suggested that Philips sell its holding', although not necessarily to Thomson, but he also quotes Gomez as saying: 'A group can have only one boss'.[19] *Libération*[20] states that Philips' refusal to withdraw was crucial both for Thomson's hesitation and the Cartel Office's decision. Therefore, a refusal of Philips to sell its 24.5 per cent remains the most plausible explanation of why Thomson had apparently lost interest in the project even before the Cartel Office made its decision. One further oddity of this episode is that Philips has links with JVC's parent company, Matsushita, but Philips and JVC are rivals while Thomson and JVC are allies.

The limits of state influence

Once the Grundig deal collapsed French government opposition to the J2T deal ended. The Grundig deal had had the personal backing of the President, yet, if our interpretation is correct, the administration was unable to persuade Thomson to agree with Philips. We cannot, of course, judge which strategy was the right one. All we can say is that Thomson's continuing pre-1981 management team in consumer electronics secured the outcome they preferred while the government did not. Gomez had become part of the Thomson team and not an agent of the Industry Ministry as perhaps hoped by J.-P. Chevènement.

The affair did lead to one acute conflict between the government and Thomson over the siting of the factory intended to produce one million VCRs in France by 1986. (This objective looks very optimistic given the state of the VCR market, not to mention the impending arrival of South Korean and Taiwanese machines.) Thomson wanted to use an obsolescent black and white TV factory in Tonnerre. The government wanted to have a factory sited in Longwy in Lorraine, scene of severe disturbances over steel plant closures. After protracted negotiations Thomson agreed to split the plant between the two sites, although its latest annual report refers only to VCR production at Tonnerre.

The relationship between Industry Ministry officials and Thomson gave the former very little leeway. The DIELI (Direction des Industries Electroniques et Informatiques) had responsibility for that part of electronics not supervised by its rival the DGT. The Industry Ministry's arguments were essentially macro-economic: for example, they advocated the building of VCRs in France because they are important for France's trade deficit. Thomson, however, not only had the micro-economic and industrial data at its disposal (which it does not communicate to the government) but also was able to point out that the overriding priority assigned to the nationalized firms by Fabius, first as Industry Minister and then Prime Minister, was the restoration of financial balance by 1985.

The Industry Ministry effectively became Thomson's lobbyist and spokesman within the administration. A senior Industry Ministry official said this was entirely natural—and indeed they often had to speak up for Philips in Brussels too when the Dutch government held back.

This abdication of the Industry Ministry in the face of Thomson can be explained by a number of factors, not least *pantouflage* through which one member of the Industry Ministry's *cabinet* joined Gomez's staff and then became head of corporate planning. Grjébine, as well as Cohen and Bauer, draws attention to the fact that the ministry in effect is dependent on industry lobbyists for much of its information.[21] Consultants get their data from firms who can then use their reports as ammunition in negotiation with the state or denounce them as academic if they are inconvenient. Grjébine complains that the presence of the head of the DIELI on Thomson's *conseil d'administration* in effect means that a member of the board of Thomson was heading the supervisory agency, and challenges the traditional view that the administration can gain power by representation on boards. People serving as state representatives on boards have confirmed to us how minor their role is. The Finance Ministry, however, does have a certain power over the nationalized firms, such as Thomson, as expressed through its ability to resist demands for subsidies and ensure that multi-year financial commitments by the state are avoided and annual budgets are respected.

No other element of the state appears to have been as clear as the Finance Ministry in its goals. The government's aims have included the promotion of a francophone audiovisual sector, national technological independence, the safeguarding of employment, the balance of payments, budgetary rigour, and the promotion of European co-operation. These are all legitimate goals, but the political mechanism has not been able to assign clear relative priorities, and so the different elements of the administration face an interlocutor that, since 1982, has in some ways taken a wider view than any one state agency.

Conclusions

The sectoral evidence presented above has illustrated some striking features of government–industry relations in France which differ sharply from the patterns which obtain in the same sectors in Britain and West Germany. In the conclusion to this chapter we develop a preliminary typology of policy networks at the sectoral level in order to begin the task of locating the French case within a comparative context.

We have argued that the state should not be understood as an actor, but as a set of institutions in which individual and collective actors interact within a set of opportunities and constraints afforded by the relationship between the state system and the wider society. It is important to recognize that this relationship obtains at different levels, and the extent to which it is possible to establish and implement coherent policy objectives at one level may be constrained by the type of relationship that obtains at other levels. For example, the French policy of promoting national champions as an instrument through which industrial objectives might be realized was frustrated in the consumer electronics sector by the inability of the Industry Ministry to challenge Thomson's monopoly of legitimate expertise. Conversely, in another country, sectoral initiatives to promote a bargained policy network might be undermined by a strong competitive market ethos at national level.

The typology is an attempt to classify the range of different patterns of power-dependence expected in our research on Britain, France, and West Germany. The relationships between actors at the sectoral level are influenced, but we would argue *not* determined, by the pattern of relationships at the macro-level, and it would be possible to devise a similar typology of national policy networks. As we have observed above, there is considerable variation between societies in the legitimate role that is accorded to the state in relation to economic activity. Thus, in France, state intervention at the enterprise level is legitimate and expected. However, this does not guarantee its effectiveness.

The relationship between the firm and the state may be direct and bilateral, or it may be mediated by sectoral trade and/or employers' associations, and/or by trade unions. In some cases this mediation may take the form of collective pressure by the industry for favourable state policies; in others it might veer towards 'private interest government'[22] where in exchange for a privileged role in determining public policy, sectoral interest associations undertake to secure member firms' compliance in implementation, for example, of planned capacity reduction. What is evident from analyses of the sectoral organization of state–industry relations is the variety of forms that they can take[23] so that we should view with intense suspicion any assumption that sectoral or micro-relationships can be read off from prescriptive formulations such as '*étatisme*' or the 'social market economy'.

We do not presume that there is a necessary correspondence between ideological conceptions of the state's role and the actual characteristics of sectoral policy networks. We do, however, make some theoretical assumptions about what factors are likely to determine power-dependence relationships within them. The first variable is the extent of power and autonomy granted to or gained by the state agency. We can use, as a preliminary hypothesis, the suggestion of Atkinson and Coleman[24] that this depends on four conditions. First, that the agency has a clearly defined role and a value system that supports it, which is more likely where the agency has a functional mandate rather than one which obliges it to represent the interests of a particular clientele. Second, state autonomy is greater where the legal and regulatory framework provides barriers between the agency and the sector. Third, state autonomy will be greater where functional responsibilities for a given sector are clearly assigned to a single agency. Finally, the state agency requires independent access to expertise and information in order to act autonomously from firms and sectoral associations. The typology recognizes three positions on a continuum from low autonomy to high autonomy.

The second major variable which determines the pattern of sectoral policy networks is the degree of monopoly closure in the relationship between the state and firms and private interest organizations, which in turn is in part a consequence of the extent of market concentration, but it may also be conferred by the state. An interest structure comprising a large number of competitive organizations with overlapping interest domains is characteristic of a low level of closure; conversely, a monopolistic relationship presupposes a single organization or a small number with the capacity to capture state agencies, negotiate with them, or be used by them as agents of implementation and control, according to the extent to which state autonomy is respectively low, moderate, or high. In cases where business interest associations are weak and dominated by one or two large firms, bilateral relationships between firms and the state tend to prevail and the firms act as functional equivalents of interest associations in representing sectoral interests.

The recognition of the importance of interest associations and monopoly firms in structuring state–society relationships, through tripartite institutions at the macro-level, has been a major theme in recent literature on neo-corporatism. Corporatism involves interest organizations in *both* policy formation and policy implementation; they negotiate policies with state agencies and then deliver the compliance of their members with the provisions of the agreement. Associational systems which are conducive to the development of corporatism are characterized by vertical integration, concentration, and centralization. Macro-corporatism thus involves bargaining between the central state and peak organizations of capital and labour.

At the meso-level, interest associations representing class, sectoral, or professional interests, with a monopoly in their respective categories, may act as interlocutors between state agencies and firms, even where the conditions for macro-corporatism are absent. At a micro-level, bargaining might take the form of direct bilateral negotiation between the state and monopoly firms ('micro-corporatism'), with the difference between this relationship and agency capture lying in the greater autonomy that the state agency has in the former case compared with the latter. Agency capture arises where private interests succeed in turning public power to private ends. Bargained corporatism or 'private interest government' exists where public power derives from negotiation between state and private actors; state corporatism exists where an autonomous state creates interest monopolies through which to exercise social control.

Table 2.1 presents an outline typology based on the interaction of the variables of state autonomy and monopoly closure. Each cell represents a possible configuration of the relationship between public and private actors in sectoral policy networks. It should be stressed that these are ideal types reached through a process of 'logical purification', and empirical cases may be mixtures of these types, although it may be possible to discern a dominant characteristic which allows us to assign a particular case to a specific cell.

The prevailing conception of the role of the state in France makes it more likely that public policy strategies will be adopted which depend for

Table 2.1 A Typology of Sectoral Policy Networks

Autonomy of State Agency			
High------------ Medium------------ Low			
State Corporatist	Bargained Corporatist	Captured	High
			Monopoly closure in state–group relationship
Statist	Interventionist	Competitive	Low

their success on the creation of what we have called a statist policy net-work. In the telecommunications section we noted that the rapid develop-ment of the telephone system was achieved by granting a considerable degree of autonomy to the DGT *vis-à-vis* other state agencies and, in par-ticular, the Ministry of Finance. But this network did not prove to be stable beyond the achievement of the initial objectives. In consumer elec-tronics the Industry Ministry was relatively weak, and was only one of a number of agencies involved in contractual bargaining with the major national champion, Thomson. In some respects the relationship resembles a bargained corporatist network but, there are aspects of cap-ture in the extent to which Thomson's corporate strategy has become identified with public policy towards the sector.

A number of questions remain, not so much in explaining why state-led strategies are attempted in France, but why they fail. We have referred to Cohen and Bauer's argument that Thomson is able to maintain a 'monopoly of legitimate expertise' which implies that Thomson is able to champion its own interests, but if this is the case we are not yet able to describe in detail *how* it is done. Our evidence so far is negative: the instrument of control through the *contrat de plan* may be no more effec-tive than the planning agreements of British industrial policy in the 1970s.

A sector dominated by public procurement, such as telecommunica-tions, does not imply that the policy networks are structurally similar in each country. There is more of a risk that the purchasing agency may be dominated by the supplier within a captured network, and we have suggested the exceptional conditions which explain why this did not happen in France. One of these was the development of an independent technological capacity via CNET, which was indispensable to the DGT in organizing the market. A high level of autonomy was given to the DGT as a consequence of the political priority accorded to expanding the system. Comparable cases occur (the nuclear programme, Concorde, the TGV, space) where markets are being created and state funding is central. A commitment on the part of the government to a policy objec-tive may require the establishment of an implementation network which is characterized by a set of dependencies upon other actors for that objec-tive to be fulfilled. As the network develops, however, the agency's ability to retain some control depends, to a large degree, on its own expertise concentrated in the *corps*.

We have argued that a crucial determinant of the structure of sectoral policy networks is the autonomy conceded to or bestowed on state agencies, and their internal coherence. The rhetoric surrounding the role of the state in France, and a good deal of academic commentary, *assumes* a level of co-ordination and a capacity for concerted action within the French state which our research suggests is the exception rather than the rule. Nationalization does not by itself guarantee state access to the information held by the nationalized firm; indeed, the post-1981 nationalizations seem to have had remarkably little independent effect on the pattern of government–industry relations.

Acknowledgements

The research on which this paper is based is part of a study of government–industry relations in these sectors in Britain, France, and West Germany, financed by the Economic and Social Research Council. Geoffrey Shepherd, Kevin Morgan, and Douglas Webber have made valuable contributions. The sectoral sections are based on interviews, mainly with officials in various ministries including the DGT. Their co-operation and frankness is greatly appreciated. The authors would like to thank Henry Ergas (OECD) and Elie Cohen (École des Mines) for their help and giving access to unpublished manuscripts.

Notes

1. Interviewed for BBC Television, *Horizon*, 10 March 1986.
2. J. Hayward, 'Mobilisation of private interests in the service of public ambitions: the salient element in the dual French policy style' in J. Richardson (ed.), *Policy Styles in Western Europe* (London: Allen & Unwin, 1982).
3. H. Machin and V. Wright, 'Economic policy under the Mitterrand Presidency' in H. Machin and V. Wright (eds.), *Economic Policy and Policy-Making Under the Mitterrand Presidency 1981–1984* (London: Frances Pinter, 1985).
4. J. Hayward, *Governing France: The One and Indivisible Republic* (London: Weidenfeld & Nicolson, 1983).
5. E. Suleiman, *Elites in French Society* (Princeton, NJ: Princeton University Press, 1978).
6. J.-C. Thoenig, *L'Ère des technocrates: le cas des Ponts.et Chaussées* (Paris: Editions d'Organisation, 1973).
7. D. Green, 'Strategic management and the state: France' in K. Dyson and

S. Wilks (eds.), *Industrial Crisis: A Comparative Study of the State and Industry* (Oxford: Martin Robertson, 1983), p. 175.

8. L. Zinsou, *Le Fer de lance* (Paris: Olivier Orban, 1985), p. 73.

9. P. Birnbaum, *Les Sommets de l'état* (Paris: Seuil, 1977), p. 142.

10. E. Suleiman, *Elites in French Society* (see n. 5) pp. 176–84.

11. J. Saint-Geours, *Pouvoir et finance* (Paris: Fayard, 1979), p 206.

12. G. Dang Nguyen, 'Telecommunications' in M. Sharp (ed.), *Europe and the New Technologies* (London: Frances Pinter, 1985).

13. J. Ruges, *Le Téléphone pour tous* (Paris: Seuil, 1970).

14. Personal communication from ITT Europe.

15. A. Boublil, *Le Socialisme industriel* (Paris: Presses Universitaires de France, 1977).

16. J.-M. Quatrepoint in *Le Monde*, 17 September 1983.

17. SECAM is the French standard for colour television, which has been adopted by the Soviet Union and some Eastern European countries, by Greece, and by some of France's ex-colonies. The other two systems are NTSC (used in the United States and Japan) and PAL.

18. 21 November 1983.

19. J.-M. Quatrepoint, 'Un échec exemplaire: l'affaire Grundig', *Revue d'économie industrielle*, No. 27 (1984), p. 38.

20. 7 September 1983.

21. A. Grjébine, *L'État d'urgence* (Paris: Flammarion, 1983); E. Cohen and M. Bauer, *Les Grandes Manœuvres industrielles* (Paris: Belfond, 1985).

22. W. Streeck and P. C. Schmitter, 'Community, market, state—and associations? The prospective contribution of interest governance to social order' in W. Streeck and P. C. Schmitter (eds.), *Private Interest Government: Beyond Market and State* (London: Sage Publications, 1985).

23. A. Cawson, 'Introduction: varieties of corporatism: the importance of the meso-level of interest intermediation' in A. Cawson (ed.), *Organized Interests and the State: Studies in Meso-Corporatism* (London: Sage Publications, 1985).

24. M. Atkinson and W. D. Coleman, 'Corporatism and industrial policy' in A. Cawson (ed.), *Organized Interests and the State* (see n. 23).

Government–Industry Relations in the Chemical Industry: an Anglo-German Comparison

——— *Wyn Grant, William Paterson, and Colin Whitston* ———

In this chapter we shall seek to demonstrate that some of the conventional academic wisdom which attempts to explain the relatively good performance of the West German economy requires qualification. In particular, we shall argue that explanations which have been applied to the West German economy and polity as a whole need to be more sensitive to important differences between sectors, and that such differences between sectors can be illuminating when considering the general characteristics of the German political economy. In the course of the chapter, we shall make a number of implict, and sometimes explicit, comparisions with British experience, but the point of departure will be West Germany. The discussion will draw on our research on the chemicals (and, in particular, the industrial chemicals) industry. The chemical industry has been a leading edge of the West German economy in the post-war period, playing a major role in West Germany's record of export-led growth. In terms of its impact on world trade in chemicals, it is the world's leading national chemical industry.[1]

The recovery of the West German economy in the post-war period, and the successful creation of a liberal democratic state in Germany, has attracted widespread attention from academic commentators, not least in Britain. West Germany remains one of the world's leading economies. It invests substantially more per capita than Britain and provides a higher standard of living and a higher rate of employment for its people. Although the British chemical industry has a better performance record than much of the British economy, the West German chemical industry in 1984 had (measured in ECUs) almost twice the turnover, over twice as many exports by value, and a substantially higher level of capital investment than its British counterpart.[2]

Explanations of West German Economic Performance

In attempting to explain West German economic performance in the post-war period, one must attempt to separate out those factors which were present at one part of the period of recovery from those which, it has been argued, have had a longer lasting influence. Our discussion will concentrate on the latter factors, that is, on themes which have been drawn out by commentators on West Germany as providing, or helping to provide, a systematic explanation of West German economic performance. However, that does not mean that the more time-bound influences were unimportant in bringing about and securing the process of West German recovery. Among the favourable factors which should be mentioned are American aid in the post-war period; the availability of a large supply of cheap, reliable labour which escaped from East Germany and from areas occupied by the Russians and Czechs (sometimes whole factories were rebuilt by their owners in the West); the presence of large allied forces which boosted the economy and the balance of payments; and the undervaluation of the German mark until the world monetary upheavals of the early 1970s. Moreover, it should be noted that, despite the use of such phrases as *der Zusammenbruch* and *die Stunde O* to describe the end of the war, much of German industry escaped unscathed. Lawrence estimates that around one quarter of Germany's industrial capacity was destroyed or dismantled:[3] a considerable proportion, but something short of complete devastation of the kind which the phrases quoted conjure up. Finally, it should be noted that membership of the EEC conferred considerable advantages on West Germany; greater advantages, one might even suggest, than on other member states. German industry benefited from access to a wider market, whilst German agriculture was protected from undue disruption.

The more systematic arguments, which do not relate to any one time-period, are organized around a central theme: that West Germany has a greater capability than countries such as Britain to deal with problems of economic performance and industrial adjustment through a pattern of élite co-operation between the state, employers, unions, and finance capital. As Katzenstein points out, 'an elite cartel founded on anxiety' became 'elite collaboration based on self-confidence'.[4]

The Role of the State

Each of these supposed components of German success will be considered in turn, before returning to a more general consideration of the way in which the different parts of the system are supposed to mesh together. Handling the role of the state in West Germany poses a number of problems, two of which have been particularly contentious: is West Germany a 'weak' or 'strong' state and, despite its adherence to the notion of a 'social market' economy, has the West German government in fact been as interventionist as many other western states?

Dyson has contrasted the 'state orientation' of the German tradition with the 'society orientation' of Britain,[5] whilst, on the other hand, Maier argues that the essential characteristics of German statehood 'involve not the strong state for which Germans are criticised, but a continuing German tradition of what might be called insufficient statehood'.[6] Those who like to classify states as 'strong' or 'weak' see West Germany as intermediate case between Japan and France, on the one hand, and Britain and the United States, on the other.[7]

What are we to make of all this? First, we do not find the language of analysis of 'strong' and 'weak' states particularly helpful. After all, the UK has a centralized bureaucracy and considerable resources which can be deployed in the pursuit of a particular strategy, as the Thatcher experience shows. Moreover, the dichotomy between 'strong' and 'weak' states often seems to mean little more than the distinction between extensive, persistent and limited, intermittent government intervention in the economy. By way of contrast, a neo-liberal would argue that the hallmark of a 'strong' state is not intervention but autonomy. The West German state needed to be strong after the Second World War to re-establish market relations which had been disrupted by the Third Reich.

Nevertheless, there would appear to be in the German case a sense of organic unity, a commitment to action in the national interest which transcends the interests of individuals or particular groups. The importance of this orientation is that it allows the state to facilitate action by other actors which promotes the achievement of long-term, national goals. To put it another way, the state creates conditions which ensure that the more rewarding way to pursue self- or group-interest is through actions which are coincident with what is conceived of as the public interest. Streeck explains what happens in the following terms:

the State in the Federal Republic acts in a variety of ways as a supporting, facilitating, encouraging force in the formation and preservation of broad, encompassing, internally heterogeneous interest organisations. Ironically, but hardly unintended, the interventionist policy of the German state on the organisational forms of social interests enables it in many cases to abstain from direct economic intervention since it provides interest groups with a capacity to find viable solutions between and for themselves.[8]

A second area of contention is the question of how interventionist the Federal Republic has in fact been in relation to the economy. Economic liberals would like to claim the Federal Republic as an example of the success of their methods; selective interventionists claim that the Federal Republic has followed a clever political strategy of proclaiming its economic virginity to the outside world, whilst pursuing a strategy of careful selective intervention to protect the long-term economic interests of West Germany. One thing is clear: the 'social market economy' has become more of a slogan, and less of a reality, over time. As Donges remarks, 'during the 1950s and 1960s industrial policies were rather complementary to the market mechanism. It is only since the early 1970s that they have become more interventionistic and distorting.'[9] The present West German government is talking of privatizing some state assets, but little progress has been made in that direction so far; equally, attempts to curb the level of subsidy to state and private industries have also been largely unsuccessful.

However, it should not be assumed that West Germany has followed a similar path to that of other western countries. There have, it is true, been substantial subsidies to industries which are to be found on the 'sick list' in most European countries: coal, shipbuilding, and steel. However, apart from the steel industry, government has generally managed to avoid becoming directly involved in resolving industrial crises; these have been left to the financial sector to sort out. Moreover, nationalized industries are much more limited in scope than is the case in countries such as France and Britain. The principal nationalized industries (Deutsche Bundesbahn and Deutsche Bundespost) have been used to implement public purchasing policies which have favoured German firms.[10] However, the state has not generally used its quite extensive shareholdings in industrial companies (including a stake in VEBA, which includes VEBA-Chemie) to influence their policies. When government has intervened, it has been to support reorganization strategies, rather than to underwite a bail-out of policies that have failed.[11]

The Role of Employers' Associations and Trade Unions

Effective employers' associations, able to commit their members to bargains reached with government, trade unions, and others, are widely seen as an important element of German success. As Tylecote puts it:

British employers make their decisions on wages, as on everything else, individually and rather short-sightedly—in response to the immediate pressures upon them. German employers, on the other hand, are capable of acting collectively, and for long-term objectives, and as a result their actions cannot be predicted, or explained mechanically from immediate pressures upon them.[12]

The International Institute of Management project on business interest associations, which included Britain and West Germany as two of the countries studied, led to results which showed that the German associations were generally less fragmented, better resourced, and more able to commit their members to an agreed line of policy (although the contrasts were more marked in some sectors than in others). The British Chemical Industries Association is one of Britain's more effective business interest associations, but that is not the same thing as saying that its relationship with its members or with government is comparable to that of the VCI in West Germany. (The employers' organization function is separately organized in Germany.)

However, one must be wary of implying that there is some 'grand design' that is being worked out at the behest of the state. Business association officials in West Germany 'have no consistent idea generally of the role and status of their organisations between civil society and the state. Neither has the state itself.'[13] Public authority is devolved to associations on a pragmatic, opportunistic basis. The general picture of West German industry being 'remarkably well organised', with associations functioning as 'efficient agents of interest aggregation',[14] has to be qualified to allow for differences between sectors. 'Whether or not associations assume the functions of private governments regulating their constituents on behalf and in lieu of the state differs by issues, sectors and levels of interest aggregation.'[15] If the VCI is found to be well organized and effective, that tells us something about the chemical industry, but it does not mean that all sectors are equally well served (and the empirical evidence suggests that they are not).

German unions are generally portrayed as well organized, disciplined bodies that are accepted as legitimate participants in economic decision-making. Labour unions 'have been part of the "grand coalition" that has supported export expansion'.[16] This has certainly been true in the chemical industry where IG Chemie has been a docile and moderate union, even by West German standards. Such a co-operative union may not be an unmixed blessing. It may mean that there is insufficient discussion at an industry level of the strategies of the employers in relation to investment and disinvestment decisions. IG Chemie has access to discussions at the plant and national level, but it is less likely to participate in discussions at the European and global levels where decisions affecting the industry are increasingly being taken.

The Role of the Banks

Many commentators, however, do not see the key feature of the West German system as the interpenetration of state and civil society, or the existence of effective employers' associations, or even the prevalence of co-operative unions, relationships which are reinforced at the plant level by the *Betriebsrat* system. Rather, the really distinctive element in the picture is seen as the nature of the German financial system and, in particular, the close relationship between the banks and industry. Part of this distinctiveness is the independence of the central bank, the *Bundesbank*, although there are those who think that it has too much independence. However, at the industry level, it is the close ties between the banks and firms that are seen as essential to the successful working of the system. The most important elements of this relationship are the concept of the 'house bank' for each firm, the maintenance by banks of substantial shareholdings in firms, particulary through the mechanism of proxy shareholdings, and the presence of bank representatives on the supervisory boards of firms.

These arrangements, meant it has been argued, that:

government was insulated to a greater degree than in Britain from the complex and detailed problem of monitoring and responding to the problems of major companies. The banks served as an 'early-warning system' which identified weaknesses in industry and on occasion mounted rescue operations.[17]

They appeared to work well when the system was not under stress. They stood up less well to the difficulties that the German economy started to encounter at the end of the 1970s. In 1979 the banks pumped 930 million DM into the ailing electrical giant, AEG Telefunken, and rescheduled its debts, also bringing in a new chief executive. By 1982 AEG was in trouble again in what was described as 'West Germany's biggest indus-trial disaster'.[18] Nor is the banking system itself free of problems. The private bank Schröder, Münchmeyer, Hengst and Co. (SMH) over-extended itself by lending to industry, especially to the IBH building machinery group. In 1983, IBH was forced to make use of the *Vergleich* procedure to avoid bankruptcy. It was estimated that SMH had lent 800 million DM to IBH, compared with the bank's own capital of 110 million DM.[19] Consequently, the German banking community was obliged to hold a midnight meeting in Frankfurt to pledge over 600 million DM to keep SMH afloat. Advocates of a closer relationship between banks and industry often forget that when the two are closely enmeshed, a crisis in industry more rapidly translates into a crisis in the financial sector, or vice versa. Moreover, the extent to which the banks and industry are enmeshed with one another in West Germany may vary from sector to sector, a point that we shall develop in relation to the chemical sector.

The Importance of Sectoral Analysis

In the rest of the chapter, we shall pursue the general themes explored in the first part in relation to the particular case of the German chemical industry. These themes are perhaps best encapsulated in work by Zysman, and by Dyson, both working independently and in collabora-tion with others. Zysman argues that 'throughout the post-war years, German economic policy has rested upon a political consensus about policy and the operation of the market rather than upon an explicit political victory of one group that excluded the losers from power in politics and the markets.'[20] Dyson argues that an intellectual tradition of political economy in West Germany that has given key place to the concept of the state 'has fostered public-regarding attitudes, a deep sense of interdependency and social responsibility even in the exercise of private economic power'.[21] Problems of industrial adjustment are seen as being dealt with by tripartite bargaining between government, unions and employers, advised by economic experts, and particular industrial crises are insulated from the political arena by timely interventions by banks well informed about the affairs of industry. We would not claim that the received wisdom about West Germany is always wrong. It is sometimes right, but it draws an over-generalized picture which is insufficiently sensitive to sectoral variations.

The case for the importance of sectoral interpretation, with particular reference to West Germany, has been convincingly made by Deubner. He argues that ' "sectors" have a highly interesting role in explaining politics. The concept can make an important contribution to explaining recent West German development.'[22] Deubner points out that not all industrial sectors receive the same degree of political attention and that highly concentrated sectors have an advantage in influencing government decisions. Collaboration between employers and labour can enchance sectoral differentiation over time. Organizational variables may change more slowly than economic conditions, and employers and labour may collaborate to express sector-specific interests which are different from those of employers or labour as a whole. Deubner argues that: 'In sum, there is in West Germany an organisational potential for generating interest positions and transmitting them into government decisions.'[23]

The idea of studying particular sectors would not surprise an economist. After all, it is well known that particular industrial sectors have distinctive economic characteristics. Chemicals, for example, is a generally capital-intensive, research-intensive industry, highly internationalized in terms of the organization of production and marketing, and, after a period of rapid technological innovation and growth, now a mature industry with slower growth rates in most sub-sectors. However, analysts rarely attempt to see whether, with their distinctive economic characteristics, sectors generate their own patterns of political activity. Such political patterns will, of course, be influenced by the particular national context in which they take place, but they may also display particular sectoral features. In an internationalized industry such as chemicals, one would expect to find cross-national links, and the development of a 'policy community' at the European level, to be particularly important.

In so far as political scientists have studied individual sectors, they have tended either to study industries which are undergoing structural decline (such as steel, shipbuilding, textiles, and the automotive industry) or, to a somewhat lesser extent, glamorous 'high-tech' industries (such as microelectronics and telecommunications). Pharmaceuticals has attracted some attention because of the role of government as a major purchaser, but the chemical industry as a whole has been neglected by analysts of government–industry relations. If one simply focuses on the management of industrial crisis, one may derive a somewhat distorted picture of the different patterns of government–industry relations. One of the advantages of studying the chemical industry now is that one can analyse both the handling of the over-capacity problem in petrochemicals, which assumed crisis proportions in the early 1980s, and the more routine relationships which surround, say, the development of health and safety and environmental legislation.

The Structure of Representation in the Chemical Industry in the German Federal Republic

The view that we shall argue here, that policy varies from sector to sector, is now a new one: 'The West German policy process is extremely diversified and complex. Policy is made in different ways not only between sectors but also in the same sector'.[24] Having said this, Dyson then adopts a line of argument which is both insensitive to sectoral differences and over-sensitive to the language of declaratory policy.

At a general level it is possible to identify a shift of dominant policy style during the 1960s . . . In particular, while regulation remains an important feature of the policy process, it is no longer as characteristic of German public policy as in the 1950s.[25]

The last statement is precisely the reverse of what has happened in the chemical sector. The pressures generated by the environmental issue mean that the government is now concerned with the regulation of the chemical industry to a totally unprecedented degree.

The standard literature in English on government–industry relations tends to underplay sectoral differences in another important way. Influenced by neo-corporatist concepts, they focus on interaction between the leaders of the peak associations (the BDI, the DGB, and the government) to the more or less total neglect of the important sectoral associations. This view is best described as the *Konzertierte Aktion* fixation. For example, Dyson gives a posthumous identity to *Konzertierte Aktion* after its collapse in 1977 by arguing that two pillars of formal co-ordination emerged, one of which 'focussed on the Chancellor and on *Konzertierte Aktion*, was concerned with the problem of consensus and . . . characterised by a collaborative style'.[26] He insists that 'a central characteristic of the West German economic policy process remained a faith in the possibility of collaborative dialogue on the basis of an intellectual rationality that was rooted in, and expedited by, common interest and a "matter-of-fact" objectivity.'[27] A preoccupation with a

Sachlichkeit style of policy-making can obscure the fact that the policy-making process also involves power relations and conflicts of interest which cut across supposed common interests.

We would argue that the importance of the peak associations is not constant but variable. They were important during an SPD-led government. The strategy of the SPD necessarily involved giving the DGB an important role. The BDI, which expresses a general view, is always likely to be more important when a government is in power with which industry (i.e. the employers) have some general disagreement. When the government is seen as 'industry friendly,' the importance of the peak associations, particularly the BDI, naturally diminishes. The importance of the peak employers' organization, the BDA, is less variable as its main interlocutor is the DGB.

The chemical industry has had a sectoral association for over a hundred years. The *Verein zur Wahrung der Interessen der Chemischen Industrie Deutschlands* (Association for the Protection of the Interests of the Chemical Industry) was founded in 1877. The creation of the unified German state was a major factor, as it was in other industries, leading to the establishment of the *Verein zur Wahrung*. By this time, too, the firms had reached a size which made co-operation a likely option. The *Verein zur Wahrung* rapidly established itself as a very influential sectoral association—an importance heightened by the key role played by the chemical industry in the First World War. It also very quickly developed a network of specialist associations for particular product groups, which were able, from 1880 onwards, to be corporate members.

The chemical industry was also much more successful than other industries in preserving a privileged structure of representation in the Third Reich where it could articulate the interest of the chemical industry. This privileged position reflected the key role of IG Farben. IG Farben was created in 1925 by the fusion of the six largest chemical companies in Germany. From its creation it was the largest industrial undertaking in Germany and the world's largest chemical company, but it assumed a special importance under the Third Reich. The autarchic focus of Nazi economic policy placed IG Farben at the centre of the political economy of the Third Reich, since it necessarily entailed a concentration on the development and production of synthetic fuels and synthetic rubber. In 1934, the *Verein zur Wahrung* was integrated into a new organization, *Reichsgruppe Chemie*, an organization based on compulsory membership. However, the *Geschäftsführer* (chief functionary) of the *Verein zur Wahrung* became the chief functionary of the new group. The number of staff increased within a year from twenty-five to one hundred and fifty.

Sectoral associations for the chemical industry re-emerged fairly quickly in the British zone after 1945, but the difficulties involved in the question of IG Farben meant that it took until 1949 for a trizonal organization, the *Arbeitsgemeinschaft Chemie*, to be established. The allies had originally intended to break it up into fifty firms, but in the winter of 1951–2 three very large (BASF, Bayer, Hoechst) and one small successor company (Cassella) were founded. The Chemical Industry Association (VCI) was refounded in 1950. As is normally the case in Germany, there is a separate employers' association, formerly the *Arbeitsring*, but now known as the *Bundesarbeitgeberverband der Chemischen Industrie*.

The VCI

The VCI is often regarded as the example *par excellence* of a well resourced and efficient sectoral association. It has over 1600 direct and indirect member firms who represent over 90 per cent of the total sales in the chemicals sector. There is one major area of chemicals production which is not in the VCI. The chemicals fibres producers have their own association which is linked not to the VCI but to the associational system of the textile industry.

The total income of the VCI in 1982 was 33 million DM of which 8 million were designated for forwarding to the BDI. (The British Chemical Industries Association, CIA, had an income of under 10 million DM in 1982, with less than 50,000 DM going to the CBI.) In evaluating this figure, it ought to be borne in mind that 1982 was a relatively poor year for the German chemical industry and the boom conditions during 1984–5 will necessarily have meant a substantially increased income for the VCI.

The VCI also administers two further substantial funds which are not counted in the 33 million DM total. The more important of the two, the so-called *Fonds der Chemischen Industrie*, is designed to support research. It is raised on the basis of 0.12 per cent of sales turnover and in 1983 this amounted to 12.5 million DM. A second fund, more recently established, the *Initiative geschützter Leben*, is concerned to promote a favourable image of the chemical industry as a protector of the environment. It is mainly supported by the large firms and had a total income in 1982 of 6.5 million DM.

The organization of the VCI

Two features of the VCI's organizational structure are worthy of note. It has a territorial dimension through a structure of *Landesverbände*. These *Verbände* each correspond to a *Land*, except in the case of the *Landesverband Nord* which includes Bremen, Hamburg, Lower Saxony, Schleswig-Holstein. This territorial dimension allows the VCI to intervene at *Land* level, a point to which we shall return. The regional structure in the British CIA is of less central importance.

More important than the *Landesverbände* are the thirty-one *Fachverbände*, or specialist associations for particular products. They are nearly all actually located in the VCI headquarters in Frankfurt (25 out of 31). Their relationship with the VCI itself is very close. The presence of most of these *Verbände* in the same building clearly aids co-ordination, and monthly meetings are held between the permanent staff heads of the VCI, the *Landesverbände*, and the *Fachverbände*. Co-ordination is also much easier, according to a senior VCI official, because the big three (the IG Farben successor companies: BASF, Bayer, Hoechst) play a major role in most associations whether territorial or specialized. Nevertheless, the *Fachverbände* are probably more important to the smaller firms and dominance of the committees by the big three is not so apparent. In Britain, some of the sub-sector associations (e.g. the paintmakers) are not affiliated to the CIA and, of those that are affiliated, the relationship with the main organization is often rather distant.

Government–Industry Relations in the Chemical Industry

The relationship between the government and the chemical industry in the Federal Republic reflects the particular situation of the chemical industry rather more than some generalized concept like social partnership. As an industry with a very high degree of competitiveness internationally, the chemical industry has looked to the government not for sectoral intervention but for positive *Rahmenbedingungen* (framework conditions). These had to include, given the international character of the chemical industry and Germany's dependence on external feedstocks, a very strong emphasis by any West German government on free trade. Other framework conditions would be an energy policy beneficial to industry, and a fairly lenient tax regime.

The chemical industry constantly emphasizes its independence from government. A major case in point is research. The chemical industry in Germany has always had a very strong commitment to research. It lays great stress on the fact that 96 per cent of this research is financed by the industry itself. State support for research is confined to a joint biotechnology research initiative, and state support for research places in smaller firms. Relations with the Research Ministry were very bad during the period of the SPD/FDP coalition. The chemical industry was totally opposed to the attempts by the ministers, Volker Hauff and Horst Ehmke, to create large research projects designed to help future oriented industries. They were also very opposed to the *Humanisierung der Arbeit* research project. This caused them concern both because of its expense and because it was seen as a sop to the unions. The Research Minister in 1986, Dr Riesenhuber, is a qualified chemist by training and his perceptions mesh fairly closely with that of the chemical industry.

Relations with the federal government are almost exclusively channelled through the VCI and its associated *Fachverbände*. (In Britain, the government relations departments of major firms play a larger role.) At the *Land* level, relations with governments are handled both by the relevant *Landesverband* and by the firms themselves. In the case of the big three, they each have a close relationship with one *Land* government (i.e. Bayer: North Rhine Westphalia, BASF: Rhineland-Palatinate, Hoechst: Hesse). The anxiety of Hoechst about the appointment of a Green, Joschka Fischer, as Minister of Environment in Hesse in December 1985, means that Hoechst will cultivate even more closely their links with the Hessian Economics Ministry.

In general, the VCI takes up issues with the government itself. It is much less likely to use the BDI than in the past. Even in the SPD/FDP period of government it was less likely to use the BDI since the chemical industry was much less interested in *Konzertierte Aktion* and tripartism which they saw as giving too much influence to the unions. In the view of the chemical industry, they could manage their own unions and did not need the state or peak associations to help them. This lack of enthusiasm for peak associations also reflects the much less strongly 'national' character of the chemical industry. Neither American multinational companies nor ICI have shown great fondness for the peak associations in West Germany. The foreign-based multinationals are gaining in importance and in 1985 the head of ICI Germany became a member of the VCI *Präsidium*. A leading figure in the VCI told us that, if an issue affected more than chemicals, he was very likely to turn to his opposite numbers in the Electronics and Machine Tool industries, both based in Frankfurt, rather than go through the BDI.

The links with government are normally routed through the Bonn liaison office of the VCI. The major contact ministry is the Economics Ministry. It has a fairly small Chemicals and Rubber Section (three or four officials), which co-ordinates chemical issues in the Ministry. The equivalent section of Chemicals and Textiles Division in the DTI is much larger (fourteen officals above executive officer level). In discussion, VCI officials reacted unfavourably to the British concept of 'sponsorship' which they saw as implying too close a relationship to government. In their view the section acted as an *Anwalt* (attorney) for the chemical industry. Relations with the Economics Ministry are good. The Economics Ministry has a way of looking at things which is very congenial to the chemical industry. 'It became and remained a political spokesman for the doctrine of social market economy.'[28] It is also very useful to the chemical industry that the Economics Ministry has the day-to-day responsibility for the co-ordination of the increasingly important European policy.

The VCI is normally able to make its influence felt at a fairly early stage in the formulation of a measure. At the first draft stage of a bill which might affect the chemical industry, the relevant section will normally send a draft to the VCI for comment. The VCI then consults with the experts in the firms. Normally there is a provision for a hearing at this stage and the VCI delegation will often be made up largely of experts from the firms who will, however, speak as representatives of the VCI. There was a great deal of dissatisfaction expressed about the practice of the Interior Ministry during the SPD/FDP government, where, on proposed environmental measures, the VCI representatives would often find themselves flanked by ten or eleven environmental groups at this point. This is clearly the key stage, but the VCI normally has the right to make representations during the passage of a bill through the *Bundestag*.

This rather favourable government–industry interface for the chemical industry has been disturbed in recent years by the increasing saliency of the environmental issue and the pressures this has generated for the regulation of the chemical industry. The environment is the major area where the chemical industry is on the defensive. It is aware that its public image is bad in relation to the protection of the environment. It constantly speaks of the Janus face of the chemical industry in public perception, by which it means that the economic importance of the chemical industry is recognized but that public opinion is very critical of it in relation to the environment. In order to try and combat this perception the chemical industry spends heavily on improving their procedures to protect the environment. It claims to have spent 30 billion DM on protecting the environment in the last ten years—a figure which is twice as much in relation to turnover as the American chemical industry, and three times as much as the French. Since 1978 it has also spent very heavily on advertisements designed to impress the German public with the environmental achievements of the chemical industry (*Initiative geschützter Leben*).

The chemical industry has a number of allies in resisting environmental pressures. The Economics Ministry is an important ally and can, as we have seen, usually be relied on to support the position of the industry.[29] Those parts of the chemical industry which relate to agricultural production have an even more effective ally in the Agriculture Ministry. Another important ally is the scientific establishment. The chemical industry has constantly cultivated its contacts with senior German scientists, and it gets a great deal of support from this quarter—an important point in a country where legitimization by professorial opinion is still important. The last important ally of the industry is IG Chemie. Although concerned about safety at work, their primary concern is with the security of job places. They can be relied on to take a vehemently anti-Green standpoint.[30] Inside the SPD and the DGB they take a line which is mildly reformist on environmental matters, and they have managed to draw the teeth of those like the IG Metall who were interested in very far-reaching measures.

The Relationship with the Financial Sector

This comment by a VCI official in interview illustrates the traditional financial relationship:

> In the old days, it used to be said that 60 per cent of the representatives on the boards of German firms were from the Deutsche Bank, 20 per cent were people close to it and 20 per cent were from other banks.

The view that banks are 'the efficient secret' of 'organised private enterprise' in the Federal Republic stretches back in English writings to Andrew Shonfield.[31] It has become a major theme in the analysis of Dyson and others.

The argument that banks play an important role in guiding and co-ordinating the strategies of German industrial companies is based both on their historic relationship and some observable present-day realities. The late industrialization of Germany, and the absence of the sort of relations that Britain possessed with the United States and the Empire meant that German capital was largely invested at home. The Stock Exchange in Germany was a much less important provider of capital for industry than its counterparts in Anglo-American countries. In this situation the banks played a major role in lending capital to industry. The system of having representatives of the banks, especially the Deutsche Bank (see above), on the boards of industrial firms dates back to the Imperial period, as does the system of interlocking directorships.

The close relationship between the banks and industry continued in the post-war period. Dyson has argued that in some areas it has been strengthened—for example, in construction where outstanding credits after 1945 were converted into bank-held shares and bonds to assist reconstruction.[32] Much has been written on the role of Hermann Abs and other prominent bankers who played an important part in post-war German industry. It is often pointed out that the share of equity capital in the corporate capital structure of German companies is less than in American and British counterparts, and they are, therefore, heavily dependent on the banks for loan finance.[33] It is further argued that it is not so much the proportion of shares actually held by the banks themselves (8 per cent in 1983) but that German shareholders still continue to deposit their shares with the banks. Zysman has claimed that 85 per cent of all privately held shares are held in proxy by the banks.[34] The possession of these 'proxy shares' means the banks play a dominating role at shareholders' meetings through the exercise of their *Depotstimmrecht* (proxy voting right). In particular, this secures a major representation for the banks on the supervisory boards of the firms and by extension allows them a major say in the choice of personnel for the executive board.

Banks occupied about 15 per cent of all seats on the supervisory boards of the 100 biggest joint-stock companies in the FRG in 1974 and were represented on the boards of 75 of them. Some 57 per cent of these seats were occupied by representatives of the three biggest banks. The Deutsche Bank is represented on the supervisory boards of 38 of the 100 biggest companies, The Dresdner Bank on 23 and the Commerzbank on 14. According to the Monopolkommission, a fifth of all the chairmen of the above firms supervisory boards in 1978 come from the banks, three quarters of them from the big three and 60 per cent from the Deutsche Bank alone.[35]

Attention has also been paid to the role of the *Hausbank* and it is often argued that the close relationship with a particular bank aids the firm by providing a form of industrial early-warning system, and that it plays an important role in pressing economic rationality on a firm during the process of *Sanierung* (rationalization).

Before we turn to look at the relationship between the banks and the chemical industry, we wish to indicate a few reservations about the line of argument pursued by authors writing in English. Firstly, they have underestimated the changes at work as the German economy becomes more internationalized. German shares are now much more attractive both to foreign buyers and to the Germans themselves. More importantly, the argument that the relationship with the banks gives German firms an edge is not self-evidently true. Despite expansion overseas in the seventies and eighties, the German banking system remains less international than its British and American counterparts. Precisely because of this, the advice it offers may not always be appropriate, the German banks know German markets very well but their relative Germano-centrism may make them less prescient guides to international markets. Indeed, it could well be argued that the bank connection is one of the factors contributing to 'the rigidites' analysed by Jonathan Carr.[36] It is also by no means the case that the banks are always successful in promoting the restructuring of an industry. They failed in their attempts to bring about a rationalization of the German tyre sector through a merger between Continental Gummi Werke and Phoenix.

The Relationship between the Banks and the Chemical Industry

'The chemical branch is so liquid that the banks are just happy to have a share of the action.' This comment by a VCI official sets the tone for the discussion of this relationship.

The sheer size of the three dominating German chemical firms means that they do not have 'house banks' in the conventional sense. They are simply too large and all three have relations with a number of banks. They engage in a continuous process of bank evaluation and change the volume of business they give to each accordingly.

The key factor is the international character of the chemical industry. This has two consequences. Firstly, the companies are oriented towards global markets. It is important to bring products onto the market simultaneously. This is an area in which banks have no special expertise and they would hesitate to offer advice. Secondly, the international scope of their activity necessarily means that an important area is reserved for international banks. Bayer, for instance, sold more, in 1985, in North America than in West Germany. German banks have traditionally been less strong internationally; therefore, a certain volume of business exists for American and British banks.

The relationship with the American banks is a crucial one. The three major firms have long been established in the United States and they are all rapidly expanding their operations there. Their assets were sequestrated in both wars and Bayer lost the right to use its own name in the United States. A leading bank figure in Frankfurt said in interview: 'The relationship with the American banks was crucial for the big three restarting in the post IG Farben situation.' Good relations with the American banks were a necessity for two reasons. Firstly, to re-establish themselves on the American market. Secondly, to try and influence American policy on the dismantling of IG Farben.

American banks play an important role in the German chemicals industry, providing financial services for the external operations of German chemical firms, and for the German operations of American-based chemical firms. German banks do play an important role in financing the chemical industry, but it does not appear to be as important as in some sectors. It is generally reckoned that the proportion of *Eigenkapital* (capital created by the firm) is twice as high in the chemical industry than the normal proportion in German industry.[37] The chemical firms enjoy excellent access to all financial markets.

Data on the share structure of BASF in 1985 shows that banks and insurance firms held 19 per cent of the shares. The role of the insurance companies as providers of capital for industry in Germany has gone relatively unremarked in England, but interviews have indicated that they played quite a major role in relation to the chemical industry. Legal regulations to protect policy holders require insurance companies only to lend money to firms which are able to furnish a creditworthy certificate (*Schuldscheinfahig*). In simple terms, these are companies with a higher than normal proportion of *Eigenkapital*. This condition is particularly met by the large chemical companies. Funds provided by the insurance companies are very important for long-term finance.

The boom of the last two years has in any case further reduced the role of external capital. A favourite newspaper headline in recent years has been 'Chemie schwimmt im Geld'. The same point has been made more soberly by Herr H. Paudtke of the VCI. He has pointed out in his yearly reports that liquidity and the creation of *Eigenkapital* has improved markedly in recent years.[38] Hoechst reduced its external capital by 3.2 billion DM in the period 1982–5 despite costly rationalization measures.[39] BASF has been particularly successful in reducing dependence on external finance. Similarly, the pursuit of a reduction of the proportion of external finance constituted an important element in the speech of Hermann-Josef Strenger, the chief of Bayer, to the 1985 Annual Shareholders meeting.[40]

We have noted some difference in the financial relationship of the banks to the chemical industry from that thought to prevail in German industry, but consideration of the influence they might generally wish to wield cannot be restricted to a discussion about their role in the provision of capital. We have already argued that the nature of the chemical business is likely to reduce the role of the banks since it involves a very high level of technical and scientific expertise and detailed knowledge of international markets. Another factor is that, while the great chemical firms engage in vertical and horizontal integration, they basically stay within the area they know best (*Chemie betreibt Chemie*) and have no desire to create conglomerates. All these factors tend to reduce the role of the banks in proferring advice.

Because of the recent prosperity of the chemical industry, those who argue for the influence of the banks would not be surprised by their passivity in relation to chemicals. The prosperity of the industry is important but it is not the whole story. In the early eighties when profits were down and the industry was burdened with problems of over-capacity, they did not turn to the banks for advice. The leaders of the chemical industry have a very strong feeling of group indentification (the solidarity of the chemical industry) and a tremendous pride in being chemists. All speeches by leading members seem to conclude with the comment that, if they had their time over again, they would choose to study chemistry. Herr Strenger, the head of Bayer, is the first head of one of the IG Farben successors not to have a doctorate in chemistry; most, indeed, have been professors. He has spent all his working life with Bayer but the fact that his qualifications are commercial rather than scientific is cause for constant comment. The common background in chemistry, normally with a distinguished background in research, strengthens the view of the leaders of the chemical industry that they know best.

This determination to run the chemical industry on their own terms has already been remarked on in relation to their desire to reduce the amount of external capital. It is apparent also in their attitude to the supervisory boards. The supervisory boards of the great companies normally have two representatives of the banks in their membership. The difference is that, whereas, among the hundred leading companies, the banks often provide the chairman (31 out of the top 100 German companies in 1975),[41] the chemical companies provide their own chairman. The convention in the big three companies is that the immediate past executive chairman, on retirement, becomes chairman of the Supervisory Board. This convention, which parallels that operating in the VCI, indicates the determination of the leaders of the chemical industry to keep the matter of running the industry strictly in the hands of those they consider best qualified for the task. Given that the person promoted is invariably a long-serving company employee, and normally a scientist of some distinction, the range of choice open to the banks is very limited.

The two representatives from the banks are normally flanked by three from large industrial companies, such as Mannesmann or Metallgesellschaft, and one or two from insurance. They play a role in helping to choose between a restricted number of people for the executive board. They are also considered useful additions to export promotion delegations when the chemical industry is attempting to open up new markets such as China. Key figures in the chemical industry sit on numerous boards both in the chemical industry and in other sectors. They also seem to have no inhibitions about being chairman in other sectors in spite of not allowing outsiders to become chairman in the chemicals sector. Dr Grünewald (Bayer) is chairman of the Supervisory Board of the insurance company, Allianz Versicherung. Professor Sammet (Hoechst) is Deputy Chairman of Allianz Leben. These positions indicate the importance that the chemical companies attach to the insurance companies as a source of finance.

The banks do, however, play a much more important role in relation to the smaller firms like Merck and Boehringer. Here they are not only an important source of finance, but also of investment advice. They sometimes have joint ventures with these smaller companies and have been very helpful in providing capital for new ventures. This contrasts with the situation in Britain where smaller, innovative companies often have difficulty in raising finance, particularly for higher risk projects. The development of the Unlisted Securites Market has been of limited assistance to smaller chemical companies; only six were listed by 1985.

The Orientation towards Research

We would argue that part of the success of the German chemicals sector is to be explained by its attitude towards, and the use it makes of, research. We have already noted that the leading figures in the German chemical giants are conventionally expected to have undertaken research themselves. This same positive attitude towards research is reflected in the personnel policy of the VCI itself. Traditionally, the staff of any *Verband* in Germany was overwhelmingly composed of those who had studied law. Many who work for the VCI have been recruited from scientific research institutes and universities.

In describing the activities of the VCI, a very senior official mentioned contact with the scientific community and the promotion of research as one of the most central tasks of the VCI. Co-operation with the scientific establishment, to which, indeed, some of the heads of the chemical firms themselves belong, is extremely close. Co-operation is very intense within the procedures of the chemicals law, and the chemical industry often calls on members of the scientific establishment to defend the chemical industry when it is under attack from environmentalists.

The major forum for co-operation is the *Fonds der Chemischen Industrie* which we have already noted. This is financed by a voluntary compulsory contribution (*freiwülliger Pflichtbeitrag*) on turnover. The *Fonds* is run by the chief of the Research and Technological Development of the VCI. The board is composed of leading members of the VCI and the Society of German chemists.

The *Fonds* exists to encourage basic research in the universities. Their support is given to outstanding researchers rather than particular projects. In 1979/80, 7000 university teachers, researchers, and post-graduate students were supported by it.[42] The *Fonds* and the chemical industry generally have always been particularly concerned to encourage talented young chemists, no doubt hoping that this will be reflected in a positive attitude towards the chemical industry as well as increased innovation.

Professor Franck, the President of the VCI, announced that the *Fonds* had established a new scheme to encourage young chemists at the annual general meeting of the VCI on 18 October 1985.[43] All chemists who manage to complete their doctorate within fifteen semesters (i.e., one less than normally), and achieve the grade of 'very good', will have their names published in the specialist journals. The name of the supervisor and the university will also be published. The candidate will receive 2000

DM from the *Fonds*. This scheme is clearly designed both to maintain the standard at the universities (a subject of burning interest to the chemical industry), and to encourage close links with the industry. It will also make it easier for the big chemical companies to recruit outstandingly talented chemists.

The total investment of the chemical industry in basic and applied research is very high; for example, in 1985 it was expected to be 7.6 billion DM.[44] The total is now approximately equal to the amount spent on new plant. The spread of leasing and the move out of bulks has decreased the proportion spent on plant. It represents just over a quarter of the total spent by all German industry on research and development. This research effort of the chemical industry has been extremely success-ful. Admittedly, it is difficult to provide reliable measures of technologi-cally-based innovative capacity. The traditional measure of the import-export balance of licences and patents is less useful than it once was, as it is now often merely a dependent variable of the ownership structure. Foreign-owned firms tend to import patents and licences from their home country. The relatively good balance between imports and exports of licences in the German chemical industry, as compared with the electronics industry, probably reflects the greater international expansion of the chemical industry as much as it does the state of research.[45] However, West Germany would not be the leading world exporter in a research intensive industry such as chemicals if it did not have a well-run research effort.

Research potential is concentrated in the large firms; four hundred small firms with less than 1000 employees provide 10 per cent of the total amount spent on research at the firm level. Sixty firms employing between 1000 and 10,000 employees contribute 30 per cent, and the ten largest firms each with over 10,000 employees dominate, with 60 per cent of the amount available. Similarly, in Britain, ICI outstrips all other firms in the industry in terms of its spending on research and develop-ment, although it tends to rank below the German firms in terms of such spending as a percentage of sales.

This intense concern with research in West Germany is flanked by an equally intense concern to improve the qualifications of the workforce. In 1984 a total of 940 million DM was spent on educating and training the workforce: 700 million DM for the 32,000 apprentices and 240 million DM on short training courses for the established workforce.[46]

The chemical industry has been extremely successful in its strategy of encouraging basic research in universities, while undertaking massive applied research at the firm level. A clear view of the strategy of Bayer is given in an unpublished speech to the Friedrich-Ebert Stiftung by Professor Grünewald, then head of Bayer, who described the goal of research as being 'to develop more intelligent products and to extend to new technologies which require less resources—raw materials, energy, but which lead to a higher level of added value'.[47] The same strategy is being pursued by the other companies, especially the giants. Professor Grünewald has, however, provided fuller figures than exist for the other companies. In 1967 research and development represented 5.7 per cent of Bayer's turnover. By 1984 it had reached 6.7 per cent. More important, however, is the change in the areas in which it is spent. In 1970 research in the area of *Pflanzenschutz* (pesticides) and pharmaceuticals represented 29.8 per cent of the total Bayer spent on research; by 1983 it represented 51.4 per cent. Basic research remained constant at over 11 per cent but all other areas were sharply reduced as a percentage of the total.

The picture at Hoechst is very similar, though they also want to develop in technical ceramics. BASF are moving away more slowly from bulk chemicals but are pursuing a similar research strategy with greater emphasis on chemicals that can be used in the electronic and aerospace industries. Other companies are active in more specialized fields. The policy of self-financing of research by the industry does not apply in the same measure to smaller firms where some research places are financed by the Research Ministry.

In Britain, a report by the Chemicals EDC has questioned whether 'by comparison with our principal European competitors . . . the general level of chemical industry R and D in the UK is sufficient for the industry's future health'.[48] Moreover, it was found that 'chemical industry R and D has declined both in real, absolute terms and as a proportion of all manufacturing R and D in recent years'.[49] The report particularly drew attention to the problems faced by small and medium-sized companies which have benefited from special arrangements in West Germany. Our British research suggests that the problem is not simply one of making available additional resources but, as the Chemicals EDC recognized, the efficiency of information flows between the potential beneficiaries of research and development.

Conclusions

In our treatment of the chemical industry in this chapter we have stressed three main themes. First, the VCI is highly effective in co-ordinating, developing, and articulating the views of employers in the German chemical industry, although it should not be treated as analogous to a form of industry self-government, as has been implied by some commentators. The VCI has a particularly good working relationship with the Ministry of Economics, but has had more difficulties with the environmental issue, which has been handled by other ministries, particularly the Ministry of the Interior. Similarly, in Britain we have found that the chemical industry has a good relationship with the Chemicals and Textiles Division at DTI, but has had more problems in its relationships with other ministries which lie outside the core chemicals policy community. We see the main constituents of this community as the leading firms (especially ICI), the CIA, and the Chemicals and Textiles Division of DTI. In West Germany, it is centred on the 'big three', the VCI, the BACI, and the Economics Ministry. Secondly, we do not believe that the received wisdom about the role of the financial sector in West Germany can be readily applied to the case of the chemical industry: the 'house banks' have a less central role; the American banks are more important; and the literature has tended to underplay the importance of the insurance companies. Thirdly, we do consider that there are important differences in the way in which research and development issues are handled in the two countries; this is of considerable importance in a research-intensive industry. Comparing the chemical industry in the two countries not only tells us something about the industry itself, but also allows us both to modify some points, and reinforce others, in the received wisdom about government–industry relations in the German Federal Republic.

Notes

The authors would like to thank Professor Dr M. Groser of the University of Bamberg for the assistance he has provided to their research effort in the FRG.

1. T. Iljen, ' "Better Living Through Chemistry": The Chemical Industry in the World Economy', *International Organization* 37 (1983), 647–80, p. 654.
2. Figures derived from CEFIC, 'Situation and Outlook of the European Chemical Industry 1984–1985' (Brussels, 1985).

3. P. Lawrence, *Managers and Management in West Germany* (London, 1980), p. 15.

4. P. Katzenstein, 'West Germany as Number Two: Reflections on the West German Model' in A. Markovits (ed.), *The Political Economy of West Germany* (New York: Praeger, 1982), p. 203.

5. K. Dyson, 'Cultural, Ideological and Structural Context' in K. Dyson and S. Wilks (ed.), *Industrial Crisis* (Oxford: Martin Robertson, 1983), p. 45.

6. C. Maier, 'Bonn ist doch Weimar: Informal Reflections on the Historical Legacy of the Federal Republic' in A. Markovits (ed.), op. cit. (n. 4), p. 188.

7. Ilgen, op. cit. (n. 1), p. 661.

8. W. Streeck, *Industrial Relations in West Germany* (London: Heinemann, 1984), p. 145.

9. J. Donges, 'Industrial Policies in West Germany's Not so Market-Oriented Economy', *World Politics* 3 (1980), 185–204, p. 189.

10. Ibid., p. 193.

11. Streeck, op. cit. (n. 8) pp. 64–9.

12. A. Tylecote, *The Causes of the Present Inflation* (London, 1981), p. 155.

13. W. Streeck, 'Between Pluralism and Corporatism: German Business Associations and the State', *Journal of Public Policy* 3 (1983), 265–84, p. 279.

14. M. Kreile, 'West Germany: the Dynamics of Expansion' in P. J. Katzenstein (ed.), *Between Power and Plenty: Foreign Economic Policies of Advanced Industrial States* (Cambridge Mass.: Harvard University Press, 1978), p. 201.

15. Streeck, 'Between Pluralism and Corporatism' (see n. 13), p. 279.

16. Kreile, op. cit. (n. 14), p. 202.

17. K. Dyson, 'The Politics of Economic Recession in West Germany' in A. Cox (ed.), *Politics, Policy and the European Recession* (London: Macmillan, 1982), p. 39.

18. J. Esser, W. Fach, and K. Dyson, 'Social Market and Modernisation Policy: West Germany' in K. Dyson and S. Wilks (eds.), op. cit. (n. 5), p. 119.

19. *Financial Times*, 9 November 1983.

20. J. Zysman, *Governments, Markets and Growth* (Oxford: Martin Robertson, 1983), p. 256.

21. K. Dyson, 'The Politics of Economic Management in West Germany' in W. Paterson and G. Smith (eds.), *The West German Model* (London: Frank Cass, 1981), p. 54.

22. C. Deubner, 'Change and Internationalisation in Industry: Toward a Sectoral Interpretation of West German Politics', *International Organization* 38 (1984), 501–35, p. 501.

23. Ibid., p. 519.

24. K. Dyson, 'West Germany: The Search for a Rationalist Consensus' in J. Richardson (ed.), *Policy Styles in Western Europe* (London: Allen & Unwin, 1982), p. 17.

25. Ibid., p. 21.

26. Ibid., p. 41.

27. Ibid., p. 35.

28. Loc. cit.

29. As shown by its constant support during the passage of the Chemicals Law of 1980. See M. Zimmermann, 'Struktur und Einfluss de Chemie-industrie auf die Umweltpolitik', Diplomarbeit am Otto-Suhr Institut der Freien Universität Berlin, pp. 155–83.

30. See the declaration by IG Chemie about the Hesse coalition.

31. A. Shonfield, *Modern Capitalism: the Changing Balance of Public and Private Power* (Oxford: OUP, 1965), especially Chapter 11.

32. K. Dyson, 'West Germany: the Search for a Rationalist Consensus' (see n. 24), p. 19.

33. Zysman, op. cit. (n. 20), p. 124.

34. Ibid., p. 264.

35. D. Webber, 'Framework of Government Industry Relations in the FRG', typescript, University of Sussex, 1985.

36. *Financial Times*, 23 October 1985.

37. *Wirtschaftswoche*, 20 May 1983, p. 106.

38. H. Paudtke, 'Chemie im Spiegel der Bilanzen', *Chemische Industrie Suplemean*, No. 1, 1985.

39. *Neue Züricher Zeitung*, 15 May 1985.

40. *Neue Züricher Zeitung*, 9 May 1985.

41. Dyson, 'West Germany: the Search for a Rationalist Consensus' (see n. 24), p. 39.

42. W. R. Streeck, *Chemische Industrie: Strukturwandlungen und Perspektiven* (Berlin, 1984), p. 80.

43. *Chemie Nachtrichten*, 18 October 1985.

44. Ibid.

45. For the relevant data see 'Entwicklung des Patent-und Lizenverkehrs mit dem Ausland in den Jahren 1982 und 1983', *Monatsberichte der Deutschen Bundesbank*, 36, Juli, 25–40.

46. *Chemie Nachtrichten*, 18 October 1985.

47. In the Institut der Deutschen Wirtschaft Archive, Köln, p. 18.

48. Chemicals EDC, 'Support for Research and Development in Small and Medium-Sized Firms in the UK Chemical Industry' (London: NEDO, 1984), p. 5.

49. Ibid., p. 6.

4

Government–Industry Relations in Japan: Access, Communication, and Competitive Collaboration

Richard Boyd

The figures are eloquent testimony to an incontrovertible fact, the huge industrial success of Japan. Consider the following: at a time when the USA's share of world GNP has declined from 33 per cent in 1960 to 22 per cent in 1980, and is continuing to decline, Japan's share has more than tripled (1960: 3 per cent; 1980: 10 per cent). Japan's annual real growth rate was 5.2 per cent in the 1970s and a figure of 4 per cent per annum is projected for the rest of the century. The sluggish USA only managed 3.1 per cent in the 1970s, and the projection until AD 2000 is 2.5 per cent per annum. When the Japanese and British performance is set against that of the USA, the dynamism of the one and the stagnation of the other is apparent: real GDP per employed person in 1950 (own country price weights) was 13.5 per cent in Japan and 47.2 per cent in the UK (USA = 100), 42.1 per cent and 50.3 per cent in 1970, and 58.4 per cent and 54.5 per cent in 1980.[1]

Calculate it as you will, the conclusions are the same: while Britain and Europe accustom themselves to higher unemployment than in the worst years of the depression, Japan's workforce of approximately 59 million has only 2.6 per cent unemployed (1,540,000). While the USA contemplates a decade without real improvement in productivity, the Japanese continue to predict annual increments of 5 per cent. These advantages have not been offset by runaway inflation hereto, and, compared with both the USA and the UK, Japan has a better economic performance.

Trade is central to the economic achievement of Japan. A notorious dependence on the import of raw materials (28.2 per cent of energy requirements, 99.8 per cent of iron ore, 96.8 per cent of copper, 98.5 per cent of tin, 87.5 per cent of lead, and 100 per cent of needs in aluminium and nickel) is offset by a success in exporting her manufactures, which makes the Japanese miracle not only a marvel to be applauded, but a threat to be countered. The challenge posed by the West's most formidable industrial competitor cannot be overemphasized. The value of Japan's export of manufactured goods was $12 billion in 1968, $34 billion in 1973, $134 billion in 1982, and $165 billion in 1984. A relatively insignificant market such as the UK (worth only 2.7 per cent of Japan's exports in 1984) consumes almost $5 billion-worth of Japanese exports annually. Superior labour productivity, a more effective use of energy (in 1973 Japan used only 57 per cent as much energy as the USA for each unit of GNP—a percentage which had fallen to 43 per cent in 1980, and continues to fall),[2] and a relentless search for new products and new markets means that the challenge is here to stay and that the urgency of the question, 'How do the Japanese do it?', grows ever greater.

Analysts mindful of Japan's precise targeting of industries and its demonstrated ability to adjust to changing international economic circumstances—to focus efforts in one decade on making the steel, auto, and shipbuilding industries world beaters, and then in the next to attempt the same for computers, banking, and biotechnology—claim that Japan's success is to have found a formula for close government–industry collaboration in the management of the economy. Political leaders on both sides of the Atlantic agree and have asserted that 'the basis for the restoration of the US economy is the development of an industrial policy'.[3] In the UK senior figures from both sides of the House of Commons are confident that what Britain needs is a guiding administrative hand modelled on Japan's Ministry of International Trade and Industry.

The model is not well understood. Old myths die hard. 'Japan Inc.' lingers on and even gains new recruits:

Frankly, too few Americans—even those with a deep interest in forcing Japan to come to terms with us—really understand the closely interwoven monolith that rules Japan. This is not the phantom 'Japan Inc.', which is only a distorted attempt to 'name the beast' that confronts us. The actual monolith is part and parcel of Japan's traditional—that is pre-war—ruling elite.[4]

When they pass they are replaced by newer, more sophisticated myths. 'Administrative Guidance'—the power enjoyed by the Ministry of International Trade and Industry (MITI), and other agencies, to determine the behaviour of the private sector in the absence of any specific legal entitlement or sanction—is the critical means which enables MITI to work the Japanese economy by remote control. What does the device run on? Culture,[5] or the 'MITI knows best' syndrome?[6] Or (and without any qualification or apology) bureaucratic bullying: the public service has the means to get even with recalcitrant industrialists?[7] On the other hand, does it exist at all? 'No', say Namiki;[8] 'No, not since 1963', says Noguchi;[9] 'Yes, since 1963', says Johnson.[10] And in the self-same book to which Namiki contributed, the editor writes, 'No one denies that Japanese ministries issue a large amount of guidance in various forms to achieve their policy goals and perform their administrative functions'.[11]

The explanatory devices, as much as the mechanisms they purport to explain, approximate to the mythical. Take culture. At its best, it is argued that the coincidence of an acute scarcity of resources (food, energy, and raw materials), physical density (born in the first instance of the pressure of a large population on a small land mass, and exacerbated by the mountains and forests which make much of the land unusable), and a harsh and unforgiving environment of natural disasters (typhoons, earthquakes, volcanoes, tidal waves, floods, and mud-slides) has taught the Japanese to view the world in Darwinian terms: to triumph over inherent weakness and manage adversity.[12] These physical and geographical characteristics reinforce a social history of groupism, a profound sense of mutual interdependence (reinforced by the exigencies of rice cultivation), which has made debt and obligation critical values. 'The fact is, Japanese citizens have been forced to cope with social interdependence and close living for centuries. As a result, there has been great capacity to transfer rural values to urban living.'[13] Not least of which is the consequence that the search for consensus and a harmonious resolution of conflict is seen as imperative: an imperative widely acknowledged to be of significance for the formulation and implementation of industrial policy in contemporary Japan.[14]

Explanations in terms of culture which operate at this level of generality are unhelpful and all but imposible to test empirically. A more detailed enquiry will often reveal culture to be a 'black box' drawn around unexamined instrumentalities, as such it is an obstacle to understanding. Caution is in order too, because culture precludes any distinction between the actual attitudes, expectations, and aspirations of the individual members of society, it obscures ideology and the persuasive rhetoric of special interests.

Government–Industry Relations in Japan: the Argument

Culture is no explanatory panacea, but plainly the government–industry relation is informed by a complex of historical, social, and geographical factors. If culture is understood as a shorthand for this matrix, then it can be argued that close collaboration between industry and government in pursuit of 'national' economic goals is historically and culturally sanctioned. Industry expects government to approach it and initiate, while government does not demarcate the public and private spheres in the fashion which is assumed by the Western notion of 'intervention'. Indeed, intervention and non-intervention are seen as two styles of regulation. There is a popular expectation that both industry and government will come to agreement, so much so that public expression in the media of failures to agree results in the resignation of those responsible.

At the same time, the government–industry relation is in no sense the simple manifestation of a peculiar culture. Consider the principal instruments of industrial policy: they include measures to keep the cost of capital low; manipulation of the foreign exchange rate so as to keep the value of the yen and thus the price of Japan's exports artificially low; tax exemptions and other special tax advantages; extensive subsidization and preferential capital allocations; industrial and technological targeting; formal and informal protection of home markets and domestic producers; closed public procurements; guaranteed or riskless investments; government-inspired cartels and government sponsorship and organization of large-scale, national research projects for the development of new technologies and with a view to their subsequent commercial development.

Few, if any, of these are unusual, let alone exotic. Few are utilized more extensively than in the West—with the possible exception of cartels. The US is more reliant on NASA and Pentagon procurements, France subsidizes high technology (particularly telecommunications) more than Japan, and Europe, in general, depends upon import quotas and tariffs to protect its industries. Nor, for that matter, is the existence of intimate, systematic, and goal-oriented government–industry relations in Japan evidence of a 'Japan Inc.' conspiracy. It is well to assume (until demonstrated otherwise) that the Japanese businessman is motivated by much the same concerns as the Western businessman, and defines his interests similarly. If, then, he is predisposed to collaborate with government, it is not because he is patriotic or typically Japanese (although he may well be both), but because he or his company or industry association has learnt that such collaboration can be of material benefit.

Communication between government and industry is good—indeed more important than particular instrumentalities. What, it can be hypothesized, underpins industrial policy and is the condition of its effectiveness, is the existence of a series of linkages and privileged points of access and communication between government and industry, the effect of which is to integrate the industrial policy community, and to facilitate the movement of ideas, the formation and representation of interests. The linkages themselves are not remarkable: many similar channels exist in other industrial nations. What is distinctive is the extensive use made of them. This is a consequence of the insulation of the industrial policy-making and implementation process from public debate. The government and industry relation is private, and considerable benefits accrue to the principal parties to the relationship because of that privacy which it is in their interests to protect. Effectively, they are constrained to use the channels that exist to come to agreement, lest the open expression of disagreement publicize the process and invite the involvement of otherwise excluded parties with conflicting interests to represent (namely, the labour unions, environmental groups, opposition parties, women, small and medium enterprise associations).

Such is the argument. Consideration will first be given to Japan's experiment with 'industrial policy' in the late nineteenth century, in the belief that the current practice of government–industry relations is informed by a particular historical legacy. Subsequently, the principal actors in contemporary government–industry relations will be introduced and their interrelations will be adumbrated. Finally, some of the principal instruments of industrial policy will be surveyed.

Government–Industry Collaboration: the Historical Legacy

Historically, it has long been believed by the Japanese that:

Our people are particularly lacking in daring, to encourage them to overcome this weakness, and to study industry and overcome its difficulties is a responsibility the government must assume.[15]

In late nineteenth-century Japan, 'industrial policy' was a desperate stratagem to preserve national integrity and to escape the disastrous cycle which was the seemingly inevitable concomitant of meetings between the industrial West and the agrarian economies of Asia—'a cycle that led through ruined handicrafts and financial instability to foreign political encroachment'.[16] Japan threatened to be no exception: the imposition of unequal commercial treaties in 1858 and 1866 stripped Japan of tariff protection and triggered the cycle. A flood of imports (in 1863 only 34 per cent of total trade was accounted for by imports; by 1871 it was 71 per cent) swamped the handicraft industry. The price of rice soared (¥ 5.70 per *koku* in 1877, ¥ 9.40 in 1879, and ¥ 12.20 in 1880), as did that of gold (it doubled in terms of notes between 1873 and 1881), which was drained from the country.[17]

Armed resistance was not a serious long-term option, which left only one alternative, a political and economic transformation of Japan which would enable her to deal on equal terms with the West. This option, encapsulated in the phrase 'Fukoku Kyōhei' (rich country—strong army), was the only alternative to dependence upon the West, but this did not mean that it would be exercised. The scarcity of private capital, the traditional and prescribed conservatism of the merchants, exacerbated by their ignorance of 'technology and production, of foreign tastes and markets, of shipping and landing and warehouse charges outside Japan, of international financial practices',[18] allied to the problems identified by Ōkubo Toshimichi, meant that if Japan was to respond to the imperative of catching up with the West, it would have to be at the instigation of the government or not at all.

That the Meiji oligarchs took the initiative was a consequence of a complex array of factors which had less to do with culture and tradition and rather more with compelling domestic political pressures (industrial development afforded the possibility of accommodating, as producers, a dispossessed and discontented *samurai* class and of relieving a hard-pressed and rebellious peasantry).

State intervention was facilitated by the existence of established channels of economic control, which dated from the Tokugawa period (1603–1868), and 'made the Japanese economy far more amenable than most to official direction and technical guidance'.[19] These were systematized, extended, and enforced in the Meiji period, as the state borrowed private capital and invested it in the development of strategic industries (mining, shipbuilding, armaments, communications, and textiles), which it operated itself and subsequently transferred at knock-down prices to private interests. Perhaps the Kōjō Haraisage Gaisoku (Regulations on the Transfer of Factories), 5 November 1880, was Japan's first encounter with the politics of privatization.[20]

The flow of benefits was not just one way. The critical dependence of the fledgling state upon the merchant houses (which as a result, in part at least, of government transfers were becoming 'industrial') was regularly demonstrated. The armed revolt at Satsuma in 1877 was put down by a conscript army, transported by Mitsubishi's ships, supplied by Mitsui

Bussan, and paid by Mitsui Bank.[21] Indeed, the processes of industrial development and state-building were interdependent.

The symbiosis of state and industry was not always cosy, but it was always imperative. Moreover, it was congruent with cultural imperatives in the late nineteenth and the twentieth centuries. These were inimical to the ethical foundations of classical free enterprise utilitarianism—the belief that the operation of choices based on individual utility or profit maximization produces the optimum allocation of resources. Such a view was regarded as unacceptably selfish in Japan and 'some other socially more acceptable justification for business activity had to be developed in terms of service to the community and to the state'.[22] The fact of government–business interdependence, dictated by a coincidence of material interest, fitted neatly with these expectations.

That relationship and its justification has even survived Japan's involvement in the Second World War. Whereas the allied powers identified the 'Zaibatsu', or financial conglomerates, as the inspiration of expansion overseas and war, the Japanese speak of 'militarists', and view the democratic constitution of 1947 and the anti-war clause (Article 9) as a guarantee against their return. The war has, if anything served as a reinforcement of the 'catch-up' lesson—Japan lost the war because she had not attained the same level of economic development as the USA.

As for 'business', it has emerged from the war with its selfless credentials intact. It is the 'architect of reconstruction', the champion of growth, the agent of Japan's return to a position of prominence in the world. That it remains mindful of the need to present its activities in culturally appropriate terms is evidenced in the 1970s in its adoption of an ideology of social responsibility with which to dress up expensive anti-pollution measures imposed by the government.

The Leading Players in Government–Industry Relations

Intimate government–industry relations have the sanction of history and culture, it has been noted, and, in the absence of any serious challenge to such collaboration, extensive channels of communication have developed between the principal parties to the relationship. Formal and informal consultation is the norm, rather than the exception and is facilitated by a practice of élite recruitment from Tokyo University. Advisory councils and policy clubs (more accurately, dining clubs) bring together officials, politicians, and industrialists on a regular non-accountable basis. Trade and industry associations are another link in the communication chain. Inter-firm groups or 'Keiretsu' linkages integrate the industrial constituency and provide a transmission belt for ideas in both directions: from and to the key bureaucratic agencies.

The bureaucracy's penetration and control of these networks is striking and has encouraged talk of bureaucratic dominance. Specifically, the practice of 'amakudari', which moves retired bureaucrats from MITI and MOF into the Liberal Democratic Party where many become ministers and even prime ministers (ex-bureaucrats constitute at least 30 per cent of the membership of the LDP membership in both houses of the Diet—Japan's Parliament),[23] into the public corporations, the Bank of Japan, commercial banks, trade and industry associations, and the boardroom of private enterprise, is said to guarantee these agencies a voice and a receptive ear in the range of bodies which make up the policy community. In this view, 'whatever the role of bureaucracy in the formal policy-making process, it actually makes policy through the use of "administrative guidance", bureaucratic ordinances, directives and informal persuasion.'[24] Serious deliberation by a 'working parliament' is substituted by deliberation in councils attached to the bureaucracy and stuffed with 'names' drawn from the peak associations of big business, journalism, and the universities. Even the most important of these councils—the Economic Council (Keizai Shingikai), the Industrial Structure Council (Sangyō Kōzō Shingikai), and the Foreign Capital Council (Gaishi Shingikai)—serve the purpose of their parent bodies, respectively the Economic Planning Agency, MITI, and MOF.[25] The extent of the relationships is illustrated in Figure 1.

The bureaucracy *is* important but reference to a 'puppet Diet' and representation of the heads of industry as bureaucratic stooges is fundamentally misleading. The relationship between the leading players is one of interdependence. The bureaucracy cannot act without the legitimating seal of the Diet, and is, in consequence, constrained to co-operate with the Liberal Democratic Party which controls the Diet. The Conservative politicians exploit their brokerage skills and privileged access to the goods and services collected and produced, managed and distributed by the bureaucracy to cultivate their electoral constituency and look simultaneously to the particular interests of industry with a view to the maximization of political contributions which are in Japan the condition of electoral success. At a minimum the activities of the LDP politicians ensure a closer fit between bureaucratic measures and popular expectations.[26]

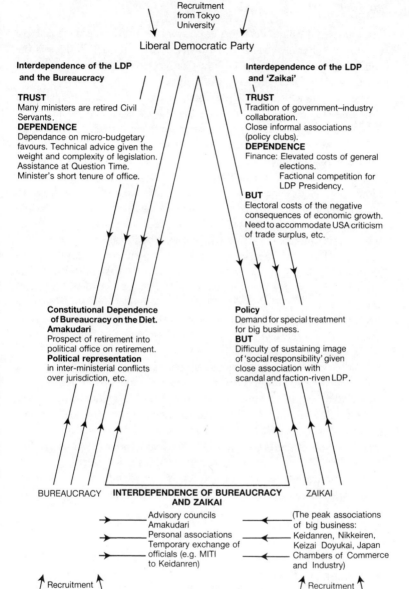

Figure 1. The Leading Players in the Government–Industry Relation: Relations of Dependence and Interdependence[a]

[a] Adapted from T. Tsurutani, *Political Change in Japan*, pp. 94–108.

For its part the bureaucracy must deliver a high level of growth and so a margin of material rewards to be distributed by the LDP. This is the condition of its partnership with the Conservatives, and a guarantee that it will be attentive to the wishes of industry.

The benefits which accrue to industry by virtue of its participation in this three-way relationship are considerable as is its dependence. The partnership permits the 'depoliticization' of the industrial policy-making process: the end, economic growth, is beyond question and public debate, while the means to that end are seen as a set of technical choices best left to the élite bureaucratic cadre. The business of keeping the industrial policy process out of politics is intensely political. It involves the search for valent slogans which harmonize with the hundred-year-old imperative of 'catching up with the West', conduce to a sense of national mission, tap a range of factors which make the Japanese a 'mobilizable' people, and have the effect of insulating a 'transcendental' administration from the demands of the public. Ikeda was the first post-war Prime Minister who resorted to this stratagem.[27] His 'Income-doubling Plan' was followed by Tanaka's 'Plan for Remodelling the Japanese Archipelago'. Nakasone's call for 'Administrative Reform' and the creation of a 'Dynamic Welfare Society', has been challenged by prime ministerial candidate Miyazawa's 'Asset-doubling Plan'.

Plainly, it would be foolish to assume such a division of labour as invariably harmonious; it is not. Even when it works well, it is at the level of 'social formation' and not the individual firm, and frequently it is tense and difficult. The Lockheed scandal exposed the best efforts of business to project an image of social responsibility; business externalizes its costs and the resultant pollution damages the Conservatives electorally. The strident demands of the USA and the EEC for a reduction of trade surplus produces conflicts of interest which divide an embarrassed cabinet and threatens exporters, not to mention the Foreign Ministry and MITI.

The Ministry of International Trade and Industry and its Bureaucratic Rivals

There has been too great a willingness to construe the Japanese economic system in terms of an economic Leviathan with MITI as the grey matter.[28] MITI is, of course, important but its precise weight within the state apparatus is difficult to determine and has changed over time.

The Ministry of Finance (MOF) has long been a rival. It is, in a sense, the most important government agency involved in industrial policy, since the principal instruments of industrial policy are direct budget and revenue items over which MOF has final approval. MOF control of the budgetary process, which is unchallenged by any other agency or groups, sets broad limits on the scope of industrial policy and simultaneously permits a detailed review of changes in the foreign exchange rate, tariff and customs policies, access to cheap government loans, subsidized expenditures, and selective tax measures—namely the whole gamut of industrial policy tools.

In particular industrial sectors MITI does not enjoy exclusive responsibility: shipbuilding is the domain of the Ministry of Transport. The importance of Japan's farmers as the electoral constituency of conservatism has made agriculture, forestry, and fisheries a sensitive sector, and the Ministry of Agriculture a formidable political broker. The special relationship between the faction of former prime minister, Tanaka, and the Ministry of Construction has given the latter considerable weight for more than a decade.

The period from the recession of 1965 to the post-oil-shock recession (1974) was a time of crisis for MITI, when it suffered from 'the greatest bureaucratic infirmity of all—fulfilment of mission and loss of function'.[29] The negative consequences of high growth were apparent and, in the case of industrial pollution, politically damaging. MITI's partial eclipse was the occasion for the re-emergence of MOF as a serious rival. US criticism made the undervalued yen and the implementation of capital liberalization key issues to be resolved: resolution threatened controls upon which MITI's efficacy had long been predicated and invited the leadership of MOF, whose preserve these issues were.

MITI redefined its mission and in part re-established itself in the mid-1970s. However, MITI officials continue to doubt—publically and privately—the extent of their control, and there is some evidence that the nature of MITI's relations with industry has changed to become more political.[30]

The Business World

The congruence of policy directives which emanate from the bureaucracy with the interests of the 'business world' or 'Zaikai', raises basic questions about 'bureaucratic dominance'. 'Zaikai' is shorthand for the peak associations of big business, the Federation of Economic Organizations (Keidanren), the Federation of Employers' Associations (Nikkeiren), the Committee for Economic Development (Keizai-Dōyūkai), and the Japan Chambers of Commerce and Industry. It is also an amuletic word which evokes successful post-war reconstruction, and the movement of Japan to the centre-stage of world economic affairs, and identifies as responsible a handful of familiar and respected figures who are shown in favourable light, even in the comics and story books of children and adolescents. The constituents of the Zaikai network are shown in Figure 2.

Keidanren is the principal institutional referant for Zaikai. Its general significance is universally acknowledged, it precise role little understood. The labour unions have no doubts: Keidanren is the power centre of Japanese society.[31] It is not a bad judgement. Keidanren has a membership of more than 100 industry-wide associations, delimited by trade, finance, transportation, manufacturing, mining, etc., and a further 800, or so, large corporations.

These are organized with the representation of members rather less in mind than agenda-setting. The thirty 'basic' committees include general policy, economic adjustment, industrial policy, reform of the government, energy policy, transportation, shipping, fisheries, forestry, industrial technology, small and medium-size enterprises, environmental policy, agricultural problems, finance, taxation, capital, economic controls, foreign capital problems, industrial capital, trade policy, international finance, economic co-operation, problems with the EEC, liberalization, tariffs, international problems, and world peace.

Keidanren makes only modest claims about its function, which is to adjust and mediate differences of opinion among its various member industries and businesses, and to submit proposals to the government regarding policies to stimulate the economy.[32] The claim is perhaps too modest. Keidanren has a bureau with a remit to consider how best to improve government, and has on occasion made spectacular interventions to change the terms of the public policy process *in toto*. Most remarkable in this regard was its orchestration of the merger of the Japan Democratic Party and the Liberal Party to form the Liberal Democratic Party in 1955. Simultaneously, and again at the instigation of Keidanren, the Economic Reconstruction Round Table (Keizai Saiken Kondankai, which later became the Kokumin Kyōkai) was set up as a channel through which flowed more than 90 per cent of the LDP's officially reported income in the 1960s and 1970s. Keidanren also acts as a

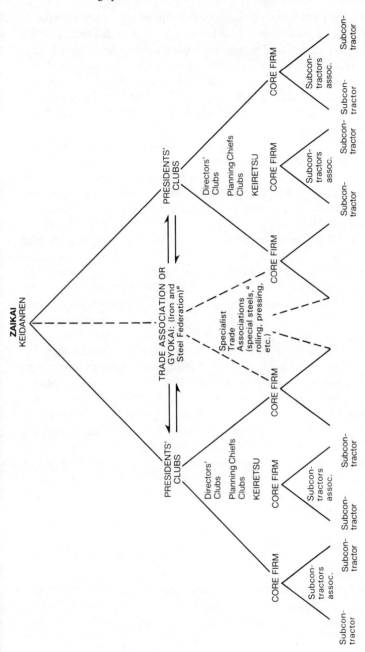

Figure 2. Horizontal and Vertical Communication in Japanese Industry

[a] The 'Iron and Steel Federation' and 'special steels, rolling, pressing, etc.' are examples of Trade Associations (Gyōkai) and Specialist Trade Associations respectively. The pattern of communication is of general significance.

pressure gauge to signal when it is time to operate the safety valve, drop
the incumbent prime minister, and introduce a new face. The request for
'a change in the political climate'—a request countersigned by the other
peak associations of business, the Japan Federation of Employers'
Associations (Nikkeiren), the Japan Committee for Economic Development (Keizai Dōyūkai), and the Japan Chambers of Commerce and
Industry—triggered the collapse of the Kishi cabinet and the installation
of the Ikeda cabinet in 1960.

The power, influence, and authority of Keidanren derives not only
from massive financial contributions to the LDP, but also from its ability
to mediate conflicts and to secure agreement about the broad limits of the
business interest. Its capacity to do this depends in turn upon an
industrial structure which facilitates horizontal and vertical communication and co-ordination.

The relatively great dependence of Japanese firms on external and
indirect financing (namely, loans from financial institutions which have
collected funds from the public in the form of deposits) rather than
internal (out of depreciation funds and profits held over) and direct
financing (the issue of shares and debentures), has produced close
exclusive relationships of mutual dependence between a group of firms
and their specialist, effectively 'in-house', city bank.[33] Mitsubishi,
Mitsui, and Sumitomo are examples of more tightly integrated, and Fūji,
Sanwa, and Dai-Ichi Kangyō of more loosely integrated inter-firm groups
or Keiretsu. Most of the bank loans of Mitsui OSK Lines, Mitsui
Shipbuilding and Engineering, and Mitsui Tōatsu Chemicals, for
example, are provided by the Mitsui Bank. Other members of the group
are substantial shareholders in any individual group member, which will,
in turn, own the stocks of other group members. The groups straddle all
industrial sectors ('From Noodles to Atomic Power' was the boast of the
Mitsubishi Group), and represent nearly one-third of the total economy.
The relatively greater importance of customary transactions in Japan
than in the US or Great Britain, suggests that these percentages do, if
anything, underestimate the purchase of Mitsubishi, Mitsui, Sumitomo,
Fūji, Dai-Ichi Kangyō, and Sanwa (popularly known as the 'Big Six') on
the Japanese economy. See Table 4.1.[34] The presidents of the member
firms participate in what is perhaps a group policy-making organ,[35]
possibly an important channel for collaboration of new ventures and a
forum for resolving disputes among members,[36] and without doubt a
point of communication and exchange within the industrial group. See
Table 4.2.[37]

Table 4.1 The Status of the Big Six (1977) %

	Total assets	Capital	Sales	Current profit	No. of employees
Big Six	24.99	19.13	15.16	26.66	6.05
All corporations	100.00	100.00	100.00	100.00	100.00

Table 4.2 Horizontal Communication and Co-ordination within the Keiretsu

Keiretsu	Presidents' club	Number of constituent firms	Lower levels of horizontal integration within the Keiretsu
Mitsubishi	Kinyōkai	28	Getsuyōkai (Heads of General Affairs Division) (Buchō) Kayōkai (Heads of General Affairs Sections) (Kachō)
Mitsui	Nimokukai	24	Getsuyōkai (Executive Directors (Jōmu) 62 companies Sanmokukai (Planning, Technology Heads) 8 companies
Sumitomo	Hakusuikai	21	Hakusenkai (OB Club) Gomokukai (Vice-Presidents' Club) Senkai (General Affairs Heads) Mokuyōkai (Heads of Personnel)
Fūji	Fuyokai	29	Funikai (Vice-Presidents) Fusuikai (Planing Divisions) Fusōkai (General Affairs Heads)
Dai-Ichi	Sankinkai	45	
Sanwa	Sansuikai	39	Kurōbākai (Vice Presidents, Managing Directors, Executive Directors) 40 companies

At a second level, the inter-firm group member is itself the nucleus of a group of small and medium-size companies (subcontractors and parts suppliers), by virtue of which relationship vertical channels of communication extend beyond the immediate reach of the Keiretsu itself to the myriad companies which make up the second face of Japan's dual-structure economy. Ninety-eight per cent of manufacturing companies in

Japan have less than a hundred employees.[38] And much as the Keiretsu has its 'steering committee', so do the subcontractors: Toyota's 133 sub-contractors are organized in the Kyoho-Kai within which 'they confront and solve their problems jointly'.[39] It can be imagined that the presence on the boards of these firms of directors from the core-firm is an induce-ment to do precisely that. Moreover, the subcontractors will often also be financially dependent through loans and stock ownership on the parent firm.[40]

The importance of the Keiretsu linkage in the dense web of govern-ment and industry is increased by the inevitable sensitivity of the presidents' club to the 'in-house' bank. The house bank is, in turn, susceptible to the influence of the Bank of Japan in consequence of the 'contractual agreement' by virtue of which the BOJ enforces monetary policy (interest rate policy, open market operations, reserve deposit requirements) and the practice of 'window guidance' (the BOJ does not fully satisfy the city bank demand for central loans but actively and daily engages in credit rationing and seeks to control the amounts loaned to customers of the city banks in a practice known as 'window guidance'). The small number of city banks facilitates the BOJ's daily fund guidance and loan controls—controls which are offset on occasion by *Fukumi-Kashidashi* ('hidden' or off-balance sheet loans) which reflect the profit-maximizing motives of the commercial banks. In another direction the Banking Law of 1927 gives MOF right of supervision and 'guidance' of private and government financial institutions. The movement of personnel at retirement between the MOF, BOJ, and the city banks serves to reinforce these ties.[41]

The Liberal Democratic Party

The LDP specializes in winning elections and is successful to the extent that a simple majority (256 of the 511 seats in the House of Representa-tives) is seen as a catastrophic failure, the sin to be expiated by public apology and even loss of office by the incumbent prime minister. 'Victory' occurs somewhere in excess of 280 seats at which point the Party controls not only the House but also the committees.[42] Its uninterrupted tenure of office (since its creation) is the indispensable con-dition and guarantee of the government-industry relation in Japan. The LDP holds the ring while the bureaucracy and business sort out their affairs: part promoter (and certainly a net beneficiary of a 'good gate' and a 'successful' contest), part 'cornerman' (and richly rewarded for advice which enables business to handle the bureaucracy), sometimes protagonist (particularly if there is an electoral dimension to the exchange), the LDP is also a referee who tries to keep the contest within bounds and who, paradoxically, takes responsibility whenever the fight spills out of the ring.

Winning elections is expensive. The Party has no machine and not much policy. The vote is mobilized by chains of personal connections which, extending from the centre, reach local notables at the periphery. The traditional expectation of gift-giving requires that key influentials who can deliver votes be rewarded: an expectation that shades easily and often into vote-buying and corruption—particularly in rural areas. The Party itself is a coalition of personal factions eager to bolster their representation and so their claim on seats in the Cabinet. The multi-member, single, non-transferable vote electoral system, which means that the LDP will run three candidates in many districts, gives the factions their chance and at a stroke increases the cost of elections to the Diet. Factional competition is fiercest and probably most expensive in the biennial contest for the presidency of the LDP, which by virtue of the LDP's in-built majority in the Diet carries with it the premiership. The guarantee of access to considerable patronage, and so a means of increasing factional strength fuels the competition and 'justifies' the expenditure of ever greater sums of money.[43] A measure of the successful LDP politician is his ability to raise the necessary funds. This rather than any legislative track record is the condition of his advancement.

Funds are provided by big business to the Party and to individual politicians, and while it may seem reasonable to wonder what return business gets on its annual multimillion pound investment, political scientists have, in the main, contented themselves with platitudes about preserving the 'free enterprise system' from the Communist and Socialist menace. If there was ever any substance to the argument it has been eroded by the persistent decline and deradicalization of the major opposition party, the Socialists (from a peak of 29 per cent to a current 20 per cent); the isolation of the Communist Party, which in the 1980s has been shunned by potential coalition partners, commands only minority support (less than 10 per cent of the electorate), and has itself deradicalized over a twenty-five-year period; and, finally, the fragmentation of the opposition into a number of small parties which seem more eager to ally with the LDP than with each other.

Policies and Instruments

Industrial policy has been accorded a very high priority throughout the post-war period in Japan. However, the objectives, the instruments, and in consequence the very nature of the government–industry relation has changed (the latter within the limits indicated in the preceding section). The first period of *reconstruction* and *high growth* extends roughly from the end of the Second World War until the middle to late sixties—at this time the government–industry relation upon which industrial policy was predicated could be characterized as the 'governmental industrial guidance model' (*seifushudōkata*). This was MITI's heyday: the time of extensive subsidization and preferential capital allocations, high tariffs to protect home markets and domestic producers, bureaucratic control of access to foreign capital, pervasive licensing powers, and so on.[44]

It is difficult to locate precisely the point at which the second stage began, because industrial policy changed in accordance not only with the logic of economic evolution, but also in response to new political circumstances which made themselves apparent in 1969. Throughout the period of rapid growth the LDP relied on and cultivated a shrinking and over-represented rural electorate to secure its parliamentary majority and neglected the urban areas; a move both electorally rational and in tune with the interests of a business community unsympathetic to large expenditures on the urban infrastructure. Socially and economically marginal groups in the towns and cities, bypassed by the economic miracle and subject to the negative consequences of the headlong pursuit of growth, turned to the opposition parties in large numbers. The LDP majority was regularly eroded, and Communist and Socialist mayors proliferated. Citizens' movements and other consumer groups flourished and entered the political arena, for the first time, to secure favourable decisions from the administration with respect to anti-pollution measures and improved social welfare. These were rammed through the Diet in the teeth of MITI's opposition in 1970.[45] At the same time, and perhaps of even greater significance as a symptom of the changing government–industry relation, was Mitsubishi's decision to join with Chrysler in the creation of a new car company—a decision taken without reference to MITI and at a time when MITI favoured and believed it had sewn up a Mitsubishi-Isuzu deal. MITI acknowledged henceforth a new 'private sector industrial guidance model' (*minkan shudō kata*).[46]

On the economic front, changes began with the demand for capital liberalization in the mid-1960s, which heralded the forthcoming internationalization of the Japanese economy and some erosion of bureaucratic controls, and culminated with the 'oil shock' of 1973, which triggered the transformation of Japan's industrial structure, and to many commentators signals the end of the first phase. A second oil crisis at the end of the decade gave the problems of adjustment and the management of industrial decline a new urgency, and has perhaps ushered in a third stage.[47]

Some of the more significant instruments of industrial policy have persisted through much of the post-war period, and merit special attention. They include public procurement policy, cartels, and regulation of the financial system.

Public procurement policy: the case of Nippon Telephone and Telegraph

MITI has effectively no public procurement budget. The Defence Agency has a budget which, although large in absolute terms (¥3,137.1 billion in FY 1985—and 6 per cent of General Account Outlay), is a relatively low proportion of GNP (approximately one per cent). Twenty-five per cent of this is used for the purchase of weapons. The Ministry of Construction has a larger budget than the Defence Agency (¥3,871.4 billion, FY 1985), and it contains a substantial procurement element. Construction is a highly politicized Ministry which does not lend itself to control by MITI and the orderly pursuit of economic ends. On the other hand, the procurement budget of the Ministry of Transport was, in an earlier period, of significance in making Japan's shipbuilding industry a world beater.[48]

Public corporations also have significant procurement budgets; that of the Nippon Telephone and Telegraph has been used with effect in the promotion of the semiconductor industry. The corporation is far from readily amenable to MITI's guidance. The sturdily independent NTT has no maufacturing facilities of its own. It secures more than $3 billion-worth of procurements annually from a 'family' of firms: Nippon Electric, Fūjitsu, Hitachi, and Oki Electric. These firms subcontract with specialist family firms, many of which depend almost exclusively on NTT contracts. These family firms have little or no need to develop marketing and basic research and development capacities, which reduces their costs and increases their dependence on NTT. NTT's own engineers take responsibility for basic research while the 'family' can focus its expenditures on application and production. NTT 'know-how' is not generally available, but is traded with the family firms on a confidential disclosure basis. Moreover, the family firms are privy to the regulations and standards which are the means by which NTT has kept theoretically open markets (the terminal or interconnect market) closed. Foreign firms (and non-family Japanese firms) are required to meet certain specifications for approval; it has been NTT policy not to divulge what the standards are.[49] Family ties are reinforced by substantial transfers of senior NTT personnel into executive positions in the leading related firms. One executive of a family firm is quoted as saying that it is harder to get into the NTT family than Tokyo University, but 'once you are in, nobody flunks out'.[50]

Benefits which accrued to the family were multiple: NEC has done more than $500 million-worth of business a year with NTT and has thereby been afforded significant economies of scale; privileged access to NTT basic research released significant sums for other and further R. & D., for the development of new markets, products, and technologies; membership of the family signalled to the city banks that loans advanced to NEC were secure: and these benefits most likely spilled over from the telecommunications to the semiconductor and computer industries (in 1981, 12 per cent of NEC sales were in telecommunications; 17.8 per cent in semiconductors).

Family ties were first ruptured in December 1980, when after protracted, occasionally bitter and heated US–Japan negotiations, and the retirement of the NTT president, Japan agreed to open $8 billion-worth of government procurement to international competition on a non-discriminatory basis. Nearly half of this ($3.3 billion) was accounted for by NTT procurements[51] in a three-track system which inversely related openness and technological sophistication: the least sophisticated items (worth $1.5 billion in 1980) would be secured by open-bidding procedures; more sophisticated items would be supplied by designated 'reliable supplier' through negotiated bids and joint research and development leading to procurement ($2.8 billion). US firms, if appropriately qualified, would be allowed the designation 'reliable supplier'.[52]

The NTT was able to defeat the best efforts of the principal bureaucratic agencies to compel it to open its procurements: the NTT has traditionally enjoyed considerable independence from its nominal parent ministry, Posts and Telecommunications—in part as a consequence of weak *amakudari* linkages; the Ministry of Finance was reluctant to move against a profitable concern, particularly since NTT's large surpluses (after 1977) reduced its reliance on government loans and so the effectiveness of MOF of leverage; finally, NTT chooses to pursue technological development within its own laboratories and in collaboration with its four leading partners in the private sector, and so escapes even MITI's best efforts to control, for example, the computer industry. In the event, only political pressure from the highest level and mediated by an NTT 'old boy'[53] turned Foreign Minister, was sufficient to secure NTT agreement.

The rate of change accelerated in June 1985 when, as part of Prime Minister Nakasone's drive for administrative reform, NTT was privatized. Newcomers to the field (Daini Den Den Inc., Japan Telecom Co., and Teleway) plan to lay telecommunication cables. The Ministry of Posts and Telecommunications aims to introduce access charges that are advantageous to newcomers who seek to link their trunk cables (for example, between Tokyo and Osaka) with NTT city cables (which remain an NTT monopoly). Joint ventures are planned with the Japan IBM Corporation and the Industrial Bank of Japan. None the less, it is interesting to note that since the 'opening' of the telecommunications procurement market, foreign firms have made inroads worth less than 5 per cent of the total market value. Moreover, NTT has already set up eleven subsidiaries financed by its head office and four others financed by its regional headquarters—primarily in equipment leasing, software development, and systems engineering. A further one hundred subsidiaries are planned and targeted, amongst these are a substantial number of the erstwhile 'family' subcontractors.

Cartels

The legal culture which makes administrative guidance possible also figures in an analysis of the part played by cartels in the industrial policy of Japan. The organization by MITI of cartels has been a persistent feature of Japan's industrial policy. In periods of rapid growth, firms competed to expand output and market share; price competition was fierce; the investment race hectic; and MITI would seek to impose investment quotas. In times of recession, government-sponsored recession cartels were introduced, 'legalized' by the 1953 Amendment of the Anti-Monopoly Act. The industry associations collaborate closely with MITI in the organization of such cartels, which are geared, Magaziner and Hout[54] tell us, to such purposes as:

(i) Long-term rationalisation of production (bearings and car-parts industries);

(ii)   Orderly reduction of excess capacity (aluminium);
(iii) Promotion of vertical integration (small, downstream textiles companies);
(iv)   Short-term production allocation (used in recessions in chemicals and steel);
(v)   Export price floors during trade crises (textiles, steel, and other industries).

The successful operation of the cartel policy depends upon a generous interpretation of anti-trust regulations by the Fair Trade Commission. Public tolerance of the questionable legality of the cartels and MITI's role in their orchestration came to an end in the early 1970s. Price-fixing cartels in the electric appliances industry produced televisions, the cost of which on the domestic market was three times the export price.[55] Illegal cartels, established with and without MITI's assistance, proliferated after 1973. Most notorious of all were the activities of wholesalers of petroleum products, engaged in 1973 in large-scale price-fixing to take advantage of OPEC actions. The public anger as the Diet discovered and the media revealed the machinations of the wholesalers (who resorted to secret codes and other elaborate measures to deceive) led to a demand for a tightening up of the Anti-Monopoly Act. The limitations and leniency of the legislative amendments proposed by the Fair Trade Commission (FTC) issue on the proposed revisions was criticized by both economists and lawyers. A qualified version of the FTC's proposals was passed by the Diet in 1977.[56]

The efficacy of the new measures was tested by the Tokyo High Court in September 1980. The casuistical judgment which resulted was greeted with dismay by consumer groups, and disbelief by academic lawyers and economists.[57] However, it was upheld by the Supreme Court (February 1984). MITI was encouraged to deal exclusively with individual firms rather than with a group of firms or an industry association, and to instruct those firms not to talk to each other! Similarly, even these measures might be waived if it was in MITI's view 'essential' or 'justifiable'. Neither the High Court nor the Supreme Court ruled on what constitutes 'essential' guidance. Industrial policy has not usually depended upon legal instruments, and has not usually been constrained by law.

The number of cartels has decreased by nearly half in a decade (976 in 1971 down to 505 in 1982), and it was reported in 1983 that there were no longer any rationalization cartels.[58] Moreover, the policy objectives pursued here changed; the remaining cartels (more than 400 of them) are designed to protect small and medium-size enterprises from the giant

Japanese corporations, or to undertake environmental protection measures.

Cartels geared to the promotion of new technologies have not been challenged in the courts, even when they do not benefit from a temporary enabling law such as the Law Concerning Temporary Measures for the Promotion of the Electronics Industry, 1957. It was on this basis that, at MITI's prompting, the Japan Electronic Computer Corporation (JECC) was established by seven companies at the forefront of Japan's fledgling computer industry. JECC was set up as a rental company which purchased computers from the founding companies (Fūjitsu, Toshiba, Mitsubishi, Oki, Hitachi, and an NEC-Toshiba sales company) and rented them to Japanese customers. It was a beneficiary of government 'financial, tax and moral support', which meant it could borrow from the Japan Development Bank and received 'an implicit guarantee of its loans from city banks'. JECC relieved the manufacturers of both a substantial investment and a risky involvement in a new and competitive rental market. JECC afforded the Japanese computer industry valuable breathing space—for example, its leasing arrangements undercut those of IBM—and is still of importance to the industry.[59]

Government regulation of the financial system as an instrument of industrial policy

Both macro-economic policy and financial regulation have been characterized as instruments of industrial policy. 'Growth required high rates of investment and export promotion if capacity was to be expanded rapidly and imports were to be financed. But Japan's capital stock was extremely small and only the banks had the necessary funds. Therefore the government, through the Bank of Japan, encouraged the debt financing required for high investment rates.'[60] The argument hinges upon an assumed necessary connection between 'overborrowing' and 'overloan'. 'Overborrowing' refers to the financing of the corporate sector and indicates a particularly heavy dependence on bank borrowing which itself reflects low reliance on internal financing and the low contribution of the issue of securities (increases in equity capital or bond issues) to external financing. The phenomenon of 'overloan' refers, at the macro level, to the indebtedness of the banking system as a whole to the Bank of Japan ('net bank reserves (equals vault cash plus deposits with the Bank of Japan minus borrowing from the Bank of Japan, or vault cash plus deposits with the Bank of Japan minus external liabilities) being negative').[61]

Whereas it is almost certainly the case that characteristics of the Japanese financial system have proved of benefit to business, it would be a mistake to reduce all of these to the dictates of industrial policy. 'Overborrowing' is a case in point; its origins are to be found in the organization of industry and Japan's recent economic history.

The role of the government in the phenomenon of overloan is more apparent. MOF has kept the official discount rate below the short-term money market interest rates. Accordingly, banks would, whenever possible, borrow directly from the central bank and avoid the more expensive short-term money markets and have little incentive to repay the central bank. MOF's restrictions of the equity and bond markets, and MOF–BOJ control of a range of interest rates (the time deposit interest rate, the bank lending rate and the terms of insurance for bonds) have left city banks with little investment opportunity other than lending to companies where the requirement of compensatory deposits permits the movement of real rates and the possibility of investment returns in excess of the official discount rate.[62]

The interdependence of bank and firm within the Keiretsu, the acceptance by both of low rates of return on equity investment, the official policy of keeping interest rates low, a taxation policy which contributed to the highest marginal propensity to save in the world, and a long-standing insulation of Japan from the international capital market, have combined to keep the cost of capital low and afforded Japanese enterprises a comparative advantage in competition in international markets. It would be a mistake, however, to explain that advantage simply and directly in terms of industrial policy.

Moreover, although the final impact on the cost of capital is unclear, fundamental characteristics of Japan's financial structure have changed in recent years. In the high growth period, corporate sector deficit was large, overborrowing was characteristic. In recession and recovery to modern growth (by Japan's standards, at least), the corporate deficit has declined, while the public sector deficit has ballooned. It seems inevitable that corporate overborrowing will diminish as deficits against public bond issue accumulate in an equation of significance for regulations governing interest rates. Simultaneously, the utility and political feasibility of a policy of low interest rates geared to growth has been called into question, by the fall in the rate of savings (real interest rates or funds invested by householders were negative in 1973–5), the internationalization of the Japanese money markets, the deregulation of capital movements within and without Japan, and by the explosion—as yet unchecked—of government debt issues.

Conclusion

At a critical juncture in Japan's recent history, the extensive involvement of government in industrial development was decisive in saving the country from a crippling economic and political dependence upon the industrial West and in creating the conditions for a phenomenal economic success. That success has legitimized close government–industry collaboration in the management of the economy. Remarkably, the legitimacy of the relationship has not been fundamentally impaired in the hundred years or so since the Meiji Restoration of 1868, despite the enormous social and political costs (domestic and foreign) of Japan's forced march to economic pre-eminence.

Nor for that matter has the attainment of levels of production second only to the USA, and of high standards of living which are widely enjoyed, done much to reduce the sense of mission, the urgency of catching up. Quite simply, the industrial policy imperative has survived the accomplishment of successive goals of industrial policy.

Why this should be so is difficult to say: certainly the oil shocks of the 1970s have played their part in dispelling complacency, and reminding the Japanese of the fragility of their economic achievement. However, a full explanation would require careful consideration of the relationship between 'culture' and 'ideology', and of the role of a highly centralized education system in the dissemination of élite values, and the manufacturing of popular beliefs and aspirations.

The case should not be overstated: the government–industry relation has been challenged—albeit briefly—by environmentalists and citizens' movements in the late 1960s and again—if with little success—in the wake of the Tanaka-Lockheed scandal in 1976. These challenges come from without hegemonic élite circles: within them, while the terms of the government–industry equation are constantly disputed, the equation itself, like industrial policy, is non-contentious. Industry resists 'control' (*tōsei*) but regards regulation (*chōsei*) as indispensable; free-market purism is confined to the academy.

The relationship is highly pragmatic: the parties to it may well subscribe to a rhetoric of the national interest, but this does not inhibit their pursuit of particular interests. At the same time they are constrained to collaborate by their common interest in preserving the insulation of the policy process, and so the exclusion of other competing interests. The rhetoric of the national interest is, in fact, only one of a myriad factors which 'close off' the policy process.

Above all, it is the dominance of the LDP which has limited and contained challenges to the existing government–industry relationship and to related networks. Its electoral position seems unassailable: it continues to benefit from an inequitable electoral system, and is no longer so dependent on a traditional and rural constituency, but has established itself firmly in the urban areas. The opposition remains fragmented and seemingly incapable of sustaining any serious claim to power. Certainly there are problems: the political costs of restructuring declining industries are potentially greater than those which result from economic management in a context of high growth. The need to accommodate US criticism of Japan's trade surplus threatens to reveal a conflict of interest between the LDP and industry, much as the demand for 'administrative reform' might conceivably open a rift between politicians and bureaucrats. None the less, there is as yet no evidence that any of these problems are threatening the LDP's tenure of office, and until such time as they do, the essential condition of the relationship between government and industry in Japan remains intact.

Notes

Japanese surnames are in bold type so as to permit family name and personal name to appear in the same order as in the original publication.

1. **Keizai Kōhō** Centre, *1985* (Tokyo 1985).
2. D. **Yergin**, 'Beyond the next oil shock', *New York Times Magazine*, cited by C. J. **McMillan** in *The Japanese Industrial Sytem* (Berlin and New York: de Gruyter 1984), p. 3.
3. Senator **Kennedy**, cited by Bruce **Bartlett**, 'Industrial policy: Crisis for liberal economists', *Fortune*, 14 November 1983, pp. 83–90.
4. F. W. **Richmond** and M. **Kahan**, *How to Beat the Japanese at their own Game* (Englewood Cliffs: Prentice Hall, 1983), p. 26.
5. **McMillan**, op. cit. (see n. 2) pp. 36–41.
6. I. C. **Magaziner** and T. M. **Hout**, *Japanese Industrial Policy* (London: Policy Studies Institute, 1980), p. 34.
7. C. **Johnson**, *MITI and the Japanese Miracle* (Stanford, Cal.: Stanford University Press, 1982), pp. 242–74.

8. **Namiki** Nobuyoshi, 'Japan Inc: Reality or Facade' in **Murakami** H. and J. Hirschmeier (eds.), *Politics and Economics in Contemporary Japan* (Tokyo: Japan Culture Institute, 1979), p. 113.

9. Y. **Noguchi**, 'The Government-Business Relation in Japan: The Changing Role of Fiscal Resources' in K. **Yamamura** (ed.), *Policy and Trade Issues of the Japanese Economy* (Seattle: University of Washington Press, 1982), pp. 123-42.

10. Johnson, op. cit. (n. 7), pp. 242-74.

11. K. **Yamamura**, op. cit. (n. 9), p. 83.

12. M. F. Deutsch, *Doing Business with the Japanese* (New York and Scarborough, Ontario: New American Library, 1983); C. Pegels, *Japan vs. the West* (Dordrecht: Kluwer Nijhoff, 1984).

13. McMillan, op. cit. (see n. 2), p. 23.

14. Believers are legion. For an excellent overview of some of the uses of culture see Yoshio **Sugimoto** and Ross Mouer, *Japanese Society: Sterotypes and Realities* (Papers of the Japanese Studies Centre, La Trobe University, 1981).

15. Ōkubo Toshimichi cited by T. C. Smith, *Political Change and Industrial Development in Japan: Government Enterprise, 1868-1880* (Stanford, Cal.: Stanford University Press, 1955), p. 41.

16. Ibid., pp. 23-7.

17. Ibid., pp. 25-7.

18. Ibid., pp. 39-41.

19. Sydney Crawcour, 'The Tokugawa Heritage', in W. W. Lockwood (ed.), *The State and Economic Enterprise in Japan* (Princeton, NJ: Princeton University Press, 1965), p. 44.

20. There is an enormous Japanese literature, much of it Marxist, on the early development of industry and 'state-building'. The works cited here are representative of the genre: **Hirano** Yoshitarō, *Nihon Shihongshugi Shakai no Kikō* (Mechanisms of Japan's Capitalist Society) (Tokyo: Iwanami Shoten, 1934); **Kajinishi** Mitsuhaya, 'Nihon Jūkōgyō no Seisei—Meiji Ishin no Saikento to Kanrenshite' (The birth of heavy industry in Japan: With reference to a re-examination of the Meiji Restoration) in *Shihonshugi no seiritsu to hatten: Tsuchiya Kyōju Kanreki Kinen ronbunshū* (The Rise and Development of Capitalism: Essays in Honour of the Sixtieth Birthday of Professor Tsuchiya) (Tokyo: Yūhikaku, 1959), pp. 1-24.

21. J. G. Roberts, *Mitsui* (Tokyo: Weatherhill, 1973), p. 114.

22. S. Crawcour, 'Japanese Economic Studies in Foreign Countries in the Post-war Period', *Keizai Kenkyū*, vol. 30, No. 1 (January 1979), pp. 49-63; B. K. Marshall, *Capitalism and Nationalism in Pre-war Japan: The Ideology of the Business Elite, 1868-1941* (Stanford, Cal.: Standford University Press, 1967).

23. C. Johnson, 'The Re-employment of Retired Government Bureaucrats in Japanese Big Business', *Asian Survey* 14 (November 1974), pp. 953-65.

24. E. Krauss and Michio Muramatsu, 'Bureaucrats and Politicians in Policy-making: the case of Japan', *American Political Science Review*, vol. 78 (1984), pp. 126–45, especially pp. 128–9.
25. Johnson, *MITI*, op. cit. (n. 7), pp. 47–52.
26. **Kawanaka** Nikō, 'Nihon ni okeru Seisaku Kettei no Seiji Katei' (The politics of the policy-making process in Japan) in **Taniuchi** Ken *et al.*, *Gendai Gyōsei to Kanryōsei* (The Modern Administration and the Bureaucratic System), vol. 2 (Tokyo: Tōkyō Daigaku Shappankai, 1974), pp. 7–8.
27. This is not to suggest that the Income-doubling Plan was no more than a symbolic act. It was this, but it was also of considerable economic significance.
28. E. Vogel, *Japan as Number One* (Cambridge, Mass.: Harvard University Press, 1979), is a famous instance of this.
29. Johnson, *MITI*, op. cit. (n. 7), p. 275.
30. **Komiya** Ryutarō, *Nihon no Sangyō Seisaku* (Japan's Industrial Policy) (Tokyo: Tōkyō Daigaku Shappankai, 1984), pp. 1–24.
31. The findings of the survey have been widely reported. I saw it in N. Sasaki, *Management and Industrial Structure in Japan* (Oxford: Pergamon Press, 1981), p. 99.
32. Keizai Dantai Rengōkai (ed.), *Keizai Dantai Rengōkai Sanjunenshi* (A Thirty-year History of Keidanren) (Tokyo, 1978).
33. *Miyazaki* Y., 'Rapid Economic Growth in Post-war Japan with special reference to "excessive competition" and the formation of keiretsu', *The Developing Economies* v., (June 1967), pp. 329–50.
34. A Survey on the Status of Industrial Groups, FTC 1979, cited by Sasaki, op. cit. (n. 31), p. 98.
35. **Sumiya** Toshio, *Nihonkeizai to Roku Daikigyō Shūdan* (Tokyo: Shinhyōron, 1982), pp. 121–35.
36. R. E. Caves and M. Uekusa, *Industrial Organisation in Japan* (Washington: The Brookings Institution, 1976), p. 65.
37. Adapted from Sumiya, op. cit. (n. 35), p. 12.
38. *White Paper on Small and Medium Enterprises* (Tokyo: Small and Medium Enterprises' Agency, 1983).
39. Sasaki, op. cit. (n. 31), pp. 10–24.
40. *Kigyō Keiretsu Sōran* (Kigyō Keiretsu—a survey) (Tokyo: Tōyō Keizai, 1979); *Industrial Groupings in Japan*, revised edn. (Tokyo: Dodwell, 1984); *Keiretsu no kenkyū* (Studies of the Keiretsu) (Tokyo: Keizai Chōsa Kyōkai, 1979).
41. Y. **Suzuki**, *Money and Banking in Contemporary Japan* (New Haven and London: Yale University Press, 1980), pp. 173–81.
42. H. Baerwald, *Japan's Parliament* (Cambridge University Press, 1974).
43. N. B. Thayer, *How the Conservatives Rule Japan* (Princeton, NJ: Princeton University Press, 1969); Nagamori Seiichi, 'Seiji Kōdō no Keishiki' (Form

in political behaviour) in *Kokugakuin Hōgaku*, vol. 21; 2 (September 1983), pp. 107–48.

44. M. **Shinohara**, *Industrial Growth, Trade and Dynamic Patterns in the Japanese Economy* (Tokyo: University of Tokyo Press, 1982, pp. 3–56); **Komiya** Ryutarō, *Nihon Sangyō Seisaku* (Japan's Industrial Policy) (Tokyo: Tōkyō Daigaku Shappankai, 1984), pp. 1–24.

45. K. Steiner, E. Krauss, and S. Flanagan, *Political Opposition and Local Politics in Japan* (Princeton, NJ: Princeton University Press, 1980).

46. **Suzuki** Yukio, *Keizai Kanryō ShinSangyōkokka no Purōdyūsa* (Economic Bureaucrats: Producers of the New Industrial State) (Tokyo: Nihon Keizai Shimbunsha, 1969).

47. **Komiya**, op. cit. (n. 44), pp. 4–11.

48. G. O. Totten III, 'The Reconstruction of the Japanese Shipbuilding Industry', pp. 130–72 in R. L. Friedheim *et al.*, *Japan and the New Ocean Regime* (Boulder and London: Westview Press, 1984).

49. T. J. Curran, 'Politics and High Technology: the NTT case', pp. 185–242, in I. M. Destler and H. Sato (eds.), *Coping with US–Japanese Economic Conflicts* (Lexington, Mass.: D. C. Heath, 1982), pp. 188–92.

50. Nikkei Sangyō Shimbun, 4 April 1974, cited by Curran, op. cit. (n. 49), p. 194.

51. Ibid., pp. 194–6.

52. Ibid., pp. 234–5.

53. Well, not quite, the father-in-law of Foreign Minister Okita had been the first president of NTT and founder of the NTT family system of procurement. Okita himself was, by training, an electrical engineer and so doubly trusted. Curran, op. cit. (n. 49), p. 233.

54. Magaziner and Hout, op. cit. (n. 6), p. 36.

55. M. H. Kirkpatrick, 'Consumerism and Japan's New Citizen Policies', *Asian Survey* 15 (March 1975), pp. 234–46.

56. The paragraph relies heavily on K. Yamamura's excellent account of cartels in K. **Yamamura** (ed.), *Policy and Trade Issues of the Japanese Economy* (see n. 9). Yamamura makes detailed reference to a wide range of the best Japanese sources.

57. A **Negishi**, 'Regulated Industries and Competition Policy' in *Keizai Hōgakkai Nenpō*, vol. 25, No. 3 (1982), pp. 61–8.

58. US International Trade Commission, *Foreign Industrial Targeting and its Effects on US Industries Phase I: Japan* (Washington, DC: US Trade Commission, October 1983), p. 76.

59. D. **Okimoto**, T. **Sugano** and F. B. Weinstein (eds.), *Competitive Edge: The Semi-conductor Industry in the US and Japan* (Stanford, Cal.: Stanford University Press, 1984), p. 156.

60. W. V. Rapp, 'Japan's Industrial Policy', pp. 37–66, in I. Frank (ed.), *The Japanese Economy in International Perspective* (Baltimore and London: The John Hopkins University Press, 1975), p. 46.

61. *Suzuki,* op. cit. (n. 41), p. 5.
62. Suzuki suggests that the Bank of Japan and its credit supply policy is the nub of the matter: 'To put it in extreme terms as a result of the credit rationing which inevitably occurs due to the artificial low interest rate policy, the relationship between the Bank of Japan and the city banks and in their turn the city banks and the export-oriented investing enterprises, is so inextricable that it preserves the overloaned position of the city banks and the imbalance of bank liquidity', ibid., p. 17.

5

Government–Industry Relations in the United States: an Overview

David Vogel

Introduction

Over the last five years, a lively debate has been waged in the United States over what role—if any—the American government should play in improving the international competitiveness of American industry. Much of this debate has revolved around the issue of industrial policy.[1] Those who favour the adoption of such a policy want the American government to play a more active role in channelling resources into industries in which the United States can create and maintain a comparative advantage.[2] They commonly cite Japan as an example of a nation in which close business–government co-operation at a sectoral level has enabled a number of its industries to improve dramatically their global market share. Critics of such a strategy, on the other hand, contend that the vulnerability of the American government to interest group pressures makes the adoption of a coherent and consistent set of policies toward industry impossible.[3] Not coincidentally, they attribute Japan's economic success to the soundness of its macro-economic policies and argue that the United States can most effectively assist its industry by improving its policies in this area and letting the market-place do the rest.

In spite of their different policy prescriptions, both perspectives share similar assumptions about the nature of business–government relations in the United States. Both assume that the American government has not had a coherent set of policies toward industry; instead they view American economic policy as a series of inconsistent and shortsighted responses to the demands and pressures of particular firms, industries, and regions. Both therefore conclude that the American government lacks the institutional capacity to define and implement policies that can improve the ability of particular industries to adjust to changes in the international economy. One perspective regards this inability as inherent in the American political system, while the other advocates the adoption of new institutions to enable the government to make its sectoral policies more like those of America's major competitors.

The purpose of this paper is to challenge this accepted understanding of business–government relations in the United States. Specifically, I want to argue that the role of the American government in promoting the development of American industry has been far more extensive—and far more important—than has been commonly assumed. As a result, much of the debate over whether the United States should develop an industrial policy is beside the point. The United States does have a relatively extensive set of policies towards industry: it does, in fact, target 'winners' and encourage the movement of capital and labour away from 'losers'. Contemporary America certainly does not resemble Japan in the latter's single-minded commitment to economic development; American public policy since the New Deal has had a far broader range of objectives. But, over the last half-century, America has pursued sectoral policies no less vigorously—or less successfully—than its major industrial competitors.

If one defines industrial policy exclusively in terms of explicit governmental efforts to promote the international competitiveness of particular industries, then America has had relatively few industrial policies. But then, by like token, neither has much of Europe. Many of the sectoral policies pursued by the French government, for example, have been informed by a variety of objectives, ranging from national prestige to energy independence. Even in the case of Japan, many of the industries promoted by MITI in the 1950s and 1960s were not originally intended to become leading exporters. America is not unique in having its sectoral policies motivated by objectives other than that of international competitiveness. Moreover, many of America's indirect forms of support for industry have been as successful as the more explicit interventions of the governments of other nations. While the intentions of policy-makers do matter, there is little to be gained by deciding whether or not a particular set of sectoral policies qualify as an 'industrial' policy solely on the basis of the objectives of those who formulated it.

The implication of this argument is that both the weakness of the American government and the strength of the 'adversary relationship' between business and government in the United States have been exaggerated.[4] While many policies affecting business have been made in a relatively adversarial setting, their implementation has usually been highly sensitive to the long-term interest of American industry. Due to the importance policy-makers have attached to economic growth, the thrust of America's foreign and domestic policies has been no less supportive of the interests of industry than those of other capitalist states. On the other hand, the American state is much less weak than most students of comparative business–government relations have argued. It has demonstrated an impressive capacity both for resisting the demands of declining sectors and regions for assistance and for taking the initiative in defining and redirecting the focus of corporate research and investment. In brief, the differences between the pattern of business–government relations in the United States and those of other capitalist polities are less important than has been commonly assumed.

But why, then, has the idea of industrial policy provoked such contention in the United States? And why has the extent of government assistance to industry in the United States been overlooked by students of both comparative and American politics? There are a number of reasons. First, the range of policy instruments available to the American government to shape the structure of the American economy are different than in other capitalist polities. For example, in contrast to all other capitalist nations, the United States has made extremely limited use of government ownership as a strategy to shape industrial development. (Both for this reason and because of the limited scope of America's welfare state, government expenditures as a percentage of GNP are relatively low in the United States.) In addition, because of the strength of private capital markets in the United States and the autonomy of America's financial institutions, America lacks an institutional mechanism for allocating capital to particular firms and industries as in other capitalist nations, most notably France and Japan. Thirdly, many of the most important efforts of the American government to promote industrial development have taken place not at the federal level, but at the state and local one, making them somewhat less visible to students of comparative politics.

On the other hand, the United States makes more extensive use of private–public partnerships, both at the local and federal level, than other capitalist nations. And American defence contractors, in spite of being privately owned, function as much as an instrument of state policy as any nationalized firm in either Western Europe or Japan. The United States also relies far more heavily on the tax code as a means of shaping the direction of private sector investment than any other nation except Japan. And instead of nationalization, America has traditionally employed government regulation as a means of directing the development of particular sectors.

Finally, America's industrial policies have tended to be implicit rather than explicit. American political culture frowns upon close ties between government and any interest group—including business. Given Americans' historical mistrust of corporate power and suspicion of business–government co-operation, government officials have understandably been reluctant to justify particular policies on the grounds of their benefits to a particular industry. Instead, they have defended them on other grounds, such as national security or regional development. Moreover, in many cases, these alternative explanations were, in fact, quite genuine: it is a peculiarity of governmental assistance to industry in the United States that it has frequently been both the unintended and unanticipated consequence of policies designed to achieve other objectives.

American history is replete with examples of this phenomenon. The purpose of the anti-trust laws enacted in the late nineteenth and early twentieth centuries was to prevent monopoly. Yet because of the way they were enforced by the courts, their *result* was to make American firms both larger and more efficient than their counterparts in Europe, since in America, unlike in Europe, companies were forbidden to form cartels as a means of reducing competition.[5] Similarly, the purpose of American agricultural policy since the New Deal has been to stabilize the income of farmers; in this sense American agricultural policy is indistinguishable from that of the European Community or Japan. But the *result* has been to make American farmers more efficient than in any advanced industrial society. The most important and striking example is, of course, American defence spending. The purpose of the Department of Defense is to maintain and promote the nation's security. Yet the *result* of America's large military budget has been to give American firms important competitive advantages in a wide variety of high-technology sectors. Likewise, the American space programme was promoted for reasons of both national prestige and military security, yet its commercial impact has been substantial.

A third reason why the extensiveness of American assistance to industry has been obscured is an ideological one. America exhibits in an extreme form a syndrome in which a nation's ideology of business–government relations bears virtually no relationship to its practices. Unlike on the Continent and in Japan, economics in America is dominated by a neoclassical faith in the efficacy and effectiveness of market-based mechanisms of capital allocation.[6] The conventional wisdom of American economists—shared across the political spectrum from Charles Schultze to Milton Friedman—is that, except in highly unusual circumstances, comparative advantage can only be created by the market. It therefore follows that the government cannot pick 'winners'; it can only retard the movement of capital and labour away from 'losers'.

Yet, not only can American neoclassical economics not account for Japan's successes; it cannot even account for many of those of the United States. In fact, the Department of Defense, the National Aeronautics and Space Administration, the National Institutes of Health, and the Department of Agriculture have proven no less—or more—capable of picking winners than has MITI. Moreover, the gap between rhetoric and practice has widened considerably under the Reagan Administration. No Administration in recent times has been so committed to the rhetoric of limited government and market-place allocation, yet none has acted more aggressively to reshape the structure of the American economy. To understand business–government relations in America, we need to pay less attention to what American economists and politicians contend government can and cannot do, and examine more closely what the American government has actually done. That is the primary purpose of this paper.

Historical Background

The rejection of Alexander Hamilton's 'Report on Manufacturing', which recommended that the federal government actively commit itself to a policy of promoting manufacturing, is often viewed as having signalled the unwillingness of the new nation actively to support economic development. In fact, however, it merely reflected the decision of the nation's political leadership to place priority on agricultural rather than industrial development.[7] During the first six decades of the nineteenth century, both the state and federal governments actively intervened to increase the volume and lower the costs of agricultural output; indeed, this constituted the major focus of the nation's foreign and domestic policies in the ante-bellum period.

While the American government played a decisive role in making the United States into the world's most important exporter of agricultural products during the first half of the nineteenth century, from the 1870s through to the 1930s the importance of sectoral policies in the United States diminished considerably. On balance, the *industrial* development of the United States was managed, directed, and financed primarily by the private sector. For example, the level of direct government subsidy for railroad construction significantly declined after 1873, after only one-third of the nation's ultimate railroad capacity had been completed. The main contribution of the federal government to the growth of industry during the industrial revolution was a negative one: high tariffs protected American industry from foreign competition, while the federal courts severely restricted the ability of those adversely affected by the rise of big business from having their grievances redressed. However, the federal government played little direct role in the development of the nation's major industries through the 1930s. Compared with those of other capitalist nations, America's steel, electric, textile, food processing, automobile, and chemical industries grew with relatively little direct government assistance. Only in the area of agriculture did the federal government pursue a relatively active sectoral policy during the last third of the nineteenth century and into the first third of the twentieth.

As I have argued elsewhere, this half-century was critical in shaping the social and political outlook of the American business community.[8] Precisely because the American government played a relatively passive role in shaping American industrial development, America's industrial élite developed an ideology that was highly critical of government intervention. Yet, ironically, for all the adversarial rhetoric that surrounded business–government relations during the industrial revolution, the political and economic triumph of large-scale industry took place more easily in America than in any other capitalist nation. America's farmers, workers, and small businessmen may have been extremely vocal in their denunciations of 'big business', but, unlike their counterparts in virtually every other capitalist nation, their efforts to restrict or to curtail the development of industrial capitalism were noticeably unsuccessful. No other nation made so few efforts to protect its traditional sectors during its period of rapid industrial growth.[9]

The New Deal is commonly and correctly viewed as a major discontinuity in the history of business–governmental relations in the United States. Most accounts of the expansion of the role of government in the economy during the 1930s have tended to emphasize its macro-economic dimensions, including the significant expansion of the welfare state, the introduction of Keynesian policy, and the recognition of the right of workers to join unions. Each of these policy initiatives was extremely controversial and was strongly—and unsuccessfully—opposed by the majority of the nation's business community. Their enactment made the relationship between business and government during the 1930s relatively adversarial.

Yet there is another dimension of the relationship between industry and government during the 1930s that also needs to be emphasized. The New Deal played a critical role in promoting the re-emergence of sectoral policies in the United States. Notwithstanding the demise of the National Recovery Administration, contemporary American industrial policy essentially dates from the 1930s. The Tennessee Valley Authority represents America's most ambitious effort at government-sponsored regional economic development in progress. In a large variety of sectors, including energy, shipping, trucking, communication, banking, power generation, housing, airlines, and agriculture, the New Deal significantly—and in most cases permanently—expanded the scope for government intervention. With a handful of exceptions, the New Deal's sectoral policies—in contrast to its macro policies—tended to be strongly supportive of and supported by the industries directly affected by them. And this pattern of business–government co-operation was significantly enhanced during the Second World War, when the basis was laid for the government's post-war support of the defence and aerospace sectors of the economy.

Contemporary American Industrial Policies

Agriculture

Agriculture provides virtually a textbook case of American industrial policy.[10] The primary thrust of the New Deal's agricultural policy was to improve the living standards of America's farmers—then the most impoverished group in American society. It established an elaborate system of price-supports and output-controls through the Agricultural Stabilization and Conservation Service and a system of subsidized credits through the Farmers Home Administration. It also subsidized the costs of providing electricity to farmers via the Rural Electrification Administration and significantly expanded the construction of public works designed to supply both power and water to farmers in the Tennessee Valley and the West. These efforts were expanded during the 1950s, when the Foreign Agricultural Service of the Department of Agriculture was established to help domestic producers respond to overseas market opportunities.[11]

Lawrence and Dyer write:

For some time . . . our largest and most successful industry in terms of employment, assets, sales, and export value has been agriculture. Yet America was not always 'the bread basket of the world'. Fifty years ago farming was a big business, but a highly fragmented and uncertain one that kept most of its practitioners at or near a subsistence income and made only a handful of them rich. How the United States became the most reliable and productive supplier of food is not widely understood.[12]

The role played by the American government in this transformation was a decisive one. By shielding farmers from the instability of fluctuating prices, the government made it possible for them to invest in expensive farm machinery, fertilizers, and pesticides. In addition, scientists from the USDA and land-grant institutions developed new fertilizers, pesticides, herbicides, and crops; the results of their research were then rapidly and effectively disseminated to individual farmers through agricultural extension services. The result was an astonishing improvement in agricultural productivity: between 1949 and 1959, agricultural output per farm worker per hour increased 85 per cent, between 1959 and 1969 by 77 per cent, and between 1969 and 1979 by 92 per cent—a rate of productivity improvement far in excess of the nation's industrial sector. These advances were made possible by, and, in turn, stimulated demands for, various industrial products: it is not coincidental that agricultural chemicals represent the only high-technology export in which American producers gained world market share betwen 1965 and 1980,[13] or that until recently America was the world's major exporter of agricultural machinery. As *The Economist* recently noted, 'When their combine makers, fertilizer suppliers, rail freighters and so on are counted, farmers are America's biggest business.'[14]

Housing

The pattern of government assistance to industry in the United States is often characterized as an irrational array of subsidies, tax expenditures, and loan guarantees, bearing no relationship to any coherent set of objectives. But this assessment is inaccurate. For one sector has received more direct and indirect assistance from the federal government than all others, namely housing.[15] Loans and loan guarantees to the housing industry totalled nearly $160 billion in 1980 while the housing industry has been the recipient of more tax subsidies than the rest of the economy combined. Housing is not normally regarded as an example of industrial policy, since it does not produce anything that is internationally traded. But it certainly provides another demonstration of the ability of the

American government to develop a coherent sectoral policy.

Government assistance to the nation's housing sector began during the New Deal. In order to prevent foreclosures on existing mortgages and restore the health of the nation's banks, the New Deal established three institutions: the Home Owners Loan Corporation, which purchased defaulted home mortgages and then replaced them by new loans, the Federal Housing Administration, which insured mortgages issued by banks, thus enabling banks to issue mortgages with lower down-payments and interest rates, and the Federal National Mortgage Association, which established a secondary mortgage market, thus increasing the number of banks willing to issue mortgages. Each of these programmes was significantly expanded following the Second World War and in addition, a special subsidized loan programme was established for veterans.

During the 1950s, the federal government began to provide massive support for highway construction, thus making additional land available for housing construction, while state and local governments co-operated by providing funds for community infrastructures. The combination of subsidized mortgages and subsidized highway construction led to a six-fold increase in the rate of new housing construction. Moreover, the substantial increase in the demand for new housing enabled builders to produce homes in much greater volume: the result was that output per employee grew at an annual rate of 2.3 per cent between 1947 and 1965.[16] As in the case of agriculture, American sectoral intervention in this industry has been highly successful: one-third of US gross domestic fixed investment has gone into housing since 1970 and a higher proportion of Americans own their own homes than in any other industrial nation.

Defence and space

The most important focus of sectoral intervention by the American government over the last forty years has been in the area of defence and space. While there is considerable disagreement about the aggregate impact of the substantial funds dispersed by the Department of Defense and the National Aeronautics and Space Administration in the post-war period, there is little question that they have played a decisive role in creating a comparative advantage for the United States in a wide variety of sectors. The most obvious impact of DoD on America's industrial competitiveness has been to make the United States the world's major producer and exporter of weaponry. Between 1970 and 1985, America's share of world arms transfers more than doubled; currently, 840,000 jobs in the United States are generated by foreign military sales.[17] As with agriculture, government support for this industry has been accompanied by government protection of it: the pronounced bias of American defence procurement towards firms both owned and located in the United States constitutes America's most important non-tariff barrier to trade.

The federal government has also played a critical role in developing the American aerospace industry—the only high-technology sector in which America's share of world exports remains as high as 50 per cent. Prior to World War II, the National Advisory Committee on Aeronautics, NASA's predecessor, built facilities where companies could test new designs, while the Post Office was the airlines' first important customer. The Civil Aeronautics Board established a legally sanctioned cartel for the airline industry, thus providing an important civilian market for commerical aircraft. As late as 1950, military purchases still accounted for 92 per cent of aerospace sales, while during the 1950s and 1960s, the Defense Department underwrote the research and development costs of each new generation of civilian aircraft. Between 1925 and 1975 the federal government channelled more direct support for technological research to aviation than to any other industry. In 1977, 70 per cent of its R. & D. was funded by the federal government.[18]

The Defense Department also played a central role in the development of both the computer and semiconductor industries.[19] While the transistor was invented in 1947 by Bell Laboratories, independently of military procurement, until 1955 virtually all computer-related research was government funded. IBM made two breakthroughs in the late 1950s that were responsible for making it into the world's leading manufacturer of computers—namely the random access magnetic-core memory and transistorized computers. Both were federally funded; indeed, until 1960, the government was the major purchaser of computers. In addition, NASA's willingness to pay for the developmental costs of semiconductors played a critical role in the development of this industry, helping to reduce the costs of an integrated circuit twenty-five fold between 1962 and 1968 and encouraging a number of new firms to enter this market. NASA and DoD accounted for more than one-third of semiconductor sales in 1967 and for over 70 per cent of annual sales during the first four years of integrated circuit production.

Robert Reich concludes:

The U.S. government has responded to emerging industries primarily through its national defense and aerospace programs. Notwithstanding that the goal of

economic adjustment has not been an objective of these programs, they have contributed to U.S. leadership in world sales of aircraft, communication satellite
technology, hard plastics, synthetic rubber, computers, semi-conductors, lasers,
fiber optics, radio and television communication equipment, robotics, optical
instruments, scientific instruments and many other products.[20]

Under the Reagan Administration, the role of the Defense Department
in promoting industrial development increased substantially.[21] Defence
spending on research and development doubled between 1980 and 1985.
DoD's 1985 budget allocates $35 billion for research and development in
new technologies—roughly one-third of all anticipated research and
development expenditures in the United States—while DoD procurement of electronics components and systems is scheduled to triple
between 1982 and 1987. In 1979 the Defense Department initiated a
joint development programme with nine computer and semiconductor
manufacturers to develop large-scale integrated circuits: nearly one
billion dollars has been budgeted for this programme over the next
decade. The Reagan Administration has also established a $1 billion pro-
gramme to develop a 'super-computer' over the next five years, DoD is
also becoming more heavily involved in funding research for advanced
lasers, advanced computer software, and fibre optics; it is also currently
the major purchaser of these products. The Administration's Strategic
Air Defense Initiative, with a projected budget of $26 billion, will fund
basic research in a number of technologies with important commercial
applications; hence the considerable eagerness of a number of European
high-technology companies to participate in it.[22] Indeed, SADI has been
described as an industrial 'martial' plan.[23] As one government official put
it, 'Defense research presses the limits of science and technology.'[24] And
in his 1986 State of the Union address, the President announced a programme of government support for the development of a
transatmospheric vehicle, or 'space plane'. This vehicle, dubbed the
'Orient Express', would have important military applications, and is
intended to help restore the pre-eminence of the United States in
aerospace technology. NASA and Pentagon funding is scheduled to total
more than $350 million by 1988.

Perhaps even more importantly, the Pentagon has begun to play a more
active role in improving the efficiency of American manufacturing.[25]
Man Tech, as it is called, has promoted laser welding, and the development of photogrammetry, an optical system for measuring the precision
of machine cuts. The Pentagon is currently working with Westinghouse
Electric to develop robotic assembly systems, and is supporting the

development of software that will link computer-aided design and computer-aided manufacturing into integrated, factory-wide systems; the latter represents an effort to develop an automated 'factory of the future'. DoD is also providing financial incentives for American defence manufacturers to develop sophisticated manufacturing systems which hold the promise of dramatically improving productivity in the manufacture of high-technology products with relatively short production runs.

The Reagan Administration's most explicit effort to use public resources to improve the comparative advantage of American industry involves space.[26] In announcing a national policy to accelerate the commercial development of space, the President stated that, 'The benefits our people can receive from the commercial use of space literally dazzle the imagination.'[27] Indeed, the Administration's programme in this area has frequently been compared to the role played by the federal government in developing the nation's railway system more than a century earlier. As one observer noted: 'Anyone who was sitting around in 1840 thinking about this railroad thing couldn't begin to imagine a fraction of the economic potential that would eventually be realized by opening up the West.'[28]

The government's space programme has already produced its first industry, satellite communications, whose annual sales volume is currently $3 billion. A second industry, based on the information provided by remote sensing satellites, has begun to emerge; already one firm provides daily crop-supply predictions that have proved valuable to both farmers and the Department of Agriculture. Each year NASA publishes a list of the products produced by its researchers that are in commercial use. The list already includes robotic systems, high-temperature lubricants, and, most importantly, solar technology. However, the really ultimate commercial potential of space lies in manufacturing. There are a considerable number of products, including various drugs, devices for measuring microscopic electronic components, and semiconductors made from gallium arsenide crystals, that can be manufactured far more cheaply and accurately in space than they can on earth. The Center for Space Policy predicts that space-related activities may involve sales of $855 billion per year by the year 2000—not including the resources spent by NASA or the military.

Given the considerable expense and risk involved in space manufacturing, virtually all the initial development costs have been financed by the federal government. NASA has already spent $200 million to create the infrastructure needed to exploit space and continues to charge companies far below the marginal costs of each shuttle flight. NASA has already turned over both rocket launching services and remote sensing to the private sector and hopes that eventually the shuttle programme will be privately owned and managed as well. Initially, private firms were hesitant to become involved in space manufacturing and experiments; the first twenty shuttle flights included only ten experiments for American companies. But this is beginning to change: already five business–university research centers have been established to design programmes in this area and corporate interest is increasing.[29]

Nor are America's current initiatives in industrial policy exclusively defence and space-related. America's biotechnology industry, now beginning to become commercially viable, was literally created by the federal government. While universities, venture capitalists, scientists, and entrepreneurs have all played a role, the support of the National Institutes of Health for basic research has been decisive. One source notes:

NIH created the knowledge and personnel base, actively worked to transfer a technology from the laboratory to the market and invented a quasi-regulatory oversight system that encouraged research. Together, these elements have amounted to a national industrial policy for biotechnology, even if NIH did not deliberately set out to create the industry that exists today.[30]

Likewise, the American pharmaceutical industry significantly benefited from military spending during the Second World War and, more recently, federal spending has played a major role in the development of new medical technologies in the United States: the government is the major purchaser of medical technology through its multibillion subsidy of medical treatment, and has also funded the development of specific innovations, such as the artificial heart. In short, it is not coincidental that virtually all of the sectors in which American industry continues to enjoy a competitive advantage have been the beneficiaries of direct and substantial governmental assistance.

Implications

This brief survey of American industrial policies requires us to reassess some of the arguments that have been advanced to explain why the development of strategies designed to improve the competitiveness of particular sectors is beyond the capacity of the American government. For example, it has been suggested that American Civil Servants lack both the technical capacity and political authority necessary to engage in sectoral planning. Yet officials in both the Department of Agriculture and the Department of Defense are both highly knowledgeable and enjoy considerable political autonomy. Their ties with their counterparts in the private sector are every bit as extensive and co-operative as those between MITI and Japanese individuals, and French Civil Servants and big business in France. It has also been argued that the vulnerability of government officials in the United States to interest group pressures makes them incapable of exercising authority over the private sector. Yet neither the space nor the defence programme was initially established as a response to industry pressures; on the contrary, it was the government which was responsible for channelling substantial private and public sector resources into these sectors in the first place. If anything, the DoD has displayed far more initiative in its dealings with industry than MITI, with whom it is frequently compared: its needs have been the driving force behind the research and development programmes of the private sector.

In the case of agriculture, defence, and space, American industrial policies benefit a relatively small proportion of the nation's business firms—and, indeed, impose considerable short-term costs on the rest of the economy. And yet the privileged position enjoyed by these sectors has not been subject to serious political challenge for nearly forty years, thus suggesting a relatively high degree of consistency in public sector resource allocation in the United States in the post-war period. Moreover, American agricultural policy clearly demonstrates that American government intervention need not degenerate into pork-barrel politics. Undoubtedly, some agricultural policies make little economic sense and serve mainly to transfer wealth from consumers to agricultural producers. This is certainly true of dairy price supports and of various import restrictions. But they are hardly typical of the broad thrust of government intervention in this sector. And the notion that the federal government cannot make choices among industries or regions is difficult to square with the observation that agricultural assistance goes to less than five per cent of the population. It is Europe and Japan, not the United States, that illustrate the 'pork-barrel' nature of government support for farmers.

Finally, it has been argued that the ability of American firms to secure funds through private capital markets deprives the American government of an important source of leverage over capital allocation by the private sector.[31] Yet, by manipulating the tax code, providing special loan guarantee programmes, and—in the case of agriculture and housing—establishing a special set of financial institutions, the American government has demonstrated an impressive capacity to redirect the flow of capital in the United States.

What of the capacity of the American government to resist the demands of declining or non-competitive sectors for assistance? Here again, the American government has proved far stronger and more independent than has commonly been assumed. Direct government subsidy to non-competitive firms or industries is less common in the United States than in Europe. The number of firms that have been bailed out by the American government over the last decade can be counted on the fingers of one hand, and, to date, most of these bail-outs have been costless to the taxpayer. Compared to the governments of other capitalist nations, the United States has provided much less protection to its small business sector. Thanks to the weakness of its trade union movement, America has made relatively few efforts to protect its workers from job losses due to international competition. For example, the United States is the only capitalist democracy that does not have legislation limiting plant closures. Ironically, France and Japan, the two nations whose states are considered the 'strongest' of any capitalist democracy have played a much more active role in protecting their small business and agricultural sectors from domestic and international market forces than has the United States.

Certainly the American government has yielded to the demands of a number of non-competitive sectors for protection from foreign producers. But the significance of the American retreat from free trade must be placed in perspective. Most obviously, America in the post-war period has been and remains less protectionist than any other major industrial economy. Moreover, in sharp contrast to the Europeans, who have provided an extensive array of subsidies to workers in sectors such as steel, shipbuilding, automobiles, and textiles—often via nationalization—for the most part, the intervention of the American government has been limited to restricting imports. But while these policies have raised prices for American consumers, they have not interfered with the adjustment of these sectors to international competition. In spite of import restrictions, both employment and investment in domestic steel, automobile production, and textiles have continued to decline. Moreover, although the United States is the only nation whose legislature is primarily elected on a regional basis, America's assistance to its declining and depressed regions has been considerably less than in Britain, France, Sweden, and Italy. In addition, the deregulation of financial markets, telecommunications, and transportion has been more extensive in the United States than in any other capitalist nation, thus demonstrating the ability of the American state to overcome the political pressures of the firms in those sectors that were committed to the regulatory status quo.

Finally, those who classify the American government as 'a weak state' would do well to consider the course of business–government relations under the Reagan Administration. Thanks in large measure to the strong dollar, substantial segments of the American economy, particular midwestern agriculture and eastern and mid-western heavy industry, were literally decimated during the first half of the 1980s. And yet the Administration was remarkably unresponsive to their demands for assistance. Whether intended or not, the Administration's fiscal and monetary policies have an important sectoral component. By making the dollar overvalued, they rapidly shifted capital and labour away from those so-called 'sunset' industries in which America does not appear to be able to maintain a comparative advantage. More recently, the Administration's efforts to reduce the level of government support for agriculture and housing, on the one hand, and increase expenditures for space and defence programmes, on the other, are clearly intended to help shift resources away from the former two sectors and expand the size of the latter two—thus engineering precisely the kind of politically directed sectoral adjustment that we usually associated with the Japanese.

The Distinctiveness of the United States

The relationship between the American government and American business—particularly big business—has been generally regarded as an adversarial one, in sharp contrast to the more co-operative relationships that appear to be more common in other capitalist societies. Yet it is by no means clear that the relationship between business and government in the United States is as distinctive as most scholars have assumed. Certainly popular antagonisms toward large firms is not a uniquely American phenomenon; it has also characterized domestic politics in other capitalist societies, including Germany, France, and Britain. Compared with other capitalist nations, the relationship between workers, farmers, and small businessmen, on the one hand, and big business, on the other, have not been noticeably conflictual in the United States. American unions have been relatively weak and moderate, American farmers have accommodated themselves to the imperatives of large-scale industrial development since the 1920s, and, except in a limited number of policy areas, American small businessmen have not been an important factor in American politics for nearly a century. Only middle-class reform groups have been more influential in America than in other capitalist nations. On balance, it would be hard to make a case that large firms in America enjoy less political influence *vis-à-vis* other sectors of the economy than their counterparts in other capitalist polities.

What, then, is distinctive about business–government relations in the United States? America does remain unique in the scope and complexity of its laws and regulations that restrict management prerogatives in a wide variety of areas. The most obvious example is anti-trust policy: no other capitalist nation has sought to establish such a wide variety of legal controls over the terms of competition. As a former chairman of the board of Du Pont put it, 'Why is it that my American colleagues and I are being constantly taken to court—made to stand trial—for activities that our counterparts in Britain and other parts of Europe are knighted or given peerages and comparable honors for?'[32] Likewise, no other capitalist nation has established so many rules that restrict exports of goods and services. These range from the Foreign Corrupt Practices Act to a variety of trade embargoes and restrictions on the sale of particular products to specific countries.

Yet, while these restrictions may be annoying to particular firms, their aggregate impact on the competitive position of American industry is rather modest. The enforcement of America's anti-trust laws has been highly selective and has not resulted in levels of market concentration significantly different from those of other capitalist nations. In recent years, the American government has not hesitated to encourage mergers on the part of marginal firms or permit co-operation among firms in the more dynamic sectors of the economy. And while some rules and regulations have certainly restricted exports, on balance, American foreign policy over the last half-century has been highly supportive of American foreign trade and investment.

It is true that over the last two decades, the level of conflict between government officials and corporate managers over the making and implementation of policy in areas such as occupational health and safety, environmental and consumer protection, and equal employment has been substantially greater in the United States than in any other capitalist nation.[33] No other capitalist nation has provided middle-class reform groups with such extensive opportunities to participate in the policy process nor erected so many legal and procedural obstacles to prevent business–government co-operation in the making and enforcement of regulatory policies. As a result, the politics of government regulation of corporate social conduct in the United States have been relatively adversarial.

Yet, at the same time, if one compares the actual implementation of regulatory policy in the United States with that of other capitalist nations, it does not appear that, in the final analysis, American officials have been any less sensitive to the costs of compliance than their counterparts in other capitalist nations. As in the case of anti-trust policy, American controls over corporate social conduct may be far stricter than in other capitalist polities, but their enforcement has been highly selective. For all the numerous, and well-documented, 'horror stories' about the effects of particular regulatory policies on various firms and industries, the burden they have placed on the American economy does not appear to differ significantly from those imposed on firms in other capitalist nations; indeed the United States spends a smaller proportion of its GNP on pollution control than does Japan. It is the way American regulatory policies are made, not the costs of complying with them, that distinguishes government regulation in America from other capitalist nations.

Moreover, it is important to keep the nature of conflict between business and government in America in perspective. Government regulation represents one of the relatively few areas in which there has been considerable antagonism between business and government in the United States. But, even in this policy area, conflict has been the exception, not the rule. Most importantly, economic regulation in the United States has only rarely challenged management prerogatives; in most cases the initiative for regulation came from the regulated industries themselves. America's current efforts at economic deregulation primarily involve conflicts *among* particular firms and industries, not *between* business and government. Prior to the mid-1960s, the regulation of corporate social conduct was handled primarily at the state level and for the most part it was relatively co-operative. It only became relatively adversarial in the mid-1960s, and the level of conflict has diminished considerably since the late 1970s. The close quasi-corporatist ties between defence contractors and the Department of Defense, farmers and the Department of Agriculture, real estate developers and builders and the Department of Housing, and bio-enginering firms and NIH are the norm, not the exception, of business–government relations in the United States.[34]

Moreover, business–government relations in America have always been relatively co-operative at the state level. During the first half of the nineteenth century, state and local governments played a critical role in promoting the expansion of American agriculture, primarily through financing and organizing the development of the nation's infrastructure: more than two-thirds of the 4,000 miles of canals constructed in the United States prior to the Civil War were financed by state governments. From the outset of the industrial revolution, states competed actively with each other in seeking to attract new investments, while, over the last century, creating a good 'business climate' has been a majority priority of most state governments. Although a few states did pursue anti-growth policies during the 1970s, more recently virtually all states governments have become much more active in seeking to improve the performance of their economies.[35] The emergence of Silicon Valley in northern California has created a model of government–business–university co-operation which other states are now trying to duplicate. Every state now has some form of an economic development agency; in thirty of the fifty states, this agency has cabinet-level status and in several states its budget exceeds $100 million. Such agencies typically employ a variety of means of attracting investment, including direct financial assistance, tax incentives, training assistance, and special programmes, such as the establishment of low-cost industrial sites.

Corporate Political Participation

What also makes the pattern of business–government relations in the United States distinctive is the nature of corporate political participation. Unlike in other capitalist nations, where there exist a wide array of official and quasi-official channels through which business can regularly communicate its views to public officials, in America corporate political participation tends to be much more *ad hoc* in nature. While in other capitalist nations the consultation of industry by government is assumed, in America it must constantly be asserted; business enjoys few privileges not enjoyed by other interest groups. Business may be no less influential in the United States than in other capitalist nations, but in America its influence comes at a price: companies must invest substantial resources if they are to affect public sector decisions.

For example, if a company or trade association wants to affect a government regulatory policy, it must prepare expert testimony for both congressional committee hearings and agency rule-making proceedings, hire lawyers who can then take an appeal against an agency decision to the federal courts, and then, if necessary, entrust its lobbyists to seek to have the regulatory statute amended in the legislature. The later strategy may require the company to enter into alliances with other interest groups, mobilize its shareholders and employees to write to or visit their representatives in Washington, and mount a nation-wide public relations campaign designed to influence press coverage of the issue. Each of these efforts involves a considerable expenditure of corporate resources.

By any index, the scope of government intervention in the economy has increased enormously over the last two decades. The American government has become more active in both regulating and promoting business than at any time in its history. As a function of the deregulation of banking and telecommunications, the increase in government spending as a proportion of GNP since 1965, the expansion of social regulation, the growing internationalization of the American economy, and the significant expansion of the Defense budget, the corporate strategy of American firms has become increasing dependent on government decisions. From this perspective, Reagan has not so much reversed the direction of the New Deal as accelerated it.

The result has been an unprecedented expansion in the amount of resources business firms devote to the political process.[36] For example, in 1961 only 130 firms were represented by registered lobbyists in Washington, DC, and of these only 50 had their own Washington staffs. By 1979, 650 firms had their own registered lobbyists and 247 had full-time employees in the nation's capital. While only a small minority of *Fortune* 500 companies had public affairs offices in 1970, a decade later more than 80 per cent had established such units. In 1974 there were 89 corporate political action committees; by 1982 there were 1,555. Corporate public relations programmes and efforts to build 'grass roots' support among employees, stockholders, and community groups were relatively rare prior to 1970; they have now become an important component of virtually every effort on the part of the business community to influence public policy. In addition, the American business community has devoted enormous resources toward influencing the climate of intellectual opinion, through its sponsorship of conferences, publications, and academic research.[37] These efforts have, on balance, proved extremely effective. The relative degree of political power exercised by business at both the federal and state levels increased significantly between 1977 and 1985. Business became much more successful both at shaping the political agenda and in influencing the outcomes of a variety of particular public policies, particularly in the areas of tax policy and government regulation.

America continues to differ from other capitalist nations, not only in the resources companies devote to affecting public policy, but also in the decentralized nature of that participation. In spite of its heightened politicization, the American business community, like all other interest groups in American society, remains politically fragmented: there is no peak organization capable of representing the views and interests of American business as a whole.

Over the last century, a number of organizations, including the Chamber of Commerce during the Progressive Era, the National Association of Manufacturers during the 1930s, the Committee for Economic Development during the 1960s and the Business Roundtable during the 1970s, have sought to play such a role. But their efforts have invariably floundered. Even trade associations in America have been far less important than in Europe or Japan; their role atrophied still further during the 1970s as companies became more diversified. In fact, over the last fifteen years, the nature of corporate political participation has become even more fragmented, with individual firms themselves becoming the most important policial units. Yoffie and Badaracco write:

A company with a politically active senior executive, a corporate public affairs staff, a PAC, its own media identity, a Washington law firm, and a Washington office or lobbyist has an independent apparatus for political action. It has its own information, contacts, and bargaining chips. It can lobby in Congress, negotiate with executive agencies, and take court action. Such a company can still work, in the traditional ways, through its industry association or through umbrella groups like the Chamber of Commerce. But it can also act on its own.[38]

Finally, compared to other capitalist nations, business–government relations in America have also been less stable. Over the last century the United States has experienced three major changes in the role of government in the economy. The first, associated with the Progressive Era, occurred between the turn of the century and the First World War. The second was the New Deal, which dominated American politics during the 1930s. The third, which still lacks a convenient label, took place between the middle of the 1960s and the middle of the 1970s; it was associated with a major increase in the scope of federal controls over corporate decisions in the areas of personnel policy, environmental and consumer protection, and occupational health and safety. The political turbulence associated with the reforms instituted during each period served to reinforce the long-standing belief of American corporate executives that the American political process is both unpredictable and potentially threatening to their prerogatives. As one executive put it at a business meeting in 1975, at the height of the most recent reform period,[39] 'My industry is regulated up to its neck. You are regulated up to your knees. And the tide is coming in.' Since then, of course, the influence of business over public policy has significantly increased, yet the perception of vulnerability expressed in this quotation remains a permanent feature of American business culture.

Conclusion

This paper has argued that business–government relations in America have been less distinctive than has been commonly assumed. It has primarily focused on the area of industrial policy, since students of business–government relations have frequently argued that it is precisely the inability of America to develop a coherent set of sectoral policies that reveals the distinctiveness of the American political system. We have suggested that America does have a highly developed set of industrial policies, which, on balance, appear to be no more or less coherent, consistent, or successful than those of its major industrial competitors. It now appears that the period of *laissez-faire* capitalism, far from establishing the future course of business–government relations in America, may instead come to be seen as a historical anomaly. In many respects we have come full circle: American business–government relations over the last half-century increasingly resemble the pattern of 'state mercantilism' of the first half of the nineteenth century. The only difference is that the former period of co-operation took place primarily at the state level, while, in recent years, the federal role has become much more important, Yet, in a sense, the fundamental dynamics are similar: just as the states financed the construction of canals and roadways in order to enable their citizens to compete more effectively with those of other states, so can many of the recent promotional policies of NASA and the Department of Defense be viewed as an effort to enable American industry to become more internationally competitive.

What does continue to make America distinctive is not so much the effect of its public policies on business as the way in which they are made. Precisely because American politics are highly pluralist and fragmented, companies have been forced to devote substantially greater resources to public affairs than in other capitalist nations. While some firms have cut back on their political activity since Reagan's election, the overall level of political involvement of American business remains extremely high by historical standards. And it is likely to remain so in the foreseeable future—particularly as issues surrounding the international competitiveness of American industry continue to occupy a prominent place on the nation's political agenda. The increased politicization of business represents one of the most significant changes in business–government relations in America over the last two decades.

Notes

1. See, for example, Chalmers Johnson (ed.), *The Industrial Policy Debate* (San Francisco: Institute for Contemporary Studies, 1984).
2. See Robert Reich, 'Making Industrial Policy', *Foreign Affairs*, September 1982, pp. 852–97; Robert Reich, 'An Industrial Policy of the Right', *Public Interest*, Fall 1983, pp. 3–17.
3. See Charles Schultze, 'Industrial Policy: A Dissent', *Brookings Review*, Fall 1983; J. L. Badaracco, jun. and D. B. Yoffie, 'Industrial Policy: It Can't Happen Here', *Harvard Business Review*, November–December 1982, pp. 96–175.
4. For the argument that the American state is weak, see Andrew Shonfield, *Modern Capitalism* (New York: Oxford University Press, 1965). For a formal classification of states in terms of their relative strengths and weaknesses, see Peter Katzenstein, 'Domestic Structures and Strategies of Foreign Economic Policy' in *Between Power and Plenty*, edited by Peter Katzenstein (Madison: University of Wisconsin Press, 1978). For more on the adversarial relationship, see Thomas McCraw, 'Business and Government: The Origins of the Adversary Relationship', *California Management Review*, Winter 1984, pp. 33–52.
5. This argument is made by Thomas McCraw in 'Mercantalism and the Market: Antecedents of American Industrial Policy' in Claude Barfield and William Schambra (eds.), *The Politics of Industrial Policy* (Washington, DC: American Enterprise Institute for Public Policy Research, 1986), pp. 33–62.
6. For both an eloquent summary and extensive critique of this position,

see Bruce Scott, 'National Strategies: Key to International Competition' in Bruce Scott and George Lodge (eds.), *U.S. Competitiveness in the World Economy* (Boston: Harvard Business School Press, 1985), pp. 71–143.

7. The one notable exception was in the area of military procurement. Eli Whitney, whose development of a system of manufacturing on interchangeable parts was critical to the development of the 'American system of manufacturing', attributed his innovation to government contracts and financing. The Springfield Arsenal was described as 'the most respectable private establishment . . . in the United States': William Diebold, jun., 'Past and Future Industrial Policy in the United States' in John Pinder (ed.), *National Industrial Strategies and the World Economy* (London: Allanheld, Osmun & Co., 1980), p. 163.

8. David Vogel, 'Why Businessmen Distrust their State: The Political Consciousness of American Corporate Executives', *British Journal of Political Science*, January 1978, pp. 45–78.

9. For the rather different European experience, see Suzanne Berger, 'Regime and Interest Representation in the French Traditional Middle Classes' in Suzanne Berger (ed.), *Organizing Interests in Western Europe* (Cambridge: University Press, 1981).

10. This section is based on Paul Lawrence and Davis Dyer, *Renewing American Industry* (New York: The Free Press, 1983), Chapter 5: 'Agriculture: The American Miracle'.

11. See also Ezra Vogel, *Comeback* (New York: Simon and Schuster, 1985), Chapter 5: 'Agriculture: Export Promotion'; Lawrence and Dyer, op. cit., p. 119.

12. Lawrence and Dyer, op. cit. (n. 10), p. 119.

13. John Young, 'Global Competition: The New Reality', *California Management Review*, Spring 1985, p. 16.

14. 'Elephant-High Farm Debts', *The Economist*, 14 September 1985, p. 17.

15. See Scott, 'National Strategies' (n. 6), pp. 133–4.

16. Ezra Vogel, op. cit. (n. 11), p. 212.

17. Ann Markusen, 'Defense Spending as Industrial Policy' in Sharon Zuken (ed.), *Industrial Policy* (New York: Praeger, 1985), p. 76.

18. See Reich, 'Making Industrial Policy', (n. 2), p. 864.

19. See Reich, 'Making Industrial Policy', (n. 2), p. 865; also Thomas Egan, 'The Case of Semiconductors' in Margaret Dewar (ed.), *Industry Vitalization* (New York: Pergamon Press, 1982), pp. 121–44; and Ezra Vogel, op. cit., (n. 11), p. 196.

20. Reich, 'Making Industrial Policy', p. 864. And Ezra Vogel adds: 'One survey of private scientists and engineers conducted in the mid-1970s put the commercial value of NASA's contributions up to that time in four fields—integrated circuits, gas turbines, multilayer insulation, and computer simulation—at between \$2.3 billion and \$7.6 billion in 1974

dollars.' Ezra Vogel, op. cit. (n. 11), p. 196. Michael Schrange notes: '[The Defense Department] was responsible for much of the funding for the most important work in computer graphics, computer networking, artificial intelligence and man-machine interfaces. The Defense Department was the driving force behind the development of numerically controlled machine tools. And Pentagon research is woven throughout the technological advances in the domestic airline industry.': Michael Schrange, 'America's Ministry of International Trade and Technology', *The Washington Post National Weekly Edition*, 27 August 1984, p. 31.

21. This section draws upon Reich, 'An Industrial Policy of the Right', op. cit. (n. 2). See also Schrange, op. cit. (n. 20).
22. 'The selling of Star Wars to Businesses Abroad', *Business Week*, 15 July 1985, pp. 68, 72.
23. Robert Kuttner, 'Blind Faith in Free Trade Doesn't Pay', *Business Week*, 14 October 1985, p. 22.
24. Bruce Steinberg, 'The Military Boost to Industry', *Fortune*, 30 April 1984, p. 45.
25. See Steinberg, op. cit..
26. This section is based on David Osborne, 'Business in Space', *The Atlantic*, March 1985, pp. 45–58.
27. Ibid., p. 45.
28. Ibid., p. 52.
29. Ibid., p. 45.
30. Neil Henderson and Michael Schrange, 'Our Biotech Industrial Policy: Will NIH's Baby have to Walk More on Its Own Now?', *The Washington Post National Weekly Edition*, 31 December 1984, p. 6. See also Susan Bartlett Foote, 'Coping with Conflict: Public Policies toward the Medical Product Industry', University of California, Berkeley: Center for Research in Management Working Paper, September 1985.
31. This argument is made by John Zysman in *Governments, Markets and Growth* (Ithaca: Cornell University Press, 1983).
32. Quoted in Diebold, op. cit. (n. 7), p. 165.
33. The next two paragraphs are based on David Vogel, *National Styles of Regulation: Environmental Policy in Great Britain and the United States* (Ithaca: Cornell University Press, 1986).
34. This argument is also made by Theodore J. Lowi, *The End of Liberalism* (New York: W. W. Norton, 1969, 1979) and Grant McConnell, *Private Power and American Democracy* (New York: Random House, 1966), although the conclusions they draw differ from mine.
35. See Mel Dubnick and Lynne Holt, 'Industrial Policy and the States', *Publics*, Winter 1985, pp. 113–29.
36. This section draws upon David Yoffie and Joseph Badaracco, jun., 'A Rational Model of Corporate Political Strategies', A Working Paper, Division of Research, Harvard Business School, 1984. See also David

Vogel, 'The Power of Business in America: A Re-Appraisal', *British Journal of Political Science*, January 1983, pp. 19–44.

37. See Thomas Byrne Edsell, *The New Politics of Inequality* (New York: W. W. Norton, 1984).

38. Yoffie and Badaracco, op. cit. (n. 36), pp. 3, 4.

39. Leonard Silk and David Vogel, *Ethics and Profits* (New York: Simon & Schuster, 1976), p. 52. For a detailed analysis of the changes in the pattern of political influence of business in American politics since 1965, see David Vogel, ibid.

6

The Cost-Containment Issue: a Study of Government–Industry Relations in the Pharmaceutical Sectors of the United Kingdom and West Germany

Keith MacMillan and Ian Turner

Introduction

The arrival in London, in January 1985, of the chief executives of three of the largest pharmaceutical companies in the world, American Home Products, Eli Lilly, and Pfizer, accompanied by senior staff from the US Pharmaceutical Manufacturers Association (PMA), was intended to signal their concern about British government policy towards the industry. Subsequently referred to as 'the charge of the US cavalry' by both industry and government officials, the delegation had sought in vain for a meeting with the Prime Minister to protest at what they saw as a dramatic and adverse change in government–industry relations which had taken place over the previous eighteen months.

A number of government measures had put pressure on firms' profitability, with the result, so senior industrialists claimed, that the UK was no longer as attractive as it had been to locate new R. & D. or manufacturing investment. There was now great uncertainty and suspicion about future government intentions. From the industry's point of view it seemed that the government had shattered the broad understanding about objectives and relationships which had served both the industry and the National Health Service well for two decades.

This paper is the product of over a year's research into the pharmaceutical industry and its relations with government in Britain and West Germany. Over that period we have talked with government officials, representatives of trade and professional organizations, politicians, journalists, academics, and pressure-group activists. Above all, we have visited a wide array of pharmaceutical companies both in the UK and West Germany and have discussed with company management their perceptions of government and the pressures they face.

By its very nature, much of the information which we gleaned from government and industry sources was supplied to us on a non-attributable basis, and we have felt bound to respect this condition. Wherever possible, however, we shall indicate in our references, at least in general terms, where specific information originated. Where information has also been published in official documents, or in the media or trade press, we have acknowledged this as a source.

Our purpose in writing this paper has been to analyse the development and current state of government–industry relations in the pharmaceutical sectors in three main ways. Using the introduction of selective prescribing guidelines, the 'limited list', as a case-study, we shall first attempt to place the observed pattern of influences which characterize government relations with the pharmaceutical industry in a theoretical and historical context. We shall then draw a contrast with the situation in West Germany, where the industry has not been subject to such dramatic changes in policy, despite some similarities in the socio-political pressures it faces. Finally, we shall speculate on the significance of the recent British experience for the ways in which companies manage their relations with government.

The Role of Government and the Pattern of Government–Industry Relations in the United Kingdom

Governments in all countries have powers which can impact directly upon the operations of pharmaceutical companies. At a general level, governments uphold the rule of law, conduct fiscal and monetary policies, maintain the infrastructure, and produce economic incentives and disincentives for industry. More specifically, drug companies are affected by government in three main ways. Governments control the licensing procedure for the marketing of new medicines, they can determine the length of patent protection for drugs, and, in most countries, they directly or indirectly affect the prices at which companies sell their products. All of these areas involve companies in a significant expenditure of effort, all can have a substantial impact on the balance sheet, and all can influence the type of behaviour companies adopt. How national governments conduct policy in these areas and how successful they are at creating a stable operating environment for the industry will influence whether and to what extent a multinational pharmaceutical company invests in the country.

In the United Kingdom the pattern of relations between the government and the pharmaceutical industry is essentially a post-war phenomenon, owing its origins to the foundation of the National Health Service (NHS) and the discovery and increasingly widespread use of powerful new drugs after 1945.[1] The original supporters of the NHS believed that demands on the service would eventually recede once the backlog of past neglect had been treated. It quickly became apparent, however, that demand for services at zero or near zero cost was virtually limitless, a fact that caused the bill for drugs consumed on the NHS to rise in what to government eyes was an alarming manner.

In an effort to stem the increase in drug costs, the then Ministry of Health entered into talks with the Association of the British Pharmaceutical Industry (ABPI) in 1954, over the establishment of an effective regulatory system.[2] The result was the forerunner of the Pharmaceutical Prices Regulation Scheme (PPRS), currently in force, whose principal hallmark is that it does *not* regulate pharmaceutical prices. Instead, it controls the profitability of companies by regulating the overall return on investment (ROI) permitted on sales through the NHS General Practitioner prescriptions. The preamble to the PPRS commits the industry and the DHSS to ensuring the provision of medicines 'on reasonable terms to the National Health Service' but also under conditions favourable for a 'strong, efficient, and profitable pharmaceutical industry in the United Kingdom'.[3] In practice, it is up to the DHSS to determine the overall ROI for the industry. To guide it in its decision it can refer to the prevailing rate of return set by the Review Board on Government Contracts and can take into consideration any recommendations made by the Public Accounts Committee of the House of Commons which periodically scrutinizes the operation of the PPRS.[4] Factors such as the rate of inflation and the average return for manufacturing industry as a whole clearly play a role in fixing the ROI, but ultimately the decision is a matter of subjective judgement by the DHSS.[5] Within the terms of overall ROI, individual companies then negotiate with the Department a rate of return for drugs sold on the NHS, on the basis of the annual financial returns and forecasts for the coming financial year, which they are required to submit. How much profit a particular company is permitted to make under the scheme is a function of its ability to accumulate the so-called 'Brownie-points' awarded by the DHSS. Points are scored if a company can demonstrate a significant contribution to the UK economy in terms of investment. R. & D., value-added in manufacture, and exports from Britain.[6] At the same time the DHSS also limits the amount a company may spend on promotion of drugs to the NHS. The exact weighting of the Brownie points is never divulged by the DHSS, and how much profit each company is allowed to make is also carefully concealed by the Department. Companies argue that this secrecy strengthens the hand of the DHSS in its dealings with industry, and allows it to play off one company against another. This is because companies who believe they come off well under the scheme have an interest in concealing their permitted return in order to preserve the edge over their competitors.[7] On the other hand, the DHSS claims that foreign companies manipulate the figures they present to the Department by transfer pricing and are thus able to conceal their true profits in the UK.

Until quite recently the PPRS served the pharmaceutical industry well. The ROI for the industry was typically higher than for manufacturing industry as a whole, reflecting the recognition of the high costs of developing a product and the size of the risks involved. True, government regulation failed to check the rise in the cost of drugs in absolute terms, but, in an era of high inflation and rising public expenditure, the pressure on the DHSS to effect savings through the PPRS was less acute. Moreover, the United Kingdom pharmaceutical industry waxed strong and prosperous throughout the 1960s and 1970s, with a significant positive trade balance and an unparalleled record in new product innovation. Companies like Beechams, Glaxo, ICI Pharmaceuticals, Boots, Wellcome, and Fisons were proof that, at least in one industrial sector, Britain could still compete on equal terms with the rest of the world.

The strength of the links which developed between the DHSS and the ABPI over profit regulation should not be allowed to obscure the underlying weaknesses in the ABPI's position, however. The PPRS is negotiated, non-statutory agreement: in effect an agreement to agree. It assigns monopoly rights for renegotiating the scheme to the ABPI, but the benefits conferred by the PPRS are available to all companies and cannot be used in Olson's terms as selective inducements for collective action by the Association.[8] In the past, this has led to repeated cases where pharmaceutical companies, particularly foreign multinationals, have disputed the legitimacy of the scheme. The Swiss companies, for example, only agreed to abide by the original regulatory scheme in 1960. A year later, the American company Pfizer refused to adjust the price of one of its products and was threatened by Health Minister Enoch Powell with the import of cheap substitutes from overseas. Perhaps most notable was the case of Roche who in 1973 withdrew from the scheme in response to government pressure to reduce the price of Valium and Librium.

The DHSS does devolve other regulatory tasks to the ABPI, such as the policing of company advertising. But this too confers little organizational power, as the scrutiny is in the form of a post-marketing response to complaints.[9] The ability of the ABPI to manage the diversity of its membership and to retain organizational autonomy—to operate in Schmitter and Streeck's terms under the 'logic of influence'[10]—is dependent on the provision of services to members, on the supply of information and intelligence on government action, and, where necessary, on the exercise of peer group pressure within the Association. Despite the weaknesses in the ABPI's position, however, it is true to say that companies have, until recently at least, preferred to rely on the ABPI to represent their interests to government. In exchange for the dilution of a company's specific interests, which participation in the ABPI inevitably entails, the Association provides guaranteed access and influence with government. Moreover, companies in general favour the flexibility inherent in the PPRS to the alternative of direct government controls.

The relationship which grew up between the DHSS and the ABPI, therefore, during the period from 1957 to 1983, adheres closely to the characteristic pattern of government–interest group relations described by Richardson and Jordan in their study of British pressure-group activity.[11] A 'routinized' and 'regularized' relationship was established to resolve issues of mutual concern. Government officials, seeking to avoid conflict with the industry, supported the ABPI. In an effort to preserve a stable operating environment for the industry, the Association cultivated a close relationship with the DHSS. Out of mutual interest was born a sense of community and a tendency to accommodation and compromise: the necessity for stability was reconciled with the need for change by bargaining and adjustment. In this way the 'rules of the game' for dealings between government and industry were established: the recognition of the legitimacy of respective interests, the willingness to consult and give prior notice of action, the prevalence of informal communication, the sensitivity to the needs and constraints of the other partner, and the preference for negotiation rather than legal action.[12]

Our research design posits the existence of 'policy communities', whose members all share a 'policy focus', in the sense that they are interested in a particular product, service, technology, market, or industry. It also distinguishes 'policy networks', which are the exchange relationships established between participants in the policy community over a particular 'policy issue'. Such a policy network was clearly established between the ABPI and the DHSS over the issue of drug costs.

It would be a mistake, however, to view the network in isolation from the relations established with other members of the pharmaceutical policy community. Because of the characteristics of the pharmaceutical market, the manufacturer is more than in other industries dependent upon the services of other intermediaries to get his product to the consumer. Thus the wholesale distributors, the pharmacists, and the doctors are links in the chain of distribution from manufacturer to patient. These intermediaries have a political as well as a functional role. As can be seen from Figure 3 they are represented in their relations with external organizations by what can be a bewildering array of trade and professional associations.

Each of these organizations is concerned with maintaining, extending, or defending its domain. At a functional and operational level this means they act to internalize the elements of instability in their environment, as, for example, when pharmacists join together to form a co-operative wholesale distributor.[13] As the boundaries of their domains are often laid down by law and controlled by the state, however, much organizational energy is expended in negotiating with government in an attempt to expedite or prevent the shifting of boundaries, or in warding off incursions into their domain by the state itself. A classic example of this sort of boundary dispute is the clash between the dispensing doctors and the rural pharmacists over the right to dispense drugs in rural areas. Parallels exist here with the legal profession where incursions by the government into the solicitors' monopoly rights to conveyancing have provoked conflict with barristers over their respective roles. Of the resources that these interest groups can command in their bargaining with government, the most powerful, under the currently prevailing climate, is the ability to offer financial savings. An outstanding example of this sort of deal is the current set of talks on the future role of the pharmacist. The pharmacist's traditional, manipulative role in dispensing drugs has been eroded by technological developments in manufacture and packaging. In order to recoup lost status, the chemists are pressing for a return to their pre-NHS advisory and diagnostic role. This could save the government money by diverting patients from NHS GPs, but would run the risk of transgressing the traditional boundaries with the medical profession.

From the point of view of the pharmaceutical manufacturers, such bargaining is of more than academic interest since it can fundamentally alter the nature of the business they are in: the doctor's advocacy of generic substitution and the pharmacists' desire for greater over-the-

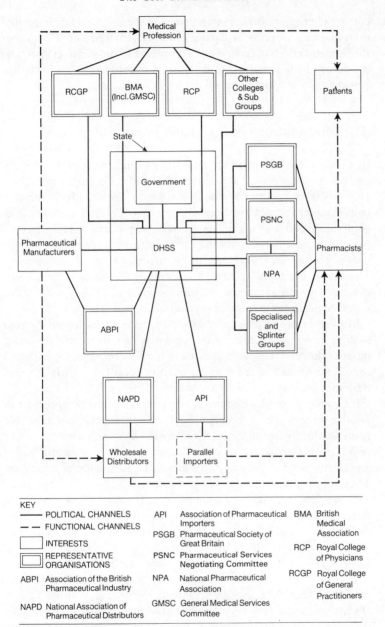

Figure 3. An Overview of the Pharmaceutical Policy Community in the UK

counter pharmacy sales are two prime examples of this. How important these interests can prove in practice will be evident from our case-study of the limited list. First, however, we must look at the social and political pressures which underlie the relationships in the pharmaceutical policy community and which generate the forces for change.

The Intensification of Social and Political Pressures

In recent years, the relations between government and the pharmaceutical industry have been subject to considerable stress from extraneous social and political forces. Perhaps most significantly, health-care costs in most countries have been rising rapidly. This reflects both demograpic and technological changes. As older people, who have the greatest per capita consumption of health care, constitute an increasing proportion of the population, there will be increased demands on available resources. Additionally, new developments in medical technology enhanced people's expectations of possible treatments and further reinforce pressures to increase expenditure.

Most governments have an interest in increasing value for money from health-care services. This may be because the government is the major buyer of these services, as in the case of the UK, or because it wishes to control the burden on the economy of rising contributions to the health insurance scheme, as in West Germany.

Expenditure on pharmaceuticals represents around ten per cent of health-care costs in both countries, but other costs are mainly attributable to the employment of staff, where cuts are less politically acceptable. As a result, the industries in both countries have recently been experiencing greater attempts to reduce pharmaceutical costs, some of which are described in later sections of this paper.[14]

In addition, the industry has increasingly been the object of criticism from pressure groups and the media on a number of issues. Following the thalidomide tragedy in the early sixties and despite more restrictive licensing procedures, there have been further cases in which the harmful side-effects of drugs have received wide publicity, such as those associated with a number of non-steroidal anti-inflammatory compounds.[15] Often these cases are associated, by the media, with criticisms of what is regarded as lavish promotion to doctors, implying that this may reduce their objectivity when prescribing. Thus, concerns over product safety reinforce public perceptions of the rising costs of drugs and the scale of profits made by pharmaceutical companies.

While most adverse publicity for the industry is to be found in advanced countries, several of the most pointed criticisms have recently referred to company practices in developing countries. It is claimed that excessive promotion by companies means that powerful, and often inappropriate, medicines are too widely available at excessive prices.[16] Several charities, church and consumer groups have formed alliances and are currently lobbying, *inter alia*, for a marketing code to be instituted by the World Health Organization, and also for increased controls to be levied on exports by pharmaceutical companies from advanced countries to the Third World.[17] In addition to this wide range of governmental pressures and adverse publicity, the industry is also criticized by animal rights groups for the use of animals in toxicity tests during new product development. Methods of direct action by some members of these groups have become increasingly militant and have added to the volume of criticisms of the industry.

Why should criticism of this type be significant? It is our supposition that the climate of opinion generated by these critical groups, particularly amongst the opinion-formers in society and the higher socio-economic classes, can and does affect the way government handles the pharmaceutical industry. We may hypothesize that when contemplating action a politician will try to select a course which offers the maximum political advantage for the minimum cost. Our interviews with government and industry representatives have led us to conclude that politicians will seek to avoid measures that can be portrayed as detrimental to the health service and patient care in particular. The medical lobby in Britain is widely acknowledged as one of the country's most influential pressure groups. It has professional legitimacy, grass-roots support, and can rely upon health service unions to support its opposition to any government move with unfavourable employment implications. Restrictions imposed on prescribable drugs, of course, also have an impact upon patient treatment and can affect industry employment. But here the target was much softer due to the pharmaceutical industry's image, so that the potential costs of moving against it were, therefore, perceived as much lower. Our case-study of the limited list will provide some evidence to support this hypothesis.

The Limited List

Background

The changing economic and political environment for the UK pharmaceutical industry in the early 1980s was reinforced by the Conservative government's increasing concern with controlling, and if possible reducing, public expenditure. Thus cash limits first introduced in the 1970s were enforced upon many sectors of NHS activity,[18] and a system of health service managers was established with the aim of improving efficiency. The cost of medicines, like the Family Practitioner Services in general, however, remained a thorn in the Treasury's side: because the bill for drugs was determined by the needs of patients and was, therefore, essentially open-ended, it resisted budgetary control by the Treasury. Within the DHSS, too, there was growing awareness of the need to make economies. From 1981 the department began to examine how other countries were dealing with the problem of costs, and in 1982 a committee of eminent representatives from doctors' and pharmacists' associations, under the chairmanship of Dr Greenfield, published a report advocating, *inter alia*, a system of generic substitution, whereby a cheaper non-branded good could be dispensed when the general practitioner indicated that he had no objection.[19] The government, however, remained unconvinced. The potential savings were thought to be relatively small and uncertain, and the DHSS therefore accepted the ABPI's argument that generic substitution would damage the research-based industry, and instituted, instead, a general price cut of 2 per cent from August 1983 followed by a price freeze until April 1984—measures which were designed to realize savings of £25 million.[20]

Throughout 1983 it was apparent that the future of the PPRS and the ROI-allowed companies was under review by the DHSS. This process was given further impetus by the change of political direction at the Department in 1982, the June 1983 General Election, and the deliberations of the House of Commons Public Accounts Committee, which concluded in July 1983 that reductions should be made in company profits on NHS sales. As a result, the DHSS announced in December of that year a cut in ROI from 25 per cent to 21 per cent, with a reduction in allowable promotional expenditure from 10 per cent to 9 per cent for the 1985/6 financial year (effective from April 1984).[21]

At this point, the pressure from the Treasury's Public Expenditure Survey[22] coincided with the DHSS's own search for economies in the

NHS drugs bill. The outcome was what ultimately became the limited list. Rightly or wrongly the DHSS now believed that attempts to achieve further savings on the drugs bill via the PPRS alone would be undesirable, and, bearing in mind the voluntary nature of the scheme, increasingly difficult to effect. Similarly, it doubted whether substantial savings could be delivered in the short-term, by limiting the quantity of medicine prescribed by GPs, without unacceptable hardship to patients. Ministers and officials within the DHSS, therefore, decided that a scheme to restrict the range of drugs available on the NHS would be most likely to deliver guaranteed savings of the order required.

Implementation of a restricted list of drugs had previously always been excluded by governments, out of deference to the combined political influence of the pharmaceutical industry and the BMA. Indeed, both the former Health Minister, Kenneth Clarke, and the former Secretary of State, Patrick Jenkin, had given assurances to that effect in the House of Commons.[23] Now, however, the circumstances had changed in response to the relentless pressure of government expenditure restriction, and the political perception that the pharmaceutical industry, by virtue of its negative public image, would be a vulnerable target for government action.

The storm breaks

After several months of secret preparation, the Secretary of State, Norman Fowler, announced in the Commons, on 8 November 1984, that from 1 April 1985 a limited list of medicines, covering seven therapeutic categories, would be enforced for GP prescription under the NHS. The list, which covered many categories for which medicines were already available over-the-counter without prescription, as well as the more controversial area of tranquillizers and sedatives, was designed to realize savings of £100 million per annum out of a total of £1.4 billion. In preparing the list, officials had consulted the World Health Organization's list of essential drugs, comprised exclusively of generic preparations. A period of consultation with interested parties was announced, terminating at the end of January, but ministers made it clear that they were only interested in detailed suggestions and not in proposals for altering the basic nature of the list.[24] Shortly after, Kenneth Clarke gave notice of further reduction in the industry's ROI from 21 per cent to an estimated 15–17 per cent, with a mandatory price reduction across the board in addition to the one per cent cut in allowable promotional spending already announced.[25]

The industry reaction

That the announcement of the limited list caused a political furore would be an understatement. Stunned by the suddenness of the move and the lack of prior consultation—an unprecedented violation of the 'rules of the game'—the ABPI and the BMA separately issued statements condemning the list in principle and refusing to consult with the DHSS over its composition.[26] As a result, the Department established its own committee of experts to review the composition of the list. From the industry's point of view, one of the most obvious features of the list as originally conceived was its differential impact on companies. Because of the categories of drugs covered, it hit companies like Roche, Berk, and Wyeth—predominantly but not exclusively foreign multinationals—much harder than established British firms like Beechams, Glaxo, ICI, or Boots. This was an unintended although apparently not wholly unwelcome effect of the list.[27]

This encouraged companies to respond individually to the threat posed by the list, and to seek a reprieve for their products. At the same time, the limited list and the cost-saving measures brought about an obvious change in the role of the ABPI towards a more adversarial position *via-à-vis* government. This was most evident in the aggressive, high-profile advertising campaign conducted by the Association in the national press. The industry's campaign gave most prominence to the claim that the limited list would create a two-class NHS with the elderly, poor, and the young in future receiving substandard medical treatment.[28] It disputed the savings that would be made, and claimed that the measure would have a devastating effect on R. & D. and manufacturing investment in the UK. In addition to the public compaign, the ABPI also conducted a tug-of-war with the DHSS for the hearts and minds of MPs. Receptions were held, briefing papers distributed, refutations and counter-refutations issued, and back-benchers implored lobby ministers to withdraw the plan. Health ministers remained adamant, however, and successfully defused opposition from Tory MPs, by a series of tactical concessions. For many companies who had in the past relied heavily on the APBI to manage their external affairs, the limited list became a political baptism of fire. For conceptual purposes the action taken by companies can be divided, following Hirschman's classification,[29] into 'voice' responses and 'exit' responses. Voice responses signify attempts to exercise political influence. Such attempts were conducted in the first place via the ABPI, but increasingly, as the logic of collective action was restored, by more homogeneous regional or national groupings of companies, like the US companies referred to at the start of this paper, or indeed by individual companies acting independently. Affected companies typically contacted MPs whose constituencies were likely to be affected or who were known to be sympathetic. Some companies, like Reckitt & Coleman and Upjohn, already retained MPs as parliamentary advisers. For others, like Roussel, it meant finding out who the local MPs were and apprising them of the situation. Representations to MPs and information to local press stressed the adverse economic effects of the list on company profitability and hence on local employment prospects. Similar points were made by trade union delegations to parliament on behalf of the work forces of beleaguered companies like Warner-Lambert, Ciba-Geigy, and Wyeth. Letters to GPs—including a very controversial one from Roche—enjoined doctors to write to MPs and to encourage patients to do the same, pointing out the damaging effect the list could have on patient health. On the practical level, companies approached the DHSS for clarification of the mechanics of the list and made representations on particular drugs to the advisory committee set up to review the composition of the list. The effectiveness of the approaches made by the companies varied enormously, but was not helped by the dearth of information on the criteria to be used by the DHSS in compiling the final list. The fact, for example, that the price of a product could be decisive was only made explicit after the final list was published, in a Commons Statement by Kenneth Clarke.[30]

Some companies, like Reckitt & Coleman, managed to rescue important products from being excluded by the DHSS. To what extent the intervention with Mrs Thatcher by the company's Chairman and President of the CBI, Sir James Cleminson, was influential in this case, can only be speculated upon. Other companies, like Dista, received a conditional reprieve for their products, or had products excluded despite pleas for exemption.

After the period of consultation had elapsed, and the committee of experts had made its judgements on the composition, the final version of the list was published in February 1985.[31] In fact, for legal reasons, the list had become two lists: a recommended list of about 100 generic and branded drugs for the seven categories covered, and a statutory catalogue of 1800 'scheduled' or 'blacklisted' products, many of which were either borderline, such as chewing-gum with nicotine, or items which were rarely prescribed in practice. As a result of the expansion of the list of permitted drugs, the DHSS now forecast savings of some £75 million—a reduction of some £25 million on the original figure.

Companies with blacklisted drugs could (like Astra and Sterling-Winthrop) await the arrival of an appeals mechanism in the hope of reinstatement, accept the inevitable and discontinue products (as in the case of Smith, Kline, & French and William Warner), or exercise the option of an 'exit' response. The exact nature of the exit, however, varied due to the complex nature of the pharmaceutical market. At its simplest, companies could elect to maintain their product on the presciption market for private prescription only: by bringing down the price to the equivalent of an NHS prescription charge and maintaining a high promotional profile to doctors, companies like Upjohn, Boehringer-Ingelheim, and Roche[32] might hope to limit the damage. For products that were already over-the-counter, like Warner-Lambert's Benylin, companies could withdraw from the prescription market completely and concentrate on general advertising to the public. In other cases, companies like Wyeth and Duphar reduced the price of their blacklisted brand-named products to the tariff price for the permitted generic compound and remarketed the product with the generic name given prominence. At its most extreme, the exit option meant cancelling planned projects in the UK, like Wyeth's £30 million laboratory at Swindon, switching attention to alternative sites in Europe, as contemplated by Merck Sharpe Dohme,[33] or scaling down UK operations, as in the case of Roche.[34]

The ABPI, in fact, claimed that £138 million of capital investment in the UK had been cancelled or deferred as a result of the list with an estimated loss of 2000 jobs.[35] The real damage, they believed, would only be seen ten years hence, when lost investment in the UK would become apparent.

The threat of exit and the long-term economic argument failed to impress health ministers however; their concerns were immediate and acute: to achieve savings in pharmaceutical spending. They were sceptical of the impact of a measure, which, they claimed, hit only some half a per cent of the total world market, and pointed to the still considerable advantages offered by the United Kingdom over some of its international rivals, in terms of political stability, scientific expertise, and lack of direct price controls.

As some leading members of the ABPI now recognize, the industry's political campaign probably lost it more friends than it gained. The emphasis given to characterizing the list as an attack on the NHS and a danger to the old and sick was, as many would now concede, a tactical error. It incensed government ministers and Mrs Thatcher alike,[36] and almost certainly lacked credibility with the public at large. Similarly, the flood of letters initiated by Roche and others, and sent by obliging GPs to MPs, provoked an angry reaction from many Conservative MPs who might otherwise have been sympathetic to the industry.[37] Perhaps most importantly, the campaign also adversely affected the working relations between the ABPI and the DHSS at official level.[38]

The response of professional groups and political parties

In order to legitimize its case against the list, the ABPI could point to the hostility the measure attracted from the other main groups in the pharmaceutical policy community. In fact, however, there were substantial differences in principle and in emphasis among the associations concerned: indeed the variety of responses would provide rich material for a study in its own right.[39] The BMA, as already mentioned, was implacably opposed to the principle of the list and maintained this position, despite rumblings from within the association, until the measure was passed by Parliament. There were indications, however, that the BMA was not comfortable in supporting the industry stand. In January 1985, for instance, the BMA Council's Chairman Dr John Marks wrote to MPs disassociating the BMA from the pharmaceutical industry's lobbying tactics. Furthermore, the RCGP, whilst officially toeing the BMA line, was more accommodating in its response to government,[40] and the Royal College of Physicians supported the limited list in principle and had only detailed reservations on the method of its implementation.[41]

The division amongst the medical associations was mirrored by the organizations representing the pharmacists. The professional body, the Pharmaceutical Society of Great Britain (PSGB), condemned the list as depriving needy patients of adequate treatment but was prepared to consult with the DHSS over particular aspects. The negotiating body, the PSNC, hopeful that the list might lead to an increased role for the pharmacist, supported the list throughout,[42] whilst the retailers' representatives, the NPA, adopted a position of masterly ambivalence somewhere in the middle. The distributors' association, the NAPD, aligned itself formally with the ABPI, but kept a low profile for fear of disrupting relations with the DHSS. For the NAPD, as for many of the professional associations concerned, the limited list issue was not to be allowed to harm progress in ongoing discussions with the DHSS over terms of contract.

Similar differences were apparent in the responses of the opposition political parties. The initial reaction had been confused by the surprise of the announcement, and the unprecedented nature of the scheme. Most of the opposition parties had commitments to generic prescribing in some form or other and were possibly misled by the wording of the announcement into thinking that the government had now embraced the principle of generic substitution. The Labour Party reaction was hesitant and unconvincing: eventually aligning itself with the industry and the BMA, the party condemned the move as misconceived and against the principles upon which the NHS was founded. Yet party advisers on pharmaceutical matters supported the list as a long overdue step to control the flood of available drugs,[43] and many back-benchers were evidently uneasy at being seen publicly to support the pharmaceutical industry.[44]

The outcome

From the government's point of view, the campaign waged against the list by the various interested groups was flawed not only by differences in emphasis but by the inability of the organizations to put forward an agreed set of alternative proposals.[45] The BMA and the PSGB urged generic substitution which was anathema to the industry. The ABPI urged savings under the pharmacists' and distributors' terms of contract, and the Labour Party, committed at various times in its history to the nationalization of parts of the pharmaceutical industry, belatedly announced its support for a limited list in principle, provided it covered private as well as NHS prescriptions.[46] Thus, the government was able to exploit the differences of interest between the various organizations concerned, in order to undermine their campaign of opposition.

The limited list was introduced by the DHSS as planned on 1 April 1985. In response to back-bench pressure, ministers agreed to work out details with the BMA for a local appeals mechanism for GPs needing to prescribe blacklisted drugs in exceptional circumstances. The agreement reached between the BMA and the DHSS on the override mechanism was, however, repudiated by the grass roots of the medical profession when they met for their annual Local Medical Conference in June. General practitioners evidently felt they would be placed under pressure by patients to obtain exemptions from the list, and this, they believed, could easily lead to unfairness in practice. In addition, the advisory committee set up to review the list was retained permanently to vet new drugs in the affected categories for prescription on the NHS.

With the co-operation of doctors and pharmacists the list is now operating adequately, although not without some resentment by harassed pharmacists, GPs, and disgruntled patients. How much the list will actually save is still uncertain. First indications were of a 25 per cent decrease in the number of prescriptions in affected categories since 1 April 1985. In early 1986 the DHSS revised its estimate of savings downwards by £10 million to £65 million.[47] The final figure will depend very much on the behaviour of doctors, patients, and companies. For the industry, the most worrying aspect of the list was the precedent it set for the future and the potential for extension to other therapeutic areas in response to further public expenditure constraints. Ministers assured companies that the list was not the 'thin edge of the wedge', and they could look forward to a period of stability—at least until the next general election.

In the mean time, however, ministers sought to maintain the momentum by encouraging greater economy in prescribing, by investigating the practice of transfer pricing by multinational companies,[48] and by scrutinizing companies' promotional expenditure more closely.

West Germany—a Contrast

Within the confines of a paper of this length it will not be possible to explore fully the contrasting situation in West Germany. Nevertheless, the absence of radical upheaval in the pharmaceutical sector, and of change in the environment facing companies on anything like the scale experienced over recent years in the United Kingdom, poses some interesting questions. Our provisional hypothesis is *not* that West German companies have been notably skilful at managing their external relations, but rather that the environment in which they operate is more permissive. In the first place, sustained high economic growth in West Germany means that pressure to constrain rising health costs is less acute than in Britain. Increases in the cost of health care—of which the drugs bill forms a prominent part—lead not to rises in government expenditure, but rather to increased contributions to the sickness funds (*Krankenkassen*), which provide some 90 per cent of the West German population with health care. As 50 per cent of contributions are paid by employers, the Ministry of Labour cannot afford to be indifferent to the effect such increases have on labour costs. But the concern is less compelling than the action prompted by the unrelenting scrutiny afforded the NHS budget by the Treasury in Britain.

This is not to say that West German pharmaceutical companies are not dependent on government in any sense. Clearly, they rely on the federal and *Länder* governments for the creation of a favourable operating environment, as other companies in other industries do. Moreover, the federal government does have the potential to intervene administratively, and through legislation in the industry's affairs by, for example, the licensing of new products or the passing of cost-containment laws. For the most part, however, the German pharmaceutical industry enjoys a substantial degree of freedom from government action.

The relative power of the drug companies in the Federal Republic, then, can be attributed mainly to systemic factors. The ethos of the social market economy, the legal and institutional framework, and the characteristics of the political system, together constitute a policy 'style' which is distinct from its counterpart in the UK, and which tends to tilt the power-dependence relationship in favour of the industry and against the government to a greater extent than in Britain.

The pattern of health care

Perhaps most fundamental to the position of the industry is the absence of all forms of direct government price or profit controls on company sales.[49] This state of affairs is justified, by the industry at least, by reference to the principles of the social market economy, the 'guiding light' of West Germany's economic policy since 1948.[50]

The compulsory sickness insurance scheme, and the pattern of health care itself, goes back still further, to the Bismarck era. This continuity in the health system has enshrined certain features in law which make it difficult for the *Krankenkassen* to control drug costs. The funds have no direct contractual relationship with drug manufacturers. Attempts to reach agreement with the industry on measures of self-regulation have, so far, broken down in the face of the inability of the trade association, the Bundesverband Der Pharmazeutischen Industrie (BPI), under German law to negotiate a settlement binding on its members.[51] Similarly, the fact that health care is provided not by one unitary health system as in Britain, but by a multiplicity of *Krankenkassen* means companies can exploit the way that the funds are compelled to compete for clients by offering ever more expensive forms of health care. Finally, the market conditions for drug firms are favourably influenced by the inability of government under German law to control the influx of doctors into the health service, a feature which encourages doctors to engage in wasteful competition for patients by offering lavish and costly treatment including the most expensive forms of drug therapy.[52]

The system of government

If the foundation of the West German industry's power position is the propitious nature of the pharmaceutical market, its influence is buttressed by the characteristics of the constitution and political system of the Federal Republic. Two features are particularly significant in this respect: the prevalence of coalition government and the dispersal of political authority through the federal system.

West German governments, at federal level at least, have almost always been coalition governments. This means that the process of formulating, deciding, and implementing government policy is pro-tracted and complex. It also means that smaller coalition partners—notably the liberal FDP—have a disproportionate influence. The pharmaceutical industry has traditionally regarded the FDP as its champion within government. FDP ministers have occupied the Ministry of Economics and have defended the industry in cabinet from cost-cutting Ministers of Labour intent on limiting its freedom.[53] Cynics might argue that this reflects the financial contributions made by the BPI to FDP politicians' election expenses.[54] In fact, the relationship is more complex than this. The FDP casts itself in the role of defender of the social market economy from dilution by either of the two larger parties, the Christian Democrats or the Social Democrats. There is thus a philosophical predilection for free enterprise which correponds to the FDP's own political base in the *Mittelstand*, the traditional professional and small business class. This is reinforced by personal links between the FDP, the industry, and, in particular, the pharmacists. The long-serving chief executive of the BPI, Scholl, for instance, was FDP Party Chairman in the Rhineland-Palatinate and the current Treasurer and spokesman on health and social affairs, Irmgard Adam-Schwatzer, is a pharmacist by profession. It is, therefore, not so much a case of the industry capturing the FDP, as rather a recognition of mutual dependency and common aims.[55]

The second characteristic is the division of responsibility for health affairs between the federal, *Land*, and local levels of government. This inhibits effective government action in the health field on matters such as hospital costs, and, importantly from the point of view of the pharmaceutical industry, the training of doctors. It also affords the industry the opportunity, through the *Länder* representatives in the upper house, or *Bundesrat*, to delay or modify legislation inimical to its interests.

The cumulative effect of these governmental characteristics is a tendency towards government immobilism. The following examples should illustrate this more clearly. A cost-containment law was introduced in 1977, with provision for the compilation of a negative list of drugs for the treatment of trivial ailments which would be excluded from reimbursement by the *Krankenkassen*. After delays caused by legal obstacles, the list finally came into effect on 1 April 1983—six years later. Meanwhile, the government had introduced a set of thirty-two revisions to the original act in mid-1981. Of these, four were approved by Cabinet and two were finally passed by Parliament, one of which had substantial modification. Concerned at the inexorable rise in the drugs bill, Minister of Labour Norbert Blum signalled his intention in March 1985 to promulgate a new cost-containment law. The idea, however, was rejected in Cabinet, by a combination of FDP and pro-industry CDU ministers and no fundamental change in the system now looks likely, for electoral reasons, before the next federal elections in early 1987.

Future trends

The tendency towards government immobilism and political prevarication in West Germany, whilst it has assisted the industry in the past by averting intervention by the state inimical to the interests of pharmaceutical manufacturers, has not immunized the West German drugs industry from social and political pressures, or isolated it entirely from the effects of constraints on health spending.

Government action in 1985 was restricted to appealing to the industry to exercise self-restraint, by keeping the increase in drug prices below the average rise in incomes. There were, however, a number of indications that government and the *Krankenkassen* were seeking to explore to the full the powers at their disposal to constrain drug costs. Such efforts were concentrated on exercising greater control over doctors' prescribing habits. A review procedure for GPs prescribing—the so-called '*Regressverfahren*'—had long been in existence. Review boards composed of *Krankenkassen* officials and *Kassen* doctors' associations have always had the authority to scrutinize the prescribing behaviour of doctors, and, where the GPs prescribing costs had persistently exceeded 40 per cent of the average for doctors in the same situation, the *Krankenkassen* had been able to demand a refund of the excess and in extreme cases request a termination of the doctor's contract. In the past, the incidence of such cases had been extremely infrequent, the margin for excessive prescribing generous, and, bearing in mind the continuous rise in average prescribing costs, not particularly irksome to the doctors. In early 1986, however, there were some signs that this was changing.[56] Local *Krankenkassen*, acting in response to short-term shortages of funds, had been instrumental in the increasing use of a more detailed examination of doctors' case-by-case prescribing habits. Individual prescriptions were scrutinized for both economy and appropriateness, and, where branded drugs had been prescribed instead of an equivalent generic product, payment to the value of the excess could be withheld. The hard line taken by these *Krankenkassen* elicited opposition from some doctors concerned about their therapeutic freedom. The *Krankenkassen*, however, were assisted by the presence of cost-conscious 'activist' doctors on the review committees, and the use of increasingly sophisticated computer data on doctors' comparative prescribing behaviour. Some generic companies, too, were quick to latch on to this development and to use it as a marketing device to sell their products.

One other development may assist the *Krankenkassen* in their cost-containment efforts. This is the imminent introduction of price comparison lists for particular therapeutic categories. These lists are being compiled jointly by *Krankenkassen* and *Kassen* doctors' associations, and reportedly categorize products into three groups according to their perceived cost-effectiveness. If used rigorously in conjunction with the review procedure, these lists could take the West German market a significant step towards a positive list of prescribable drugs. Only time will tell how effective these measure will be, however, in the face of opposition from the industry and the medical profession.

It is clear that drastic changes in the pharmaceutical market in the Federal Republic will, for political reasons, only take place after the general election in January 1987. The governing coalition has already flagged its intention of implementing a fundamental reform of the sickness insurance scheme.[57] The proposals are designed to introduce more consumer choice and increase the market element of health provision, in order to make the participants more cost-conscious. Significantly, such reforms are also supported by the pro-market FDP, but, given the strength of vested interests in West Germany, and the susceptibility of government policy to political pressures, it may confidently be predicted that the final outcome will fall short of the announced proposals.

A far greater threat is posed by the possibility of a change in government at federal level. An SPD government maintained in power by the parliamentary support of the Green Party is a conceivable, if not probable, result of a general election. The SPD has already floated plans for the establishment by the *Krankenkassen* and doctors' associations of an independent drugs institute to compile a positive list of prescribable drugs, and, whilst the Green Party is reportedly dismissive of the Social Democrats' preference for bureaucratic solutions, the party is on record as favouring the introduction of therapeutic superiority or relative efficacy as a criterion for licensing of drugs.

Discussion and Conclusions

The paper has attemped to analyse the pattern of relations that grew up between government and the pharmaceutical industry in the UK in the post-war period. In so doing we have paid particular attention to the role of the industry's principal trade association, the ABPI, in mediating between companies and the DHSS. We have also shown how the organizational limitations of the ABPI and the presence of the other interest groups in the pharmaceutical policy community have made it difficult for government and industry always to maintain unity of purpose. The Association is subject to internal tensions from the member companies, whilst the Department must respond to the needs of the other professional and commercial groups, as well as being subject to political direction and Treasury constraints. As a result, the policy network established between government and the pharmaceutical industry, can be disconnected by shifts in government policy brought on by changes in the social and political environment. We believe that the industry is particularly vulnerable to such shifts due to the activities of critical pressure groups, and their ability to transmit a negative image of the pharmaceutical industry and its methods to key opinion-formers in society. The climate of opinion which is thus created can facilitate government action hostile to the industry. Such groups and the pressure for change which they generate—often in ways that are tangential to their purposes—are not confined to the UK. But our researches in West Germany have made us aware of the particular characteristics of the British system which enable these pressures to take effect.

At this point it may be appropriate to look a little more closely at the constraints under which some of the main actors in the pharmaceutical policy community operate, in order to gain some insight into how the pattern of relations is likely to develop in the future. Let us look first of all at the government, which, until the next general election at least, looks set to remain Conservative.

The dilemmas of government

The irony of the situation for the government is that it finds itself, of necessity, locked in a firm embrace with the pharmaceutical industry in a way which contravenes the market principles upon which government–industrial policy is supposedly based. Given that the government is committed to the NHS, and given that, for electoral reasons, it will be unwilling to introduce thoroughgoing reforms on the demand side of the health system to make doctors and patients more conscious of cost-effectiveness in the use of drugs, it must perforce maintain control on the supply side in order to moderate the costs of medicines to the state. There are several ways it could do this, but, traditionally, British governments have preferred voluntary schemes to statutory price regulation, as they involve less expenditure on administration and have greater likelihood of eliciting compliance by the companies. Whatever means is chosen, however, involves the state in an essentially arbitrary decision about the balance to be struck between maintaining a prosperous industry and getting the best deal in cash terms for the NHS. The DHSS is thus in the invidious position of being both the sponsor department of the pharmaceutical industry and its main customer in the UK. The Department is clearly well aware of this dilemma and the Health Minister reportedly attempted to divest the DHSS of its sponsorship to the Department of Trade & Industry in 1983, but was blocked by the Prime Minister's veto. Most ministers are not unaware of the economic value of the pharmaceutical industry, but its national significance in political terms—the total number of people employed in the UK is some 81,000[58]—does not weigh as heavily, say, as the motor industry. Moreover, in the present climate, the need to effect financial savings is often pressing, whereas the potential damage to the economy from offering the pharmaceutical industry an inadequate return will take years and possibly decades to materialize.[59] The ironic result is that the Conservative government—acting in accordance with one of its philosophical principles—distanced itself from the industry, in order to introduce by central direction a mechanism for restricting the choice of drugs which consumers can be dispensed under the NHS. In so doing, it introduced an element of coercion which was at odds with another element of party doctrine: its avowed distaste for state compulsion.[60]

The dilemmas of the industry

All of which did not bode well for the industry and, in particular, for the ABPI. Deprived of its previous close relationship with the DHSS, the Association became much more responsive to the demands of its membership and had to adopt a higher public profile. It is significant that the Association agreed, under pressure from the American-owned companies, to increase its budget for public affairs activities in 1986 to some three times the level of 1985. This was in stark contrast to what happened in 1980 when a comprehensive public relations plan for the industry had been produced by the ABPI but was virtually ignored by the member companies. It must be stressed, however, that the public relations activities of the Association reflected not power but weakness. As Richardson and Jordan have expressed it: 'campaigns are the currency of unsucessful groups; permanent relations are the mode of the successful'.[61]

Within the ABPI, tensions have increased between the smaller and the large companies as a result of the government action. At the time of writing, the Association is conducting protracted negotiations with the DHSS over the future of the PPRS. Prime targets, from the Department's point of view, look likely to be the expenses which companies can write off under the PPRS for promotional and R. & D. activity.[62] Both these aspects will exacerbate divisions within the ABPI. Smaller companies will be disproportionately affected by a percentage reduction in allowable promotional spending—believed to be from the current nine per cent to seven and a half per cent—given the threshold costs of establishing a national presence in the market-place. Large companies, on the other hand, will be hit by a reduction in R. & D. allowance as they rely heavily on new product innovation for a competitive edge. This conflict recently came to a head at the 1985 annual conference of the ABPI held at Gleneagles. As a result, the smaller companies were compelled to accept a change in the constitution giving the larger companies a much greater influence in the Association's affairs, in order to prevent the British companies and their corporate allies from breaking away to form a separate organization.[63]

Another bone of contention within the ABPI is the issue of transfer pricing. By 1986 there were indications that the DHSS was poised for a crackdown on this, and American companies, in particular, were concerned that the Department was to seek further justification of their import prices where products seemed to be available cheaper elsewhere. In an effort to dissuade the DHSS from this course of action the PMA reportedly pressed the American Department of Commerce to threaten retaliation against British companies in the USA. The US group of companies in the UK, moreover, worried by the ABPI's apparent indifference to the transfer pricing issue, has now attempted to establish its own direct links to the DHSS independently of the Association.

How the role of the ABPI develops in the future depends on how the Association manages to resolve the outstanding issues with government and reconcile the conflicting tensions from within. To be successful, the ABPI requires a close relationship with government to provide it with access to information and influence that it can use on behalf of its members. Without this function the Association relinquishes autonomy to the logic of membership. The government, for its part, prefers to deal with a single industry representative and must, therefore, provide the ABPI with sufficient resources in terms of influence and concessions to enable the Association to deliver the compliance of its membership. The mechanics of this are clearly visible in the renegotiation of the PPRS. Agreement on terms too favourable to the DHSS could present the ABPI with real problems in ensuring compliance of all its member companies. On the other hand, failure to agree a new scheme would seriously undermine the position of the Association as sole representative of the industry with government. The ABPI's main hope must be that, however bad the new PPRS turns out to be for the industry, the alternative—direct price control or even exclusion of high price drugs from NHS use—would be even more unpalatable for member companies. If the Association can extract some concessions from the government over other such salient issues as patent life extension, transfer pricing, or the control of animal experimentation, it could yet recover some of its lost influence.

The company perspective

At the outset of this paper we instanced the 'charge of the US cavalry' as a measure of the anxiety of major international pharmaceutical companies over the change in UK government policy towards the industry. The question that remains to be answered, however, is why firms of this size should become so agitated by the measures taken by the UK government. After all, research-based pharmaceutical companies are archetypal multinational enterprises, operating globally to increase their return and minimize risk.[64] The UK market ranks only sixth in the world, well behind the United States and Japan, accounting for less than 4 per cent of total sales. Even if the DHSS had been successful in achieving £100 million savings on the NHS drugs bill, it would still have affected only 0.0016 of the world market, and not all of that would have been a complete loss to companies since they could have pursued alternative marketing strategies.

Nevertheless, the limited list and the other measures imposed on the industry by the DHSS since 1983 have clearly had a damaging effect on company finances, particularly on those companies whose products were suddenly and arbitrarily excluded from prescription on the NHS.[65] The full impact, we would suggest, is probably much wider and, at the same time, less tangible. It has to do with the creation of uncertainty where once there was stability, of suspicion where once there was trust. The UK has traditionally been regarded by companies as a haven of moderation by international standards and attracted much investment as a result.[66] A marked change in the UK environment of the kind recently experienced, however, could cause the top management of multinational companies to look elsewhere when locating their manufacturing or R. & D. facilities in the future. Some examples of this, indeed, have already been noted, although it will take time for the full effect to become apparent.

The influence of the multinational pharmaceutical companies, therefore, derives ultimately from their international mobility. If they dislike what is happening in the UK then they can transfer their operations elsewhere. In reality this option is more limited. Clear differences between national regimes, as we have seen in West Germany, do still remain. The deterioration in the operating environment for pharmaceutical companies, however, is an international phenomenon. Management in these companies must compare the circumstances in the UK with conditions obtaining in other countries, and, in most cases, it would appear that the climate is becoming less favourable. The agitation of critical pressure groups operating internationally for a restrictive range of drugs at cheaper prices, appears to coincide with the pressure on governments of developed and non-developed countries alike to seek savings in their publicly funded health schemes.

Conclusion

The research on which this paper is based is still continuing. It has, nevertheless, been possible to identify both a broad policy community concerned with the pharmaceutical industry, and a rather more discrete policy network related to the issue of cost-containment. Taking a comparative perspective with West Germany has led us to recognize that there are distinct similarities in the issues and pressures facing the industry in both countries, but that the way these are manifested differ, mainly due to differences in market, government, and party systems which themselves are legacies of different constitutional and legal cultures.

The findings have underlined the dynamic nature of government–industry relations, and, at the time of writing, there appears to be considerable strain on the pattern of relationships which has obtained over recent decades in the UK. The similar pressures in Germany are also occasioning change, but to a lesser extent. In both cases, however, new expectations on the part of both government and industry are emerging and these reflect wider concerns about the costs of health care generally. It may be that on this issue a new pattern of relationships will evolve which will be more pluralistic than in the past. If so, individual companies may play a larger role in relations with government, with industry-level associations declining in relative importance. This is not to deny that many social and political issues are of common concern to companies. It is, therefore, unlikely that industry associations will be completely eclipsed by this change of emphasis. Nevertheless, it will be instructive in a future phase of the research to focus more closely on individual companies, to examine how differences in corporate context and strategy may be associated with different approaches to government relations and public affairs.

Notes

1. See R. W. Lang, *The Politics of Drugs* (Farnborough; Saxon House, 1974).
2. Ibid., pp. 66–7.
3. ABPI/DHSS, *Pharmaceutical Price Regulation Scheme* (April 1978), p. 1.
4. See: House of Commons, *Tenth Report from the Committee of Public Accounts, Dispensing Drugs in the National Health Service, Session 1982-3*. (London, 1983), (= *PAC Report*, 1983); House of Commons, *Twenty-sixth Report from the Committee of Public Accounts, Dispensing Drugs in the National Health Service, Session 1983-4*. (London, 1984), (= *PAC Report*, 1984), and House of Commons, *Committee of Public Accounts, NHS Suppliers and the Pharmaceutical Price Regulation Scheme, Minutes of Evidence, Session 1984-85*, (London, 1985).
5. *PAC Report*, 1983, p. 6, para. 6.
6. Ibid. For a good review of the workings of the PPRS, see J. A. Sargent, 'The Politics of the Pharmaceutical Price Regulation Scheme' in W. Streeck and P. C. Schmitter (eds.), *Private Interest Government* (London: Sage, 1985), pp. 105–27.
7. Interview with government official and finance director of a multinational pharmaceutical company.
8. M. Olson, *The Logic of Collective Action* (New York: Harvard University Press, 1965). In simple terms, Olson's thesis is that associative action will be unlikely to occur unless there are selective inducements for the membership, as a rational, self-interested actor will prefer to 'free-ride' on the efforts of others.
9. See J. Sargent, 'The Organisation of Business Interests in the UK Pharmaceutical Industry', International Institute of Mangement Paper IIM/LMP 83-6 (Berlin, 1983), and ABPI, *Code of Practice for the Pharmaceutical Industry* (London: ABPI, 1984).
10. See P. C. Schmitter and W. Streeck, 'The Organization of Business Interests', International Institute of Management Paper IIM/LMP 81-13 (Berlin, 1981). The authors analyse the organizational tensions which trade associations are subjected to from the pressures of satisfying a diverse membership—'the logic of membership'—and from achieving organizational aims and autonomy—'the logic of influence'.
11. J. J. Richardson and A. G. Jordan, *Governing under Pressure* (Oxford: Martin Robertson, 1979).
12. See pp. 304–7.
13. One of the largest UK distributors, Unichem, is a pharmacists' co-operative. Interestingly, attempts by manufacturers to absorb the distributor's role have proved less successful.
14. M. L. Burstall with I. Senior, *The Community's Pharmaceutical Industry—Evolution of Concentration, Competition and Competitivity* (London: Economists Advisory Group, 1985), pp. 8–11.

15. Most prominent perhaps is Lilly's Opren which has since been withdrawn following the association of the drug with over a hundred fatalities amongst elderly people. More recently, phenylbutazone pain-killers have been banned from general use in the UK after reputedly being associated with over 1500 deaths in Britain.

16. See, for example, D. Melrose, *Bitter Pills—Medicines and the World Poor* (Oxford: Oxfam, 1982); C. Medawar and B. Freese, *Drug Diplomacy* (London: Social Audit, 1982); C. Buxton, D. Jones and A. Mohamed, *Drug Pushers* (London: Tower Hamlets International Solidarity, 1984) and F. Rolt, *Pills, Policies and Profits* (London: War on Want, 1985).

17. See P. Barnacal and M. Barber, *Better Pills—The Right Kind of Medicines*, Scrip Report (London, 1984).

18. R. Klein, *The Politics of the National Health Service* (London: Longman, 1983), pp. 106–10.

19. DHSS, 'Initial Report on the Informal Working Group on Effective Prescribing' (London: DHSS, 1983).

20. Information from industry and government sources. See also ABPI, *Annual Report 1982-83* (London: ABPI, 1984), p. 10.

21. ABPI, *Annual Report 1983-84*, p. 10; *PAC Report*, 1984.

22. Interviews with government officials. See also the reports in *Doctor*, 7 February 1985, and *BMA News Review*, February 1985.

23. See *Hansard*, 22 November 1983, col. 114 and the extract from a speech made by Patrick Jenkin as Secretary of State in 1981 and quoted in a letter sent by Dr Michael Wilson of the BMA to the chairman of all Local Medical Committees, 5 February 1985.

24. *British Medical Journal* (= *BMJ*), 5 January 1985.

25. *Financial Times*, 13 April 1985. ABPI, *Annual Report 1984-85*, p. 8.

26. For the ABPI, see *Financial Times*, 15 November 1984; for the BMA, see *BMJ*, 17 November 1984.

27. Information supplied by a government source.

28. See *Lancet*, 8 December 1984 and the article by two leading officials of the ABPI, John Griffin and David Taylor, in the *Pharmaceutical Journal* (= *PJ*), 12 January 1985.

29. See A. O. Hirschman, *Exit, Voice, and Loyalty—A Response to Decline in Firms, Organizations, and States* (Cambridge, Mass., Harvard University Press, 1970).

30. See *BMJ*, 16 March 1985, and *PJ*, 16 March 1985.

31. *PJ*, 2 March 1985.

32. *Medical News*, 4 April 1985; *General Practitioner*, 19 April 1985.

33. Cited in evidence by Lord Ennals, quoted in *PJ*, 30 March 1985.

34. As reported by the *PJ*, 20 April 1985.

35. Taken from the results of the joint ABPI/Peat Marwick Mitchell survey published in the *PJ*, 9 February 1985. See also the overview in *Financial Times*, 12 June 1985.

36. Information provided by back-bench MPs. See also the reports in *BMJ*, 19 January 1985; *PJ*, 12 January 1985 and 9 March 1985, and *General Practitioner*, 15 March 1985.

37. Information provided by back-bench MPs. See also *BMJ*, 23 February 1985. Notably vitriolic was the reaction of MP Richard Hickmet, Chairman of the Conservative back-bench Trade and Industry Committee, who announced his intention to expose the pharmaceutical industry 'for the self-interested money-grabbing cartel it is'. See *PJ*, 9 March 1985.

38. Information supplied by a government offical.

39. Of interest in this context is the contrast in the editorial lines taken by the two leading medical Journals, the *BMJ* and the *Lancet*, and the divided state of GP opinion, revealed by a survey of doctor's views published in the *PJ*, 2 February 1985.

40. Interview with government official. See also the report in *Pulse*, 16 February 1985.

41. Interview with Sir Raymond Hoffenberg of the RCP, 13 February 1985. See also his letter to *The Times*, 15 January 1985.

42. Interview with Mr A. J. Smith of the PSNC, 21 February 1985. See the comments of their President, Mr Stephen Axon, as reported by the *PJ*, 21 January 1985.

43. See *PJ*, 2 March 1985 and the article by Joe Collier and Charles Medawar in the *Guardian*, 17 December 1984.

44. See, e.g., reports in *BMJ*, 19 January 1985; *PJ*, 2 February 1985, and *Medicine in Society—The Socialist Journal of Health Studies*, vol. ii, No. 2 (Summer 1985), pp. 9–10.

45. Interviews with government officials. See also the report in *General Practitioner*, 22 February 1985.

46. *Lancet*, 16 February 1985. *PJ*, 26 January 1985.

47. *Scrip* (Richmond, Surrey: PJB Publications Ltd.), 10 February 1986.

48. Interview with government official. See also *Scrip*, 12 August 1985.

49. *Scrip*, 1983, 'The Pharmaceutical Market in West Germany'.

50. See, for example, H. Hannse, 'Arzneimittelpreise' in W. Hamm *et al.*, *Aspekte zur Pharmaokonomie* (Mainz: Gustav Fischer Verlag, 1984), p. 36.

51. BPI, *Pharma Jahresbericht 1984–85* (Frankfurt/Main, 1985), pp. 23–4. The industry subsequently agreed a voluntary two-year price-freeze backdated from April 1985.

52. See J.-M. Graf v.d. Schulenburg, 'Die Arzteschwemme und ihre Auswirkungen auf die ambulante Versorgung', International Institute of Management Discussion Paper IIM 85-6 (Berlin, 1985).

53. This division of functions between a number of ministries is itself a significant difference from the UK where the DHSS combines the role of sponsor and main customer.

54. See e.g., the exposé of the so-called 'School Affair' in *Der Spiegel*, 24 June 1985, 1 July 1985, and 8 July 1985.

55. Interviews with BPI and FDP representatives. The authors are indebted to Geoffrey Roberts for his observations on the FDP.

56. Interviews with German, Swiss, and British companies. See also *Scrip*, 23 December 1985.

57. Interview with FDP and CDU representatives in Bonn. For details, see BPI, *Pharma Jahresbericht 1984–85*.

58. ABPI figures quoted in *Scrip*, 25 September 1985.

59. This is the traditional theory used to explain the mismatch of political and industrial requirements. See S. Wilks, *Industrial Policy and the Motor Industry* (Manchester: University Press, 1984).

60. The irony of this has not escaped the government's intellectual supporters. See D. G. Green, *Which Doctor?* IEA Research Monograph 40 (London, 1985), pp. 27–30.

61. Richardson and Jordan, 1979, p. 123.

62. Interviews with government and industry representatives. See also *Scrip*, 2 September 1985 and 23 September 1985.

63. Interviews with ABPI representatives. See also *Scrip*, 16 October 1985.

64. The largest twenty pharmaceutical companies account for over half of world sales. This may overestimate the degree of market power in individual market segments, however, where technological and market leadership can change quite rapidly. See S. Slatter, *Competition and Marketing Strategies in the Pharmaceutical Industry* (London: Croom Helm, 1977).

65. Roche (UK) Ltd., reportedly the worst hit by government measures, lost 70 per cent of its NHS pharmaceutical business as a result of the delisting of its benzodiazepines and vitamin products, but this amounted to only 10 per cent of the firm's total busintess (*Scrip*, 22 April 1985).

66. See US Dept. of Commerce, *A Competitive Assessment of the US Pharmaceutical Industry* (Washington, 1984).

Legal Culture, Product Licensing, and the Drug Industry

Leigh Hancher and Matthias Ruete

Introduction

This chapter is concerned with the role of law in the implementation of product safety regulations for prescription medicines in the Federal Republic of Germany and the United Kingdom. We begin with an examination of the two dominant legal approaches to the relationship between law and public policy, and explore their respective short-comings. Using the German and British experiences of the control of medicines as a point of departure, we argue that only a systematic comparative analysis of the socio-legal context of a regulatory programme can reveal the potential significance of law in the policy process. We compare the legal background to the development of drug licensing in each country and assess the contribution of legal factors to its current scope and design. We then move on to explore two recent issues in drug-licensing policy which, we suggest, illustrate the capacity to mobilize law in different legal cultures. We examine the 'second licence application', an issue which has arisen in Germany but not in the UK, and the tensions created in the latter country by the recent Review of Medicines. We argue that it is important to realize that the form of *articulation* of a problem may be as much a feature of an administrative and legal tradition or culture as the style of its *resolution*, and that it is only from this perspective that the role of law in comparative policy analysis can be understood. We then go on to offer some tentative conclusions about the impact of administrative and legal traditions on policy implementation.

Legal Analysis of Public Policy

Two approaches

At the risk of over-simplification, legal writing on public policy can be classified into two schools of thought. On the one hand, we have the 'constitutionalist' school of public law, which, in the United Kingdom at least, has tended to treat recent policy developments in the relations between government and industry with disdain, claiming that such events are so 'influenced by economic and political vicissitudes that the most appropriate commentator is the journalist'.[1] The predominant theoretical concerns of this school reflect their commitment to liberal constitutional values, in particular, the legal protection of the legitimate interests of private groups and individuals. For some writers within this school, freedom from the potential oppression of state intervention could only be secured through a comprehensive system of judicial review,[2] but, as faith in the effectiveness of the courts as a neutral mechanism for controlling potential abuses of discretionary power has weakened and the so-called 'polycentricity' or complexity of modern decision-making processes has received greater attention, the universality of the judicial method of dispute resolution has been questioned.[3] Alternative methods of controlling discretionary power are considered, including participation in the decision-making process.[4] Two themes recur throughout this literature: discretion is viewed with suspicion, and justice to the individual is the yardstick against which all government activity is measured.[5] As a result, British constitutional lawyers have given little thought to 'the part played in decision making by moral, political, organisational and economic values'[6] and, in particular, to the role of law in the policy process.[7]

The German '*Rechtswissenschaften*' tradition, continued and strengthened in academic legal writing in the modern Federal Republic, has always laid claim to a more comprehensive approach to the legal aspects of government–industry relations, as illustrated in recent work on 'economic law'.[8] The problem of administrative discretion has been analysed in terms of the constitutional constraints on the exercise of discretionary powers, and, in particular, in terms of the potential application of concepts such as proportionality and equal treatment. This has meant that moral, economic, political, and organizational values are considered if they can be expressed as 'constitutional' values. Analysis of the policy process, albeit wider than in the UK, still remains grounded in

distinctly legal values and discretionary power is viewed as a phenomenon to be controlled rather than explained.

In consequence, it is perhaps surprising to discover that the second
school of thought to which we want to make brief reference has equally
little to offer on the topic of administrative discretion. The 'regulatory'
school, as its name suggests, is primarily concerned with the growth of
regulation and its impact, and attempts to offer solutions to a perceived
'crisis of regulation'.[9] Regulatory law is characterized by certain features
which set it apart from traditional legal forms, such as the common law or
civil code. It is purposive and goal-oriented rather than conditional.[10] It is
coercive rather than facilitative, implying an adversarial relationship
between state and citizen. Classic examples of regulatory laws are health
and safety, and environmental legislation. This type of legislation is seen
to comprise highly centralized sets of rules or standards which increasingly bear little or no relation to the individual firm's capacity for compliance.[11] This approach to regulation implicitly denies that discretionary
power is or could be problematic, the self-proclaimed task of recent
analysis being to measure the perceived costs and purported benefits
which might be attributed to the adoption of a regulatory programme.
The concern here, then, is not with individual justice, but with the
societal cost of the programme. While narrow legal values were seen to
dominate the framework adopted by public lawyers, the writers of the
regulatory school appear motivated by the prescriptions of welfare
economics and a perennial search for Pareto optimality.[12] Any departure
from individual freedom of contract, as guaranteed by the remedies of the
common law, must be justified in terms of societal gains which outweigh
the costs of regulation.

To illustrate this approach we can point to the vast body of medical,
economic, and political science literature on the effects of the 1962
amendments to the *Food, Drug and Cosmetic Act* on drug innovation in
the USA.[13] This literature has been used as the basis for a legal analysis of
licensing procedures, in particular,[14] and of the regulatory process, in
general.[15] To summarize an extremely complex debate, the stricter
testing and approval standards introduced in 1962 are alleged to have
resulted in a 'drug lag', that is, that the USA has experienced a relative
fall in the rate of the introduction of new drugs as compared both with the
rates of introduction prior to 1962 and with the rates in jurisdictions with
more lenient licensing laws.[16] Obviously, the presence of drug lag itself
suggests no normative judgement, but if its cause is as alleged—stricter
regulation—and if the effect is not a societal gain in terms of safer and

more effective drugs, but a delay in the introduction of valuable new drugs, or, perhaps, increased concentration in the pharmaceutical industry, leading to enhanced monopoly powers and higher prices,[17] then alternative, less 'costly' measures of consumer protection warrant consideration.[18]

If European levels of innovation have indeed proved healthier, this might provide a useful point of departure for our study of the Medicines Act 1968 and the German equivalent, the *Arzneimittelgesetz* 1976. American writers have praised the voluntary system of safety-testing introduced in the United Kingdom in the wake of the thalidomide tragedy in 1962, the inherent flexibility and informality of which was seen to be the key to Europe's superior performance with regard to innovation.[19] A recent British cost–benefit analysis of the formal regulatory system, which replaced the voluntary system in 1968, does in fact suggest a causal link with the subsequent decline in the rate of new drug discovery.[20] This finding might serve to justify an analysis of the extent to which German and British licensing legislation has indeed become more purposive and rigid, in line with the American system. However, we feel that, for a number of reasons, such an approach could only be of very limited value.

In the first place, the evidence that stricter regulation has indeed been a cause of drug lag is inconclusive. As Baily and later Grabowski have argued, it is difficult to disaggregate the effects of regulation from non-regulatory factors, such as the international depletion of research opportunities.[21] Secondly, even if stricter regulation is one of a number of factors contributing to the decline in drug innovation, do the costs outweigh the gains? This is a difficult calculation to make, not only because the final consumer, the patient, neither selects nor pays for the product, but also because it involves an estimation of the supposed therapeutic value of drugs which *might have* been developed and marketed but for the stricter system of regulation.[22] Thirdly, and most importantly in legal terms, we think it necessary to call into question the very model of regulation employed in this mode of analysis. It has been argued that this model reflects the fact that 'the dichotomy of an autonomous market system governed only by common law principles and by anti-trust legislation and a superimposed regulatory grip over the market place [is] deeply rooted in US economic, political and legal thinking'.[23] An uncritical transplantation of this model would ignore the question of its relevance to the European situation where, historically, government and industry have not necessarily maintained a similar adversarial relationship.

Furthermore, regulation is assumed to be coercive, so that any general advantages regulation may bring to industry, perhaps in terms of raising barriers of entry into a market, and hence encouraging voluntary co-operation, are ignored.[24] Finally, the regulatory model implies that, by the adoption of purposive language, the goals of a programme can be clearly determined in advance—a valuable attribute not apparently shared by the common law—and unproblematically assumes full compliance. Costs can then be calculated and benefits assessed. The relationship between these new forms of law and the older forms which have been replaced is never examined, a factor which we feel can only lead to impoverished comparative analysis, if not to a distorted picture of the legal process.

A reappraisal

Recent work on sector-specific forms of regulation, especially on environmental law, has come to question two implicit assumptions in the work of the regulatory school, that law is self-enforcing and that full compliance is assured. A number of empirical studies have underlined the prevalence of non-legal sanctions,[25] and attempts have been made to incorporate non-legal sanctions into a theory of regulatory enforcement which embraces 'bargained' or 'negotiated' compliance.[26] This new approach has led to the important recognition of divergence in national styles of regulatory enforcement. West Germany and the United Kingdom are seen to prefer bargained or negotiated solutions, and neither country has adopted the rigorous specification standards so typical of American environmental legislation.[27] Much of this work has, however, been confined to an examination of the perceptions and practices of actors in the policy process, be they bureaucrats or industrialists, with the result that little attention has been given to the structural or institutional factors which contribute to bargained outcomes in the concretization of policy goals. As a result, bargaining over enforcement is discussed in terms of whether or not sanctions are applied to deviant behaviour, and not in terms of how legal factors contribute to the specification of policy goals.

It is this latter feature of the role of law in the implementation of public policy that we wish to consider in the remainder of this chapter. Applications to market a new drug in either West Germany or the United Kingdom must meet the standards of safety, efficacy, and quality demanded by the relevant licensing authorities. Such standards must always be relative, and cannot be easily specified in legislation. They will vary over time as knowledge and scientific techniques change. Drug companies have an obvious commercial interest in contributing to the determination and application of any current standard. It must further be remembered that governments pursue two irreconcilable objectives in their dealings with the industry. The first is to protect the consumer by ensuring that drugs are safe, effective, and reasonably priced. The second is to maintain the economic well-being of its domestic pharmaceutical industry. Bargaining and negotiation over the scope of safety and efficacy standards appear inevitable but that is not to say that bargaining will only take place over whether or not to apply a legal rule or standard. It is important to realize that bargaining may take place within law, and hence to examine the impact of important variations in legal and administrative cultures which determine the nature of that bargaining process. Even if the end result produced in national systems appears to be similar, in that an overall balance between the objectives of government and those of industry is achieved, the mechanisms utilized in the process may be very different. We contend that the role of law in the policy process should be approached from this angle, and not from the narrow value-oriented concerns of the constitutionalist school or the economic preoccupations of the regulatory school.

Recent work on comparative policy implementation has suggested an important distinction in the administrative cultures of the United Kingdom and Germany. Whereas Britain is portrayed as having a flexible, bargaining culture, which is evident across a range of policy programmes, the Federal Republic is characterized by its formal, legalistic approach to policy implementation.[28] In this context, the regulatory schema introduced by the Medicines Act 1968 would appear aberrational in the extent to which it regulates the manufacture and commercialization of a new drug, as well as providing for considerable procedural protection in the event of an unfavourable licensing decision.[29] An assessment of the impact of divergent legal cultures involves more than an analysis of the design and structure of regulatory programmes: it involves a consideration of the propensity of actors to *mobilize* law in different legal systems.[30] Arguably, it is no less difficult to challenge the legality of a policy decision in the United Kingdom than in Germany, but it remains true that very few conflicts over policy issues find their way into the British courts.

In the remainder of the chapter we argue that the continued influence of legal and administrative traditions is to be discerned by means of a careful analysis of the different bargaining or rule-oriented styles of decision-making, as reflected, firstly, in the types of problems posed by the introduction and functioning of the regulatory programme and, secondly, in the manner in which those problems have been resolved. This, in turn, leads to a reappraisal of the structural parameters of bargaining and negotiation. Whereas the two approaches to public policy discussed above posit a straightforward dichotomy between legal and non-legal styles of decision-making, so that bargaining is assumed to take place *outside* law, we would argue that a comparative assessment of the impact of legal culture suggests that there are important *legal* aspects of negotiated compliance with regulatory goals, so that the potential for bargaining to take place *within* the respective legal frameworks created by the Medicines Act 1968 and the *Arzneimittelgesetz* must also be recognized.[31]

The Pharmaceutical Industry and Safety Legislation in the United Kingdom and the Federal Republic of Germany

Introduction

The pharmaceutical industry is economically powerful and politically well-organized in the United Kingdom and West Germany. Its economic importance is reflected in the current position on world markets occupied by German and British-based multinationals. Of the world's top fifty companies, six are German, including the two chemical giants, Hoechst and Bayer, as well as the two 'pure' pharmaceutical companies, Boehringer Mannheim and Boehringer Ingelheim, and five are British, including the Imperial Chemical Industry, Glaxo, Boots, and the Wellcome Foundation.[32] The continued growth in demand for pharmaceutical products, both domestically and internationally, has ensured the immunity to this sector from the post-oil-crisis recession. In fact, it has continued to sustain a high level of product innovation, to provide an important source of employment for skilled and semi-skilled labour, as well as contributing significantly to the balance of payments in both countries.

The multinational structure of most of these large pharmaceutical firms in itself ensures considerable commercial autonomy and freedom from effective state control. The industry in each country has, however, maintained consistently close links with the government, initially as a powerful actor engaged in the production of chemicals, but with the post-war socialization of health care and the explosion in demand for branded prescription products, the pharmaceutical sector has developed its own independent channels of communication with government.[33] At the level of associative activity, the Association of the British Pharmaceutical Industry (ABPI) represents the interests of some 150 companies engaged in the manufacture of prescription drugs, while the Bundesverband der Pharmazeutischen Industrie (BPI) provides a similar service for its 506 members. Both organizations maintain close links with other sectoral associations, to the extent that the BPI shares both premises and expertise with the German Chemical Industry Association (VCI).

Given the importance of pharmaceutical products and the peculiar structure of the market for prescription drugs, where price competition is virtually non-existent, most governments keep a watchful eye on the level of public expenditure on drugs. Whereas the concerns of the British government date back to the inception of the National Health Service (NHS) in 1948, the more recent explosion in the rate of growth of public expenditure on health care has prompted a reappraisal of the hitherto non-interventionist policies of successive governments in the Federal Republic.[34]

In the following sections we will examine the legacy of the British government's early preoccupation with cost-related matters and the system of voluntary price regulation which was introduced in 1957. We argue that this system of control has produced a distinctive style of government and industry relations which reflects the institutionalization of a particular set of interdependent relations. The actual process of implementation of legislation on testing and licensing of new drugs, introduced in the wake of the thalidomide tragedy, can only be understood in this context. We compare the reactions of the German drugs industry to the introduction of a similar legislative programme and we suggest that, in the absence of an institutionalized structure of dependent relations, German industry has sought to mobilize legal rights to pursue an essentially similar objective, that is, the preservation of its commercial autonomy in product-marketing decisions. A comparison of the legal aspects of these two policy processes reveals an important, though often neglected, aspect of government and industry relations in this sector.

The United Kingdom

The aftermath of thalidomide The introduction of comprehensive drug safety legislation in the United Kingdom can be traced to the impact of the thalidomide tragedy in the early 1960s. As was remarked in the House of Commons in 1963: 'the House and the public suddenly woke up to the fact that any drug manufacturer could market any product, however inadequately tested, however dangerous, without having to satisfy any independent body as to its efficiency or its safety'.[35] Hitherto, the manufacture, sale, and administration of only a limited range of drugs had been regulated, so that if a product was neither a biological substance nor a poison it could be marketed without prior testing.[36] To remedy this situation, the Conservative government requested its internal, expert, advisory body, the Joint Standing Committee on Health (Cohen), to investigate alternative methods of testing and screening new drugs. The Committee proposed that for an interim period of two to three years, manufacturers should continue to be responsible for testing new drugs prior to clinical use, but that an independent body, working on the basis of voluntary compliance by the industry, should review the evidence and offer advice to the Minister of Health on the toxicity of new products, and collect and collate evidence of adverse reactions of marketed products.[37]

The informal and voluntary nature of the proposed arrangements appears to have been the result of a compromise. The ABPI had earlier expressed support for consolidation and rationalization of the existing controls over medicinal products, but advocated the creation of an independent, voluntary trust to advise industry.[38] The ABPI's aim was to make clinical trials more acceptable to the medical profession, but, at the same time, limit the ambit of any controls to criteria based on safety and quality of products, rather than considerations based on the comparative efficacy of particular products. Provided that a new product could be demonstrated to be prima facie safe, in the sense that known risks were outweighed by claimed benefits, the industry would be free to determine the rate of supply of new products, as well as combinations and variations of established drug substances, irrespective of considerations based on need or comparative cost.[39] The Cohen Committee's contention that public concern would only be alleviated by the creation of a government-appointed body, resulted in the setting up of the Committee on the Safety of Drugs, albeit without statutory powers to compel the submission of data or to prevent the marketing of products which had not been subjected to its scrutiny.[40]

With the benefit of hindsight, the introduction of a voluntary system of drug approval and the subsequent activities of the Committee on the Safety of Drugs (CSD) can be seen as a perpetuation of an existing structure of dependent relations between government and the drugs industry. Furthermore, the voluntary system provided the industry with a valuable 'breathing space' in which to consolidate its position on an independent system of drug approval, prior to the introduction of the statutory scheme envisaged in the Cohen Committee's final report.[41] In order to understand this chain of events and to appreciate fully their significance to industry, it is necessary to examine briefly the nature of the existing relationships between government and the drugs industry, on the one hand, and between government and the ABPI, on the other.

It should be recalled that the main market for the British drug industry's products is the NHS. If the architects of the NHS paid little attention to the problem of controlling drug costs,[42] alarm at the rapidly increasing size of the overall health bill prompted action on three fronts. In 1949 the government took powers to levy prescription charges, and in the following year an internal body, the Joint Standing Commitee on the Prescription of Drugs, was charged with the task of categorizing drugs in terms of their therapeutic efficacy, and to advise the medical profession accordingly. In its second Annual Report, this body recommended that all drugs which could not be categorized as therapeutically superior to standard or generic preparations should only be prescribed subject to a satisfactory agreement being concluded with industry on the matter of their price.[43]

This report led to the introduction of the third and most important method of tackling the problem of drug expenditure—the Voluntary Price Regulation Scheme (VPRS). It is not possible to describe in any detail the nature and operation of this scheme but certain of its features are worthy of note.[44] The scheme itself was, in fact, based on a proposal submitted to the Minister of Health by the ABPI, following an announcement by the former of his intention to place the purchase of prescription drugs on a par with other non-negotiated government supply contracts. The ABPI objected that this method of profit control, based on the calculation of an allowable rate of return on capital, was inappropriate to the phamaceutical sector which needed a higher rate to guarantee continued investment in research and development. The ABPI persuaded its members that some form of administered price control was preferable to the unbridled use of the Minister's monopsonistic powers.

The Joint Standing Committee had suggested that the reasonableness of prices should be calculated on the basis of a comparison with the prices of generic products, but the government's initial attempts to do so had been fraught with problems, caused in part by a complete absence of statistical evidence of product demand, and of price formation generally.[45] The ABPI's suggestion that a comparison of domestic prices with those prevailing on a number of export markets would provide a suitable measure of the reasonableness of the prices paid by the NHS was accepted, despite the lack of evidence to suggest that in a market comprising a patchwork of international patents and cross-licensing agreements such prices were in any way objective. Indeed, evidence of export prices was to be supplied by the individual firm, and the Ministry of Health would then address itself not to the prices charged for individual products but to the overall rate of profit on each firm's total NHS sales. No sanctions were envisaged against recalcitrant firms, nor was there any mechanism available to 'claw back' past excess profits. Instead, the ABPI gave a voluntary, written undertaking, on behalf of its members, only to increase prices in the event of rising costs. This agreement was legally unenforceable, either by the Minister of Health against the ABPI, or by the latter against its members. Membership of the ABPI has never been made conditional on adherence to the VPRS and, indeed, there have been occasions when companies have refused to participate in the scheme.[46] On the whole, it would seem that the somewhat disparate interests of the Swiss, American, British, and the other European companies, already united in any event by the common external threat of an alternative, state-imposed scheme, were further consolidated by a process of internal reorganization of key committees.[47] A separate committee, comprising representatives of the leading manufacturers of branded products, was entrusted with the task of negotiating the first and subsequent versions of the VPRS, while a Public Relations Policy Committee was charged with the task of keeping government departments, health-care professionals, and the general public informed as to the functions, aims, and achievements of the pharmaceutical industry.[48]

Despite Treasury scepticism and the disapproval of the House of Commons Committee on Public Accounts, the Minister of Health publicly welcomed the co-operation of industry and the ABPI.[49] It should not be forgotten that this was a politically weak Ministry, without cabinet status, and considered a backwater by Civil Servants.[50] The ABPI, on the other hand, formed in 1930, could rely not only on its own organizational sophistication, but also on the close links and good record of co-operation with government, established in the course of its participation on the

Minister of Labour's Central Pharmaceutical War Committee, to present a convincing case for self-regulation in the matter of price control.

Co-operation on profit control served the ABPI and its membership well, both in the short and the long term. The system of profit control itself was not onerous, yielding little in the way of direct savings for the NHS,[51] and yet it allowed the industry as a whole to demonstrate its commitment to self-policing, entrusting to the ABPI the task of promoting and maintaining the good image of the sector. The cost and share of branded products, as a proportion of total public expenditure on drugs, continued to rise steadily despite the VPRS and its successors, but ministerial attention was effectively deflected from the issue of the comparative efficacy of one product over another. Although the Joint Standing Committee continued to classify products for the benefit of prescribing doctors, industry was free to introduce and to promote new products irrespective of criteria based on need or, indeed, cost. Further evidence of the drug industry's early assertion of control over the policy agenda can be evinced from the government's readiness, in 1958, to respond to public and parliamentary criticism of the industry's promotional activities by accepting a further measure of industry self-regulation—the adoption of a Code of Practice on advertising by the ABPI.[52]

In conclusion it is suggested that by 1962 an identifiable policy network had emerged, comprising the Ministry of Health, advised by a number of professionally qualified experts on the therapeutic aspects of prescribing, but with industry and its trade association, the ABPI, playing the dominant role on issues of cost. Secondly, one can point to established 'rules of the game' in the Minister's relations with the latter, based on an *implicit* division of responsibilities: the ABPI assumed responsibility for maintaining the adherence of its members to the philosophy of the VPRS, and for enforcing the Code of Practice, while the Minister would make use of his various legal powers to influence prices only in the last resort. Co-operation on a flexible and informal basis ensured the maintenance of a stable policy network.

The thalidomide tragedy expanded the policy agenda to include matters of safety and quality as well as cost, but the ABPI was by now well placed to secure the exclusion of issues of comparative efficacy. By its terms of reference, the CSD was entrusted with the task of advising on the safety and efficacy of new products prior to marketing. In 1962 the ABPI had set up its own working party on clinical trials, which by 1963 had become the Study Group on Clinical Trials. The then Minister of Health, Enoch Powell, had given an undertaking that, in return for its collaboration with the CSD, the ABPI would have access to the Committee at all times and would be invited to participate in the evaluation of criteria by which safety factors would be assessed.[53] The first memo to be produced by the CSD's sub-committee on Clinical Trials was the product of long deliberations with the ABPI Study Group. The strategic importance of this sub-committee should not be understimated. As Professor Wade, a member of one of the other three sub-committees, recalled:

Looking back I see only one major error in our performance. We were so aware of the enormous co-operation we received from the drug industry that the main Committee made every effort it could to see that submissions were handled as rapidly as possible. As a result, Frazer's sub-committee (on Toxicity) and Hunter's sub-committee (on clinical trials and efficacy) had a much higher priority for staff than did the Adverse Reaction sub-committee, and I think the work of that committee suffered.[54]

The ABPI were able to use their considerable expertise and influence over matters relating to clinical trials and therapeutic efficacy to ensure that the CSD's attention was focused on the former issue rather than the latter, despite the Committee's terms of reference. Indeed, the Chairman of the CSD, Dunlop, emphasized the role of his Committee as being primarily concerned with safety matters: 'its purpose is not to act as arbiter of therapy'.[55]

Furthermore, the ABPI went to some lengths to ensure that the CSD had the full co-operation of industry in discharging its duties. While neither the Committee nor the Minister had statutory powers to prevent a new drug being either marketed or submitted for clinical trial, in a circular to all members of the medical profession, the Minister of Health undertook to alert doctors of any product not approved by the CSD.[56] In most cases, 'any difficulties encountered by the Committee were reported to the ABPI who would then notify members and attain [sic] co-operation', presumably by exerting pressure.[57] With an average of 600–700 applications per annum to process, the small staff at the Ministry was heavily dependent on the co-operation of the ABPI and industry in general, and of necessity considerable faith must have been placed in the reliability of the industry's data. Indeed, the CSD accepted the ABPI's proposal to introduce a short, abridged form of licence application for products containing established drug substances, applications which could be processed by the Committee in less than one month. The industry, in turn, used its good record of voluntary compliance with the CSD to improve its own public image, and to ensure the extension and consolidation of the existing rules of the game as far as licensing matters were concerned.

The Medicines Act 1968   The voluntary system of control was only intended as an interim measure, but the success of the CSD was such that the Labour Government's 1967 White Paper on the statutory scheme promised to preserve the status quo:

The introduction of a statutory licensing system with sanctions necessarily involves making detailed requirements with regard to the particulars to be supplied, the conditions to be satisfied, the provisions attached to licences and the circumstances in which licences can be refused or revoked, but the intention is to retain the flexible administration which has been so effective under the voluntary scheme ... with co-operation and mutual confidence, legal proceedings should be exceptional.[58]

By the time the Medicines Bill was introduced into the House of Commons, in February 1968, certain important developments had occurred, and the Bill itself contained proposed new controls over the quality and content of promotional material, as well as provision to base marketing approval on criteria of efficacy in addition to those of safety and quality. Both proposals can be attributed to the recommendations of the Sainsbury Committee, appointed in 1966 to report on the relations between the NHS and the pharmaceutical industry. In its Report the Committee advocated, *inter alia*, the creation of a single, all-purpose Medicines Commission which would exercise responsibility for matters of safety as well as cost. Brand names were to be abolished, prices determined for individual products, and doctors informed of the usefulness of new products, on the basis of a uniform system of classification drawn up by the Medicines Commission.[59]

Questions as to the therapeutic efficacy of various products already on the market were also being raised by the successor to the Joint Standing Committee on Prescribing, the MacGregor Committee, appointed in 1963 to reclassify drugs with a view to encouraging doctors to prescribe more economically. MacGregor recommended that a fundamental distinction should be made between drugs containing a single active ingredient with an acceptable degree of efficacy, and those containing a fixed ratio of active substances, the so-called 'fixed combination drugs', which should only be prescribed in limited circumstances. As with previous committees, its recommendations were advisory only, being contained in a new governmental publication, *Proplist*. The ABPI actively opposed this system of classification, seeking a number of meetings with the Minister of Health, but to no avail.

If all the recommendations of the Sainsbury Committee had been accepted or fully implemented by the Labour government, the existing relationship between the industry and the Minister of Health, a relationship evolved through the implementation of several voluntary price regulation schemes and nurtured during the CSD's interregnum, would have been drastically altered. An interventionist, active, regulatory authority, the Medicines Commission, equipped with a battery of statutory powers over each and every stage of the process of drug development, marketing, and promotion, would have made substantial inroads into the industry's commercial autonomy. The self-regulatory system based on voluntary co-operation between government and industry would have been replaced, and the 'buffer' role occupied by the ABPI, with its codes, guidelines, and study groups, effectively displaced.

In the final event, the devaluation of sterling and a general downturn in the economy prompted the Labour government to reassess the risk of seeing this highly mobile sector move to more favourable regulatory climates. Many of Sainsbury's proposals were either abandoned or modified extensively, but interestingly, the fate of the proposed system of comprehensive classification, although of crucial importance to the industry, was not resolved until the second reading of the Medicines Bill.[60] The Minister of Health made it clear that the test would not be a comparative one, but would continue to be interpreted in relation to safety matters only. At a meeting shortly after this, the ABPI impressed upon the Minister the redundancy of any further system of classification based on efficacy for the benefit of prescribing doctors. Such a classification could only be based on an evaluation of *comparative* efficacy, and would, therefore, be inconsistent with the Minister's earlier assurances that such a test would not be used.[61] Furthermore, it would harm exports. The Bill was subsequently amended in standing committee to ensure that comparative efficacy between one medicine and another would not be a determining factor.

In successfully opposing the introduction of a statutory system of classification, the industry was able to remove the issue of comparative efficacy from the policy agenda. The former members of the CSD took up positions on the new advisory Committee on Safety of Medicines, which, in turn, absorbed the functions of the MacGregor Committee. Responsibility for control over safety was kept quite separate from issues of cost, the former being entrusted to a newly formed Medicines Division within the Department of Health. Undoubtedly, the statutory schema of licensing, enacted in 1968, enhanced the government's formal powers to exclude certain products from the market. It is now a criminal offence to supply a medicinal product without a licence, and the Minister of Health has considerable powers to withdraw, vary, or revoke product licences. These powers are, however, seldom used, most products being voluntarily withdrawn by industry. Moreover, the criteria applied in assessing an application, the essentially reactive approach of the regulatory authority, as well as the continued *ad hoc* participation of the ABPI in discussions on policy issues—in other words, the operational elements of the system—remain unchanged.

If the process of obtaining a product licence is more cumbersome than hitherto, this would seem less a reflection on the formalization of the licensing process and more a consequence of the development of higher scientific standards and more sophisticated methods of testing new products. The operative rules of the game remain unaltered, as does the division of responsibility between government and the ABPI as far as regulating the industry is concerned. Self-regulatory codes of conduct and ABPI guidelines continue to play an important role in the overall regulatory picture and have, indeed, been strengthened by the ABPI as an alternative to stricter formal regulation by government, as in the case of advertising.[62] In return for the industry's agreement to stricter controls on pricing and promotion, the Labour government announced the abolition of the special provisions relating to compulsory patents for drug products in 1977.[63]

While successive governments have been slow to adopt and utilize the extensive legal powers contained in the 1968 Act, industry has been equally reluctant to make use of the various legal provisions in the Act to challenge government decisions. We shall go on to explore the only occasion where a legal challenge has in fact been mounted in the courts, but at this point it is relevant to compare the evolution and current application of the German licensing system.

The Federal Republic of Germany

The modern legal framework of drug licensing in the FRG is determined by a number of Acts, the most important and detailed being the *Gesetz uber den Verkehr mit Arzneimitteln* of 1976 (hereafter AMG), which in turn provides the legal basis for a considerable body of delegated legislation. As drug licensing is an administrative activity, several further general Acts, including the *Verwaltungsverfarhengsgestez*, the *Verwaltungsprozessordnung*, and, ultimately, the Constitution, have some bearing on the licensing process.[64]

The early history Prior to the enactment of the AMG, drug manufacturers had only been required to register their products with the Federal Health Authority—the Bundesgesundheitsamt (BGA)—by means of a notification procedure, under the terms of the Drug Act 1961. Although the thalidomide tragedy was soon to highlight its ineffectiveness, the 1961 Act was seen as a substantial breakthrough. A coalition of the industry, retail and wholesale pharmacists, and the medical profession had, since the days of the Kaisereich, successfully argued that the federal government's legal power to regulate the marketing of drugs was limited to determining which drugs could be sold outside pharmacies. In particular, the Reichsgesundheitsamt (RGA), the BGA's predecessor, had been opposed to comprehensive regulation, preferring to see itself in the role of expert scientific adviser to government on general health matters. Apart from the more interventionist legislation enacted during the Nazi period, endowing regional administrative authorities with the power to issue manufacturing licences, numerous efforts to introduce a comprehensive licensing period met with failure.[65] Following the creation of the Federal Republic in 1949, renewed attempts to regulate the industry culminated in the submission of legislative proposals to the Bundestag in 1950. The scheme, drawn up by industry and backed by the BGA, conceded the need for a system of manufacturing licences, but proposed an automatic registration procedure for pharmaceutical products.

Some impetus for the adoption of a comprehensive scheme was, in fact, provided by a series of judgments in the Constitutional Court. The Court ruled that the existing system of manufacturers' licences was unconstitutional, thus depriving *Länder* health authorities of their only means of gathering information on the types of drugs being marketed. However, in a later decision the Court ruled, *obiter*, that in view of the revolution in manufacturing techniques, and the shift in production away from pharmacies, statutory measures aimed at regulating product safety could no longer be considered as a potential infringement of Article 12 of the Basic Law which guarantees the freedom to choose a profession.[66] Deprived of an important legal weapon, industry conceded partial defeat.

Although the regulatory powers subsequently accorded to the BGA, under the terms of the 1961 Drugs Act, were minimal, being confined to a refusal to register drugs known to be harmful, the expertise which the BGA could potentially bring to bear on an assessment of the safety of new drugs was considerable. The expertise of the old RGA in this area had been developed in the period between 1924 to 1938 when it had been entrusted with the duty of issuing export licence certificates for certain products. These certificates were only provided subsequent to analysis, by the RGA, of the safety and efficacy of the particular product. It was the former licensing division of the RGA—the Opiumstelle—which provided the institutional foundation for the specialist medicines division within the BGA—the Institut fuer Arzneimittel—subsequently entrusted with responsibility for the new registration procedure.[67]

The 1961 Act was amended in 1964, following the thalidomide tragedy, but the changes introduced were merely cosmetic. Producers were required to give assurances to the BGA that their products had been tested in accordance with established scientific methods,[68] but the criteria for assessing safety and efficacy were not established by statute. Instead, voluntary guidelines were drawn up by the medical profession. Following a number of deaths attributed to the appetite suppressant Menocil, a new series of guidelines was issued by the Minister of Health in 1971, instructing the BGA not to permit registration unless clinical trials on the products met with certain standards.[69] The standards were drawn up by an *ad hoc* committee of experts, whose remit was modelled closely on the UK's Committee on the Safety of Medicines, and though binding on the BGA were not legally binding on industry, nor did they apply to generic products or drugs already on the market. However, the introduction of these guidelines can be seen as a decisive shift towards a system of comprehensive product licensing and, in turn, marked a substantial increase in the size of the Institut fuer Arzneimittel, and in the scope of its activities.[70] This period has been described as a phase in which the BGA's 'professional scientific knowledge was established and enlarged but with the minimum of regulatory powers'.[71]

The Medicines Act 1976 The regulatory powers hitherto denied the BGA were to be provided by the AMG 1976, which introduced a more interventionist style of regulation not dissimilar to the American and British regimes. While the strengthened majority secured by the SPD–FDP coalition in the 1972 elections increased the SPD's chances of success in securing parliamentary approval for a stricter regulatory system, it would seem that by the early seventies, the political parties were no longer polarized on this issue.[72] In addition, it has been observed that the passage of the Act was accompanied by vigorous debate on the constitutionality of its proposals, leading to the 'legalization' of the policy debate ('guidifizierung der politik formulierung').[73] Developments at the European level were also forcing industry's hand. The 1965 Directive, [74] requiring national governments to set up a system of marketing authorizations for medicinal products, further provided that such authorization should only be granted on the basis of documentary evidence of the product's safety, quality, and therapeutic efficacy. Earlier, the Christian Democrat governments had vehemently opposed the inclusion of this last phrase, but without success.[75] The provisions of the 1976 Act, in fact, approximate closely to the requirements of the Second Council Directive, the final text of which was eventually adopted in 1975.[76] In addition, the Act made provision for a state-financed system of compensation for victims of drug-induced injuries.

It should be noted that the BPI and industry did not actively resist the introduction of the 1976 Act. A system of product licences, harmonized at the European level, was seen as an important means of securing easy access to an increased share of the highly lucrative European market, as well as maintaining existing shares in the international market. Industry's attention was, instead, directed at preventing the introduction of more stringent controls, and ensuring that the opportunities for the BGA to make use of its substantial expertise were kept to a minimum. There are, in fact, three distinct fetters on the BGA's powers, each of which affords industry some influence over the implementation of drug-licensing policy.

All new drug products are assessed by the Institut fuer Arzneimittel, which is now organized into six divisions, including one devoted to drug approval. In assessing the documentation submitted to it, the BGA can make use of its own scientific findings, consult with specialists, or commission certified reports, but all new preparations must be endorsed by an independent committee of experts—the Zulassungskommission—which assesses the full documentation and holds a hearing on the application. The final decision on an application rests with the Institut fuer Arzneimittel, but there appears to be considerable bargaining between it and the Zulassungskommission, with disagreement arising in only 29 out of 706 cases in the last four years.[77] The Committee is composed of nine members, selected by the Minister of Health from names submitted by the governing bodies of the health professions and industry. As Murswieck has commented, 'the formal sovereignty of the regulatory agency is integrated in a network of procedures which guarantees . . . the participation of social interest organisations [specified in the AMG] in the decision making process.'[78]

In the event of disagreement, the BGA must give reasons to support its decision. It is at this point that the rules of general administrative law come into operation, providing a second and highly significant fetter on the BGA. A dissatisfied applicant may invoke these general principles and request an administrative court review of the reasonableness of the BGA's decision. The applicant may submit new evidence to substantiate its case within one month of notification of intent to appeal. At this point, the administration has to review its own decision and can provide its own remedy. This is the task of the legal department of the BGA. Whereas the test of unreasonableness is primarily a procedural one under British administrative law, in German law that test is a substantive one, so that the legal department can effectively substitute its own decision for that of the Institut fuer Arzneimittel, thus providing a 'secondary judicial licence'. By holding back evidence until the appeal stage the company may often demonstrate that, at least on legal grounds, the initial decision was unreasonable.

The centrality of the role of lawyers to the BGA's work cannot be overlooked. Although a minority in a technically oriented administrative agency, lawyers occupy many of the key positions in the BGA.[79] Companies have sucessfully mobilized legal arguments to counter adverse decisions. That this has worked to industry's substantial advantage is demonstrated by the success rate obtained on appeals. Between 1978 and 1984, the Institut fuer Arzneimittel licensed 4,374 drugs and refused 364 applications. The legal department dealt with 362 of these, invariably granting the licence, although with certain conditions attached. Between July 1984 to July 1985—the only period for which concrete figures are available—of the 95 objections dealt with by the legal department, 77 were decided partially, or totally, in favour of the objector.[80]

The link between this 'secondary judicial licence' and the third fetter on the BGA's underlines the impact of administrative law on the implementation of the 1976 Act. In examining the initial decision on a licence, the legal department applies as a yardstick the general guidelines on the assessment of safety and efficacy issued by the Minister of Family, Labour, and Health in the exercise of its supervisory powers. These guidelines are themselves the product of formal deliberations between representatives of the Ministry of Health, the Bundesrat, the health professions, and industry. Finally, the legal department may make use of expert opinions provided by industry and the BPI in exercising its substantive control over the BGA's decisions on individual products.

The German licensing process has been characterized as displaying a 'low level of intervention coupled with a high degree of legalistic attitudes and bureaucratic formalism'.[81] We have suggested that the formalism introduced by the 1976 Act has worked substantially in industry's favour, achieving a none too dissimilar result to the maintenance of informal rules of the game in the United Kingdom. Indeed, as we shall go on to argue, the 'juridification' of the German licensing system appears to offer significant long-term advantages to industry.

Mobilizing Law and Policy Implementation

The United Kingdom

In our analysis of the introduction of the statutory licensing scheme in the United Kingdom, we argued that the existing rules of the game remained almost unaltered, despite the vesting of legal powers of enforcement in the Minister of Health. Moreover, we argued that industry had ensured that issues of comparative efficacy had been excluded from the policy agenda. A further test of the durability of these rules was occasioned by the Labour government's announcement in 1975 that, in order to comply with the aims of the two EC Directives on medicinal products, the 30,000 products which had been awarded an automatic licence of right in 1971 would have to be subjected to a full review if they were to remain on the market after 1990.[82]

In order to supervise the arrangements made to meet the Community deadline, and to examine the documentation which companies were now obliged to supply in support of the claims made for their products, a new advisory committee, the Committee on the Review of Medicines (CRM), was set up in late 1975. This Committee resembles the CSM in that it is staffed by independent medical experts and is serviced by the Medicines Division at the DHSS. Whereas the CSM considers applications for full licences on an individual product basis, the CRM started its reviews on the basis of a systematic examination of individual therapeutic categories, each of which might cover a potentially large number of products. The CRM began by tackling the largest and most important categories of substances,[83] using separate sub-committees to scrutinize the data supplied by companies. On the basis of these findings, the CRM issued provisional recommendations on a therapeutic substance, which were then subject to a two-month consultation period. A final definitive recommendation on the drug substance could then be issued as a prelude to the formal consideration of an individual firm's products.

The first review—of analgesics—was generally acknowledged to be a success in terms of its end result, but as a process, the multi-stage procedure proved slow and cumbersome, especially at the consultation stage. Problems were greatly enhanced when the CRM commenced its review of individual products on the basis of the systematic review. The CRM, in common with the CSM, was understaffed, given the nature of the task in hand. But whereas the industry was prepared to co-operate with the latter, which after all had something to offer, in the form of a marketing authorization, the CRM was threatening to take something away, and did not enjoy such ready support for its endeavours. If the CRM recommended the variation or revocation of a licence of right, the company affected could, and often did, invoke the substantial procedural protection for applicants envisaged in the 1968 Act, but which industry had seldom used in its dealings with the CSM. A further shift to procedural formalism on the part of the CRM is evidenced by its increased dependence on its statutory powers to demand information from companies whose products were being reviewed.[84]

With progress on the review substantially hampered by the use of these cumbersome procedures, which in themselves encroached further into the CRM's already over-stretched resources, the Minister of Health instituted an *accelerated review*, designed to run in parallel with the systematic procedure. Products thought to present special hazards were singled out by the CRM's secretariat, and a notice of the Committee's intention to revoke the licence issued without prior review of the therapeutic substance contained in the product, and hence without full consultation on this basis. This unilateral alteration in the rules of the game served to underline, at least in industry's eyes, the CRM's adversarial stance. Relations were to worsen following the CRM'S accelerated review of pyschotropics. An internal report on certain types of fixed combination drugs'—a category of products previously criticized by the MacGregor Committee—expressed considerable doubt over the safety and efficacy of these products in the treatment of psychiatric illness.[85] The CRM subsequently dispatched an unprecedented 200 notices recommending the revocation of over 134 licences of right for barbiturates, including two held by the British subsidiary of the American multinational, E. R. Squibb.

Squibb, despite a number of oral and written represensions, failed to convince the CRM of the efficacy of its products, and rather than avail itself of its statutory right of a hearing before the Medicines Commission, took the highly unusual step of seeking an application for judicial review of the CRM's recommendation.[86] We have noted that formal challenges to the legality of the decision of the licensing authority have become a standard method of overturning the BGA's recommendations under the German licensing system, but this has not been the case in the United Kingdom. The mere fact that a company was prepared to seek judicial review, and thus depart substantially from the British rules of the game, would appear symptomatic of the extent to which relations between industry and the licensing authority had broken down. The Chairman of the Medicines Commission herself commented that 'one could not unnecessarily [sic] say that the regulatory authority and industry were drifting into an adversarial attitude over the Review'.[87]

Various reasons were put forward for this unwelcome development. The burden of producing documentation in support of well-known products did not always seem justifiable. Clinical trial records which would satisfy modern medical standards were often not available. However, we would suggest that the primary reason for this breakdown in relations can be attributed to the shift in the balance of power which the Review process itself entailed, the full extent of which is made clear in judgment in the Squibb case. The company claimed that the CRM had formed its opinions on the basis of its own internal report, ignoring the company's oral representations. The CRM had, in fact, considered Squibb's claims along with those made by the manufacturer of an identical rival product whose licence was also under threat. Having discussed the extent to which Squibb's products differed, the CRM concluded that the latter had offered no convincing evidence of efficacy. Not only was the CRM making full use of its regulatory powers to demand information, but it was using that information to compile independent and secret reports on therapeutic substances, on the basis of which individual products would be judged. However, and this was no doubt the motivating factor behind Squibb's unusual action, the CRM had used criteria based, *inter alia*, on the comparative efficacy of one marketed product *vis-à-vis* another. The onus of proving its product's superiority to the often more recent and improved versions marketed by rival companies fell on the applicant. The CRM, perhaps unwittingly, had elevated itself to the forbidden position of 'arbiter of efficacy'.

Squibb's attempt to quash the CRM's recommendations illustrates the weakness of the British procedurally-oriented system of judicial review. The trial judge ruled that as the hearing was only advisory the CRM was not under an obligation to give detailed reasons for its decision, although these would have to be provided in support of the Minister of Health's final decision on the licence.[88] If this case had been decided under German administrative law, application of the principle of equal treatment would have undoubtedly circumscribed the CRM's discretionary power. The expense in terms of time and manpower, consequent on procedural formalization, suited neither side and, faced with continued difficulties in obtaining the information necessary to proceed with the Review as well as industry's increased lack of co-operation with the CSM, the Minister instituted a wholesale review of the Review in late 1981. Following extensive consultation in a number of *ad hoc* working parties on which the ABPI was represented, many of industry's grievances were dealt with. The systematic reviews ceased, and revocation orders were to be confined to exceptional cases so that products could be withdrawn with mininimum publicity. Finally, there was to be 'less emphasis on control so that the Review [would become] medicines oriented rather than prescribing oriented'.[89] Product licences would be reviewed on renewal, in accordance with a two-stage timetable based on company licence numbers.

The Review process will be completed by 1990, but products will not have been particularly closely scrutinized. The onus to produce the information necessary to justify the continued marketing of the drug has shifted to the individual firm, but stress is now placed on the need to modernize data rather than to prove efficacy. The role of the CRM is to assist in the task of compiling data of a requisite standard.

The Federal Republic of Germany

If the highly bureaucratic and formal licensing process introduced by the 1976 AMG has not led to hostile regulatory environment, this is not to say that all industry's suspicions as to the potential use of its considerable scientific expertise have been allayed.[90] The German equivalent of the UK Review process, which began much later and on much less ambitious terms, has not proved a source of friction, but the existence of (albeit latent) strains in the relations between industry and government have emerged in the debate over the use of the first licensee's data in support of a second and later application for a licence for a similar product.

A comparatively high proportion of the total number of products on the German market are, in fact, branded generics or 'close copies' of market leaders, and, as every drug must now be licensed, manufacturers of these products must lodge the requisite data in support of their application.[91] The tests necessary to generate this data are both time-consuming and expensive. Even when a patent has lapsed, there is often little published evidence relating to these tests in the public domain. Hence the so-called 'second applicant' has sought to circumvent the need to repeat the required tests by making reference to the files lodged with BGA by the company holding the first licence.

In claiming what is tantamount to a new form of 'property right' in the original data, the first licensee is effectively seeking to extend its monopoly of a product after the patent has lapsed, by turning the requirements of the licensing regime to its own advantage. The validity of this claim has triggered off a major constitutional debate. The BGA's policy, first announced in 1979,[92] has been to allow references to be made to tests undertaken in support of earlier licence applications, a policy vigorously opposed by the BPI, or to be precise, its research-oriented members. The ensuing battle has been fought by means of an exchange of legal opinions, commissioned by the leading protagonists, and has resulted in a government amendment to the BGA, currently at committee stage in the Bundestag.[93]

The draft amendment appears to offer a compromise solution to the extreme positions hitherto adopted by the BGA and the BPI. The latter argued that any reference by the former to data lodged in support of prior applications constituted an unconstitutional expropriation and an infringement of the fundamental constitutional principle of equal treatment in economic matters.[94] The BGA and its supporters contended that an enforced duplication of tests on humans and animals, the results of which were already available, would be equally unconstitutional as it would contravene the principle of proportionality.[95] Constitutional and general administrative law principles have thus provided the operational elements which have been used to rewrite the regulatory programme of the *Arzneimittelgesetz*. The Act itself only contains the core requirements of safety, efficacy, and quality, whereas the legal debate on the second licensing issue adds a new dimension, concealing a hidden agenda. Generic substitution is seen as an important method of cost-containment by the Federal government and the *Krankenkassen*, in the face of increased drug bills, whereas industry seeks to extend its property rights as a means of promoting research and innovation.[96] The proposed amendment to the AMG, pre-empting a similar provision in the 1984 EC

Draft Directive,[97] would allow for a ten-year period of protection for the licence holder, with an absolute ban on the use of the data for the first five years and a system of compensation for the remaining period.

Whereas their British counterparts have eschewed formal legal process, and have barely troubled themselves with issues of legal principle in their dealings with the regulatory authority, the German policy debate has been conducted not only in terms of the social and economic advantages and disadvantages of the facilitation of generic licence applications, but as an essentially legal debate, conducted in terms of the application of constitutional principles. The centrality of judicial review in the Basic Law cannot be overlooked in any analysis of the implementation of government policy, this being the result of the functional duplication of constitutional law. Law does not only provide the 'technical' rules of society, including government and industry relations, but also provides the language in which policy debates are often couched. Legal arguments over the interpretation and application of constitutional law principles are thinly disguised policy debates. This functional duplication has in turn created a widespread acceptance for a flexible, result-oriented approach to legal problems. In particular, the judicial technique of '*abwagung*' or overt balancing of values and interests in determining vague principles, such as economic equality, has aroused the suspicion of UK lawyers reared on a precedent-based system.[98]

A cloak of legal language cannot disguise the essential difference between a general policy debate and a legal debate. The very subject matter of the latter debate feeds directly into the legal system and acts as a vehicle for changes in policy programmes which are themselves highly legalized. In this context the second licensing debate can be seen as an attempt to moblize both the 'policy element' and the 'legal dimension' of constitutional law. Whereas the industry's legal arguments were effectively countered by those of the BGA, the government's proposed amendment to the AMG indicates that the industry has won the policy debate.

Conclusions

In our discussion of the licensing process, we have contrasted the particular legal problems which have emerged in the two national systems, in order to throw some light on the role of law in policy implementation in each country. We have argued that, while the statutory procedures introduced by the Medicines Act 1968 and the *Arzneimittelgesetz* of 1976 might suggest an abrupt departure from the established patterns of relations between the pharmaceutical sector and government, further analysis reveals that there has been little real change. However, the processes by which stability has been maintained have differed, and we would argue that legal culture has contributed significantly to those processes.

We have argued that neither the German nor the British-based industry was fundamentally opposed to a system of licensing. The thalidomide tragedy had precipitated most nations into enacting some form of product control. That is not to say that industry would accept a substantial degree of governmental intervention in its marketing decisions. We have compared the strategies adopted in the British and German pharmaceutical sectors, and argued that, whereas the former has pursued the maintenance of a flexible, informal style of policy implementation, in which bargaining plays a central role, the latter has accepted a more formalistic legal framework, but has made full use of administrative law procedures and participation in rule-making to create flexibility *within* the legal framework.

It is in this context that we can understand why problems have emerged in the review process in the UK, which initially entailed an unusually extensive use of the licensing authorities' powers, but not in Germany, where the review process, begun at a later date, has not aroused resentment. The implementation of the UK Review marked not only a departure from the established rules of the game. The reappearance of the issue of comparative efficacy was seen also as a unilateral alteration to the policy agenda.

It would appear that German industry has not relied on informal mechanisms—such as the Council set up in 1971 along the lines of the former British Committee on the Safety of Drugs—to anything like the same extent as its British counterpart. Instead, formal legal arguments over the ownership of the data submitted in support of a licensing application—a problem which has never emerged as a legal issue in the UK—have been used to ensure that the licensing process makes a minimal inroad into industry's commercial freedom. This contrast in the way in which problems have been articulated in the two national systems can at least partly be explained by the emphasis on bargaining *within* a given legal framework in the German system, as opposed to the processes of negotiation which occur *outside* the formal framework of law in the UK.

While it is not possible to attribute policy outcomes to variations in legal culture, its impact on policy processes and bargaining styles is of some consequence. A major weakness of the British system must surely lie in the degree of secrecy which surrounds the entire licensing process—a degree of secrecy necessitated by the degree of interdependence between government and industry. It is virtually impossible for third parties, such as consumer groups, to have a sustained input into the policy process. In the German context, law can be seen as a potential means of opening up the policy process, not only by providing a common medium of communication, but also by placing decision-making in a more open and, therefore, more accountable forum. However, it should not be forgotten that legal controversy is often merely a surrogate for wider forms of societal conflicts, the resolution of which may be distorted by the imposition of a formal legal framework. Legal arguments as to the ownership of licensing data have partially obscured the underlying debate on the economics of generics.

A further consequence of legal culture on policy processes and bargaining styles is its impact on the role, functions, and cohesion of policy networks. Whereas, in the UK, a reliance on informal mechanisms of control has served to reinforce the structure of dependent relations not only between government and industry but also between individual firms and their peak association, the ABPI, so that conflicts have tended to be suppressed within the organization, this does not appear to have been the case in West Germany. Policy networks would appear to have a more direct role in the initial stages of policy formulation rather than at the later, implementation stage. The existence of legal rights, as an alternative means of realizing the disparate aims of the various members of the BPI, has allowed more open conflicts to emerge, as in the recent split in the membership over the issue of generic substitution.[99] This could have important consequences for the implementation of new policy initiatives and, as such, offers a useful insight for future research.

Notes

1. S. A. De Smith, *Constitutional and Administrative Law*, 3rd edn. (London: Stevens, 1977), p. 208, quoted in T. C. Daintith, 'Legal Analysis of Economic Policy', *Journal of Law and Society* 9 (1982), pp. 191–224, at p. 192.

2. W. Friedman, *The State and the Rule of Law* (London: Fontana, 1971) is the classic exposition.
3. J. L. Jowell, 'The Legal Control of Discretion', *Public Law* (1973), pp. 178–220.
4. G. Ganz, *Government and Industry* (Oxford: Professional Books, 1977); A. Page, 'Legal Analysis of Economic Policy', *Journal of Law and Society* 9 (1982), pp. 225–52.
5. A. W. Bradley, 'Research and Reform in Administrative Law', *Journal of the Society of Public Teachers of Law* 13 (1974), pp. 35–46.
6. R. Baldwin and K. Hawkins, 'Discretionary Justice', *Public Law* (1984), pp. 570–99, at p. 580.
7. See, however, T. C. Daintith, above (n. 1); P. McAuslan, 'Administrative Law, Collective Consumption and Judicial Policy', *Modern Law Review* 46 (1983), pp. 1–42.
8. H. J. Jarass, *Wirtschaftsverwaltungsrecht und Wirtschaftsrecht*, 2 vols. (Cologne, 1983), Vol. 2 lists the most important recent works on this topic.
9. G. Teubner, 'Reflexive Law', *Law and Society Review* 17 (1983), pp. 240–95.
10. R. Stewart, 'Regulation and the Crisis of Legalisation in the United States'. Paper presented at the Conference on Legalisation and De-legalisation, European University Institute (Florence, 1985).
11. E. Bardach and R. A. Kagan, *Going by the Book* (Philidelphia: Temple, 1982).
12. R. Posner, *Economic Analysis of Law*, 2nd edn. (Chicago, 1977).
13. S. Peltzman, 'An Evaluation of Consumer Legislation', *Journal of Political Economy* 81 (1973), pp. 1046–91; L. Lasagna and W. Wardell (eds.), *Regulation and Drug Development* (Washington DC: American Enterprise Institute, 1975); P. Quirk, 'The FDA' in J. Wilson (ed.), *The Politics of Regulation* (New York: Basic Books, 1980); J. E. S. Parker, 'Regulating Pharmaceutical Innovation', *Food, Drug and Cosmetic Law Journal* (1977), pp. 163–79.
14. S. Breyer, *Regulation and its Reform* (Cambridge, Mass: Harvard University Press, 1981).
15. L. Schriffin, 'Lessons from the Drug Lag', *Harvard Journal of Law and Policy* 5 (1982), pp. 9–118.
16. H. G. Grabowski *et al.*, 'The Effects of Regulatory Policy', *Journal of Law and Economics* 21 (1978), pp. 133–64.
17. P. Temin, *Taking Your Medicine* (Cambridge, Mass.: Harvard University Press, 1980).
18. S. Breyer, above (n. 14).
19. J. E. S. Parker, above (n. 13).
20. K. Hartley and A. Maynard, *The Costs and Benefits of Regulating New Drug Products* (London: Office of Health Economics, 1982).
21. M. N. Baily, 'Research and Development Cost and Returns; The US Phar-

maceutical Industry', *Journal of Political Economy* 80 (1972), pp. 70–85; H. G. Grabowski, above (n. 16).

22. D. Kennedy, *Drug Lag, Does it Exist?* (Baltimore, 1981).

23. N. Reich, 'The Regulatory Crisis', *Government and Policy* (1984), pp. 140–59.

24. Though many of the 'Economistic' school have opposed regulation because of this, e.g. G. Stigler, 'The Theory of Economic Regulation', *Bell Journal of Economics* (1971), pp. 3–21.

25. K. Hawkins, *Environment and Enforcement* (Oxford: OUP, 1983).

26. C. Diver, 'A Theory of Regulatory Enforcement', *Public Policy* 28 (1980), pp. 257–71.

27. A. Peacock *et al.*, *The Regulation Game* (London: Anglo-German Foundation, 1984).

28. H. Jann, *Staatliche Programme und Verwaltungskultur* (Opladen: W. D. Verlag, 1983).

29. Section 21 and Schedule 2 of the 1968 Act.

30. D. Black, 'The Mobilisation of Law', *Journal of Legal Studies* 11 (1973), pp. 125–42.

31. Peacock *et al.*, above (n. 27).

32. M. Burstall, *et al.*, *The Community's Pharmaceutical Industry* (Brussels: EC Commission, 1985).

33. J. Sargent, 'The Organisation of Business Interests in the UK Pharmaceutical Industry', IIM Discussion Paper 83–6 (Berlin, 1983).

34. OECD, *Trends in Health Care Expenditure* (Paris: OECD, 1985).

35. Paliamentary Debates, HC vol. 677; 8 May 1963; col. 448.

36. Therapeutic Substances Acts 1925–57; Poisons Acts 1908–72.

37. Ministry of Health, 'Safety of Drugs' *Final Report of the Joint Standing Committee on Prescribing* (London: HMSO, 1963).

38. ABPI, Annual Report 1962–63 (London, 1963).

39. In fact, it is only non-manufacturing countries, such as Norway, which adopt criteria based on need or comparative efficacy.

40. The so-called Dunlop Committee first reported in 1964. Its terms of reference are reproduced in Appendix One of its *First Annual Report of the Committee on the Saftey of Drugs,* (London: HMSO, 1964).

41. Above (n. 37).

42. R. Klein, *The Politics of the National Health Service* (London: Longman, 1983).

43. Ministry of Health, *Annual Report for year ending 1952*, Part 1, Cmd. 8933 (London: HMSO, 1954).

44. For a full account of the operation of the various versions of the VPRS, see R. Lang, *The Politics of Drugs* (Farnborough: Saxon House, 1974).

45. Ministry of Health *Annual Report for year ending 1955*, Part 1, Cmd. 9564 (London: HMSO, 1956).

46. J. Sargent, 'The Politics of the Pharmaceutical Price Regulation Scheme' in

P. Schmitter and W. Streek (eds.), *Private Interest Government* (London: Sage, 1984).

47. Ibid.

48. R. Lang, above (n. 44).

49. *Third Report from the Committee on Public Accounts*, Session 1956–7, HC, no. 243 (London: HMSO, 1957).

50. R. Klein, above (n. 42).

51. *Special Report and First, Second and Third Reports of the Committee on Public Accounts*, Session 1956–7, HC, nos. 75, 93, 190, and 243 (London: HMSO, 1957).

52. The Hinchcliffe Committee on Effective Prescribing, reporting in 1958, recommended that the industry should introduce measures of self-discipline on promotional expenditure.

53. ABPI Yearbook, 1962–3 (London, 1963).

54. Wade, 'The Review of Medicines' in BIRA, *Fourth Symposium on Regulatory Affairs* (London, 1984).

55. D. Dunlop, 'The Committee on the Safety of Drugs' in L. Landau (ed.), *Regulating New Drugs* (Chicago: Norton, 1973).

56. Committee on the Safety of Drugs, *Annual Report for year ending 1964* (London: HMSO, 1965).

57. Committee on the Safety of Drugs, *Annual Report for year ending 1969* (London: HMSO, 1970).

58. Cmnd. 3397, para. 143 (London: HMSO, 1967).

59. Cmnd. 3410 (London: HMSO, 1967).

60. R. Lang, above (n. 44).

61. Medicines Act, Sections 24 and 28; *Annual Reports of the Medicines Division, the Medicines Commission and the Committee on the Safety of Medicines*, 1971–8 (London: HMSO).

62. See ABPI, Annual Reports 1974–5, 1975–6, and 1977–8 for developments.

63. Parliamentary Debates, HC, vol 930; cols. 390–93; 15 April 1977.

64. The Administrative Court Procedures Act 1976, BGBL IS 1253 and the Administrative Court Procedures Act 1960, BGBL II 1960.

65. See A. Murswieck, *Die Staatliche Kontrolle der Arzneimittelsicherheit in der Bundesrepublik and den USA* (Oplanden: W. D. Verlag, 1983).

66. Judgment of 8 January 1959, B. Verf, GE 9, 83: the grounds of the case were that the principles of the Rechtsstat (rule of law) did not allow for such vaguely worded, far-reaching prohibitions on commerical activity, and judgment of 11 June 1958, B. Verf, GE 7, 377.

67. A. Murswieck, above (n. 65), p. 400.

68. Zweites Gesetz zur Anderung der Arzneimittelgesetz vom 23 June 1964, BGBL IS 365.

69. Richtlinie der Deutschen Pharmakologischen Gesellschaft (163) und Richtlinie der Deutschen Gessellschaft fuer innere Medizin. Richtlinie uber die Prufung von Arzneimitteln, Banz, no. 113 of 25 June 1971. The

standards laid down in the guidelines were mainly taken from the EC Draft Directive 12 February 1970, (DT BT DS vi/417) and adapted by the Beirat Arzneimittelsicherheit—the Council on the Safety of Medicines, set up along the lines of the UK's CSM in 1970.

70. In 1876 the predecessor of the BGA had a staff of 7, in 1926 of 120, and by 1984 employed a total of 1,676 in the different sections. In the Institut fuer Arzneimittel itself, the staff has grown from 39, in 1968, to 256. An increase to 360 is planned for 1986—see BGA Yearbook, 1981, pp. 83–9.

71. A. Murswieck, above (n. 65), p. 431.

72. Ibid.

73. Ibid. p 378.

74. Council Directive no. 65/65 of 26 January 1965 in OJ no. 22, 9.2.65 369/65.

75. N. Bel, 'L'Œuvre communautaire en matière d'harmonisation des legislations des produits pharmaceutiques', *Revue du Marché Commun* (1975), pp. 505–14.

76. Council Directive no. 75/318 of 20 May 1975 in OJ 1975, L. 147/1 and Council Directive no. 75/319 of 20 May 1975 in OJ 1975, L. 147/13.

77. BGA Yearbook, 1984 (Bonn, 1985), p. 26.

78. A. Murswieck, above (n. 65), p. 202.

79. The head of personnel, the head of public relations, and the Vice-President, as well as the former Vice-President, are lawyers, but only fourteen of the total of 1,600 staff are legally qualified.

80. Personal communication to Dr Ruete, November 1985.

81. Klaes, Seebach, und Lex, *Regulativ Politik und Politisch Administrative Kultur*, (Cologne, 1982) pp. 178–79.

82. Article 37 of EC Directive 75/319, OJ 1975, L. 147/13.

83. For a full account of the systematic review procedure see the Annual Reports of the Committee on the Review of Medicines for 1976 and 1977.

84. See the Annual Reports of the CSM, CRM, and the Medicines Commission for the years ending 1978–81.

85. *Annual Report of the CRM for year ending 1979* (London: HMSO, 1980), para 3.

86. *R. v. The Committee on the Review of Medicines, ex parte E. R Squibb and Son*, 8 April 1981, unreported.

87. R. Hurley, 'The Medicines Act—is it Working?', *Journal of the British Institute of Regulatory Affairs* 2 (1983), pp. 1–3.

88. R. Squibb, above (n. 86).

89. E. S. Snell, 'The Review of Licences', Fourth Annual Symposium of the British Institute of Regulatory Affairs (London, 1984).

90. The Institute currently employs over 280 scientific experts and plans to increase this number to 360 by the end of 1986.

91. Scrip, *The Pharmaceutical Market in West Germany: A Scrip Special Report* (Richmond: P. J. B. Publications, 1983), p. 37.

92. Bekanntmachung des Bundesgesundheitsamtes vom 30 Mai 1979: Banz nr. 106 vom 9 Juni 1979.
93. Para. 20a of AMG Bill 1986 BT BRS 10/51, 12.
94. R. Scholz, *Konkurrenzprobleme bei behordlichen Producktkontrollen* (Cologne, 1983).
95. D. Schefold, *Verfassungsfrfagen zum Verhalthis vom Erst un Nachnanmelder im Zuslassungsverfahren von Arzneimitteln* (Berlin, 1983).
96. It has been estimated that a switch to generic prescribing could save the *Krankenkassen* up to twenty-two per cent of their current expenditure on drugs. *Scrip*, No. 1086, 19 March 1986.
97. COM (84) 510 (Brussels, 1984).
98. K. H. Ladeur, *Abwagung—Ein Neues Paradigma des Verwaltungsrechts* (Berlin: Campus, 1984).
99. Five generic manufacturers have recently broken away from the BPI to form their own industry association. *Scrip*, No. 1085, 17 March 1986.

8

Adapting to Decline: Organizational Structures and Government Policy in the UK and West German Foundry Sectors

Colin Appleby and John Bessant

This chapter reviews comparative organizational structures and industrial policy outcomes in the foundry industries of the UK and West Germany. The orthodox distinction between pluralism in the UK and corporatism in West Germany is broadly confirmed but the more dramatic decline of the industry in the UK obscures a direct comparision. We conclude by comparing the industries at the level of the individual foundry company where common problems and a degree of convergence between the two systems is observed.

The Industry

Metal casting is one of the oldest and most central of manufacturing processes. Melting raw materials and pouring the resulting liquid into a mould, or die, to produce a casting is the most efficient way of shaping metal. Nevertheless, the industry has been subject to a long-term secular contraction in demand, caused by the interaction of declining customer sectors, the substitution of other materials for metal, and competition from alternative processes. The castings sectors remain, however, substantial employers with around 100,000 employees in West Germany and 60,000 in the UK. From the viewpoint of government–industry relations, a number of features of the foundry sectors are distinctive.

Production is largely indigenous, exports and imports tend to represent only a small percentage only of domestic production. Given the traditional nature of the process, foundry companies also tend to be old, with few established after 1945 in either the UK or West Germany. Production is fragmented into a large number of sub-sectors, conventionally subdivided by metals, processes, and markets. The industry is dominated numerically by small firms, which are often independent, family-owned businesses. As such, foundry producers have little market power. On the supply side, they deal with large, monopolistic public utilities for their energy and raw materials; on the demand side, their customers are often giant, multinational companies, themselves subject to the pressure of international competition. Foundries thus offer significant contrasts to sectors such as motor vehicles, consumer electronics, and pharmaceuticals. In these cases, production is dominated by multinationals, trading consumer-end products in an international market-place. Foundries are more likely to reflect a traditional and ingrained industrial culture. In addition, fragmentation of the industry enhances the role of representative associations in mediating between the industry and government. The age of the sector, and the dominance of the independent company, implies high closure costs and peculiarly intractable problems of adjusting foundry capacity to declining demand.

Much has been written on the process of de-industrialization in Western Europe and, particularly, in the UK. Foundries tend to typify many of the worst features of manufacturing decline. In the world economy, foundry capacity and output have, in fact, grown. An irony for the UK and West German industries is that much of this growth has occurred through the technical consultancy provided by their own associations. In 1984, for example, Japanese iron castings output stood at record levels, an almost 20 per cent increase on 1975, 30 per cent larger than West German levels and three times as large as UK levels of production. The other side of this coin has been contraction and recession in castings production in Western Europe. From a position in 1960, when the UK and German industries were of similar size and significance, production has declined. In the UK, however, the scale of collapse has been atypical in the European context, and much more severe than that experienced by West Germany. As Table 8.1 illustrates, in the UK most early 1980s indicators of foundry activity stood at around 50 per cent of 1975 levels. In the German case, although the rate of decline is clearly less steep and aluminium castings demand (from the automotive sector) has grown by 43 per cent, our interviews reveals a clear perception of 'crisis' in the industry.

The central aim of this chapter is to assess the importance of organizational issues in determining outcomes for the foundry sectors in UK and West Germany. An overarching question is whether the existence of a more complex system of representation in the UK has impeded responses to decline or, in a stronger version, has actually played a causal part in decline. An obviously related point is whether organizations and inter-

Table 8.1 Output, Employment, and Establishments in the UK and West Germany Foundry Industries 1975–83

	UK			W. Germany		
	1975	1983	%	1975	1983	%
Tonnage (1000 metric tonnes)						
Ferrous						
Iron	3002	1436	– 52			
				3933	3311	– 16
Steel	269	115	– 57			
Non-Ferrous						
Aluminium and alloys	170	76	– 55	227	325	+ 43
Zinc alloys	1157	36	– 37	45	42	– 7
Copper alloys	67	50	– 25	77	72	– 6
Total employees (1000s)	160	61	– 62	144	107	– 26
Total number of establishments	1651	1088	– 34	1489	1126	– 24

relationships between them *do* matter in determining policy outcomes. These are questions tackled in the conclusions.

In the case of foundries, definition of the industry is more than usually problematic. The UK Foundries Economic Development Comittee, in its 1983–4 restructuring and capacity utilization enquiries, identified fifteen 'natural groupings' within the industry, defined according to metal, volume, process, and so on.[1] Thus, it is probably best to think in terms of a 'conglomeration of industries' rather than an industry. Most sub-sectors of the industry have been subject to rapid technical change. In its early 1970s review of iron and steel castings, the UK Department of Trade and Industry commented that 'there has been as much change in the last 15 years as in the previous 50 years'.[2] The emergence of new techniques can alter the disposition of 'natural groupings' and sub-sectors within the industry. The use, for instance, of Disamatic moulding machinery, originally designed for grey iron castings, has now been adopted for certain kinds of aluminium casting. In this case, former iron casters now have the opportunity to compete in markets previously occupied exclusively by aluminium die-casting companies. Equally, the ability to melt a variety of metals in modern electric melting plant will tend to break down the conventional subdivision of the industry by metal type. Technical developments of these kinds change the basis of competition within the industry, and alter the composition of the natural groupings described above.

Foundries may be either independent companies (often family-owned), or be tied to end users, or be part of larger, more diversified holding groups. Variations in ownership are important in determining company responses to decline, participation in the policy-making community and, critically, decisions to close. All ownership types are present in the UK and West Germany, with, if anything, a tendency towards a more dominant independent sector in the UK, compared with more vertical integration (especially in the automotive sectors) in Germany. In the UK, where decline has been more pronounced, closure rates have been highest among tied foundries and those parts of holding company structures.[3] In both countries, the independent, family-owned sector has displayed immense 'stickability', often in the face of adverse trading conditions. Independent foundries often have little alternative expertise to that gained in the foundry industry, work long hours for relatively poor reward, find closure costs high, and can often utilize quite large sites for other purposes which subsidize the foundry activity. Given the numerical importance of such companies within the industry structure, and their potential for survival, the problem of adapting capacity to declining demand has been and remains an important issue in the industry.

Recent Economic Conditions

One factor which unites the 'industry', especially in the UK, but also in Germany, is the experience of decline. As Table 8.1 shows, most indicators of activity in the UK stood at around 50 per cent of 1975 levels by 1983. Castings production in the UK has declined at a faster rate than the manufacturing index and is specifically related to the collapse of demand from major UK customer sectors, notably vehicles, but also shipbuilding and mechanical engineering. This has been exacerbated by increasing competition from alternative processes and materials. Castings are competitive with machining, forging, stamping, fabrication, and powder forming as processes, and plastics, ceramics, and concrete as materials.

For the UK, the Foundry Economic Development Committee's 1982 demand forecasts[4] predicted continuing decline, with a further 25 per cent reduction in castings output during the period 1985–90; its capacity utilization survey found companies typically operating at 75 per cent of 1978 capacity and 94 per cent of financial breakeven.[5]

The UK foundry sectors seem to fall clearly into F. M. Scherer's definition of the 'sick industry' problem. The essential prerequisites for this doubtful status are 'capacity in excess of current and probable future demands and rigidities which retard the allocation of resources towards growing industries'.[6] For many types of UK casting, prices barely rose, or actually fell, between 1979 and 1982, while typical costs for oil, gas, electricity, and coke more than doubled. In these circumstances, financial performance of the sectors has been very poor. Inter-company comparisons lists UK iron foundries as 57th in rank order on rate of return on capital; non-ferrous foundries perform even worse at 59th of 60 industrial sectors.[7]

While there has been contraction within the West German industry, the decline has been by no means as dramatic as in the UK. Nevertheless, the perception of 'crisis' exists in the German industry and whilst present conditions are better, comments from both ferrous and non-ferrous trade associations indicate no grounds for complacency. In particular, although the overall health of the industry has been good there is increasing concern about rising levels of import penetration from within and outside Europe. Taken at a time when rising labour and production costs and an unfavourable exchange rate are threatening export performance, the future picture for West German foundries is by no means optimistic. Interviews with these foundries reflect their concern with issues very much in common with their UK counterparts. These include the inability to pass on cost increases as higher prices to customers, over-capacity, the breakdown of price discipline, the increasing pressure for environmental control regulation, and so on.

Putting these matters into context, however, we should consider briefly some comparative performance indicators between the UK and West Germany. The FEDC's international comparisons[8] reveal consistent differences in the performance of the two countries in productivity, marketing, and capital expenditure. For example, 1983 labour productivity in the ferrous sector was 33.2 tonnes per man year in the UK, compared with 42.8 tonnes in Germany; 8 per cent of UK output was exported, as against 17 per cent of German output; average output per foundry was almost double in Germany at 6,600 tonnes per foundry, compared with 3,500 in the UK. In European rank order the Germans frequently figure first or second and the British sixth or seventh across a variety of performance measures. The FEDC's own conclusion on this work was that the principal problem lay in reducing capacity to equal demand and increasing the volume throughput of individual foundries to compensate for the faster decline in demand in the UK. The only solution is fewer but stronger and healthier foundries and the FEDC's discussion of restructuring has clearly followed the correct path.[9]

Several reasons could be advanced for the better performance of the West German industry. Related to the FEDC's conclusion, the most obvious reason is the better health of key customer sectors. However, it is also plausible to see this difference as one more symptom of a general *malaise* which has seen the UK weaker than West Germany across a whole range of manufacturing sectors. 'Industrial structure is very similar in the two countries . . . yet the difference in performance between 1954 and 1972 was considerable . . . there was not a single major branch of industrial activity in which UK performed better over the period.'[10] Factors often advanced to account for these differences include external elements, such as banking and finance, the industrial relations system, government policy at the macro-level, the vocational education and training system, as well as elements internal to the firm, such as the roles of works councils, the higher level of technically qualified management, and the role of the *Meister* grade of supervisor.[11]

From this position it is easy to construct an argument to explain the relative difference in the performance of the foundry sectors in the two countries. On the one hand, there is West Germany, with its tradition of organized and co-ordinated industrial trade and technical representation, a coherent trade union structure, clear and unambiguous channels of communication with government, a planned and regulated vocational educational system, which ensures a ready supply of skilled manpower, a financial system specialized by sector and prepared to lend long-term, and so on. By contrast, the UK industry can be painted as one in a state of 'disintegration'. Trade and technical representation is fragmented along the many divisions within the industry, and is consequently weak; trade union representation is characterized by too many different groups, with consequent problems of demarcation reflecting traditional area and craft loyalties; there is declining support from companies for training; financial institutions are over-centralized in the City; and lending policies do not favour manufacturing industry and especially not the 'smokestack' end of the spectrum occupied by foundries. Finally, and most important, the behaviour of the industry is essentially the sum of many individualistic actors, lacking co-ordination, and the ability to speak with one voice.

Such a set of stereotyped views is attractive as an explanation for differential performance; in particular, it suggests that the co-ordinated pattern in West Germany has enabled the industry to adapt better to the serious threats facing foundries during the last thirty years. Our concern in the rest of this chapter is to explore the validity of this argument for the differences in the performance of the foundry industry between the two countries.

An Organizational Map

Our basic comparative finding tends to reinforce the sterotypes introduced immediately above. In the UK, the organizational map tends to reflect the fragmentation and diversity present in the industry (see Figs. 4 and 5). In West Germany, more consolidated representation, and a much simpler map emphasizes commonalities in the metal casting process (see Figs. 4 and 6).

In the UK there are six major trade associations, three research associations, and nine trade unions. In West Germany, we find two trade associations (reflecting the broad division between ferrous and non-ferrous sectors), one technical association, and one trade union. In geographical terms, UK organizations are spread, with major centres in Sheffield, London, Birmingham, and Glasgow. In West Germany, all representative bodies have their headquarters in Dusseldorf, and two of the major associations occupy one building.

In the Figures, we compare the organizational activities of trade associations, research associations, and trade unions in turn. We accompany this mapping exercise with a discussion of the role of industry-wide bodies in the UK. We find that the UK is atypical in this respect, with no German equivalent of the Foundries EDC and no 'desk' in the Economics Ministry providing a parallel to the Materials and Metals Division of the UK Department of Trade and Industry.

Trade Associations

In both the UK and West German foundry sectors, trade associations have a potentially important role in representing the views of a diverse industry to government and its agencies. Given the large number of fairly discrete natural groupings within the foundry sector, there is clearly a

Figure 4. An Outline Listing of UK and West German Organizations

UK
Employers Federations
Engineering Employers Federation   (EEF)
National Metal Trades Federation   (NMTF)
Trade Unions
Confederation of Shipbuilding and Engineering Unions   (CSEU)
Joint Committee of Light Metal Trade Unions   (LMTU)
Amalgamated Union of Engineering Workers, Foundry
   Section   (AUEW)
Technical, Administration, Supervisory Section of AUEW   (AUEW/TASS)
Association of Patternmakers and Allied Craftsmen   (APAC)
National Society of Metal Mechanics   (NSMM)
Domestic Appliance and General Metal Workers   (DAGMW)
Associated Metal-workers Union   (AMU)
General and Municipal Workers Union   (G & MWU)
Transport and General Workers Union   (T & GWU)
Association of Scientific, Technical and Managerial Staffs   (ASTMS)
Trade Associations
Steel Castings Research and Trade Association   (SCRATA)
Light Metal Founders Association   (LMFA)
Zinc and Allied Die Casting Association   (ZADCA)
Association of Bronze and Brass Founders   (ABBF)
British Foundry Association   (BFA)
British Investment Casting Trade Association   (BICTA)
British Metal Castings Council   (BMCC)
Research Associations
British Casting Industry Research Association   (BCIRA)
British Non-Ferrous Research Association   (BNF)
Steel Castings Research and Trade Association   (SCRATA)
Production Engineering Research Association   (PERA)
British Steel Corporation R. & D.   (BSC)
Industry-Wide Bodies
Foundries Economic Development Committee   (FEDC)
Institute of British Foundrymen   (IBF)
Engineering Industry Training Board   (EITB)
Department of Trade and Industry, Materials and Metal
   Division   (DTI)
West Germany
Trade Unions
Industrie Gewerkschaft Metall   (IG Metall)
Trade Associations
Deutscher Giessereiverband   (DGV)
Gesamtverband Deutscher Metallgiessereien   (GDM)
Research Associations
Verein Deutscher Giessereifachleute   (VDG)

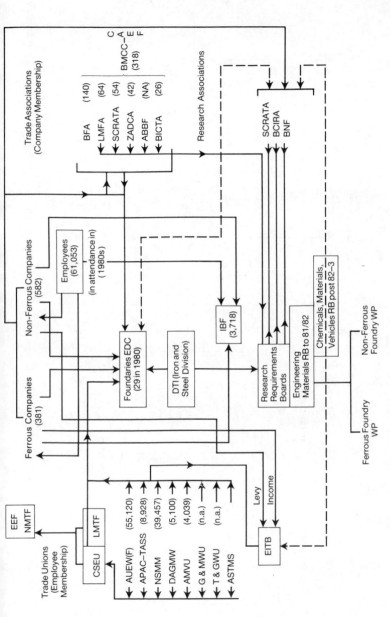

Figure 5. UK Outline Map for Foundries/Castings

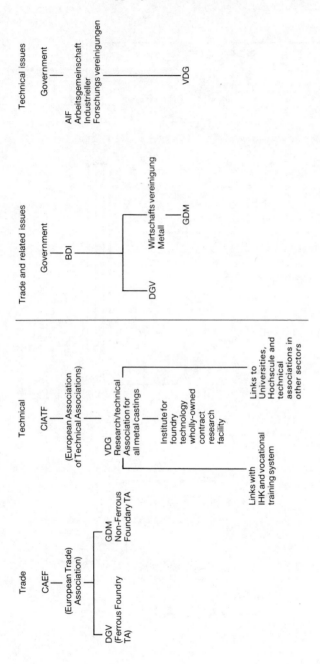

Figure 6A. Trade and Research Associations in W. Germany

Figure 6B. Government–Industry Relations in W. Germany

stark choice on the form of representation. The first option is for larger groupings, enjoying the benefits of scale and the ability to speak for the industry 'with one voice', but with the accompanying problem of encompassing a variety of diverse and often incoherent interests. The alternative is reliance on smaller and more discrete groupings, with the advantages of greater coherence and common interest among the membership.

The German case is most like the former option where representation at the trade association level is concentrated into two organizations—the Deutsche Giesserei Verband (DGV), for the ferrous sectors, and the Gesamt Verband der Deutsche Metallgiessereien (GDM), for the non-ferrous sectors. Both of these large, all-encompassing organizations have broadly similar functions and offer a similar range of services to members.

The DGV was originally founded in 1870 and the present organization dates from 1950. The tradition of co-ordinated representation has nine-teenth-century origins but the range of DGV activities has increased significantly since that time. Membership is on a voluntary basis and the DGV has around 350 ferrous foundries representing about 80 per cent of the total. In addition to activities in Dusseldorf, the size of DGV allows it to operate at the *Land* level, through a number of regional associations. Each regional grouping operates with a director and comprises around fifty foundries. Services to members include energy and raw materials advice, legal advice, external relations for the industry, company level economic analysis and advice, collation of statistical material, and liaison with the BDI and IHK (roughly equivalent to the UK CBI and Chambers of Commerce) on education and training issues. These areas are covered by eight or nine managers and, in total, over forty staff are employed in Dusseldorf.

Diverse interests within the ferrous casting sectors for different process and end-product sectors, such as steel, ductile and malleable iron castings, and automobile and rollers, as product groups, are catered for by *Fachverbande* or special interest groupings within the VDG (the tech-nical association for the industry). While there are a number of private consultancies advising the industry, it is important to note that there are no competing associations and that, as far as the foundries themselves are concerned, the DGV is the 'voice' of the industry. The DGV is able to represent the industry in national and regional policy formulation via the BDI. As far as manpower issues are concerned, they are members of the BDA (equivalent of the Employers Federation) which conducts wage negotiations with government and unions on a tripartite basis.

Reinforcing this picture of central strength, order, and consistency is the close geographical and organizational links between the DGV and the GDM (non-ferrous association). The GDM is broadly similar in functions, structure, and regional representation to its ferrous equivalent. It represents around 80 per cent of non-ferrous foundries, although this accounts for only 50 per cent of capacity, since many of the larger companies, particularly in tied groups like Volkswagen (which accounts for 10 per cent of tonnage) are not members. Reflecting the higher proportion of small companies in the non-ferrous sector (80 per cent of non-ferrous foundries in Germany employ less than 50 people), the majority of members fall into the small- to medium-sized category. A major difference between the DGV and the GDM is the nature of representation within the BDI. The DGV is a direct affiliate of the BDI, whereas the GDM belongs via an umbrella organization to the Wirtschafts Vereinigung Metalle eV (economic union for metals). Within this context, and as with the DGV, dealings with national government take place through the BDI, and the GDM is again seen by its members as the voice of the foundry sector in making inputs to this process. In addition to these internal links the DGV and GDM directly represent the ferrous and non-ferrous sectors in international matters on the European CAEF body.

In summary, on the German side there is a high level of industry support for these two major organizations; special interests are accommodated *within* their umbrella organizations; links to national government are not direct, but through the BDI; informal links between the DGV and GDM, and between these trade associations and the VDG, the single technical association, are well established by regular meetings.

In contrast, in the UK we find a more complex picture with multiple and sometimes competitive representation, lower levels of company support through membership, and the function of organizations often determined by historical accident and statutory anomaly. Many of the UK trade associations are necessarily quite small with support staff often carrying out secretarial functions only. Trade affairs and policy are often driven by a few key members, with the consequence for policy of a narrow representation of sectional interest. To an extent, this is inevitable in any trade association, but the tendency is reinforced in the UK case by fragmention into sub-sectoral interest groups. One major difference lies in the dynamics of the situation. In the UK, the organizations have been subject to the dramatic process of contraction experienced by the industry itself. In the last ten years more consolidated forms of representation have begun to emerge, often from financial necessity rather than a desire for integration.

The six UK metal casting trade associations are split by type of metal cast. Within the ferrous sectors are the BFA (British Foundry Association—mainly iron founders) and SCRATA (the Steel Castings Trade and Research Association). On the non-ferrous side is the LMFA (Light Metal Founders Association—mostly aluminium and alloys), ZADCA (Zinc Alloys Die Casting Association), and ABBF (Association of Bronze and Brass Foundries). These divisions by metal type are complicated by the anomalous position of BICTA (British Investment Casting Trade Association), where the distinctive feature lies in the 'lost wax' process which is used for both ferrous and non-ferrous alloys. A further anomaly lies in the position of SCRATA, which is both a trade *and* research association.

The picture of diversity is compounded if we examine the traditional core, and largest sub-sector of the industry, iron castings. From 1941 to 1983 the tension between a desire to 'speak with one voice' and the competing desire for common interests among discrete groups of members was catered for by the Council for Iron Foundry Associations (CFA). In this federal arrangement, individual iron founding companies belonged to one or more of a large number of autonomous regional or product or market-based, constituent associations of the CFA. Tripp, writing on the UK iron founding associations in the 1950s comments that:

The truth was that association in the industry for any common purpose was on a strictly sectional basis, of an 'ad hoc' kind and by modern standards an extraordinary muddle . . . there was no national unity and no coordinated thinking.[12]

The diversity encompassed in the loose federal arrangements embodied by the CFA gave way, for the first time, in 1983 to a direct membership body on the German model, the British Foundry Association (BFA). In part, this progress towards more centralized representation was enforced by financial necessity, as the number of active iron founders fell from 768 to 381 in the years 1978–83.[13] The accompanying financial weakening of the CFA was further and specifically exacerbated by the withdrawal of the Scottish-based BIA (British Ironfounders Association) from membership in the mid-1970s, and the further withdrawal of Birmid Qualcast, UK's largest iron founding company, in 1980. Birmid Qualcast's dissatisfaction with the CFA was given further expression in 1983 when the company became a leading member of the newly formed Association of

Independent Casting Manufacturers (AMCM), established with the
express purpose of restating the strategic case for the castings industry to
government.[14] At the same time, the new direct membership, BFA, was
formed to represent the views of iron founders to government departments, and to speak for the industry with one voice.[15] In the period
1983–5, however, many of the larger independent iron founders chose to
belong to the AMCM and a significant number of the smaller companies
remained as members of the former constituent associations of the CFA,
refusing to join the BFA on a direct membership basis. A typical early
reaction to the BFA has been 'we don't mind the industry speaking with
one voice, as long as it's ours!'[16] The power and authority of the associations clearly depends partly on the number of companies in membership.
Table 8.2 illustrates much lower membership ratios than in West
Germany. Lower membership in the UK is partly explained by the
growing financial pressure on foundry companies, partly by the persis-
tence of a self-sufficient industrial culture in the UK, but also by some
evidence of frustration at the performance of UK associations. Thus, the
FEDC's 1980 survey of small craft foundries 'revealed that many
foundries felt that their TA's were not as helpful as they might be in
representing their members interests'.[17] In a similar way, Rogers, from a
Department of Trade and Industry viewpoint, explains that 'an overall
view of the industry was difficult to obtain in the UK due to low levels of
trade association membership and the consequent absence of an accurate
representative view of the industry'.[18]

We have given here a brief review of the complexity of organizational
structures and relationships on the trade side. To an extent, Tripp's

Table 8.2 Membership of Trade Associations—1980[a]

	Approximate membership	Approximate total national establishments	TA membership ratio
CFA (1980)	300	580	.52
BFA post-1983	140	381	.37
ABBF	59	275	.21
LMFA	64	375	.17
SCRATA	54	77	.70
ZADCA	42	112	.38
BICTA	26	75	.35

[a] Source: Engineering Industry Training Board

'extraordinary muddle' for the UK persists. Organizations certainly carry out similar functions to those in West Germany, and on the ferrous side a more consolidated structure is emerging, but the dominant picture which remains is of fragmentation, anomaly, and asymmetry.

Research Associations

Turning to research and technical support, the comparative picture is essentially similar to that for trade affairs. There is one formally constituted association in Germany—the Verein Deutscher Giesserei Fachleute (VDG)—which is the technical and research association for *all* foundries, ferrous and non-ferrous. In the UK, the BCIRA has traditionally served iron castings interests, SCRATA steel castings, and the BNF, non-ferrous castings. In both countries, other engineering, university, and government departments contribute to the research effort. In the UK, independent research by individual foundry companies has virtually ceased, thus accentuating the role of the RAs in promoting technical change. The VDG is larger than its UK counterparts, has more regional outstations, but performs essentially similar functions to the UK RAs.

VDG membership covers around 2,600 individuals and 850 organizations; its structure and functions can be briefly summarized. Research activity is organized by a series of technical committees concerned with major metals and processes; two journals and an active documentation centre assist in the dissemination of research findings; the VDG has an important role in quality assurance and setting standards; the research programme attempts to combine a reactive mode— responding to the needs of companies—and a proactive role, aimed at developing technical capability within the industry. This range of activities is not dissimilar to those undertaken by the UK counterparts, although the German operation tends to be more comprehensive. For example, the UK RAs tend to leave the promotional role to the respective trade associations, and education and training to both the statutory national body, the Engineering Industry Training Board, and private organizations such as METCON, which itself encompasses trade affairs (the BFA) and training matters.

As outlined above, membership of the VDG is on a voluntary basis but the general level of support is high. A major difference between UK and Germany, and an anomaly in the UK, is that the BCIRA has historically received statutory support from the industry. From its foundation in

1921, BCIRA was supported by a levy on pig iron tonnages. Since 1966, this has become a compulsory levy on iron founding companies. This statutory support has given BCIRA a position of some strength and independence in an organizational sense. A 1982 survey of the industry, undertaken by the Department of Trade and Industry, found 90 per cent of iron foundries in favour of continued compulsory support, and gives BCIRA a somewhat firmer financial footing than SCRATA and BNF. SCRATA, as we have seen, is a combined research and trade association funded by voluntary membership of 70 per cent of companies in the steel casting sub-sector. The BNF represents a parallel body to those in Germany, where companies join the respective non-ferrous trade associations and can choose beyond this level to become corporate members of the RA.

Just as decline in the industry has precipitated reorganisation among the UK trade associations, a similar re-examination of roles has occurred over the last ten years in the RAs. The Rothschild[19] report recommended measures to increase the industrial relevance of RA research programmes. The DTI research requirements boards were established, in the mid-1970s, and grants gave way to the more commercially driven customer-contractor principle. Since 1975 and certainly in the 1980s the requirements boards have developed a more strategic and interventionist approach to the kind of research they are prepared to fund. Another major issue has been the potential for wasteful duplication, between the three castings RAs themselves and others engaged in castings research. BCIRA acknowledges the potential for collaborative work with kindred associations thus: 'preliminary discussions have taken place to investigate the possibility of collaborative joint projects between BCIRA, SCRATA and BNF'.[20] Taking a more positive line, SCRATA argued, in 1983, that: 'metal casting is a fundamental and unique manufacturing process and it deserves the most effective concentration of R & D effort for the mutual benefit of its various sectors'.[21]

The debate about a merger, between BCIRA and SCRATA, originated in the 1960s. The *Financial Times* claimed that the two organizations had been having 'desultory talks about merging for two decades'.[22] In the event, in spite of agreed plans between the two organizations and DTI waiting in the wings with £1.5 million to assist reorganization, the merger plan collapsed in 1984. This failure to achieve rationalization in the face of considerable separate financial weakening can be put down to a combination of the intransigence of some member companies, organizational problems relating to staff, and, not least, a profound suspicion by some parties of the promotional role being played by government. We are left, then, with an unreformed organizational structure in UK castings research which is clearly more fragmented than West Germany.

Trade Unions

Once again, the West German pattern appears much more simple and clear-cut. There is only one trade union responsibile for the foundry sector—the Industrie Gerwerkschaft-Metall or IG Metall. This is the largest trade union in West Germany and represents all the metal production industries and much of the engineering sector, including motor vehicles. Industrial relations in West Germany take two basic forms: issues at national or *Land* level are resolved by negotiations between employers federations and trade unions, whilst local issues are dealt with by the *Betriebsrat* (BR) (works council). In the former case, most foundry employers belong to the Verband der Metallindustrie—Federation of the Metal Industry—which is, in turn, a member of the Bundesvereinigung der Deutscher Arbeitgeber Verbande (BDA)—the German Union of Employers Federations. The *Gesprachspartner* (negotiating partner) of the BDA is the Deutsche Gewerkschafts Bund (DGB)—the equivalent of the TUC in the UK—to which the trade unions are affiliated. There is an annual process of negotiating wage settlements—the *Tarifhandlung*—and these set the standard for the industries in question within the individual *Länder*.

For the foundry industry there is something of a problem in being represented by the IG Metall. Total foundry employment in West Germany is only around 100,000 spread across a large number of small firms. In comparison with the large employers in the steel or engineering industries, the foundry sector has a very small voice, and for this reason membership tends to be somewhat low. Employers are also unhappy with the arrangement since it binds them to pay arrangements set for the more profitable industries like motor vehicles where the unions are in a stronger bargaining position. As far as the *Betriebsrat* is concerned, this provides a mechanism for resolving plant level questions and is undoubtedly one of the major factors contributing to relatively good industrial relations within the industry. However, for many of the smaller firms, especially in the non-ferrous sector, there is no legal requirement to establish a BR; even in those firms where employers have indicated a willingness, no BR has been set up.

In the UK, the diversity and extent of foundry worker representation is indicated in Figs. 4 and 5 with nine major trade unions identified. The CSEU with its foundries sub-committee acts as a peak organization in wage negotiations for the jobbing engineering sectors, the NMTF for light metal castings interests. Taking the foundry industry as a whole, there has never been a situation where one union had foundry workers as a dominant interest, and, at the same time, was sufficiently well represented to make that count. Foundry workers have found themselves either in the largest union, AUEW(F), which has become increasingly submerged within the AUEW; or as part of the giant T&GWU or G&MW; or in very small unions catering for foundry workers, which have increasing problems in remaining viable. Historically, the AUEW(F) is a descendant of one of the earliest UK labour organizations, the Friendly Society of Iron Founders, established in 1809. The history of foundry worker representation is one of gradual consolidation via amalgamation. Craft-based sectional interests have, however, continually frustrated the development of an industry-based union.

In recent times, the UK industry's workforce has declined very dramatically, from some 150,000 in 1970–1 to 61,000 in 1982–3. AUEW(F) membership fell from around 71,000 in 1958 to 56,000 in 1982 and was 42,000 in 1983.[23] This decline has weakened the union's position and led to recent merger discussions with other unions catering for foundry workers. By the end of 1983 terms and conditions for a transfer of engagements were agreed and the full integration of the foundry workers into AUEW became effective from October 1984. Despite this merger, the representation of labour interests in the industry as a whole remains extraordinarily muddled, partly due to the nature of the industry but, mainly, to the historical development of union activity in the UK.

Industry-Wide Bodies

Perhaps in response to the pattern of fragmentation within the UK foundry industry, a number of industry-wide bodies have grown up which attempt to provide some form of coherent overview of the sector. The first of these is the Foundries Economic Development Committee of the National Economic Development Council.

The FEDC has operated since the mid-1970s, and has provided an important forum for discussion of key issues relevant to the foundry sectors. Its existence lends some support to the view that the foundry sectors do, in some sense, constitute an industry. The origins of the FEDC lay in the early 1970s selection of castings as an 'important' industrial sector and the consequent operation of the ferrous and non-ferrous foundry aid schemes under Labour's 1975 Industrial Strategy Programme. The FEDC was first constituted as a Ferrous Foundries EDC and inherited the analysis of the industry carried out under DTI chairmanship entitled 'Iron and Steel Castings—Review to 1977'.[24] There were no clear reasons why ferrous castings should be 'important' and 'strategic' while non-ferrous castings were not. The Non-Ferrous EDC was thus formed, after lobbying from the non-ferrous trade associations, in April 1976, and the Ferrous and Non-Ferrous Committees were merged in November 1977 into the Foundries EDC.

Much of the early work of these tripartite committees was concerned with monitoring the effects of the ferrous and non-ferrous aid schemes (see below) which were designed to assist a process of modernization and re-equipment of foundry companies. The FEDC was reconstituted in 1980 and 1982 and has recently, in late 1985, been reorganized around market groupings related to the industry's customer sectors. The FEDC has attempted to represent all major sectors of the industry. The rough composition has been eight industry and five trade union representatives, two DTI officers, and two NEDO officers. Trade unionists are nominated by the regions to the TUC and, thence, to the FEDC. Industrialists are either approached directly, or are nominated by the relevant trade associations. On the FEDC it has been the practice to consult with the TAs. In 1980, however, the position of TA officials on the FEDC changed from full membership to 'in attendance'. This caused some annoyance among TA officials and reflected the desire of the FEDC to achieve what NEDO officals perceived to be a 'meaningful' discussion of the industry's problems and prospects. The argument is that the Committee needed members able to express an independent, informed viewpoint, without having to consult with their member companies for authority to argue in particular directions. NEDO interviewees have emphasized the important and independent role that trade union officials have played on the FEDC. Some writers have categorized the tripartite process as monopartisan with industry or government and industry as the dominant contributors to the discussion. Interviews indicate, however, that one should not underestimate the trade unions' role.

The 1982–5 programme of the FEDC has concentrated attention on the issues of future demand, capacity utilization, and international competitiveness. The FEDC in its 'Next Steps'[25] report posed pointed questions to government about the effectiveness of the market mechanism in producing a more internationally competitive sector. From the mid-1970s the FEDC became a focal point for discussion of the industry's problems. However, when action and implementation of policy was undertaken, the FEDC was not involved. One interesting feature is that many foundry companies clearly misconceive the role of the Committee. They either believe that the FEDC speaks for the industry (which it does not), or that it organizes action on behalf of the industry (which it clearly cannot).

A second and important industry-wide role has been played by the Department of Trade and Industry. A frequent general complaint is the lack of consistency in the Department's treatment of industries because of frequent changes of personnel. Foundries may prove the exception to this rule in that some DTI officers have had almost twenty years involvement with foundries. Major issues for DTI have been the administration of the sector aid schemes, the redirection of research policy via the requirements boards, provision of support for the restructuring of steel castings under the Lazard's schemes, and a supportive role in the merger of BCIRA and SCRATA. We discuss all of these issues at other points in the chapter.

What is clear from contact with DTI officials is the continuity and developing appreciation of the problems the industry was facing. These perceptions developed from the view held in the early 1970s that the problem was cyclical, to a decade or so later, and the recognition that a permanent and irreversible decline in demand for the industry's products was inevitable. What is also clear is that the DTI never pursued proactive policies towards the industry. In the case of the aid schemes, applications were reviewed in sequence and each treated equally, without discrimination. A widely held view now is that the aid schemes exacerbated the 1980s problems of over-capacity in the industry, and that the DTI's non-discriminatory approach was partly to blame. SCRATA's director, Dr Reynolds, has spoken of the 'bandwagon effect' arising from the publication of successful aid scheme applications.[26] There is also a question mark over the effectiveness of market appraisal when carried out on an individual company basis. A proactive approach might have looked at applications for new equipment in groups and anticipated likely over-capacity problems. The absence of such an approach tends to confirm the DTIs overall reactive mode. The Department has, in the last decade, been faced with a major turn-round in government policy towards the desirability of industrial intervention. The reactive mode has extended to the interpretation of policy as the 1980s has seen the shift from self-help to no help from government in restructuring the industry.

In contrast to the position of the FEDC and DTI, West Germany has *no* industry-wide body concerned with the foundry sector beyond the trade and technical associations. Certainly, there are individuals in government with some knowledge of the foundry sector, but there is no foundries desk as in the UK DTI. Similarly, the tripartite NEDO has no direct equivalent in West Germany, although the whole basis of industrial policy is essentially corporatist, with clearly defined channels and representation for government, unions, and employers. One partial exception to this is the Industrie und Handelskamer—IHK. Whereas membership of TAs and RAs is voluntary, *all* West German firms are required by law to belong to the IHK, which broadly translates to a Chamber of Industry and Commerce. The general role of the IHK is to act as a regional focus for overseeing compliance with legislation covering employee welfare and rights, education and training, and so on.

Summary

From this brief overview it would appear that the stereotyped view of the difference between the two industries is confirmed. On the West German side, organization is orderly, with clear channels of communication and delineation of responsibility. By contrast, the UK presents a fragmented picture, with some considerable confusion even amongst involved agencies as to their role, or the extent of their representation and responsibility. Having said this we should note that the seeds of more coherent structures are present in the UK. Although historically an association representing iron founders, the BFA (British Foundry Association), is now beginning to recruit amongst non-ferrous foundries and may form the embryonic core of a more united trade association for the industry. Similarly, in research BCIRA has had 'cast iron' roots but is now referred to by the logo 'BCIRA', 'International Centre for Cast Metal Technology'. This change in name again opens the possibility for a single cast metals RA in the UK. These recent developments do not, of course, change our basic conclusions that the UK organizational map has been and remains more fragmented and complex than West Germany.

We should point out, however, that what we have drawn here is a simple map of organizational arrangements. What determines an industry's health, and policy outcomes, is the way in which the constituent elements of the organizational network, and key actors within it, respond to the industry's problems. At this level, we suggest that the German industry is still, and somewhat surprisingly, dominated by an independent, firm-centred culture, and it is here that the behaviour of the sector as a whole is shaped. Despite the best efforts of West German organizations to operate in a co-ordinated fashion, in the final analysis, the picture is one in which 'Jeder will sein Suppe kochen'—everyone wants to cook his own soup! In sharing this common characteristic, the sectors of the two countries tend to converge.

Government Policy Towards the Foundry Sectors

There are marked differences in the approaches taken by governments in the two countries towards the foundry industry. Although both have increasingly sought to regulate the industry in emission controls, health and safety, and environmental protection, on other matters there has been a far more interventionist pattern to UK government involvement. An identified problem in both UK and West Germany is that of reducing capacity in line with declining demand. In both countries, there is evidence of weak prices and poor financial performance which result from excess capacity. A major contributory factor to the problem is the 'stickability' of independent companies which we referred to above. In the UK, we describe below interventionist attempts to deal with the need for restructuring; in Germany, there is no parallel to this and market forces have been left to determine the size and structure of the foundry sectors. The interventionist approach is exemplified most clearly in two major attempts to restructure the UK industry, by means of the Foundry Aid Schemes (1975–81) and the Lazard rationalization schemes for steel castings (1982–3). As background, we should note that a feature of policy formation and development in the UK has been the willingness to regard the industry's activities as in some way of strategic significance and importance to the wider national economy. The degree of strategic importance attached to the industry in the UK outweighs its importance in employment terms. Thus the AMCM, in 1983, argued that castings manufacturers were the backbone of British industry and that this multitude of companies served a vital strategic need which had to be supplied domestically if the manufacturing economy were to be sustained.[27]

Statements such as these have often predicated arguments by the industry for selective government support in the UK. Although, in theory, in Germany, the DGV or the GDM could make a case for special assistance by the state, in practice this would be unsuccessful, because it is too small a branch of the economy.[28] What direct intervention there is (and Germany has no tradition of sector-specific programmes) has gone on the larger sectors, such as shipbuilding and steel. In the view of the DGV, support from central government is largely a function of the importance of employment. Thus, the ferrous foundry industry, with some 70,000 employees, is already relatively small and fragmented. The prospect of job losses through closures and a lack of planned rationalization are, bluntly, not thought sufficiently important to warrant direct support. This lack of numerical importance, combined with the encompassing of foundry interests within broader groupings, and the national predilection for a social market approach, has led to the specific absence of selective assistance for foundries in Germany. By contrast, in the UK, specific and selective support has been available in the last decade.

From 1972–9 the UK industry's problems were largely perceived as related to cyclical fluctuations of output. This optimism begins to give way in 1978–9 to the view, given ultimate expression by the Foundries EDC demand forecasts in 1982, that the decline in demand for castings is permanent and irreversible. In the earlier period, and specifically from 1975–81, the ferrous and non-ferrous castings sectors received selective assistance under Labour's sector aid schemes. Under the Industrial Strategy Programme, foundries could qualify for 25 per cent grants for investment in new equipment, 15 per cent for new buildings, and also obtain soft loans for the rationalization of activities between companies. The schemes were offered under Section 8 of the 1972 Industry Act and provisions were made for some £80 million of aid for ferrous and £20 million for the non-ferrous sectors. In the event, by 1980–1, the schemes were substantially underspent, with £46 million committed in ferrous and £12 million in non-ferrous castings.[29]

The aim of selective assistance was not to increase capacity, but to promote the process of restructuring and rationalization, thereby creating a strong and efficient core-group of foundry companies. This view that the 'good' would drive out the 'bad' has to a large extent been confounded by events. First, large numbers of companies applied for and received support. This has led to the accusation that, in implementing the aid schemes, the DTI did not discriminate sufficiently between companies, and was not critical enough of companies' future market projections. The onset of recession in 1978–9 certainly caused much of the underspend on the schemes and by the early 1980s the schemes were being blamed by the industry for exacerbating excess capacity problems. A broad conclusion on the exercise of selective intervention in the UK is that, in the implementation stage, it was insufficiently selective. The 'rules of the game', as operated by the DTI, implied fair and equal treatment to individual private sector companies, yet the critical requirement of a situation where demand in the customer sectors was beginning to collapse was the willingness to discriminate and direct support towards the best-equipped plants. Secondly, the recession has often driven out 'good' rather than 'bad'. In short-term desperation many companies tended to underprice products, thus depriving well-equipped companies of work, and precipitating the closure of high quality foundries.

Analysis of the problems of the foundry sectors in the early 1980s has emphasized the need for 'orderly' or 'planned' restructuring of capacity to meet demand. The most significant steps in this direction have occurred in the steel castings sectors where two schemes received government support in 1982–3. SCRATA played an important analytic and catalytic role in the early stages of development of these schemes; and the merchant bank, Lazard, undertook an arms-length negotiating role with individual companies. Steel casters were required to participate as 'openers' or 'closers'; companies choosing to remain open would compensate closers for lost turnover over a five-year period. Under these general arrangements, in March 1982, in the high alloy steel casting sector, five of sixteen companies, around 22 per cent of participating tonnage, were closed with a loss of 400 jobs. In February 1983, Lazard Bros. announced a further scheme for general steel casters in which twelve participating foundries agreed to close ten of their twenty-two foundries and eliminate 25,000 tonnes of annual capacity, with a loss of 1,800 jobs. In both schemes, the Department of Trade and Industry provided assistance towards closure costs.[30]

It is worth noting that government support for these schemes was forthcoming in an era when stated government policy was to work with the grain of market forces. In this context, the Lazard schemes were viewed as self-help exercises on the part of the industry and thus worthy of national government support. A more detailed analysis of the genesis of the schemes would also point to the importance of an informal policy network, including the British Steel Corporation (with substantial steel casting interests), the Bank of England, and the Conservative government, which created a favourable political climate for government support. In a similar way to the Foundry Aid Schemes, the Lazard proposals are widely judged to have failed.[31] A major factor here has been the continued decline in demand for steel castings (1983–5), which has left the openers with continued problems of excess capacity and uneconomic operation. Following the perceived failure of Lazard's, in the autumn of 1984, government attitudes shifted from the stance of self-help of the early 1980s to no help.[32]

Reviewing the last decade of government policy towards the industry, the clear British tendency for a more interventionist approach emerges. On the West German side, the industry has faced pressures for rationalization similar to those experienced in the UK, although smaller in magnitude. The main difference is the *laissez-faire* approach of the German government towards the industry. German foundry companies and the trade associations have shown considerable interest in the Lazard schemes, which have been discussed, for example, in the Europe-wide CAEF forum. But the preference for the market approach, and, importantly, a stricter and more literal interpretation of anti-cartel legislation, has prevented development of Lazard-type organized restructuring schemes in Germany.

Conclusions

The organizational mapping undertaken in this chapter conforms broadly to pluralist-corporatist distinctions discussed widely in the political science literature. Following Streeck,[33] in the UK, pluralist systems feature (*inter alia*) multiple and competitive interest representation, voluntarism, and 'unit multiplicity'. Corporatist structures (more typical of Germany), by contrast, contain a limited number of non-competitive organizations, well supported by membership and recognized by government, with representational monopoly and 'unit singularity'. The large, encompassing institutions of Germany are contrasted with narrow, highly specific, sectional associations in the UK. More orderly and planned structures also have a more intimate and dependent relationship with the state. In similar vein, Dyson and Wilks's work on comparative industrial culture argues that German companies are more likely to view themselves as enmeshed in institutional interests, whereas, in the UK, the development of industrial association is impeded by the self-sufficient firm.[34] To a large extent, these broad findings seem well confirmed in the UK and German foundry sectors. There are, however, difficulties and, in particular, two important paradoxes we need to discuss.

First, when viewed from the level of the individual foundry company, the picture of the two national sectors begins to converge. A common set of worries among foundries includes cheap imports, the potential impact of environmental legislation, a breakdown of price discipline, and relatively poor financial performance. At company level, the independence and self-sufficiency of foundry companies in both countries is also a common factor. To an extent, this independent role tends to be forced by the economic realities facing companies with no end-products and little market power. The following quotation is from a German iron founder but it could equally well have originated in the UK:

the (German) foundry industry may not be saying 'No!' to its customers as often as it might . . . but the problem is that *it is not a united industry* and customers can play one firm off against another . . . increases in material and overhead costs should be, but are not being passed on . . . every year the industry gets weaker.

In this light we are tempted to hypothesize on the effects on German organizations of a collapse in customer demand, similar to that which has occurred in the UK. Under this 'what if?' scenario, we would speculate that hitherto quite centralized bodies would fragment under pressure from individual companies, and form sub-sectors seeking to gain independent access to government. Certainly, as the pressures of decline have intensified in the UK, the identity of interest between individual companies and the industry has become increasingly dislocated. We suspect that similar pressure in Germany would lead to a similar splinter effect. Having said this, the existing trio of German associations (the DGV, GDM, and VDG), which has been described to us as a close-knit club, does offer specific current advantages to the German industry. Not least of these is the ability to promote a co-ordinated and common image for the industry. There is no counterpart to this in organizational or functional terms in the UK.

A second paradox relates to government-industry relations. The corporatist model assumes sound and developing links; the pluralist model, a set of inconsistent and weak relationships with government, involving a multiplicity of interest groups. In contrast to this, we have found strong and developing links to government in the UK and an arms-length and generalized relationship only in West Germany. As Reynolds argues in his review of the UK castings sectors:

It is interesting to speculate on whether the British situation has been adversely influenced by too jealous a regard for sectional boundaries. This may be true at the R & D level but in many other respects Britain could show evidence of a corporate awareness as tangible as might be found anywhere else. There may be no single trade association but there is no shortage of channels through which government might be addressed, assuming the industry can agree a strategy for survival.[35]

Reynolds explains this enhanced corporate awareness with reference to UK's distinctive industry-wide bodies, such as the Foundries EDC. The FEDC has certainly been a forum for discussion and produced distinctive industry-wide analysis of policy issues. Implementation has not, however, been on an industry-wide basis and the overall impact of interventionist policies has been patchy. We would argue that the influence of organizations on policy outcomes emerges most clearly and significantly at a more fine-grained level of analysis. Within the UK, for example, SCRATA, a combined trade and research association, played an important catalytic role in winning government support for rationalization. That no such schemes emerged in iron castings, in spite of equally severe excess capacity, relates in large part to the split between technical and trade support between the BFA and BCIRA, and a consequent lack of creative and technically based input into the policy development process. Pluralist structures do not, then, prevent close relationships being established between industry and government. What they do, however, is to ensure that links will tend to be particularized and that the effects of policy intervention will be inconsistent between sectors.

Reynolds speaks (above) of a strategy for the industry. As we have seen, strategic arguments have often been advanced in the UK by sectional interest groups. From the German viewpoint, a clear finding is that foundries are unlikely to be considered 'strategic' or discussed outside of their industrial context. In this sense, foundry activity is not seen as an end in itself but more as a means to achieving broader-based manufacturing efficiency. Reinforcing this 'objective' view of the sector's contribution is the widespread acceptance by the industry in Germany that, in employment terms, it is relatively insignificant and cannot realistically hope for sector-specific support.

We are left with the overarching question of why the German foundry sectors have performed better than the industry in UK. Is organizational solidarity a factor which assists economic performance, or is it a symptom of superior performance? We would argue that the answer is yes, on both counts. Fragmentation in the UK leads to some dilution of organizational effort, whereas in Germany there is a consistency of purpose which is to the advantage of the industry in trade and technical matters. We reassert, however, that organizational solidarity in Germany could conceivably break down under a process of decline similar to that experienced in the

UK. In a sense, UK organizations and the industry are living through a vicious circle of decline which tends to reinforce a historically fragmented picture; relative industrial stability in Germany has given a stability to the organizational map, which serves to reinforce industry performance.

We are, in fact, concluding by returning to the nature of the 'industry' itself and the economic realities which bear upon companies. In much of the chapter we have spoken somewhat loosely of the industry; in reality we are speaking of a conglomeration of industries where disjointed interests are likely to become more pronounced as the financial and economic pressures of manufacturing decline assert themselves.

Notes

1. National Economic Development Office (NEDO). Foundries Economic Development Committee, 'Re-structuring: Results of Consulting the Industry' (September 1984). 'Assessment of Current Capacity Utilisation in UK Foundries' (October 1983), unpublished papers.
2. NEDO, *Industrial Review to 1977, Iron and Steel Castings* (London: NEDO, 1974).
3. For evidence on this see, for example, I. J. Smith, and M. J. Taylor, 'Take-over, Closures and the restructuring of the UK iron foundry industry', *Environment and Planning A* 15 (1983), pp. 639–61; and West Midlands County Council, Economic Development Committee, *The West Midlands Foundry Sector* (December 1982).
4. NEDO, Foundries Economic Development Committee, 'Assessment of Future Demand for UK Castings' (February 1984), unpublished paper.
5. Ibid.
6. F. M. Scherer, *Industrial Market Structure and Economic Performance*, 2nd edn. (New York: Rand-McNally, 1980), pp. 212–14.
7. Inter-Company Comparisons, *Business Ratio Reports* (London, 1986).
8. NEDO, Foundries Economic Development Committee, 'International Competitiveness' (October 1983), unpublished paper.
9. NEDO, Foundries Economic Development Committee, 'Investigation of Best Manufacturing Practice' (January 1985), unpublished paper.
10. M. Panic, *The UK and West German manufacturing industry, 1954–72* (London: NEDO, 1976).
11. See J. Bessant and M. Grunt, *Management and Manufacturing Innovation in the UK and West Germany* (Aldershot: Gower, 1985), for a detailed review of these arguments.

12. B. H. Tripp, *The Joint Iron Council 1945–66* (London: Allen & Unwin, 1966).

13. 'Benchmark Inquiry into iron foundries, 1983', Statistics Division, Department of Trade and Industry, *British Business*, 19 July 1985.

14. Press release, 'The Backbone of British Industry', *Association of Major Castings Manufacturers* (Secretaries, Heathcote and Colemon, Birmingham, 31 March 1985).

15. 'A New Voice for the British Castings Industry', Editorial, *Foundry Trade Journal*, 16 June 1983.

16. Interview with regionally-based UK iron founding association.

17. NEDO, Foundries EDC, *Small Craft Foundries: their present role and future prospects* (London: NEDO, 1980), p. 35.

18. J. A. Rogers, 'Aid to the UK Die-casting Industry', *Foundry Trade Journal*, 24 April 1986.

19. N. M. V. Rothschild, 'The Organisation and management of government R & D' in *Framework for Government R & D*, Cmnd. 4814, xxxv, 1971.

20. BCIRA, *Annual Report*, 1977–8.

21. SCRATA, *Annual Report*, 1983.

22. I. Rodger and P. Cartwright, 'Merger Plan takes place for research', *Financial Times*, 12 May 1985.

23. *The Foundry Worker*, Journal of the AUEW(F), 26 March 1983.

24. NEDO, 1974, op. cit. (n. 2).

25. NEDO, Foundries EDC, 'Next Steps' (November 1983), unpublished paper.

26. K. Gooding, 'Aid Schemes for the Industry', *Financial Times*, 22 March 1978.

27. AMCM Press release (see n. 14).

28. Interview with German trade association deputy director.

29. For more details of these schemes see C. Baden-Fuller and R. Hill, *The Case of the Lazard scheme for UK Steel Castings* (London Business School, August 1984).

30. J. T. Lambert, 'Ferrous Foundry Industry Scheme, an assessment of the effects of selective assistance', Department of Trade and Industry, Government Economic Service Working Paper No. 77 (London, 1985).

31. See, for example, M. Brown, 'Sad Story of how to profit out of closing, scheme to cut steel castings capacity has flopped', *The Guardian*, 21 February 1984.

32. This shift of policy is evidenced by the unpublished response of the DTI to FEDC queries on further government support for restructuring schemes, Autumn, 1984.

33. W. Streeck, *Industrial Relations in West Germany, A case study on the car industry* (London: Policy Studies Institute, Heinemann, London, 1984). See, for example, p. 137.

34. K. Dyson and S. Wilks (eds.), *Industrial Crisis: A Comparative Study of the State and Industry* (Oxford: Martin Robertson, 1983).
35. J. A. Reynolds, 'Precision Forming: A Policy Study, The Prospects for Metal Castings in Britain', commissioned by SERC and DTI, January 1982, unpublished paper.

9

The Implementation and Effectiveness of MITI's Administrative Guidance

Takashi Wakiyama

This chapter aims to reveal the nature and effectiveness of administrative guidance given by the Ministry of International Trade and Industry (MITI) of Japan, in the process of its implementation of industrial policy in the post-war era. Although this topic has been extensively discussed in academic and administrative circles, both domestic and abroad, many things have yet to be clarified, partly because administrative guidance is often conducted behind the scenes in the form of a series of delicate actions, and detailed information is seldom made available to outside observers. Thus, in the view of some observers, MITI's administrative guidance is as omnipotent as Aladdin's lamp: any difficult problem being solved simply by a MITI official's phone call to a company executive, as if MITI were a chief executive officer of 'Japan Inc.'. In this chapter the author intends to correct such misconceptions.

Following the definition of administrative guidance, its necessity and effectiveness will be discussed in the light of the author's experience of working for many years for MITI.

Definitions

Administrative guidance is defined as an administrator's action, without any coercive legal effect, which encourages related parties to act in a specific way in order to realize some administrative aim.[1]

Several points need to be clarified. First, administrative guidance does not have a coercive legal effect; it influences the related party only on a *de facto* basis. An interesting case in this connection is the Japanese automakers' 'voluntary' export restraint to the US, which was implemented in the 1981–5 period, as a result of MITI's guidance. At that time, it was essential to prevent extraterritorial application of the US anti-trust legislation on the grounds of the Foreign Compulsion Doctrine.[2] MITI, therefore, publicly emphasized that, if administrative guidance should fail to secure manufacturers' compliance, it would use its legal power, provided by the Foreign Exchange and Foreign Trade Control Law, to assure complete compliance, and that it would expect to avoid anti-trust litigation by promising this contingency action. The US Department of Justice endorsed this expectation of MITI. In essence, this is a rare instance where administrative guidance, contrary to its standard definition, was officially declared to be compulsory. Despite this exception, there is no disagreement among commentators on the definition of administrative guidance *de jure*. The real controversy in this regard is to what extent the affected party feels obligated to comply with the guidance on a *de facto* basis. The author intends to discuss this issue as the central issue of this article.

Secondly, in most cases, administrative guidance is implemented without specific legislative jurisdiction. Three points need to be clarified on this matter. Initially the guiding agency does have general jurisdiction, as long as its action remains within the framework of its overall organizational terms of reference. For example, MITI's Automobile Division is empowered to take necessary measures to promote the automobile industry; what is usually missing is specific legislation authorizing particular administrative guidance. Furthermore, in some cases, a law specifically empowers a particular agency to take non-binding measures, such as a recommendation or guidance. For example, a MITI minister is empowered to make a necessary recommendation to modify the petroleum supply plan submitted by a refinery, pursuant to the Petroleum Industry Law of 1962. These legally stipulated, non-binding measures should also be regarded as administrative guidance. Finally, in the process of the execution of legal powers, the administrator in charge frequently advises the related party to carry out their regulatory job efficiently. For example, when a utility company wishes to raise its tariff rates, both MITI and the company prefer to discuss the permissible margin of increase prior to the final execution of MITI's legal power. The discussion, before an application is submitted, is normally expected to be more candid, while discussion after a submission may be more rigid, and less likely to lead to a compromise. It is doubtful whether the guidance given during the pre-application discussion should fall within the definition of administrative guidance. In the author's view, such guidance constitutes a part of the implementation of legal power and should not be termed as administrative guidance. In most literature, however, this type of guidance is also considered to be administrative guidance.

Thirdly, administrative guidance needs to be a legitimate act of an administrative agency. Important administrative guidance is made pursuant to the decision of the Ministry's Director-Generals' meeting; less important guidance is made on the basis of the decision of the responsible Director-General or division head. However, when an officer below the level of division head gives advice, it is sometimes difficult to know whether the officer is acting as a representative of the division he belongs to, or is simply voicing his personal feelings. For this reason, although the definition of administrative guidance is not controversial, its actual identification is often difficult. Even a responsible division head cannot confidently tell how many times his division gave administrative guidance in the recent past. This obscurity makes a quantitative analysis of administrative guidance difficult, and attracts criticism for its occasional lack of accountability.

Administrative guidance is extensively made, not only by MITI but by many other ministries and agencies; and by local as well central government agencies. MITI's guidance is the most well-known because MITI's administration is closely watched by foreign observers, and MITI relies on it more heavily than other agencies, and more than its other policy tools.

The Necessity for Administrative Guidance

Despite the lack of the ability to coerce, MITI has relied heavily on administrative guidance for several reasons. In the first place, MITI's other policy tools, such as legal power and subsidy, which can be used to enforce its policies, are limited when compared to its extremely wide jurisdiction. It encompasses a wide range of industries from retail shops to steel manufacturing. In many cases where something has to be done, the only method MITI can use is administrative guidance. Therefore, Chalmers Johnson argues that:

During the 1950's administrative guidance was rarely mentioned in connection with MITI's actions because most of its orders, permissions, and licenses were then firmly based on explicit control laws. Administrative guidance came to be openly practiced and discussed during the 1960's, and then only because MITI lost most of its explicit control powers as a result of liberalization and the failure to enact the Special Measures Law. In a sense, administrative guidance was nothing more than a continuation by MITI of its established practices through other means.[3]

A brief description of each of MITI's policy tools, other than administrative guidance, is provided below, mainly to demonstrate their relatively limited availability and concessionality. For relevant statistics and supplementary information, particularly on legal power and subsidy, see the Appendix to this chapter.

The general consensus in the Japanese administration is that MITI's legal power base is much weaker than the other major ministries. However, an official report, submitted to the Diet in 1981, claimed that MITI's legal powers number more than 2,000, second only to the Ministry of Transportation. According to the author's count, this is partly because MITI's legal powers have increased by more than 40 per cent since 1966, while the legal powers of the Japanese government as a whole have stayed almost constant. Such a dramatic increase was caused by the increased need for consumer protection, industrial safety, environmental protection, and energy policy. Subsidy, on the other hand, has never been a major policy tool of MITI in its post-war history, at least in terms of its total size of budget appropriation. MITI's subsidy budget is one of the smallest among the major ministries of Japan, accounting for only 1.6 per cent of the total General Account subsidy and 4.7 per cent of the total Special Accounts subsidy in FY 1984.

The FILP (Fiscal Investment and Loan Programme) continues to be a major tool of industrial policy in terms of its volume of operations. MITI has constantly controlled about 30 per cent of all the FILP funds channelled through about fifteen semi-governmental entities, such as the Japan Development Bank, Export–Import Bank of Japan, and Small Business Finance Corporation, in the form of loan, loan guarantee, or equity investment. Its importance in terms of the concessionality of the assistance, however, has been declining particularly during the period of easy money supply since the late 1970s.

Tax incentives were an important policy tool of MITI until the early 1970s but have not been in recent years. Government policy is now to scale down gradually these incentives to reduce chronic fiscal deficit and to ease the growing public sentiment against these measures.

A second reason for relying on administration guidance is that, since business conditions change frequently, policy implementation also needs to be timely and flexible. A lengthy legislative process may not be completed in time and, once enacted, legislative action is often too rigid to meet changing industrial needs. As the problems of industry are often complex and delicate, a ready-made, formal solution provided by legislation does not necessarily help, while administrative guidance, with its informal nature, can provide a timely, tailor-made solution.

A third consideration is that the industries under MITI's control are relatively well-endowed with financial resources and are not necessarily eager to obtain the government's financial assistance. In many cases, they only need someone's initiative and leadership, which MITI is prepared to provide in the form of administrative guidance.

Fourthly, the typical tasks addressed by administrative guidance during the period of rapid economic growth were the avoidance of short-term, excessive competition within a particular industry, or the construction of a large-scale production facility without causing over-supply at the time of completion. Although such purposes could be achieved by forming a cartel with the authorization of the Fair Trade Commission, administrative guidance was usually preferred because of its speedy execution.

These types of problems were normally solved through bilateral discussion between MITI and the industry concerned, without inviting any serious objections or intervention from other groups in the country. Administrative guidance was very suitable for this type of bilateral problem. In the period of recent slower economic growth, however, problems have become so complicated that opinions of affected groups outside industry need to be taken more fully into account.

The more frequent interventions by politicians in recent years are mainly attributable to stronger pressure by small- and medium-sized firms facing a more severe business climate. Since such firms exist in large numbers, their vote-pulling power has always been appreciated by politicians of all parties. Politicians' interventions, inspired by electoral considerations, are tilted toward protectionism, often at the cost of economic efficiency, as exemplified by the following measure. In 1977, the Law Concerning Adjustment of Large Enterprises' Business to Retain the Business Opportunity of Small/Medium Scale Enterprises was enacted to empower the MITI Minister to make the necessary recommendation to a large enterprise if its expanded business caused or threatened to cause disruption of small or medium-sized firms' business. The Minister's legal power has never been used, but the possibility of using the power has acted as an effective deterrent when MITI resorts to administrative guidance to persuade a large firm to give up such expansion. One further factor is that socialist politicians tend to intervene at the request of labour unions in depressed industries or companies.

Although intervention had been visible even during the period of rapid economic growth, as exemplified by coal mining, it has recently become more frequent in many other depressed industries.

Fifthly, administrative guidance was facilitated by the fact that, during the period of rapid economic growth, every company had a chance to benefit. Even if an unlucky company was given a slightly smaller chance to benefit, as a result of administrative guidance, it did not constitute a life-and-death problem. Therefore, MITI's persuasion was relatively easy to accept.

The Implementation Process

The processes of formulating and implementing policies by administrative guidance is essentially the same as with the implementation of other types of MITI's industrial policy. If the policy issue is important and has an impact on many divisions and departments within MITI, the content of guidance is discussed and decided on by a regular meeting of all the Director-Generals of Bureaux, possibly in the presence of the Minister. If the issue involves the petrochemical industry, for example, the division in charge of refineries is likely to have a say from the viewpoint of the supply of naptha, a major petrochemical feedstock; so is the division in charge of pollution control, from the viewpoint of environmental protection. Any disagreement within the Ministry has to be sorted out before implementing the guidance in accordance with normal intra-ministerial procedures. If the issue is less important, a final decision is made by a Director-General, after listening to a proposal made by a division head. A number of operational issues on a day-to-day basis, however, are dealt with by division heads whose identity is usually unknown, even to MITI officials outside the division.

The way MITI decides on the content of guidance differs from case to case. Officials, however, rarely 'invent' the content and attempt to unilaterally 'impose' it on the industry. It is unanimously believed by officials that such high-handed leadership would not work, in view of the nature of administrative guidance. For the content of guidance to be acceptable and convincing to the industry, it must have some foundation in the industry's thinking. As will be explained in the following section, in some cases MITI's guidance attempts to represent a unanimous or a majority view of the industrial circle, or, at least, it needs to reflect one of the noticeable views of the industry. Therefore, for the success of administrative guidance, it is essential that officials understand well the current situation of the industry, and the view of various groups in the industry. Such knowledge can be obtained only through constant and close contact, and the candid exchange of views with businessmen.

In some cases, MITI seeks the opinion of an advisory body, consisting of such persons as industry representatives, professionals, and consumer and user representatives. This advisory procedure is sometimes statutory but is, in many cases, self-imposed by MITI. Seeking their opinion, MITI usually makes proposals or suggestions which tend to influence the course of their discussions.

If administrative guidance concerns the jurisdiction of other ministries and agencies, they need to be consulted. Such consultation, for example, has taken place frequently between MITI and the Fair Trade Commission, particularly when the issue concerns supply–demand adjustment. This controversial relationship will be discussed in a later section. Local government is occasionally guided, either as an implementing agent of MITI's policy (for example, in the case of policies for small and medium-sized firms, or as an organization directly affected by policy such as the siting of nuclear power plants).

Guidance is communicated to a responsible executive officer of the guided organization either orally or in a written document. As will be discussed later, oral communication is prone to lead to obscurity. Guidance is, however, seldom imposed unilaterally; it usually requires a continuing process of persuasion and negotiations. As the flexibility of implementation is a major advantage of administrative guidance, MITI officials are generally prepared to compromise, at least, concerning the details of guidance, without sacrificing an essential element of their objectives. When many firms are guided simultaneously, bargaining among the guided firms is also necessary.

MITI normally does not deal directly with large shareholders, labour unions, or banks, any of which may have a strong influence on a company's management. Company executives are left to persuade them. If they have objections to MITI's position, company executives convey these back to MITI. This procedure is not unique to administrative guidance but common for every instrument of industrial policy. MITI does not deem it productive to talk to those who do not have day-to-day contact with the Ministry, and therefore, have not established the rapport which is necessary for candid discussion. This indirect communication has not, so far, proved a major disadvantage.

MITI's administrative guidance is given to (a) individual firms,

(b) industry trade associations, (c) non-profit organizations related to industrial activities, or (d) local government, depending on its objective. The cases (a) and (b), which are generically referred to as 'industry' in this paper, constitute a dominant majority. A trade association is either a direct guidee or a communication channel between MITI and individual firms. If the industry comprises numerous firms, MITI cannot deal with them directly: communication through an association is the only choice. Sometimes, MITI prefers to negotiate through an association, if association executives are sympathetic to MITI's policy objectives, and competent enough to act as good mediators. Generally speaking, officials of trade associations tend to welcome the success of administrative guidance particularly when guidance calls for the industry's concerted action. Since such an action strengthens the position of the association executives, they are usually willing to help MITI persuade member companies. As will be mentioned later, the Tokyo High Court, in September 1980, prohibited MITI from using a trade association as a channel of administrative guidance for supply–demand adjustment because such a method is likely to lead to conspiracy.

Effectiveness

By definition, as well as in the light of MITI's experience, the major disadvantage of administrative guidance is the lack of ability to enforce its policy aim. A great deal of effort is needed on the part of officials to persuade industry along the lines of its policy objectives. Like many other aspects of Japanese society, without a prolonged process of forming consensus between MITI and the industry, as well as within the industrial circle, administrative guidance cannot achieve its target. MITI considers sabre-rattling or arm-twisting most undesirable, since it would harm long-term relations with industry.

This section examines under what circumstances industries can be effectively persuaded to respect MITI's guidance. For this purpose, administrative guidance needs to be classified from various viewpoints. First, it can be classified in accordance with its relationship to other policy tools. There are broadly four possibilities here. The first is that administrative guidance is sometimes made in conjunction with the execution of more powerful policy tools. As argued above, the author doubts the rationale of regarding guidance in the process of legal power execution as administrative guidance. With this reservation, this type of guidance is exemplified by the guidance given to a utility company which wishes to revise its tariff rates, as explained previously. Guidance is also given in connection with financial assistance. For example, from 1974 to 1977, computer manufacturers received aid in the form of grants to strengthen their technological ability. At that time, MITI considered it essential to provide aid to a consortium of companies carrying out a joint research project rather than to assist individual companies. Therefore, as a prerequisite for providing such aid, MITI persuaded the companies concerned to form three research consortia. When administrative guidance is not an isolated action but armed with other powerful tools, it is usually effective. The effectiveness, however, is attributable to the power of the other tools, not to the power of administrative guidance *per se*.

In a few controversial cases, administrative guidance is made under the disguise of legal power execution, on the basis of a dubious interpretation of the law. For example, according to the Petroleum Industry Law of 1962, the only legal requirement for those who wish to start an oil import business is to report pertinent matters to MITI. The law does not empower MITI to stop them from starting the business. In practice, however, if some company wishes to start an importing business, it has been MITI's policy to refuse to receive such a report and to persuade the company to give up its business plan, arguing that only fully experienced importers can meet domestic demand properly. In this case, MITI faces a difficult situation because it has to persuade a company unknown to it, on a dubious legal justification, without any bargaining chip for persuasion. Recently, MITI had prolonged disputes with gasoline retailers who insisted on starting the business of gasoline importation.

Likewise, those who wish to start a gasoline retail business are obligated to register at MITI, which is not legally entitled to refuse such registration as long as certain legally specified conditions are met. MITI, however, has often refused registration and tried to persuade the applicant to give up the plan, arguing that the existence of too many gasoline stations might cause waste of gasoline. So far, at least two persons have started a retail business despite denial of registration. MITI sued them and both cases were subsequently settled out of the court.

A second possibility is of administrative guidance armed with other powerful tools only as a last resort. As explained above, the so-called voluntary restraint of automobile export to the United States, from 1981 to 1984, was made as a consequence of administrative guidance. MITI made it public, however, that should its guidance fail to work, it would use its legal power to limit exports. Thus, legal power was declared to be a last resort, potentially available if necessary, but dormant under normal circumstances. Another example is the Petroleum Industry Law, which empowers MITI to request refineries to modify their annual supply plans. In practice, however, instead of making a formal request, MITI has always relied on administrative guidance, because its informal and flexible nature has been considered more desirable in the light of the delicate and changing market conditions. Knowing that a sword was hanging on the wall, the companies had no other choice but to respect MITI's guidance.

A third case is where administrative guidance is supported, as a lever of persuasion, by other, more powerful policy tools which are only partially or indirectly related to the purpose of guidance. This type, which constitutes the majority of cases, typifies MITI's administrative guidance. A well-known example of this type of administrative guidance is that made in 1965 to a steel manufacturer to curb its production, in order to prevent excessive supply. When the company expressed its objection, MITI threatened to cut the company's import quota of coking coal and finally persuaded the company to follow its request. Although the supply of coking coal is essential to steel production, MITI's power to allocate imports is only partially related to the issue in question of curtailing production. Likewise, MITI's adjustment of capital investment in the petrochemical and other industries using imported technologies was made through its legal power to license technology imports. In many other cases, the loans of public lending institutions, such as the Japan Development Bank, were also used as a lever. For example, in the late 1960s, MITI, supported by financial and tax incentives, persuaded the chemical industry to construct an ethylene plant producing more than 300,000 tons per year, and an ammonia plant producing more than 1,000 tons per day. Although such financial assistance, including tax incentives, is not necessarily large in amount, and is merely symbolic in many cases, it provides MITI with a useful lever in negotiating with the industry.

When MITI has a multifaceted relationship with the industry under question, it can easily find a lever, which may be only remotely related to the issue of administrative guidance. Therefore, the effectiveness of its guidance hinges on the good overall relationship with the industry. MITI's day-to-day efforts, over many years, to maintain close and extensive relationships with industry constitute the key to its success in administrative guidance.

The fourth possibility is the use of administrative guidance without any leverage. If no leverage is available, MITI's general prestige may be the only power it has over the industry. Generally speaking, this type of single-issue industry is the hardest to persuade. MITI, therefore, tends to refrain from guiding such an industry, unless there is compelling necessity, such as strong consumer pressure or public opinion. The examples of an oil importer and gasoline retailers, cited previously, testify to the difficulty of administrative guidance without a leverage.

It was suggested earlier that administrative guidence is made because other policy tools are not available. According to the argument in the preceding paragraph, however, without other policy tools which can be used as a leverage, administrative guidance is not feasible. This is a dilemma which has increasingly bothered MITI since the early 1960s, since the phasing out of other policy tools increases the necessity of administrative guidance but decreases its effectiveness.

An alternative approach to the classification of guidance is to examine the nature of policy objectives. We can consider the uniformity of objectives and the time-scale over which they are intended to be achieved. There is, initially, a distinction between uniform interests and divided interests. The effectiveness of administrative guidance differs, depending on whether the guidance pursues an objective recognized to be beneficial to every party concerned or an objective beneficial to some but costly to others. Even if every party concerned acknowledges the benefit of a particular measure, it is often difficult to put it into practice, sometimes simply due to lack of initiative. For example, suppose many toy manufacturers are making toys which are selling well but suspected to be potentially hazardous to users. Under such circumstances, every manufacturer wishes it could stop making them, but does not wish to do so until its competitors do likewise. The only thing needed is someone's initiative. Administrative guidance is most effective in this type of situation, where there is unanimous consent, and even unanimous willingness. Actually, there are many such cases awaiting the government initiative. Once it has been made, its effectiveness and compliance are almost assured. In other cases, the majority group of an industry knows something is desirable but cannot put it into practice because of the minority's obstinate objection. Under such circumstances, the majority group can use MITI as a scapegoat to persuade the minority, saying that they have been overwhelmed by MITI insisting upon every party's compliance.

On the other hand, if the companies concerned have diverse views and interests, administrative guidance faces objections from various groups within the industry. Even if guidance is reasonable and equitable, the particular companies affected tend to discount any benefits and inflate the cost of acceptance. It is, therefore, conceivable that MITI's compromise solution might appear costly and unfair to every company concerned. Under such circumstances, again, it is the long-term and overall relationship between the company and MITI, not the short-term and specific situation, that finally induces the company to accept the guidance even reluctantly.

As a corollary of this conclusion, a homogeneously structured industry is more accomodating to administrative guidance than a heterogeneously structured industry, consisting of, say, large firms and small firms, early starters and recent starters, firms with a diversified line of business and undiversified, single-product firms, or efficient firms and inefficient firms. To achieve a policy purpose under such difficult circumstances, soft-handed policy tools, such as administrative guidance, are less effective than hard-handed tools equipped with enforcing ability.

There is a further distinction to be made between emergency needs and long-term needs. Administrative guidance which attempts to meet obvious, emergency policy needs is more effective than guidance which aims at meeting less obvious, long-term policy needs. In the case of an emergency, legislation cannot be made in time and administrative guidance, which may be the only solution, is usually effective, since it is backed by the strong support of public opinion. Starting shortly after the first oil crisis in 1973, emergency administrative guidance was provided for fifty-three consumer goods, until the end of September 1974, to curb hyper-inflation. At the time of the Iranian Revolution, MITI persuaded oil importers to refrain from scrambling for inflated Iranian oil, considering the importance of the Japan–US diplomatic relationship. Emergency protection against sudden, unexpected pollution or hazardous consumer goods are other examples.

Administrative guidance for long-term policy aims is exemplified by (a) capital investment adjustment to achieve future supply–demand balance or economies of scale; (b) protection of small firms from competition with big firms; and (c) prevention of sudden trade friction with major trade partners. Over such long-term policy objectives, public opinion is divided, as are industry's views, and persuasion is successful only after persistent efforts.

Finally, the effectiveness of guidance depends, in part, on the number of companies affected. Administrative guidance normally requires face-to-face persuasion, which is not feasible if there are many companies to be persuaded. MITI cannot deal with more than, say, twenty or thirty companies. When modernization of the weaving industry, consisting of about 65,000 small firms, was carried out, from 1967 to 1974, at MITI's initiative, legislation was provided to enforce the policy purpose, although a similar purpose was achieved by means of administrative guidance in the case of oligopolistic industries, such as the petro-chemical, fertilizer, chemical-fibre, and paper-pulp industries, in the same period. Although there are more than 50,000 gasoline stations in the country, MITI first attempted, starting in 1978, to persuade each of them through their trade association to close their business on Sundays and holidays to conserve energy. As this attempt subsequently turned out to be ineffective, a law was enacted in 1982 to provide the legal basis for this measure.

Administrative Guidance and Anti-Monopoly Regulations

The relationship between MITI and the Fair Trade Commission has not necessarily been cordial. The Commission has expressed its objections, from time to time, to MITI's adjusting the output of a particular industry to keep it in line with projected demand. It once expressed the view that MITI's bilateral guidance to each company was not illegal as long as companies did not talk among themselves. The theory was later supported by the Tokyo High Court in 1980, although it is unrealistic to expect companies affected by MITI's guidance not to talk among themselves. The Commission also expressed its view, in 1966, that MITI's guidance to adjust the volume of investment in production facilities and equipment was not illegal, because the purpose of anti-monopoly legislation is to ensure free competition in the supply of goods and services, and not in the investment in production facilities and equipment. As investment in production facilities and equipment does affect the future supply of goods and services, this theory appears to be unfounded. The Commission, therefore, reversed its view in 1978.

Generally speaking, until the late 1960s, the Commission was over-whelmed by MITI's eagerness, and reluctantly interpreted anti-monopoly laws and regulations leniently. Encouraged by strengthened public opinion in support of anti-monopoly administration, the Commission gradually became more rigorous in the 1970s and 1980s. In the meantime, as the economy slowed down, industry's enthusiasm regarding massive investment for the expansion of capacity, particularly in key intermediate materials industries, was replaced by investment in pollution-control and energy saving, which did not require MITI's intervention for the purpose of supply–demand adjustment. The investment in new, leading industries such as electronics has been bullish even after the oil crisis, but demand has been growing fast in these industries and administrative guidance has been unnecessary.

Because of the growing concern of public opinion in recent years, MITI's administrative guidance has been made in a more modest manner. For example, in 1975 and 1976, eight industries had to restrain their output because of excessive supply. At that time, MITI only announced its estimate for total demand and did not indicate each company's share, hoping that individual firms would cut their supply in the light of MITI's overall estimate. This so-called 'guideline method' was a new device designed in reaction to the more critical public sentiment in the last decade.

In September 1980, considering a case of alleged conspiracy by twelve oil companies, conducted in connection with MITI's administrative guidance, the Tokyo High Court concluded, among other things, the following:[4]

(a) MITI's bilateral guidance given to an individual firm is acceptable as long as companies do not talk among themselves;

(b) Administrative guidance should not direct each company's allotment, particularly on the basis of a uniform standard, such as pro rata, except when such guidance is really essential (the Court did not specify an 'essential' case);

(c) Administrative guidance should not be made through an industry's association, because such a method is likely to lead to a conspiracy within that industry.

This High Court judgment, as well as the subsequent Supreme Court judgment in February 1984, limited the rationale of administrative guidance to certain justifiable cases, although neither judgment clarified under what circumstances it was justified. Because of these judgments, MITI has become even more restrained and careful in implementing administrative guidance.

Although administrative guidance for supply–demand adjustment was frequently made in the 1960s, despite the Commission's reluctance, it appears fair to say that it did not harm consumers' interests intolerably because during that period inter-firm competition was so fierce that the guidance only reduced its excessiveness.[5]

Problems with Administrative Guidance

As might be expected, administrative guidance is not without its disadvantages. Lack of enforcing ability is the most serious drawback. Even when MITI's guidance was strongly backed up by the detailed legal powers provided, by the Petroleum Industry Act of 1962, one of the largest refining companies adamantly rejected MITI's guidance on the oil supply plan and price setting from 1963 to 1966. Even if the guided companies promise to follow MITI's guidance, whether they actually keep their promise depends solely on their good faith, in the absence of reliable methods of verification. In the process of the anti-monopoly trial by the Tokyo High Court cited above, it was revealed that many oil refining companies were secretly departing from MITI's guidance. The possibility of such cheating is another reason why persistent efforts to secure consensus are necessary. If companies promise something reluctantly, they feel tempted to cheat MITI, thus defying the aim of administrative guidance. Therefore, a less ambitious policy objective, which is willingly accepted by every party, is better than an ambitious one, which is only reluctantly accepted.

A series of problems also arise from the perspective of the company. As previously stated, administrative guidance is feasible only when every party concerned is satisfied that it gains something. Contrary to free competition, there should not be clear winners and losers. This requirement tends to penalize an efficient company and favour an inefficient one. Since administrative guidance is often made in a very informal manner, the responsibility of an executing officer or agency is not necessarily defined clearly. Guidance is sometimes made by issuing an official letter, but is often conveyed orally to the company executives concerned, sometimes in equivocal language, by a division head or senior staff working for him, without clarifying whether such guidance reflects MITI's official position.

Besides unclear accountability within MITI, accountability between MITI and a guided party may cause a problem. If guidance should turn out to be in error, who should be blamed, MITI or the guided party? As guidance is officially defined as not binding, MITI is entitled to claim *de jure* that the final decision was made by the guided party. From a viewpoint of moral or political accountability, however, this legal excuse is irrelevant, since the degree of coercion delicately differs from case to case. Unfortunately, no one has produced a convincing theory on how to define accountability in this broader sense. At the same time, intangibility can have advantages. Since companies usually have many business secrets, they are likely to prefer the details of administrative guidance to be kept confidential. From this viewpoint, a legislative action, which usually invites or requires more publicity than administrative guidance, is less desirable. This is particularly true when administrative guidance concerns an immediate sales plan, such as price or sales volume. To an advocate of 'Government in the Sunshine', however, such secrecy is unacceptable.

Conclusion and Future Prospects

Administrative guidance typifies MITI's industrial policy, particularly with regard to its flexible and advisory nature as well as to the necessity of consensus-formation. In view of the various advantages explained above, MITI will continue to rely on administrative guidance in the future. However, some of the conditions, which formerly enhanced its effectiveness have been changing. Since the slow-down of economic growth has made industrial problems more complex and less reconcilable, bilateral talk between MITI and the guided industry is no longer adequate. The more rigorous attitude of the Fair Trade Commission, as well as public sentiment, requires MITI to implement administrative guidance in a more cautious manner.

On the other hand, industrial policy objectives have become more diversified in the last decade or so. Increased policy needs for energy policy, R. & D. policy, adjustment for depressed industries, prevention of international trade friction, consumer protection, industrial safety, and environmental control have increased MITI's power base. Because of their complex nature, these newly emphasized policy purposes call for a variety of policy tools, including administrative guidance. The guidance for these recently highlighted purposes requires hard bargaining and tough decision-making among parties of different backgrounds, and invites severe criticism of third parties including public opinion.

Therefore, the implementation of administrative guidance, in the future, needs to be adapted to cope with new situations. First, administrative guidance should be made on the basis of a clear official decision of the responsible ministry, agency, bureau or division, depending on the importance of the issue. Second, to avoid obscurity, guidance should be conveyed in a written document, and not orally. Third, opinions of all the affected parties, as well as those of an objective third party where appropriate, should be sought thoroughly before implementing administrative guidance. Similar procedures were sometimes followed previously; for example, so-called discussion groups were formed for investment adjustment of the petrochemical industry and chemical fibre industry in 1964, for the paper-pulp industry in 1965, and ferro-alloy industry in 1966, and the various committees or sub-committees of the Industrial Structure Council, advisory body of MITI, were often convened to discuss aspects of certain industries. However, there was no firmly guaranteed procedure to adequately reflect opinions of all the parties concerned.

These proposed measures may partially sacrifice the advantages of administrative guidance, such as flexibility, informality, timeliness, and confidentiality. Such sacrifice, however, is a justifiable price to be paid for the continued successful implementation of administrative guidance under changing circumstances.

APPENDIX

MITI's Major Policy Tools—Legal Power and Subsidy

Legal Power

A legal power is defined as a power that is based on legislation. Although a legal power is usually supplemented or substantiated by decrees or regulations, it must have a legislative basis. Therefore, in the following analysis, only laws are looked at. To reveal the nature and characteristics of MITI's legal powers, they are classified into three categories: regulatory powers, promotional powers, and managerial powers. To simplify the analysis, any legal power stipulated by a regulatory law is defined to be a regulatory power, a legal power stipulated by a promotional law is considered to be a promotional power, and so forth. Regulatory laws are exemplified by the Petroleum Industry Law, Electric Utility Law, High Pressure Gas Control Law, Explosives Control Law, Consumer Products Safety Law, Household Goods Quality Labelling Law, and Credit Sales Law. Promotional laws provide the legal basis needed to encourage desirable industrial activities, even if the encouragement measures are mainly financial assistance or tax incentives. Promotional laws are exemplified by the Industrial Relocation Promotion Law, Small/Medium Enterprises Modernization Promotion Law, Electric Power Development Promotion Law, Coal Mining Industry Rationalization Law, and the Law for Promotion of Specified Machinery and Information Industries. Managerial laws concern the management and operation of government-managed systems (such as the Japan Industrial Standards), industrial property rights, and commodity exchanges.

On the basis of this classification, regulatory powers account for 47 per cent, promotional powers 35 per cent, and managerial powers 18 per cent of the total powers in 1982 (see Table 9.1).

To examine a historical trend, the same count was taken for 1966, a time when the extensive legal measures specifically designed to regulate the war-devastated economy had been mostly abolished, and an industrial policy geared for rapid expansion largely initiated. According to the author's count, MITI's legal powers increased by 44 per cent between 1966 and 1982. In particular, regulatory powers increased dramatically by 69 per cent, as shown in Table 9.1.

The factors underlying such a dramatic increase in regulatory powers

Table 9.1 Number of MITI's Legal Powers^a

Purpose	Promotional 1966	Promotional 1982	Regulatory 1966	Regulatory 1982	Managerial 1966	Managerial 1982	Total 1966	Total 1982	Rate of increase (%)
Consumer safety/Industrial safety/Environment	20	0	238	404	0	18	258	422	63
International trade	90	119	34	52	0	0	124	171	38
Industry	273	375	112	182	183	214	568	771	36
Small firms	180	219	13	28	0	2	193	249	29
Utilities	10	12	177	302	0	0	187	314	68
Industrial property	0	0	0	0	111	154	111	154	39
Total	573	725	574	968	294	388	1441	2081	44
(Energy)	NA	NA	NA	NA	NA	NA	(349)	(705)	102
Rate of increase (%)	–	27	–	69	–	32	–	44	
Share in each year	40	35	40	47	20	18	100	100	

^a Source: Tentative count by the author. The figures for 'Energy' are duplicated by other items. The years are Financial Years.

include the increased need for consumer protection, industrial safety, environmental protection, and energy policy. The powers relating to the first three items combined increased by 70 per cent, and the powers relating to energy policy almost doubled during the sixteen-year period under consideration.

The question may be asked, however, whether the dramatic increase explained above is in line with the general trend of the Japanese government as a whole during this particular period. Although the precise information is not available, the number of legal powers may be assumed to be approximately proportional to the number of laws in view of the statistical Law of Large Numbers. From this viewpoint, we note that the total number of laws in effect in July 1966 was 1,528, while the number of laws in effect in July 1983 was 1,518. The number of laws has not increased but rather decreased slightly. Therefore, the sharp increase of MITI's legal powers can be judged to be a unique feature of industrial policy.

Subsidy

MITI's share in the General Account subsidy budget[6] has been almost constant in the last two decades ranging from 1.1 to 1.8 per cent, but its share in the Special Account subsidy budget has increased from 2.0 per cent in 1975 to 4.7 per cent in 1984, mainly due to the increased allocation for energy policy (see Table 9.2). MITI's General Account subsidy budget was only about 11.7 per cent of the Ministry of Construction, 9.9 per cent of the Ministry of Agriculture, Forestry, and Fisheries, and 22.0 per cent of the Ministry of Transportation in 1984.

Local government and non-profit organizations receive most of the MITI's subsidy; particularly for electric power source development and regional development, local government is by far the largest recipient. In many cases of R. & D., consortia for companies jointly conducting the research receive the subsidy.

Notes

1. Michael K. Young, 'Judicial Review of Administrative Guidance: Governmentally Encouraged Consensual Dispute Resolution in Japan', *Colombia Law Review* 84: 3 (May 1984), pp. 923–83.

Table 9.2 Main Purposes of MITI Subsidy

Billion Yen, per cent in brackets

	Total	Energy		Electric Power Source	Small/Medium Firms	R. & D.	Regional Development	Aircraft & Computers
		Oil/Minerals	Coal					
1970	118.2	2.9	56.0	0	11.4	5.7	14.4	0.8
	(100)	(2.5)	(47.4)	(0)	(9.6)	(4.8)	(12.2)	(0.7)
1975	272.3	7.4	49.4	29.4	34.2	16.8	36.8	26.7
	(100)	(2.7)	(18.1)	(10.8)	(12.6)	(6.2)	(13.5)	(9.8)
1980	527.8	140.2	49.4	123.5	60.8	19.5	39.9	17.5
	(100)	(26.6)	(9.4)	(23.4)	(11.5)	(3.7)	(7.6)	(3.3)
1984	783.1	318.6	49.4	157.9	91.0	16.4	38.6	12.4
	(100)	(40.7)	(6.3)	(20.2)	(11.6)	(2.1)	(4.9)	(1.6)

2. According to the Foreign Compulsion Doctrine, any action forced by a foreign government is immune to litigation.

3. Chalmers Johnson, *MITI and the Japanese Miracle* (Stanford, Cal.: Stanford University Press, 1982), p. 226.

4. The concept of excessive competition puzzles economists. According to MITI, excessive competition is defined as such competition that is likely to harm the national economy by creating idle capacity or an unsold stock of goods. Because of lack of preconditions for an ideal free market function, such as labour and capital mobility, freedom of entry into and retreat out of the market, and immediate adjustment action, market mechanisms often fail to achieve the optimum allocation of resources, thus causing excessive or inadequate competition.

   In the author's view, so-called excessive competition in Japan was a by-product of the period of high economic growth. During that period, every company was bullish but wanted to do what other companies were doing. As demand continued to grow for many years, the surest way of making profits was to supply the product which other companies had been selling well. To do something original was unnecessary and risky.

5. Japan Industrial Policy Research Institute, *Gyosei-shido lo Dokusen-Kinshi-ho* (Administrative Guidance and Anti-Monopoly Law), Tokyo, June 1981.

6. The subsidy budget occupied about 29 per cent of the total General Account Budget of the Government in 1984, while MITI's subsidy occupied about 24 per cent of its total General Account budget.

Telecommunications and Government: the US Experience

——————— *Manley R. Irwin* ———————

Introduction

It belabours the obvious to observe that US telecommunications is undergoing a profound transition in technology, markets, and government policy. Consider recent developments in information technology: the number of components on a silicon chip doubles every eighteen months; satellite-receiving dishes retailing at $34,000 in 1980 are priced under $2,000 today; data modem speeds of 1200 bits per second in 1972 today approach 10,000 bits per second; fibre optic repeater distances of 8 kilometres in 1982 are projected to be spaces of 150 kilometres next year; video signal compression ratios of 15–1 in 1980 are expected to approach 1600–1 this year.

Or consider random developments in telecommunication facilities and services: 1984 saw the divestiture of the world's largest telephone system, American Telephone and Telegraph, from its Bell Operating Companies; IBM purchased an equity position in an interstate telecommunication company that some twenty years ago did not exist; Merrill Lynch resells excess capacity of its fibre optic network to clients in downtown Manhattan; a package courier service buys a communications satellite for document distribution (Federal Express); a retail chain offers voice, data, and video conferencing services, via its own communication network (Sears Roebuck); five midwest electric power utilities establish a communication subsidiary via a fibre optic network (Minnesota Power and Light); a private corporate network constructs a global integrated digital services facility (General Motors/Electronic Data Systems, Inc.).

Finally, consider developments in US telecommunications policy: the industry is experiencing massive realignment of basic exchange rates and toll telephone rates in the US; there is a splintering of communication policy among federal courts, the FCC, the Department of Justice, and the

White House; the Department of Defense classifies a digital telephone switching exchange as a national security product; for three decades, state utility commissions have opposed entry in telecommunication equipment and services; and regional telephone companies have yet to recover 26 billion dollars of outstanding depreciation expenses, primarily central office equipment.

These illustrations serve as a prelude to the following arguments. First, the triad of technology, markets, and government policy is increasingly complex and interrelated. Anyone possessing the temerity to assess the US telecommunication scene inevitably must come to grips with the dynamic interplay of the three. Secondly, technology and market forces dominate, or at least pace, the US telecommunication scene, by altering the cost/revenue calculations of firms in the industry. Stated differently, policy tends to be the US telecommunication tail: market forces the US telecommunications dog.

That is not to say that policy does not pose as a critical variable in the US scene. On the contrary, a jurisdictional regulatory war has erupted between the state and the federal government, and the economic stakes are crucial. The problem is that by the time regulatory issues are sorted out, technology upsets the apple cart by creating a market discontinuity that precipitates yet another regulatory crisis. Nowhere is technological discontinuity and public policy more apparent than in the 1984 divestiture of AT&T into seven separate holding companies, an unprecedented restructuring of telephone markets, assets, and organization. True, the modified final judgement, sanctioning the AT&T/Bell Operating Company breakup, is two years old. Yet many believe, and certainly the regional Bell Operating Companies insist, that the AT&T Consent Decree has been rendered null and void by technological change and unprecedented domestic and global market forces.

How can one place the development in US telecommunications in perspective? One attempt is to impose a set of time periods upon the industry's evolution and examine whether these stages shed any light as to future trends in the industry. That is the task of this paper. We divide the industry into three periods: 1880–1956, 1957–84, and post-1984. Within each period the interplay of technology, markets, and policies are explored.

We offer the following observations. First, information technology giveth and taketh. The interaction of technology and markets emerges as a key determinant in the ebb and flow of US policy and regulation. Technology may erect formidable barriers to market entry; technology can also can erode and dissipate those entry constraints. Secondly, regulation in the US appears to adhere to a cyclical institutional pattern. The telephone industry first experienced the rise and decline of regulation at the municipal jurisdiction. A similar cycle is now discernible at the state level of oversight. My own sense is that the US will inaugurate a cyclical contraction of economic regulation at the federal level. Finally, regulation persists as an unrelenting institution growing beyond its original natural monopoly premises. Public oversight merely assumes a new form. Yesterday, regulation found justification in scale economies; today, the new rationale is 'sensitive information'—technological 'haemorrhaging' to the Warsaw pact. Perhaps that observation overly embraces the life cycle theory of regulatory bodies. Nevertheless, the concept of the 'public interest' is sufficiently elusive and ill-defined for appeals to the national interest to be able to shift public policy away from choice and diversity toward state intervention and government surveillance. The US is presently agonizing over that policy juncture.

Period I—1876–1956: Economic Monopoly: Regulatory Stability

Period I begins with the origin of the telephone industry and its evolution into a regulated monopoly. This phase is somewhat arbitrary to the extent that it covers at least three generations of technological change.

Technology

Development in telecommunication transmission, switching, and customer equipment in Period I proceeded incrementally. The telephone instrument improved in quality, cost, and maintenance. Transmission facilities, evolved from open wire, buried cable, coaxial cable systems, and microwave relay, and were secured via loading coils, multichannel, and carrier systems. Switching apparatus evolved from manual to electro-mechanical switchboards. Direct distant dialling services spread throughout the US. The vacuum tube, the transistor, the integrated circuit, the transition from electro-mechanical technology to electronics proceeded within this eighty-year time-frame; and technology penetrated the telephone.network, first as components, then products, then finally as communications systems.

During Period I, the telephone industry exercised discretionary control over the state of the telecommunication art. Clearly, the award of the patent on the telephone instrument (1876) marked the origin of the industry. Subsequently, the original Boston Bell Patent Association added to its portfolio patents on a wide range of applications that sustained the company long after the original telephone patent expired in 1894.

In 1885, Theodore Vail formed AT&T as a vehicle to render interstate long distance calls. By the turn of the century, Bell's corporate reorganization converted AT&T to a parent telephone holding company. Bell's market supremacy was challenged by competition post-1900, but not in any fundamental sense. It is true that the invention of the vacuum tube did loom as a potential threat to Bell's investment in the terrestrial wire facilities. But AT&T countered by embarking on a programme of fundamental telephone research and, by 1924, the creation of the Bell Telephone Laboratory institutionalized corporate R. & D. as an ongoing strategy. The research activity of Bell Telephone Laboratories soon attained stature and pre-eminence. By 1956, BTL essentially paced developments in the state of the telecommunication art in the US, and perhaps the world at large. The US telecommunications industry both introduced new products and systems and controlled the retirement of obsolete equipment. For the Bell System, at least, Phase I could be described as one of technology supremacy.

Markets

Several characteristics persisted during this first time-frame. First, telephone service enjoyed a monopoly in terms of geography, equipment, and manufacturing. Telephony commenced as a local service, and, under the basic telephone patents, local Bell companies were assigned an exclusive geographic franchise by the parent firm. The introduction of toll telephone services began in the mid-1880s. By the turn of the century, AT&T's long distance and local exchange facilities dominated the industry; and Bell's toll facilities linked its regional exchange operations. Monopoly in long distance soon paralleled monopoly control in local service.

Secondly, the US communication market was divided into telephone and telegraph services. Having rejected an offer to purchase the basic telephone patent, Western Union Telegraph Company started a rival telephone company in 1877. But, in 1879, Bell Telephone and Western Union reached an accommodation. Western Union retreated into telegraphy and Bell was now free to develop the voice market. Telephone historians regard 1879 as the industry's Magna Carta.[1]

Thirdly, the manufacture of telephone equipment moved from competition to a monopoly. From 1876 to 1882, Bell purchased equipment from a pool of diverse geographical suppliers. But in 1882 Bell acquired its own manufacturing affiliate, Western Electric. Following that acquisition, Western supplied equipment under Bell's patent license and operating company purchases were essentially limited to their in-house manufacturer—an integration of service and manufacturing that was to be challenged twice within the time-frame of Period I.

Public policy

Local telephone service, provided by a single firm, eventually invited some form of government oversight. At first, regulation originated at the municipal or city level. After all, early telephone service was concentrated in heavily populated centres. By the early 1900s, however, rate regulation began to migrate from individual cities to state jurisdictions, driven largely by the Bell System's preference for state commission oversight.[2] Rate-making principles became codified and standardized, providing guidelines for operating expenditures, research and development, cost of capital, rate base evaluation, depreciation schedules, and individual subscriber prices. Federal regulation commenced in 1910 through an amendment to the Interstate Commerce Commission. The ICC was primarily interested in railroad rates and service, and in 1934 Congress established the Federal Communications Commission (FCC) as a new regulatory body. Since less than 5 per cent of all telephone calls in the nation were interstate in the 1930s, federal regulatory activity tended to be eclipsed by jurisdictional decisions at the state level.

The integration of equipment and services continued to beset regulatory authorities during the latter half of Period I. How, regulators asked, could a commission approve telephone prices if the agency exercised little control over equipment costs? In the 1920s, a series of court decisions shifted the burden of proving the reasonableness of equipment prices to the telephone carriers themselves. Bell's studies insisted that Western Electric's equipment was less expensive than its rival equipment suppliers. In the 1930s, the FCC started an investigation of AT&T's Western Electric performance. The Commission sought to determine the reasonableness of equipment costs that, in turn, influenced telephone rates and service. Though many suspected that the FCC was intent on bringing Western into the fold of direct regulation, the study ended in 1939 without a Congressional request for FCC jurisdiction over equipment manufacturing.[3]

After World War II, the FCC's study reappeared in the form of an anti-trust suit. The Department of Justice alleged that Bell had taken a legal franchise in telephone service and leveraged it into an illegal monopoly in manufacturing equipment. The Department of Justice sought divestiture of Western Electric from the Bell System and the splitting of Western into three competitive companies. The anti-trust suit was settled by a Consent Decree in 1956.[4] This court-enforced order required AT&T to make available its existing patent portfolio—now of formidable proportions—to all users on a royalty free basis. In return, AT&T retained ownership in Western Electric and the company agreed to confine its future telephone service and equipment to regulated activities only.

The year 1956 thus represented a high water mark in the telephone industry. Bell's holding company organization, its integration of utility and manufacturing, the institution of state and federal regulation, emerged as the US response to the dilemmas of natural monopoly. Boundary lines separating telephone from other industries appeared immutable and long established; and the industry paced, if not con-trolled, the state of the telecommunication art.

The relationship between state and federal regulatory institutions was marked by harmony. To accommodate the state commission's desire for minimal telephone rates, the FCC embarked on an esoteric accounting process, separations and settlements, that transferred revenues from interstate toll to local basic services. In a word, toll subscribers subsidized local subscribers. In an era of regulatory good feeling, the telephone company was, essentially, given the power to tax. Private monopoly subject to public regulation was held as a policy model worthy of emula-tion if not envy. 1956 was a very good year indeed.

Period II—1957–84: Technical Challenge and Legal Upheaval

Period II witnessed an acceleration of the interaction of technology, markets, and policy. However pre-eminent in the past, the industry's technology no longer stood alone. Market boundaries, once hard and impenetrable, became soft and permeable; and the Bell System began to experience market rivalry and competition. Ultimately, an anti-trust suit separated AT&T from its regional operating companies, and a jurisdictional war erupted between state regulatory and federal regulatory agencies.

Technology

The trends perceptible in the latter part of Period I gathered speed in the second period. Technology no longer consisted of one or two disciplines, but several technologies, indeed, families of technology. The transition from an analog to a digital world was now well underway. Computers began to be tied to the telephone network and, over time, the network itself became increasingly digital and software driven. New generations of customer premise equipment, PBXs, key systems, etc., began coming on stream in the 1970s. The transition from analog to digital transmission began with telephone trunks and descended into the network hierarchy. Electronic switching introduced in the 1960s began to penetrate the industry's switching plant as well.

As technology migrated and expanded, the expertise of the telephone industry, though undiminished, was supplemented by the R. & D. effort of other firms and industries. Nowhere was this more apparent than in the national debate over commercial satellite policy in the early 1960s. AT&T proposed a medium orbit system, so as to minimize the delay inherent with satellite voice transmission.[5] The number of satellites and the complexitiy of earth stations constituted a heavy capital expenditure. The aerospace industry, by contrast, proposed a synchronous orbit system, so that the satellite appeared stationary or fixed from a ground station. Eventually this lower cost technology was to prevail. For the first time, the expertise of the nation's telephone carriers was subject to challenge and debate.

Markets

Period II might well be termed the market entry stage. From AT&T's perspective, however, that entry was asymmetrical, if not downright unfair. On one side, firms began to penetrate customer premise equipment, interstate toll services, and telecommunication manufacturing. Each challenged the industry's structure and policies. Bell opposed the attachment of customer equipment to its dial-up network, and the carrier filed tariffs requiring an interface device on non-Western products. No device was required on its own equipment. Interconnect suppliers insisted that the coupler device was anti-competitive, and demanded direct connection of their equipment via a registration programme. AT&T argued the interface device was essential to protect its network from subscriber equipment harm.[6] Bell resisted the FCC's equipment certification programme, lost its case before the FCC, and then took its fight into the courts. In 1978, the courts supported equipment certification—i.e., direct attachment of customer equipment to the telephone network. Competition now became a reality in subscriber equipment.

Entry began to erupt in the intercity transmission market, first with microwave radio relay, then satellites, then packet switching. AT&T opposed the former two services and, through its local operating companies, refused to permit equitable access to firms competing with AT&T's Long Lines Division. This market resistance set off a series of private anti-trust suits.

Finally, equipment suppliers tried to penetrate Bell's vertical integration by selling equipment to the Bell Operating Companies directly. Their failure prompted charges that AT&T's Western integration favoured its in-house supplier, irrespective of the equipment, price, cost, or technology of Western's rivals. Once again, private anti-trust suits erupted. As if this were not enough, the Department of Justice (1974) filed an anti-trust suit alleging that AT&T had monopolized the customer premise equipment market, monopolized the interstate toll service market, and, through vertical integration, monopolized equipment manufacturing. The Department sought nothing less than a massive reorganization of the Bell System—a proposed breakup of the world's largest regulated utility.

The asymmetrical side of market entry was especially frustrating to AT&T. When Bell introduced a new teletypewriter terminal, the computer industry claimed that that product was moving into non-regulated equipment and services. Bell, they insisted, was violating the conditions of its 1956 Consent Decree. AT&T insisted that its terminal was a communication device and that its prices had been approved by state regulatory commissions. IBM took exception to AT&T's tariff filing and appealed to the US Supreme Court on grounds that Bell had overstepped the 1956 Consent order. That theme, the definitional content of the 1956 Consent Decree, began to haunt AT&T from 1974 to 1982. Whether in PBXs, electronic funds transfer, packet switching equipment, or computerized yellow pages, the company's adversaries resurrected the Decree as blocking Bell's ability to diversify into non-regulated activities. From AT&T's perspective, firms could diversify into telecommunications, but the telephone company could not move into computers. What had constituted a management coup in the mid-1950s now emerged in the 1970s as a strategic nightmare.

Public policy

As technology and markets began to unravel, the consensus between state PUCs (Public Utility Commissions) and the FCC began to fragment as well. The estrangement of the state PUCs and the FCC erupted first in the mid-1960s when the FCC began to explore the growing inter-dependence of computers and communication. Would such a trend, asked the FCC, call for new policies, new programmes, new approaches, new investment? Should public policy encourage market entry in digital technology? The state commission resisted the policy implication of these questions—and so generally ignored what was to be called Computer I.

Later, the FCC began to accommodate customer requests to tie their own equipment to the telephone network, to sanction the entry of firms into the intercity transmission market, including microwave and satellite companies; and the FCC began to question whether Bell Operating Companies were securing Western Electric equipment on the basis of price and performance only. In each of these matters the state commissions opposed, resisted, and fought the policies of the FCC. State commissions voted against customer equipment ownership, MCI Inc., specialized carriers, domestic satellite carriers, valued added networks, sharing and reselling, Xerox X-10 digital microwave, cellular radio competition, fast depreciation write-offs, inside wiring deregulation, customer premise equipment deregulation, non-dominant carrier deregulation, cable TV interconnection, Execunet/local loop interconnection, and satellite master antenna dishes. State PUCs, focusing on local telephone rates, feared that entry into the long-haul market would dissipate profits employed to subsidize local subscribers. Entry threatened, in short, to destroy the delicate balance between toll rates and local rates; and state commissions resorted to judicial appeal on a massive scale.

The Federal Courts invariably favoured the FCC. The result saw a 'federalization' of US telecommunications policy on such issues as domestic public land mobile radio service, private radio system–public telephone network interconnection, cellular mobile radio, owner-ship of customer premise equipment, customer premise equipment deregulation, enhanced services deregulation, non-dominant domestic carrier deregulation, one way paging, non-wire line cellular radio, telephone sharing and resale, receive-only satellite dishes, telephone access fees, inside wiring, cable TV interconnection, specialized communication carriers, satellite master antenna systems and optical fibre/private microwave systems.[7] State commissions began to experience an enlargement of FCC regulatory power and a concomitant loss of their own jurisdictional reach. At the regional operating company level, state PUCs continued to forfeit regulatory power even after the Bell breakup. In disposing of some twenty-three Bell Operating Companies, 90 billion dollars of assets and 800,000 employees, AT&T secured freedom to diversify into non-regulated or information services and equipment.

But what of the future of the remaining Bell Operating Companies? Now organized into seven holding companies, the operating companies are precluded from diversifying into interstate toll services and telephone equipment manufacturing. The Federal District Court, assisted by the Department of Justice, has exercised jurisdiction over the enforcement of the anti-trust settlement. The result is both a concentration of federal regulation in the United States, and a splintering of public policy between the FCC, the Courts, the Department of Justice, and the White House.

In a word, the experience of Period II revealed that the telephone industry's technology was no longer pre-eminent, that industry boundary lines were softening, that the entry process was gaining momentum, that AT&T was inhibited from diversifying, that Bell's resistance to competition precipitated anti-trust suits that led to the system breakup. The chasm between Period I and Period II represented a quantum leap of unprecedented proportions.

Period III—Post-1984: Dilemmas of Regulating Markets in Eruption

The US is embarking on its post-1984 phase. Despite the absence of total clarity, some trends are becoming discernible. Technology is now global, market boundaries continue to be eroded, products and services are now international, and state regulation is less cohesive and monolithic. The jurisdictional war between the state PUCs and the FCC has not diminished, and federal policy is split between the Courts, the Department of Justice, the FCC, and the President.

Technology

Technological confluence, productivity, and globalization continue to accelerate. The line between computers and communications is virtually indistinguishable. Technology is pervasive to the extent that expertise includes telecommunications materials, integrated circuits, communications satellites, computers, software, and particle physics. The convergence of voice and data is giving birth to the concept of the integrated service digital network (ISDN). Moreover, productivity continues unabated. The number of components per chip doubles every eighteen months; each generation of satellites embodies more and more voice channels; the distance between fibre optic repeaters continues to multiply. Finally, technology is now global. Expertise resides in the Far East, North America, and Europe. No one firm, no one industry, indeed, no one country possesses total exclusivity in developing the state of telecommunications and the computer. As a result joint R. & D. ventures are becoming the order of the day.

Markets

The phenomenon of boundary erosion continues without interruption. Distinctions between local and toll are no longer clear-cut, as fibre optics, satellite dishes, broadcast techniques, shared tenant services, intelligent buildings, teleports blur local and toll service. Competition, by exploring technological options, lowers communication costs by going around or circumventing carrier facilities. In the US such technical competition, known as telephone bypass, can erupt within local, regional, or long-haul facilities. This bypass of telephone investment raises the fear that competition will lift rates for the local exchange subscriber. Increasingly, long-haul communication carriers themselves, including AT&T, are exploiting local bypass opportunities.

Computer and communication markets now overlap. Under the 1982 Consent Decree, AT&T is moving into unregulated, computer information services, both at home and abroad. And IBM's acquisition of a PBX supplier and a specialized carrier, MCI, accelerates its move into telecommunications. Even the distinction between domestic and overseas markets is less clear-cut. Domestic carriers are moving into overseas voice and data markets, and overseas carriers are diversifying into domestic services. A satellite dish today constitutes an international gateway, and private satellite and fibre optic consortia are seeking to expand offshore telecommunication facilities in the Atlantic basin.

Within the US, the entry process is now generic. The distinction between software, banking, retail, telephone, computers, insurance, brokerage houses, is fast becoming a memory. The dynamics of the process are instructive.[8] First, a firm weighs the option of leasing facilities from a carrier, or buying equipment and providing the services internally—the classic lease/buy decision. For some firms, technology is increasingly tipping the option away from leasing carrier facilities. The 'buy' option is an investment decision that satisfies the internal demands of the corporation, whether in computers, software, electronic mail, voice, video conferencing. But, invariably, the firm experiences excess capacity. Idle plant, in turn, sets the next stage. The firm now begins to sell excess capacity to outside customers, sometimes via a separate subsidiary, sometimes within the same corporate structure. In any case, the firm taps external markets and customers.

The firm now finds itself in a new market. Sears, for example, is selling voice, data, and video conferencing services; Merrill Lynch reselling fibre optic capacity in Manhattan; Rockefeller Center reselling telecommunications facilities; Federal Express—document distribution; Boeing Aircraft offers telecommunication facilities; General Motors is reselling its global telecommunications capacity, at least in the UK. A firm has jumped industry boundaries, and injected competition into new markets. Indeed, some firms are in the process of redefining themselves and their markets. And, of course, weakening boundary lines intensify the number of competitors and the degree of market rivalry.

The result is the evolution of global markets in telecommunication equipment, stock quotations, printing services, insurance, computer aided design, computer aided manufacturing, electronic offices, electronic mail. Time and geography are becoming increasingly irrelevant. As one Chief Executive says, given communication satellites today, there is little place for a modern firm to hide.[9]

Public policy

Period III exacerbates the tension between state regulatory policy and federal regulatory policy. Both invariably square-off over fundamental questions of market entry, competition, depreciation, expenses, rate regulation, and cost of capital. Nevertheless, some provocative future developments are in the offing. First, information technology confers additional options to a firm's investment and plant location decisions. Secondly, state regulatory policy is experiencing greater diversity; and thirdly, within regions of the US competition is intensifying. Finally, state Public Utility Commissions may experience a loss of authority, as state governors step in to attract investment in order to generate jobs and employment. Let us consider each point briefly.

Technology is both centralizing and decentralizing investment decisions in the US. Factories are smaller in size and production cycles are shorter. Some 90 per cent of the machined products in the US occurred in batches of less than fifty units. Process technology is obsolete within four years. Product life cycles are contracting, the rate of technical product and process innovation is accelerating. The pace of obsolescence suggests that scale economies are no longer the only answer to manufacturing success. Computer aided design and computer aided manufacturing further contracts the time between product conception and product development. Vertical integration is often perceived as limiting flexibility rather than promoting corporate efficiency.

The office today is becoming modular, interactive, decentralized. Not unlike the factory, offices are interlinked by communication lines, domestically and internationally.[10] Retail stores are putting up micro-satellite dishes for two-way data exchange, fibre optics are so pervasive that copper technology for telephone trunk lines appears limited in application. Networks and services are altering boundaries, modifying business strategy, shifting corporate location. Clearly, information technology is the driving force behind telephone bypass—the circumventing of telephone investment in switching and transmission hardware. Indeed, bypass is not without its global aspects. Canadian firms hub telephone calls to the United States and then back to Canada thus circumventing the 3,000-mile Canadian telecommunication investment. The potential of private, fibre optic, and satellite systems overseas, particularly in the Atlantic basin, provides yet another invitation for technological bypass. Stated differently, bypass fuels technical, economic, and global competition.

Secondly, regulatory harmony among and between state commissions is no longer a constant. Some commissions intend to regulate future services as in the past—employing the old formulas of rate base rate of return, operating expenses, rate cross subsidy. But other states are assessing the option of deregulating telecommunications. Some are going so far as to contemplate entry in local exchange service, an idea considered heretical only five years ago. Other states impose jurisdiction over intelligent buildings and teleports; while still others are exercising regulatory forbearance. Some state Public Utility Commissions promote interstate competition within their borders; others forsake market entry. The US,is beginning to witness an unprecedented pluralism among state PUCs, their policies, and practices. Why the diversity? One answer is that the regional Bell Operating Companies are no longer a single, monolithic system. Each regional Bell Operating Company, now independent and autonomous, elects to pursue its own strategy, its own market, its own diversification. Some Bell Operating Companies are content to rely on traditional telecommunications services. Others are forming subsidiaries to diversify into national competition. Some other Bell Operating Companies are exploring entry into equipment manufacturing and into interstate telephone service. And yet other companies are acquiring software subsidiaries, or forming joint ventures in the Far East or Europe. Differentiation and pluralistic strategies now mark the regional Bell Operating Company scene in the US.

Inevitably, that redefinition has spilled into state regulatory attitudes and policies. Given the options for industry location, given the diversity of regional Bell Operating Companies, competition among and between the states is beginning to intensify. No state can remain immune from the consequences of its own tax, regulatory, and telecommunication policy. If, for example, Florida imposes a unitary tax on IBM, IBM will expand its operations in adjacent states. If New York imposes interest rates on credit cards, Citicorp will move its operations to Sioux Falls, South Dakota, and transmit the data to New York by its own satellites. If the State of New York places constraints on bank diversification into insurance, New York Banks will migrate to Delaware or South Dakota. If North Carolina attempts to regulate customer premise equipment, IBM will threaten to move its research facilities out of the state. If California fails to lift its unitary tax, Japanese electronic firms will relocate to Oregon. Capital mobility constitutes a new variable in the state regulatory equation.

Offices no longer need to be located adjacent to their corporate headquarters or their suppliers. Smart buildings are linked by satellites or terrestrial facilities, domestically or globally. The university, the science park, and the quality of life influence research, office, and plant location decisions. Regional competition is thus intensified within the US; smart buildings vs. smart buildings; intelligent buildings vs. teleports; unitary taxes vs. non-taxes; income taxes vs. their absence. Alternatives breed rivalry, and state commission policy will be challenged by other state policy.

Investment mobility is not without its international dimension as well.

Rivalry between the European PTTs is intensifying. The UK's deregulation of telecommunications and financial markets beckons firms to hub their communications computer networks in London. National Semiconductor and the Bank of America are pulling back from the restrictive practices of European PTTs. Even German banks are placing computer centres in the UK. Just as US state utility commission policy no longer resides beyond market accountability, European policies are no longer immune to market forces. Paris, Brussels, Frankfurt, and Zurich now compete with the financial centres of New York, Tokyo, and London. Singapore and Hong Kong advertisements inviting corporations to locate within their information infrastructure provide evidence of a shrinking world.

Policy pluralism between state PUCs tends to dissipate united opposition to federal regulatory policy. After all, state PUCs no longer offer a monolithic telecommunication front *vis-à-vis* their federal counterpart. Indeed, one can visualize states teaming up with the respective regional Bell Operating Companies, both of whom might challenge federal government policies in the future. Just as federal regulation policy will experience new competition from regional Bell Operating Companies, so federal policy is fragmenting at the same time. The District Court overseeing the Bell breakup is under pressure to relax the constraints imposed in interstate toll and manufacturing activities. And markets continue to move on a deregulatory track; witness AT&T's petition for deregulation of its communications affiliate, and IBM acquisitions of AT&T's major intercity rival, MCI.

Increasingly, the federal government will find itself addressing the international trade aspects of equipment and services. The issue of protectionism in telecommunication manufacturing services is very much on the policy agenda. Negotiations to open up overseas procurement markets and service exports are likely to continue in the foreseeable future; and it is uncertain whether the FCC's power will be enhanced or diluted in matters of foreign trade. Clearly, however, there are emerging players on the block: the Commerce and the State Departments—not to mention the White House.

In sum, Period III has begun to unfold. Its content, direction, and rate of change, though speculative, suggests a coalescence of technology, an erosion of industry boundary lines, a softening of domestic and global markets. The breakup of the Bell System, the diversification of IBM are signal institutional events. State commissions' policies are less monolithic under pressure from the regional Bell Operating Companies.

Information technology accords the office, factory, bank, and store greater choice and flexibility. Market forces continue to intercede at the state, federal, and international level of the industry. As the US moves into the 1990s, diversity at the state level, and fragmentation at the federal level, may be a prelude to a decline of telecommunications regulation.

Conclusion

Our industry overview suggests that the cycle theory of regulation—inception, youth, maturity, decline—appears a compelling model. We have seen the regulatory cycle at the municipal level, the state level, and perhaps at the federal level. If the cycle thesis is valid then one can assert that if, in the past, technology provided the rationale for monopoly and regulation, technology today generates the rationale for deregulation. And to the extent that information technology is global, one might speculate that the forces experienced in the United States may very well be replicated by other nations as well.

Yet, having embraced the cycle theory of regulation, there is some evidence that the US is embarking on a new regulatory era. Telecommunication is the hallmark of an information intensive economy. Remote data banks, stocks, electronic funds transfer, medical records, computer modelling, corporate records, banks, designing, are very much part of the information scene. Commercial data banks and information technology are increasingly vulnerable to theft and access by the Soviet bloc. The US Department of Defense asserts that the national security in information technology resides not only in classified information but is grounded in 'sensitive information' as well.[11] Since on-line information is vulnerable to theft, pilfering, and unauthorized access, the 'public interest' resides in the preservation of data and information integrity. Once any agency asserts its concern for the public interest, the seeds of regulation are sown. Is it possible that information technology, in eroding the rationale for economic regulation, now provides the basis for national security regulation. To the extent that products, industries, and economic sectors are becoming permeable, the jurisdictional reach of a new regulatory agency appears limitless and perhaps unrestricted.

Clearly the export of military information to our adversaries constitutes an issue of national import. The problem is that technology is blurring the distinction between commercial and military products. The ability to disentangle or separate products and services is bound to become more elusive over time. One may classify VLSI chips, radar, microwave satellites as critical military systems today. But are ball bearings, Apple II computers, heart pacers, robots, and telephone central office exchanges similarly embedded with national security content? And is the US the only supplier of these products? If 'sensitive' information is susceptible to Pentagon review, what facet of an economy's infrastructure does not invite security oversight and defense regulation? And does not the opportunity cost of information regulation bias the US economy toward economic concentration with its attendant diminution of economic performance? Whatever the answer, the US is searching for a balance between information freedom and information regulation.

Notes

1. Manley R. Irwin, *Telecommunications America: Markets Without Boundaries* (Westport, Connecticut: Greenwood Press, 1985) p. 10.
2. Robert N. Garnet, *The Telephone Enterprise (The Evolution of the Bell System's Horizontal Structure, 1878-1909)* (Baltimore, Md.: Johns Hopkins University Press, 1985), p. 130.
3. FCC, *Report on the Investigation of the Telephone Industry in the United States*, HR Doc. 340, 76th Congress, 1st Session (1939).
4. *Consent Decree in United States* v. *Western Electric*, Civ. no. 17–49, DNJ, 23 January 1956.
5. FCC, In the Matter of an Inquiry into the Administrative and Regulatory Problems Relating to the Authorization of Commercially Operable Space Communications Systems, Docket 14024, *Response of American Telephone and Telegraph Co.*, 1 May 1961.
6. Alvin Von Auw, *Heritage and Destiny: Reflections of the Bell System In Transition* (New York: Praeger, 1983), p. 141.
7. M. R. Irwin, op. cit. (n. 1).
8. For an elaboration of the process, see M. R. Irwin: 'U.S. Telecommunication: Borderless Markets and Corporate Redefinition', paper, *American Economic Association* (New York: Transportation and Public Utilities Group, 29 December 1985).
9. Peter Wilson-Smith, 'Master of Change Welcomes City's Inevitable Revolution', *The Times*, 14 December 1984, p. 27. Also, W. Wriston, 'The Information Standard', *Euromoney*, October 1984.
10. Office of Technological Assessment, *Automation of America's Offices*, Library of Congress (Washington, DC: GPO, 1985), p. 211.
11. House of Representatives, Computer Security Policies Subcomittee on

Transportation, Aviation and Materials, *Committee on Science and Technology*, 99th Congress, 1st session, 27 June 1985; Office of the Undersecretary of Defense for Policy, 'Assessing the Effect of Technological Transfer on US/Western Security—A Defense Perspective', February 1985, Washington, DC.

Telecommunications: a European Perspective

—————————— *Klaus W. Grewlich*[1] ——————————

Telecommunications and computer-based informatics—part industry, part services—have been identified as the very basis of the 'third industrial revolution'. While telecommunications was seen in the 'old days' as a piece of useful infrastructure, *telematics* (meaning the convergence of electronic switching, optical fibres, satellites, and information processing) is seen as a make-or-break ticket to economic, cultural, and political development. Thus, the international competition in telecommunications has ceased to be a game among merchant princes, and has become a high stakes race. Domination of key techologies or systems-knowledge in the field of the information economy is seen as a matter of economic security. The stakes in the high-tech race are not just markets, as such, but a perceived need of the major technological powers of the West to capture a share of world production in growth sectors to offset the inevitable decline in others.

It is probably due to such perceptions that in many countries and regions government-industry relations oriented towards positive structural adjustment have become intrinsic to a competitively oriented modernization strategy. This involves regulation and technology policy and, in both, telematics is central to the strategy. European telecommunications strategy could lead to a 'high-tech pull' in Europe and enhance technological, economic, and social innovations. The envisaged projects include a European strategy for digitalization (Integrated System Digital Network, ISDN) and a Europe-wide broad-band glassfibre network, including mobile telephony and satellite links.

Increasing liberalization of the terminals market and of services, and the harmonization of the relevant norms on the basis of CCITT (Committee Consultatif Internationale Telegraphique et Téléphonique) and CEPT (Conference Europeanée des Administrations des Postes et des Telecommunications) standards should go hand in hand with such major projects. Public-sector procurement markets would continuously be opened up, the European telecommunication industry would strengthen technological co-operation and, as necessary, establish consortia.

This strategy would be boosted by the simultaneous intensification of efforts to create a homogeneous market for information services, notably specialized information, data banks, machine translation, and a bid to realize a common market for media products (such as TV and video). The goal of such European co-operation in information and communications technology products and services is not a technologically self-sufficient Europe, but one which competes and co-operates equally and in partnership with all nations and regions of the world, in the spirit of independence. Thus, it is not the objective of a European information and communication policy to reverse existing global telecommunications alliances, but quite the opposite, to strengthen market and technology access.

Challenges and Opportunities

The Information revolution

The main trends and interrelationships in the field of telematics are complex but can be briefly summarized. As information processing systems are linked with information delivery systems, fundamental changes are starting to occur: no longer is a telephone simply an instrument for voice communications, but rather an information terminal, a means of accessing and exchanging information. No longer is a television simply a passive instrument for receiving news and entertainment, but rather an interactive communications device. No longer is a PABX (Private Automatic Branch Exchange) simply an instrument for routing telephone calls in and out of offices, but rather a multipurpose office management system, supporting a variety of operations from inventory control to energy management. Telephone lines are evolving into multipurpose information systems, linking people to people, people to machines, or machines to machines; and communications networks increasingly permit users to transmit information in a variety of electronic forms, volumes, and speeds. Sophisticated private networks are also evolving to meet the specialized needs of business and government users, whose operations have become heavily dependent on advanced communications and information processing. Emerging satellite and cellular radio systems offer new alternatives to traditional landline communications systems. Figure 7 contains a survey of the technological continuum of the three generations of telecommunication services.

Industrial growth

The information processing and telecommunications industry—which includes everything from electronic office typewriters and copiers to computers, satellites, and telecom hardware and services—will, according to some estimates, take it from about $350 billion, in 1985 revenues, to an incredible $1,000 billion in annual revenues by 1995. This annual growth rate of more than 20 per cent will, however, not be enough to support all the current players. There will be winners and losers—or to put it more carefully, some will win more than others. Telecommunications equipment accounts for a substantial part of this growth: the international market for telecommunications equipment is expected to increase from about $47 billion in 1982 to more than $100 billion by the end of the current decade. Of this equipment market

Figure 7. Three Generations of Telecommunications Services

Two Way Communications:

Basic Services	**New Services**	**Advanced Services**
(First generation)	(Second generation)	(Third generation)
Current basic telecommunications infrastructure	Enchancement of basic telecommunications infrastructure	New telecommunications infrastructure
Telephony	Integrated basic services	Videotelephony
Telex, teletext	with some speed	Videoconferencing
Low-speed data	enchancement (ISDN)	Fast facsimile
Mobile telephony	Digitized voice	Bulk document transfer
Low-speed facsimile	Textfax	High-speed data
	Audiographic	On-line graphical design
	teleconferencing	Remote printing and
	Electronic mail	publishing
	Wider availability of	Dynamic computer
	mobile telephony	load-sharing
	Higher resolution	Burst-mode host-to-host
	videotex	transfer

(growing at 8 per cent per year), 92 per cent is at present oriented to telephony and slow-speed data telecommunications services. By 1992, according to current trends, these will still represent at least 85 per cent of the total market, although by then most equipment sold will be digital. In addition, it is likely that the emerging telematics market for products bridging the telecommunications and information processing worlds will present a major opportunity.[2]

Communications as a resource

The timely, rapid, and efficient introduction of new telecommunications networks and services in close connection with data processing has a broad horizontal effect on the general economic structure. It will create a strong growth impulse for the economies of those countries in the position to produce and market advanced telecommunications equipment and telematic services early. The ability to create, store, and transfer 'information'—the decisive resource of the future, next to energy and raw materials—both nationally and transnationally[3] leads not only to new products but to new manufacturing processes as well. The result of this is not only the creation of new sectors—as, for instance, software[4]—but, to some extent, also the renewal and strengthening of traditional industries. This applies, in particular, to the service sector—banks, insurance companies, consulting, and so on. The sale of information will increasingly become an interesting business. About 10 to 15 per cent of all international data flows are of a commercial nature. This share is expected to increase rapidly. For on-line information, for instance, a yearly increase in turnover of 20–30 per cent is expected in this decade.[5] The United States has a strong position in this field. It dominates the electronic information markets of the world; some have, therefore, described the US as the 'OPEC of information'.

Job creation

Communications technologies destroy jobs, but they also create new jobs. It should be food for thought for the Europeans that, in the last ten years, the United States has been able to create more than 15 million new jobs—though of varying quality—while about 3 million jobs have disappeared in Europe. According to estimates (which, however, say nothing about the extent of laid-off workers) at least 2 million jobs could be created in Europe in the next ten to fifteen years, and a further 2 million could be retained if the Europeans could master and apply the modern communications technologies early on, and if they could corner about 20–25 per cent of the international information and communication technology market—a share comparable to the size of the European communications market.[6]

Implications for government

Because of the strategic importance of communications technologies, the nature of government-industry relations is particularly relevant in this field. Governments employ, to varying degrees, and often unintentionally, different means to promote pertinent high-tech industries. Among the most important are, first, subsidies in the pre-competitive phase of long lead-time research; secondly, application-oriented 'technology and industrial policies', promoting high-tech sectors of the economy as, for instance, the development of indigenous micro-electronic capabilities, or of data bank capacities. Instruments include direct subsidies, advantageous regulatory 'flanking measures', indirect measures via, for instance, government contracting (in such fields as space, the military sector, transport, and telecommunications), or, through judicious mixtures of incentives and disincentives, including 're-regulation' policies and public procurement. Thirdly, commercial policy can be implemented in such a way as to protect high-tech industries, in some cases by resorting to the 'infant industry argument'. Another approach to preserving the technological edge could be to subject high-tech exports, notably enabling technologies and high-tech data, to restrictions and controls. There is, however, no evidence that this is happening in a systematic way, at present, within the OECD area (the COCOM-arrangements, which are justified by considerations of Western security, are a different case).[7] This list is augmented by so-called 'cultural protectionism', i.e. the protection from 'alienation' through foreign media of what is known as 'cultural identity', through means such as quota systems for the import of media products. These culturally motivated protective measures might possibly have some justification in the purely cultural sector; but in some instances they may be promoted by economic considerations.

The use of these different measures in the struggle for top positions in the high-tech race could, in the foreseeable future, considerably strain relations within the US–Japan–Europe triangle, unless these partners succeed in agreeing on some kind of effective 'political code of conduct' or 'rules of the game' which took the edge off the potential for conflict. On no account must the economic-technological race, on which the technological powers of the West have embarked, degenerate into ruinous cut-throat competition. Reducing the capacity gap in the field of information technologies, achieving a fair division of labour, and strengthening high-tech co-operation on the basis of equality would be the ideal safeguard against economic conflicts and protectionism. Concretely, this presupposes, in particular, that the Europeans will ensure and firmly hold their place among those in the technological vanguard.

Crucial Issues in Safeguarding European Competitiveness

As to the technological competitiveness of the more advanced nations of Western Europe, there have been plenty of analyses in the past three years,[8] some lachrymose or dramatizing, others deliberately minimizing potential dangers. A more balanced view now appears to have crystallized along two lines of thought. First, the economic–technological capacity of the more advanced countries in Western Europe is, at present, underestimated. There are, however, dangerous gaps in such vital fields as micro-electronics and major data processing.[9] Their closing will require an all-out effort. Secondly, for some of these strategically important areas of advanced technology, the Europeans need transborder co-operation and, above all, a bunching of Europe's own prowess. The decisive factor is not to tackle high-tech issues as isolated elements but in the broader context of socio-economic policies[10] and European internal market policy.

Telecommunications is one information technology sector where the overall situation of Europe's industry and infrastructure seems favourable. Notably during the seventies, the technological performance of the telecommunications sector in Europe was remarkable. It was in the countries of the European Community that time-switching systems were developed and then put into service in the networks. Moreover, Community operators, both industrialists and carriers, lead the field in the development of broad-band networks.[11]

The European telecommunications industry dominates the Community's internal market in the telecommunications field. A total of a dozen European firms satisfy most of the requirements of a market which, taken as a whole, accounts for approximately 20 per cent of the world market. Whereas imports account for only 15 per cent of production, Community firms succeed in exporting about 25 per cent of their telecommunications equipment production, though the EC share of the total telecommunications export market has been steadily declining, at an average of one per cent per year, over the past ten years. A number of factors render this comparatively satisfactory situation, however, more fragile in the medium and long term, notably the compartmentalization of the European market, the semiconductor deficit, and constraints in the field of 'framework policies' (i.e. regulation and standardization). We can consider each of these in turn.

Unfortunately, the total size of the European market means little for the individual European company, because each European nation usually has a preferential buying policy to support its local firms. No individual market in Europe comes close to matching the scale of those in the United States and Japan. The carriers, whether public or private, strongly influence the development of the telecommunications industry (hardware and software manufacturers), and the behaviour of the users of the services (both businesses and individuals); carriers exercise their strongest influence in the field of switching and transmission equipment. With the transition from electromechanical to digital telecommunications equipment and the increasing importance of software, the cards on the national and world markets are going to be reshuffled. Innovation cycles are shortening; the obsolescence of equipment is increasingly rapid. Economies of scale, on the basis of an internal market of continental dimension, become a major condition for economic and technological success.

Both the fragmentation of the European markets (too small to form a solid basis for economic success) and the number of telecommunications firms (too many with small markets) are a disadvantage in international competition. Consider the cases of central office switching (COS), the PBX market, and the European performance in data communications network. These three strategic areas clearly show that Europe is confronted with two major investment difficulties. Recovering R. & D. expenses will become increasingly difficult to guarantee, and this will adversely affect the development of new products and their price. In central office switching, for instance, the cost of developing a complete range of digital switches has risen, in Europe, to over $600 million. This level of investment has to be recovered over the market life of the product; today ten years, as compared with thirty years for electromechanical switches. This can only be done if the supplier has around 4 per cent of the world market. If he has less than this, or his development is just two years later to the market than competitors, he cannot recoup the research and development costs, unless there is a 'price umbrella' in a protected market. The same pattern is emerging in the field of large PBXs, where a fourth generation switch will require about $25–50 million of R. & D. The supplier must have around 3 per cent or more of the world market to recoup his R. & D. costs.

It is not difficult to understand why even some of the more advanced European countries are seen as lagging behind in a number of areas, as far as investment in telecommunications equipment and infrastructure for advanced telematic services is concerned. This is notably also the result of the inability to develop and produce at competitive costs because of insufficient economies of scale; thus, European switches cost about 35 to 50 per cent more than those in the US. There are obviously limits to the financial capacity of national carriers to support national telecommunications manufacturers via procurement. As a result, the average growth of the equipment market appears likely, on the basis of current trends, to be appreciably slower in Europe (5 per cent per year) than, for instance, in the United States and Japan (about 8 per cent per year). In order to compete with the average Japanese telecommunications company, the European firms would not only need bigger markets, but they would have to co-operate to such an extent that, instead of the eight larger and a few smaller European telecommunications firms, only four combines would be left. In order to cope with the American competitors, notably AT&T and IBM, collaboration would have to go so far that only three combines would remain.[12]

The so-called 'semiconductor deficit' constitutes a second weak point. Europe is vulnerable in the field of basic technologies which determine the development of networks and services, particularly micro-electronics and data processing equipment. This weakness could hamper the EC's commercial prospects in the 'systems' sector. The EC imports most (83 per cent) of the micro-electronic components which will be used increasingly in telecommunications equipment; they already account for about 20 per cent of all micro-electronic components consumed in the EC. Thus the EC telecommunications sector is vulnerable to non-availability or delays of deliveries. Innovation in services and in supporting systems and networks is increasingly reliant on performance in advanced integrated circuits. Although a great number of European firms are present in the fields of the critical technologies necessary for the development of the second and third generation telecommunications services, none of them is in the position of having achieved world-wide leadership in any of those technologies.

A third major problem of Europe's development of communications results from constraints in the field of 'framework policies', notably regulatory policy and policy for norms and standards. Most PTTs (Postal Telegraph and Telephone Authorities) in the EC have a *de facto* monopoly over nearly all civil telecommunications activities. Together with this monopoly privilege come regulations that govern the operations of the monopoly, which specify obligations and place responsibilities and constraints on the PTTs. Those regulations governing the PTTs operations are, in many cases, more important than market forces and technology trends in determining the PTTs overall behaviour and their relationships with users and suppliers. In general, regulations govern the operations of the telecommunications carriers. They control what services a user has access to, and the conditions of use. This regulated environment strongly influences the relationship of telecommunications manufacturers both with the carriers and with the user.

When measured against their charters and the regulatory environment, the PTTs, in general, perform well. If this behaviour is less appropriate as market forces and technology change, it is the charters and the regulatory environment that should be modified so that, in turn, the behaviour of the PTTs changes. A process in this direction of effective 're-regulation', though at varying speed and depth, is under way in several European countries. The UK clearly has a leading position in this development, having, as a matter of industrial policy, undertaken a bold re-regulatory process. It seems that this re-regulation has, at least initially, improved the position of the UK services industry. But here and elsewhere there are a series of financial constraints and supply restrictions which raise important issues of regulatory policy.[13]

Many telecommunications carriers have limits to their financing resources that in turn limit their investment levels. The severity of these limits, and the way they are imposed, varies greatly between EC member states. In some countries, the net cash generated by the national telecommunications carrier is absorbed into the overall national budget, and requests have to be made for an allocation from this budget for telecommunications investment. In other EC countries, PTTs are more independent, but have to transfer certain parts of net cash generated to the national budget. Another important factor in some member states is that the losses on postal services are supported by the profits of the telecommunication services. For some PTTs, this substantially reduces the funds available for investment in telecommunications. The result is that, in 1981, in EC member states the average overall telecommunications investment levels (PTTs and private users) per capita was 79 per cent of that in Japan and 40 per cent of that in the US. Over a longer period, this may lead to a lower penetration of basic services and a weakening of the telecommunications manufacturing industry.

Most PTTs in the EC are, according to their charters, obliged to order their investments in networks and services in the light of net return within a short period. Thus, each investment must normally pay for itself. There are exceptions to this—as, for instance, in the Federal Republic of Germany—but, in many cases, such a policy prohibits PTTs from aggressively trying high-risk new services. This pattern may, in fact, slow down certain forms of innovation, as the PTT is more likely to 'procure' immediately usable equipment rather than more risky innovative equipment with a longer technology policy perspective. On the other hand, advanced ISDN planning shows that PTTs may be innovators.

In most EC states the PTT has a monopoly over the type of services that are provided by the telecommunications infrastructure. Increasingly, however, there is a growing market need for a greater variety of services. But, even if the PTT decides not to offer a particular service, other organizations are often not allowed to step in. Compared with the US, such (second and third generation) services are, indeed, becoming available only to a more limited degree in the EC, although national policies vary considerably. Many European PTTs discourage, for instance, private data communications networks. It is alleged, notably by users and service providers from the US, that the most important restrictions include measures to: abolish private leased lines at fixed monthly fees and force users to employ public switched lines, based on a volume sensitive pricing system; require some local processing of information, so as to reduce savings from remote data processing; prohibit the establishment of independent transmission facilities; forbid the resale or re-use of capacity on private leased lines (sharing extra capacity on a leased line with another user); require use of PTT supplied equipment for the 'first phone' on a line or the modems for data communications; forbid connecting private leased lines to the public switched network. Such regulations and policies are normally designed to discourage 'cream-skimming' and justified by the PTTs' social obligations to be able to provide cheaper rates to residential telephones, which must be balanced by higher revenues from business communications. Though there might be some virtue in the latter argument, it must be recognized that, in a number of European countries, the late and low level of availbility of second generation telecommunications services might slow the development of the market for telematics. Often the telecommunications infrastructure may be only a small cost element, but could effectively open up major opportunities in Europe.

The realization that opportunities for advanced services exist and are to some extent being missed will make the relationship between European governments, PTTs, manufacturers, and users more complex in the future. At the same time, the pressure from outside, notably from the US, to open up the telecommunications and data services markets will increase. Users representing the future microcomputer-dominated information environment may enhance the intense latent demand for workable local-area network (LAN architecture). Superior computing hardware thus creates demand for increased telecommunications capability. Future wide-area broad-band nets have to serve distributed applications running on new machine architectures. There will be demand for high-speed and high bit-rate services. Thus, in most EC countries, the present relationship between the main actors in the field of telematics might be modified by some adjustment in terms of judicious re-regulation in certain fields and complete deregulation in others. Not only the EC member states but also the EC Commission will have a vital role in this process (see below).

The re-regulation debate also extends to issues pertaining to norms and standards, both in terms of functional standards (designed to connect the networks and to guarantee the communication of terminals) and of operational standards (concerning the inner workings of the different telematic devices). The fragmentation of markets is aggravated by national standardization and type-approval policies. The economic impact of international telecommunications services and equipment standards has grown, as the distinction between the computer, broadcasting, and telecommunications industries blurs, and growth of the 'information' sector of the world economy continues. Current debates on standards for direct broadcast by satellites, high definition television, integrated services digital networks, and open systems interconnection, illustrate the dynamics of international standardization. Important standardization efforts are underway, including those within the framework of the International Telecommunications Union and the International Standards Organization, specifically the seven-layer reference model for open systems interconnection (OSI). Similarly, the European Commission has recently produced proposals for standardization in the field of information technology and telecommunications.[14] Nevertheless, the lack of an overall standards policy taking into account the technological continuum of telecommunications, data processing, and audio-visual media leads to narrow markets that may fall below the economic optimum.

Current standard-making processes are becoming increasingly inappropriate because there are separate processes for telecommunications, data processing, and communication and information services, while standards are needed in the interface-areas. Furthermore, innovation is speeding up, while the increasing complexity is slowing down standard-setting. Overall, there is the problem that technology is allowing an increasing diversity of equipment and services, while present standard-making processes (national and international) try to reduce both functional and operational standards, thus hampering, in some cases, technological development. The lack of standardization has, in sum, not only caused the loss to manufacturers of a substantial business opportunity, but, more importantly, denied users, the European business community, a potentially significant new service.

The OSI model[15] and the ISDN concept (also reflecting the OSI approach) are designed to overcome these problems. There is a controversy between IBM's SNA (systems network architecture) and the supporters of the OSI model, perceived as an anti-IBM standardization effort. The debate is over two different approaches to standardizing a market—on the basis of consensual international agreement, on the one hand, and a proprietory technology (*de facto* standardization), on the other. In principle, European firms and public authorities back the OSI standard as an alternative to IBM's SNA, but is there a real commitment to a European dimension when important investments are to be made and operational decisions taken? Some recent events show the complexity of the question. The German Bundespost, for instance, has decided, in one specific case, to adopt for the network of mail offices the SNA standard.

ISDN planning is occurring simultaneously at national levels, as the standardization work is progressing, under comparatively strong European influence, in Study Group XVIII of the CCITT, the relevant organ of the ITU. ISDN planning is the most ambitious and far-reaching of attempts to achieve standardization. At the most fundamental levels, there is some international agreement on what ISDN comprises: a network that may evolve from an integrated digital telephone network to provide complete end-to-end, digital connectivity (switches and paths), so that it may provide services on an integrated basis, including voice, non-voice, data, video, and other services. Beyond this basic description there is a wide spectrum of views on what an ISDN should be and why it is desirable to move in global telecommunications towards ISDNs. There is a debate between those who see ISDN as a device for maintaining monopolies and others who view it as a force for diversity. In European countries, it is generally easier to plan for the ISDN, due to the centralized administration of communications.

Thus, progress towards an ISDN environment in Germany is exceptionally well-planned, with milestones for technological developments and digital upgrading foreseen well into the next decade, contemplating eventual convergence of broad-band and narrow-band ISDNs.[16] France concentrates its ISDN planning on the digitization of the local loop. In the Netherlands, ISDN planning is based on the integration of telecommunications and existing cable television facilities. Belgium has begun with an intercity overlay network. Each of the European countries have their plans for the introduction of ISDN.

From comparison of these ISDN plans it is, however, evident that only the general concept of ISDN is common. In terms of the dates for introduction of new services, the specifications of the services, and specifications related to the network, there are significant differences from one country to another, acting as constraints for a European dimension. Certain European countries are already launching experiments, others do not foresee the introduction of ISDN before the mid-1990s. Today, not one teleservice which exploits the potential of ISDN is sufficiently well defined, not even the simplest of teleservices—the telephone! Under these conditions the terminal markets may remain, to a large extent, national markets. For a European terminal market, precise interfaces are indispensable, both between PABXs and terminals, and between terminals and the public exchanges. Today it is difficult to recognize any common policy in the ISDN strategies of the different countries in the EC.[17]

If the ISDN policies of the different European countries continue without any co-ordination, telecommunications markets, notably terminal markets, will remain national markets and thus of restricted size compared to a European market, hence sacrificing economies of scale which are of great importance during start-up phases. The lack of compatability of networks also presents particular difficulties to the operations of transnational enterprises, who are expected to be among the first major users of national ISDN services. A Europe thus divided will be faced by two other countries, whose internal markets are considerably larger than any national market in Europe. The European Commission argues that Europe might lose a strategic development if it does not achieve a rapid convergence in the introduction of the ISDN.

The Internationalization of the European Industry

Corporate strategies are of great relevance for development towards the creation of a European dimension for telecommunications. The framework in which individual firms define their industrial and commercial strategies includes novel threats and opportunities. Information and communications industries and markets are in a state of flux. It is impossible to predict the shape of the emerging telematic networks, services, and user equipment configurations. It is difficult to indicate whether telecommunications manufacturers are better positioned to make inroads into the office equipment sector or vice versa. It is probably in the European interest that telecommunications companies take the lion's share. Business communications, the integrated communications system of the future, are at the centre of the battle in which the giant rivalry between IBM and AT&T is repeated at lower levels by intensifying competition between firms with varying size and technological capacity.[18] It is not only this 'telematic syndrome', a merger of telecommunications with information technologies, but also the change in relative importance between telecommunications hardware and software[19] needed to drive the systems and guarantee inter-operability that produce links and mergers, acquisitions and participations, between equipment manufacturers and software houses.

An equally complex picture emerges in the area of market access. Despite the privatization of NTT, it seems at present difficult for foreign firms to secure major access to the Japanese telecommunications market. American firms thus seem to increase even more their interest in the European telecommunications market, and there is a growing pressure from the United States to obtain a more open telecommunications market. On the other hand, all major telecommunications firms have realized that a substantial breakthrough on the American market—40 per cent of the world telecommunications market—is an indispensable component of their strategy. European telecommunications enterprises indicate that they experience difficulties in accessing the 'deregulated' American market via trade, but direct investment and, notably, industrial alliances are considered promising ways. Are these alliances in the interest of Europe? Will they promote or hamper the developments towards a European telecommunications dimension? How can the European component in the emerging global industry be given as high a profile as possible?

For reasons of access to markets and/or access to technology, even giants like IBM and AT&T have not adopted a go-it-alone approach. Thus, IBM has secured its strategic bridgehead through the acquisition of Rolm, the PABX manufacturer. But European firms have also begun searching for 'global alliances'. BT, with the acquisition of CGT and Mitel of Canada, and Olivetti, with market access and technology agreements with AT&T and links with Toshiba and Xerox, are not the only European firms strengthening their potential for the battles to come. Thomson of France has concluded a deal with DEC on office communications and PABXs, while the new telecommunications group Alcatel-Thomson has signed an agreement with Fairchild. Siemens, for its part, has raised its stake in Telecom Plus of the US, is expanding its fibre optic joint venture (Siecor) with Corning Glass, and has agreed upon collaboration with GTE, a major US telephone operating company. Though authorities in Paris on the other hand support proposals for a European telecommunications alliance, the state-owned CGE appears interested in collaborating with AT&T.

The European monopolies have not so far favoured alliances by community-based firms via procurement policy. The second suppliers have normally been telecommunications firms with headquarters in the United States. But there are now attempts to strengthen the European component. Notably France is pushing in this direction. The French are said to have taken the lead in setting up the agreement between CIT-Alcatel, Italtel, Siemens, and Plessey on joint R. & D. efforts for sub-systems and components for digital switches. Yet the French Direction Générale des Telecommunications (DGT) has also taken up contacts with NEC of Japan and ITT as possible second suppliers of digital exchanges after the now merged Alcatel-Thomson group. European firms are prepared to work together in R. & D. programmes such as ESPRIT (European Strategic Programme for Research in Information Technologies) and RACE (Research for Advanced Communications in Europe). The ESPRIT programme was jointly formulated by Europe's electronics industry, the EC Commission, and the representatives of the EC member nations (with participation by the subsidiaries of transnational corporations, such as IBM and ITT, operating and actually doing research work in Europe). A recent assessment by an independent group of the available results of ESPRIT has, in the view of the European Commission, been quite positive.

The 'technology push', resulting from ESPRIT should be bolstered by the emergence of an increased 'high-tech pull' in Europe, primarily as a result of the development of telecommunications innovations. The RACE programme is designed to introduce a definition phase for the pre-paration of the 'integrated broad-band network', a revolutionary concept to provide comprehensive switched broad-band services for Western Europe by the late 1990s. It remains to be seen whether this co-operation will continue in the transition from development to application. It is possible that the new EUREKA initiative will generate, through a 'bottom-up approach', some of the conditions for a lasting and effective co-operation among European firms designed to achieve global competi-tiveness in advanced technological processes, services, and products.[20]

The European Community and Industrial Coherence

The Commission of the European Communities has emerged as a major factor in charting the course towards a European telecommunications dimension. In recent years the Commission has taken a leading role in formulating a coherent European approach to telecommunications covering the continuum from base technologies (ESPRIT) and infra-structural applications to services (both bearer and information services) and media policy.[21] The latest step in this endeavour is the programme RACE which involves three phases: a definition phase; a series of R. & D. programmes (including very large integrated circuits, high complexity integrated circuits, integrated opto-electronics, broad-band switching and communications software development); and pilot projects for broad-band equipment and services. The RACE programme is part of a Commission action plan submitted to the EC Council in May 1984.[22]

The first element in this action plan is the strengthening of a Com-munity-wide market for telecommunications in the terminal and network components area, on the basis of uniform standards and type-approval procedures. The Commission entered into a letter agreement with CEPT to work together on equipment standardization issues and to formulate a European perspective on such issues. On 12 November 1984 the EC Council adopted a recommendation that member governments ensure that telecommunications administrations and carriers provide opportunities on a non-discriminatory basis for tenders for (a) all new telematic terminals and conventional terminals, for which there are common type-approval specifications, and (b) contracts for switching and transmission apparatus and conventional terminal apparatus for which there are no common type-approval standards for at least 10 per cent in value of their annual orders.[23]

A second element of the action plan is the establishment of important joint telecommunications infrastructure projects, including a broad-band pilot network to link the decision-making centres in the Community, a second-generation transnational cellular telephone service, and joint investment in the main trans-Community lines for an integrated services broad-band network. The RACE programme is designed to contribute to such infrastructure investments. The Commission attempts to place the issues pertaining to a European telecommunications dimension at a political level and remove it as far as possible from the realm of technical discussions among the PTTs. One result of this effort is that EC member countries are prepared to ensure that all telecommunications services introduced from 1985 are 'on the basis of a common harmonised approach'; notably, digital switches ordered after 1986 should take account of common standards.[24] As to the ISDN development, the Senior Officials Group for Telecommunications, a group from European ministries of economics, industry, telecommunications, and foreign affairs has approved important first-stage proposals. The Group's task is to advise the Commission in the elaboration of proposals to the Council and they have approved a report proposing services (bearer services, tele-services, supplementary services, first and second generation, and adaptors) to be defined and specified in detail by the end of 1986 and provided in 1988 in all EC member states as a first step in a comprehensive ISDN strategy.[25]

The third element of the action plan dealt with joint research, notably RACE. The RACE staging and timetable, proposed in February 1984, anticipated the creation of an Integrated Broad-Band Communication System, which would first be demonstrated in 1988 and be fully operational by 1996.

The Commission is also concerned with the creation of more favourable conditions for the development of the European information market (including data banks, trade in information products, and new media, such as TV and video).[26]

In addition to its role in encouraging standardization and R. & D., the EC has considerable regulatory powers. If member states adopt protectionist norms, they may be in breach of Community law and the Commission has to act against such infringements of the EEC Treaty. Moreover, the Commission may have to adopt considered action to adapt to today's market the monopoly power of national PTTs, who control about 70 per cent of the EC telecommunications market. So far, the Commission has taken limited but decisive action in this field. It has acted to prevent the extension of PTT monopoly power to new product and service areas under Article 37 (and Article 86) of the Treaty of Rome. The Commission has initiated a number of complaints to encourage free and open competition in the telecommunications market. Its most notable involvement was its anti-trust case against IBM. The action was settled in return for commitments by IBM that it would release information about equipment standards, thus ensuring that private industry standards do not limit competitive opportunities for European manufacturers. In an attempt to limit the PTT monopoly in new products and services, the Commission has also filed a complaint against the German Bundespost alleging an 'abuse of dominant position' under Article 86 of the Treaty of Rome. The Commission's role in enforcing competition policy was recently given impetus by the March 1985 decision of the Court of Justice of the European Communities, upholding an earlier Commission decision in which the Commission held that British Telecom had abused its dominant position by prohibiting private message forwarding activities to the UK. The Court's decision in the British Telecom case may accord the Commission rather broad discretion to challenge activities or practices by PTTs that it views as impediments to competition. Another field where the Commission may have to act is state aid for the telecommunications sector, with a view to limiting deliberate distortion of competition while promoting the common interests of the Community (in pursuit of Article 92 of the Treaty of Rome). From a strictly legal point of view one may indeed conclude that the Community has an overriding duty to act in telecommunications, and that—given the supremacy of EC law—it has the tools at its disposal to contribute substantially to the creation of a European telecommunications dimension.

Conclusions

Telecommunications is a technology-intensive growth sector of strategic importance, where the more advanced countries of Western Europe remain competitive with the US and Japan. The objective of a European

telecommunications dimension is to consolidate this position. The parameters of a Community telecommunications policy are set by at least four
constraints: developments in the world market and competitive positions
in the techno-industrial race between the US, Japan, and Europe, the
regulatory framework in the EC member states, corporate strategies, and
the role of the EC Commission and of Community law.

These constraints and opportunities have to be considered in the context of overall telecommunications policy developments, driven notably
by fast technological change in the advanced countries of the West.
Deregulation has triggered off a wave of pricing adjustments, both at
national and international levels; telecommunications are becoming the
object of bilateral talks and are under the attention of the GATT; acquisitions and mergers, both at the national and the international level, will
derive from the efforts of companies to face the challenges of innovation
and competition; users will play an increasing role, both at the national
and the international level, as new telematic services develop and
pressure is put by users on national (and international) regulatory authorities for rationalization and for the introduction of flexible approaches.

Two basic attitudes emerge in this period of transition in telecommunications. The first draws on the US experience of the divestiture of
AT&T and favours 'liberalization', both in the telecommunications
infrastructure and in services. The second attitude favours 'integration'.
It stresses the positive elements of 'natural monopolies' and is based on
the conviction that monopoly power may be effectively used to promote
standardization, introduce new equipment and services, and to
strengthen transborder co-operation. It could, therefore, service the goals
of economic, industrial, and technological policy and thus contribute to
the enhancement of competitive positions in the international innovation
race.

The latter attitude, stressing the benefits of an integrated approach, is
dominant in continental Europe. The EC RACE programme is an
example of an integrated approach, although there remain, to some
extent, diverging views among the more advanced EC member countries
as to the the proper orientation of this initiative leading to an integrated
broad-band network in Europe.

In practice, there may not be one best approach. Neither integration
nor liberalization may be pursued as a pure solution, and compromises
will most probably characterize the transitional stage in telecommunication policy. In any case, greater reliance on competition does not eliminate the need for efficient re-regulation: the liberalization process must

be kept under some control to avoid, for instance, exploitative monopolies. It will also be necessary to find a balance between standard-setting, allowing an improvement of interconnection, and standards that may be perceived to act as technical barriers to trade; or, to give another example, a balance will have to be found between some effective supervision of the service providers, on the one hand, and providing them with the necessary degree of autonomy, on the other. There is, thus, wide scope for the adjustment of regulatory devices which, in a situation of constant change, must aim at a suitable balance in the relationships between 'facilities' and 'services'; between 'basic' and 'value added' services, and between 'enhanced services' and 'informational' or 'transitional' services.

One of the questions of overriding importance for European policy-makers, and notably for the EC Commission, is whether the development of a European telecommunications dimension will be centrally directed and co-ordinated or whether it will evolve a 'bottom up' approach from 'channelling' initiatives at the national level into European co-operation at the enterpreneurial level. The EUREKA initiative could, ideally, become a pragmatic framework for efforts designed to promote market-led co-operation and integration, and hence to the European presence in global telecommunications markets. In any case, European telecommunications strategies will evolve from institutional arrangements different from those in the US and Japan.

It certainly cannot be the objective of a European telecommunications dimension to hamper or reverse co-operation with enterprises originating from the US and Japan. The EC market must be an open one. But there is a need to give the European component in the emerging global telematic industry as high a profile as possible. A stronger European position could be boosted by joint R. & D. co-operation, joint ventures, and important telecommunications infrastructure projects where a European dimension is required (in view of high risk and large investment tasks ahead). Examples for such projects are the transition from narrow-band to broad-band ISDN, and the new generation of mobile radio and their integration into the network. The example of the space industry shows that European co-operation does not exclude co-operation with the US and Japan, but that such co-operation is fruitful and leads to genuine partner-ship, because, united, the Europeans can offer more.[27] This may also apply to telecommunications and telematics.

The impetus behind a European telecommunication policy is something more complex than the often cited stereotyped view of American electronics advantage, paced by space and military quantum leaps, or Japanese industry being perceived in a simplistic way as subsidized by MITI. What matters for Europe is, first, to create an entrepreneurial and innovative economy by facilitating positive adjustment policies, creating functioning markets for risk capital, and introducing fiscal policies that encourage innovation. This is part of the European internal market policy. In addition, further progress is needed in introducing new forms of co-operation between universities and industry, and in setting up models of equality-based co-operation between corporations already established in the market and creative research workers and young entrepreneurial blood willing to take risks. Secondly, considering the extent of the challenge and the massive capital investment involved in the international high-tech race, a purely decentralized approach will not suffice. If the European dimension—the vast internal European market, Europe's economic-technological-cultural potential, and the political institutions that arise from Community treaties and policies—is ever to be used, then the time to do so is now! The years to come will show the Europeans taking an active part in shaping the worldwide technological change and in assuming political responsibilities for it. Telecommunications and telematics are central to this effort.

Notes

1. The author is writing in his private capacity and the views expressed are his personal views
2. See Arthur D. Little International, *European Telecommunications—Strategic Issues and Opportunities for the Decade Ahead*, Final Report to the EC Commission (November 1983).
3. Klaus Grewlich, 'Free Electronic Information and Data Flow?', *German Foreign Affairs Review* 1985: 1.
4. OECD, *Software—An Emerging Industry* (Paris, 1985).
5. Federal Ministry for Research and Technology, *Specialized Information (Fachinformation)* (Bonn, 1985).
6. EC Commission (FAST Report), *EUROFUTURES—the challenges of innovation* (London, 1984).
7. See Heinrich Vogel, 'Technology for the East' (Technologie fur den Osten—ein leidiges Problem), *German Foreign Affairs Review* 1985: 2.
8. See e.g. EC Commission, *The Competitivity of the Industries of the European Community* (Luxembourg, 1982); Commissariat Général du Plan, *Quelle*

Strategie Europeanée pour la France dans les annees 80? (Paris, 1983); Klaus Grewlich, 'EG-Forschungs—und Technologiepolitik' in Herbek Rudolf und Wolfgang Wessels (eds.), *EG-Mitgliedschaft ein vitales Interesse der Bundesrepublik Deutschland?* (Bonn, 1984); Brendan Cardiff, 'Impact of High Technology on European-American Relations—High Technology Trade Indicators' (December 1984, unpublished).

9. See the preparatory papers for the European conference, 'A Competitive Future for Europe', Erasmus University Rotterdam (12–13 December 1985).

10. Klaus Grewlich and Finn H. Pedersen (eds.), *Power and Participation in an Information Society* (Luxembourg: EC Commission (Fast), 1984).

11. EC Commission, *Communication on Telecommunications*, Doc. COM (84), 277 (final), 18 May 1984.

12. See C. J. Van der Klugt, 'Prospects for Collaboration and a Common Industrial Policy in Europe for the High-Technology Industries' (Speech at *Financial Times* Conference, London 21–2 June 1983).

13. See also Arthur D. Little International, *Telecommunications Regulatory Policy in the European Community, USA and Japan*, Final Report for the EC Commission (Brussels, 1983).

14. EC Commission, *Proposal for a Council Directive on Standardisation in the Field of Information Technology and Telecommunications*, Doc. COM (85), 230 (final), 25 June 1985.

15. The seven layers of OSI are (1) physical, (2) link, (3) network, (4) transport, (5) session, (6) presentation, and (7) application. The first three, or lower-level, layers describe the control of, and interaction with, the network by terminals. These layers describe 'network', rather than 'service', whereas the higher layers, five to seven, describe services, i.e. communications between users.

16. See *Jahrbuch der Deutschen Bundespost*, vols. 35 and 36 (1984 and 1985).

17. EC Senior Officials Group, Telecommunications/Analysis and Forecasting Group, 'Proposals for the Coordinated Introduction of ISDN in the Community', Brussels 1985 (unpublished).

18. See e.g. European Research Associates (Robert Taylor), 'Corporate Strategies and Government Policies in Telecommunications', Brussels 1985 (unpublished). This section draws extensively on the results of this study.

19. Five years ago a big switching station represented a mix of 75% hardware and 25% software in value added; today, the split is about 50–50; five years from now it is likely to be 25% hardware and 75% software, see Klaus Grewlich, 'EUREKA-eureka?', *German Foreign Affairs Review* 1985, 1, p. 23.

20. See the 'Declaration of Principles' and the concrete projects resulting from the 'second EUREKA conference at ministerial level', Hanover, 5 and 6 November 1985; the third EUREKA conference is to take place in the UK.

21. For an economic and political analysis of this approach see Gilbert-François Caty & Herbert Ungerer, *Les Télécommunications—nouvelle frontière de l'Europe* (Futuribles, December 1984), p. 29 ff.; Klaus Grewlich, 'Information and Communication Technologies—A European Answer', *Transnational Data Report*, vol. VIII, No. 3 (1985); Maurice English & A. Watson Brown, 'National Policies in Information Technology—Challenges and Responses', *Oxford Surveys in Information Technology*, vol. 1, 1984.

22. EC Commission, *Communication on Telecommunications*, op. cit. (n. 11), 18 May 1984.

23. Council Recommendation of 12 November 1984, *Official Journal of the European Communities*, No. 1, 298/51, 16 November 1984.

24. Council Recommendation of 12 November 1984, *Official Journal of the European Communities*, No. 1, 298/49.

25. EC Senior Officials Group, Telecommunications/Analysis and Forecasting Group, op. cit. (n. 17).

26. EC Commission, *Discussion Paper on a Community Information Market Policy*, SEC (84) 1928, 15 February 1985; EC Commission, *Television without frontiers*, COM (84) 300 (final), 14 June 1984; EC Commission, *Work Programme for Creating a Common Information Market*, COM (85) 658, 29 November 1985.

27. Klaus W. Grewlich, 'Information Technologies', *German Foreign Affairs Review* 1985: 2.

Conclusion: Comparing Government–Industry Relations: States, Sectors, and Networks

Stephen Wilks and Maurice Wright

As its broadest, government–industry relations is concerned with the grand issues of what used to be termed 'political economy'. The giants of classic political economy each had some conception of the actual and proper relationship between government and industry. For Adam Smith, government was unproductive and the 'profusion of government must, undoubtedly, have retarded the natural progress of England towards wealth and improvement'.[1] Nevertheless, he accepted necessary minimal functions for government in the provision of public goods, mainly public works. For Marx, government in capitalist society was seen as an instrument of the ruling class, and, in the famous formulation of the Communist Manifesto, 'the executive of the modern state is but a committee for managing the common affairs of the whole bourgeoisie'. While contemporary Marxist analysis rejects a simple mechanistic or deterministic relationship between capital and the state (or between industry and government), such theoretical positions, in their modern guise, continue, in an extraordinary way, to define much of the agenda of the contemporary debate, at least in Britain, where highly idealized principles of market economics and socialist planning are incorporated into party-political positions. Similarly, post-war political economists, like Schumpeter[2] and Lindblom,[3] discuss issues of governmental control and industrial autonomy.

At the other end of the spectrum, government–industry relations exists, and can be studied, over a number of narrow and often prosaic areas. Studies of corporate taxation, sponsored training, or government procurement illustrate the variety of government's relations with industry and the fundamental, constitutive foundation for industrial activity provided by the multiple activities of the state.

The objectives of the ESRC research initiative are far more modest than those of the great political economists, but more ambitious than a series of detailed substantive studies. We are not directly concerned with the detailed analysis of policies or industries, nor with interpreting political outcomes, explaining relative industrial success, nor with prescribing suitable ways of improving industrial or governmental performance. Our primary concern is with the understanding and analysis of the *processes* of government–industry relations: how the various organizations interact; what goals the key players pursue; how they construct their strategies; and how they influence one another. Our contention is that there is virtually no systematic ordering of material in this area, and the production of reliable interpretation and valid generalizations about processes will supply an important tool for contributing to an understanding of the substance, outcomes, relative success, and prescriptions for government–industry relations. Thus, while the empirical studies reported in earlier chapters are important as industry studies, they are more important as extended case-studies of how the processes of government–industry relations actually operate. The eventual theoretical challenge will be to integrate these individual analyses into a manageable framework of concepts which distinguish the characteristics of the processes of government–industry relations, between countries and between sectors, by reference to a series of accessible variables. The building blocks of one such possible framework are elaborated later in this chapter.

The general approach of the ESRC research initiative, and of this volume, was outlined in the Introduction. Since the emphasis is on relationships and processes there is a bias towards issues defined by reference to political science and policy concerns. The three consistent themes identified were, first, the urgent need to break away from system-level macro-generalizations and to move towards empirically-based analysis, second, the comparative focus, and third, the effort to contribute towards a more productive theoretical approach. In order to illustrate some of the drawbacks in the existing literature, and the relative absence of directly applicable theory, we go on to review some of the more influential interpretations of comparative government–industry relations. The generalizations that emerge from the existing political science literature are compared with the research findings reported in earlier chapters, and we conclude that it may be more correct to see the research initiative as a departure from, rather than as an attempt to 'build upon', previous work. In the spirit of such an enterprise, we present an adaptation of an interorganizational framework of policy communities and networks. Some of the research findings are reinterpreted in this light to illustrate that we have here a productive middle-range research tool, which can generate creative, consistent, and relatively rigorous analysis. The chapter ends with a note of warning: both government and industry share a concern and a responsibility for industrial growth, and the concern with growth forms an unspoken semi-normative bias in much academic analysis. Government also, however, must have regard to societal and environmental implications of industry's economic success. The analysis of government–industry relations should not lose sight of societal and distributional issues.

Comparative Industrial Adaptation

A literature on comparative government–industry relations is beginning to emerge and there have been some extremely useful summaries.[4] It would not be strictly true, however, to say that there is an extensive or focused literature, since this subject area had been delineated in its present form mainly as a result of the ESRC research initiative.[5] There are several substantial bodies of literature which bear directly on the question of comparative government–industry relations without necessarily addressing it directly. Thus, for instance, work on industrial relations, economic history, business strategy, and macro-economic management has much to offer for an understanding of comparative issues. More directly, much of the recent writing on corporatism is explicitly comparative, and frequently deals with relations between business, labour, and government. This literature is particularly relevant because its major concern is with the organization and institutionalization of interest 'intermediation'. When this perception is applied to business and labour we can find incisive analysis of the detail of relations between government and industry.[6]

Over the past decade, there has developed an intense interest in how states and economies have adapted to a far less favourable economic environment. The 'oil shocks', slow growth, monetary instability, rising unemployment, and rapid technological change have presented a series of challenges to economic management. Different states have reacted in different ways and with varying degrees of success. An important element in their reactions has been 'industrial policy', which can be said to have come of age during the seventies. The study of industrial policy has expanded rapidly among academics, and in international institutions like the OECD,[7] and this expansion has been fuelled by a keen interest in 'how they do it elsewhere'. The German social market model has been widely admired, and perhaps less widely understood, by British Conservative ministers, while, across Europe and the United States, the competitive strength of the Japanese has fostered a masochistic curiosity in the extent to which the Japanese state has promoted its industry.

While the undertaking is still inchoate, there have, nevertheless, been several recent studies which address comparatively the issue of industrial policy, and, hence, government–industry relations. Since the focus is typically wider than policy programmes as such, and, in fact, is concerned with the ability or inability of the state to respond to economic challenges,[8] it would be more accurate to describe the literature as dealing with 'comparative industrial adaptation'. These studies cannot, for the sake of space, be reviewed exhaustively here. On the other hand, it is necessary briefly to consider their content and their relevance to the research undertaking, for two reasons. First, the research on GIR is not being undertaken in a theoretical vacuum. Researchers are clearly influenced by the prevailing body of ideas and concepts which are available to be validated, invalidated, or perhaps discarded as irrelevant. Secondly, there is some evidence that the concepts presented in much of the existing literature are indeed irrelevant to disaggregated, detailed research into the government–industry relationship. To an extent, research approaches, tools, and concepts are being developed from scratch. Researchers are not building upon or testing previous theoretical work, they are abandoning it as misleading. If this is the case, then the theoretical disjuncture needs to be made explicit and, to some extent, delineated.

The best place to start is with the common-sense observation that, in some countries, state-intervention in industry is customary and unremarked: the state is expected to involve itself in industrial activities; in other countries, intervention is contested and regarded as intensely controversial: the state is expected to stay aloof from industrial activity. At this hugely generalized, but nevertheless recognizably accurate, level we, therefore, have a contrast between assertive interventionist states and non-interventionist, market-dominated states. The prime examples of interventionist states appear, of course, to be Japan and France. They also have enjoyed conspicuous industrial success over the post-war period. The non-interventionist states are, in contrast, the USA and the UK; in these cases, coincidentally or not, industrial success has proved more elusive. Somewhere in the middle ground lies West Germany, which is economically highly successful but where state agencies certainly profess not to intervene. This broad generalization finds confirmation in a variety of summary country studies of industrial policy and industrial adaptation.[9] Simple observation, journalistic generalization, and anecdote can also, of course, give rise to dangerous caricatures of industrial adaptation, which generate glib references to 'Japan Inc.', to French '*étatisme*', to America as a corporate economy, or to the British liberal bias.[10]

If this broad intervention/non-intervention spectrum could be freely accepted as describing consistent, nationally homogeneous approaches to the role of the state in the economy, then much of the agenda of research on government and industry would be predefined. In particular we would expect to be able to test a series of hypotheses about how government relates to, or engages with, industry. We could, for instance, expect to find the features shown in Table 12.1 as typical of the government–industry relationship. Before any attempt could be made to apply such a model, or to examine the hypotheses it embodies, we would need to identify the causal theories which have been advanced to explain variations in intervention.

The most widespread, influential, and sophisticated theoretical explanation for variations in governmental intervention in the process of industrial adaptation is centred on an interpretation of the role of the state in society. The argument is historical/cultural and draws on the way in which political history has fashioned state forms, and the way in which economic history has drawn the state into sponsorship of industrial development. A particularly articulate exponent of this position is Kenneth Dyson who argues that societies have a distinctive industrial culture which expresses traditions of public authority and the historical processes of industrialization. Hence these industrial cultures 'help to explain some of the deep and subtle differences between the character of

Table 12.1

Interventionist states	Non-interventionist states
discriminatory policy	even-handed non-discrimination
firm level intervention	industry level intervention
proactive government	reactive government
business co-operation	business suspicion
regular and stable contact	irregular and *ad hoc* contact
informal consultation	formal consultation

government–industry relations in Britain and the United States on the one hand, and France, Italy and West Germany on the other'.[11]

In the continental countries, it is argued, policial history has been one of conflict and insecurity. In Germany and France (and the argument might be extended to Japan), absolutist rulers defended the integrity and coherence of the state, by reference to their personal qualities, by asserting the primacy of national interests and the need to maintain secure borders. In these states, succeeding regimes have inherited and built upon legal and administrative traditions which stress the importance of national solidarity, the importance of allegiance to state priorities, and the requirement for the state to lead or authorize major economic developments. A contrast can be drawn with Britain and the United States, which have enjoyed relatively peaceful political traditions and gradual, bloodless evolution of the political system. These states have liberal political traditions which emphasize free association, consent, and a government which reacts to, rather than dominates, the popular will. This contrast emerges in the work of a variety of authors. Dyson, for instance, draws a contrast between 'state' and 'state-less' societies.[12] State societies are marked by a deference to the authority of state organs and implicitly, therefore, intervention is, if desired, regarded as a legitimate use of public authority. But such state societies are also characterized by a respect for order, a sense of the pre-eminence of public obligations, and a legal tradition (in continental Europe) of regulation of social relationships and industrial organizations. Britain and America are, however, 'state-less' societies. There is widespread scepticism of the ability or right of government to provide industrial leadership and 'neither administrative nor business culture has absorbed the concept of a benevolent "public power"—the state—acting in the name of the common good'.[13]

The second element in the formation of industrial cultures derives from the work of economic historians. In the work of Alexander Gerschenkron, and succeeding writers of this school,[14] it is suggested that the later a country industrializes (or the more 'backward' it is), the more important and assertive must be the role of the state in facilitating industrialization. Thus, the early industrializers, especially Britain and the United States, experienced a market-led, company dominated industrial revolution, in which the role of government was minimal and the functions of the state embraced only the classic *laissez-faire* responsibilities of monetary and commercial regulation. Later industrializers, however, relied upon the state to mobilize capital, to invest, to build protective trade barriers, and even to engage directly in industrial production. The prime examples, here, are France and Japan. In these states, government's positive role in industrial activity was essential for industrial growth; the leadership and intervention provided by the state was regarded as necessary and entirely legitimate. As Dyson again puts it, 'the central thesis . . . is that the character . . . of industrial cultures are rooted not just in social structure and in political and legal tradition, but also in the historical conditions of industrialisation'.[15]

Dyson is, of course, expressing, in an admirable and accessible synthesis, a widespread view which has the hallmarks of a theoretical orthodoxy. Its origins lie in the early 1960s, when Britain's relative industrial decline first became fully apparent and analysis of its causes became a preoccupation. Thus, in 1963, Brian Chapman pointed to the lack of any British concept of 'the State', and hence identified an institutional origin of Britain's decline. He remarked upon 'the genuine lack of doctrinal significance attached to the concept of public service in Britain. There is no sentiment that public office should involve public responsibility, or that public power should involve the exercise of dispassionate and disinterested judgement.'[16] In 1965, Andrew Shonfield took a not dissimilar line. His influential study put emphasis on the role of public authorities in fostering economic success. He stressed the importance of 'the management of the institutional apparatus which guides Western economic life',[17] and he detected a process of convergence, especially over the use of economic planning. In the detail of his comparative analysis, Shonfield constantly referred back to traditions of public power and the historical origins of industrialization. Taking a more recent example, Andrew Gamble similarly emphasizes the weakness of the British state and its inability to pursue 'industrial modernisation'. His theme, as with several other writers,[18] is that of the 'unfinished revolution'. Early industrialization, and the post-civil war subordination of the state to private interests, meant that 'the planning for future growth and the anticipation of the long-term needs of capital accumulation, was provided for neither by British civil society . . . nor by the British state, which remained wedded to the liberal conception of its role in the national economy.'[19] According to such writers, therefore, there are considerable variations in the national autonomy and authority of the state apparatus, which, in turn, affects the competence of the state to facilitate, to lead, or simply to involve itself constructively in the process of industrial adaptation and economic growth.[20] Such variations are historically determined over a span of centuries. Gamble can refer back to 1688, commentators on France regularly cite an interventionist tradition which stretches back to the *ancien régime*, while writers on Japan may stress the more recent Meiji restoration of 1868.

In a comparative context, the most impressive deployment of this theme is to be found in Katzenstein's 1978 collection.[21] The analytic focus is on the distinction between state and society, but the collection also delineates 'ruling coalitions' and distinct policy networks within each state. An attempt is made to identify the distinctive national state forms within which networks operate, since 'the ways in which state and society are actually linked is historically conditioned and that link determines to a large extent whether modern capitalism is atomistic, competitive, organised or statist'.[22] For purposes of analysing foreign economic policy, Katzenstein is able to group the advanced industrial states into three categories. The first, occupied by Britain and the United States, is marked by devotion to objectives of a liberal international economic order and possesses relatively few policy instruments. Japan, in contrast, has an overwhelming objective of economic growth and a multiplicity of policy instruments. The continental states of France and West Germany constitute a third, hybrid pattern. These patterns are also marked by variations in 'the degree of differentiation which separates state from society'.[23] Overall, 'the role of the state in policy networks is strongest in Japan . . . The role of the state is also strong in France . . . Suffering from different liabilities, the American, British, West German and Italian states have fewer instruments at their disposal.'[24] There is a danger in over-simplifying to the point which does violence to the caution and subtlety of Katzenstein's analysis, but the implication is certainly that variations in industrial adaptation are to be explained essentially by features which generated 'strong' states in some countries and 'weak' states in others. The vocabulary of strong and weak states is used explicitly by Krasner in the same collection, who does unambiguously assert that:

the defining feature of a political system is the power of the state in relation to its own society. This power can be envisaged along a continuum ranging from weak to strong . . . Japan comes closest to the pole of strength . . . the United States is probably closest to the pole of weakness.[25]

Thus, it can be said that an orthodox explanation of variations in the comparative role of government in industrial adaptation, with all that is implied for government–industry relations, would propose a simple typology of strong and weak states. Britain and the United States are 'weak' states marked by liberal traditions, a reactive government which intervenes very reluctantly, and national attitudes which strongly reject any need for the state to intervene extensively in the market. France and Japan, by contrast, are 'strong' states with authoritarian traditions, where the market is regarded as suspect, and government intervention is regarded as in the natural order of things. In these cases, the state performs a leadership role by means of routine, unremarked sectoral and financial policies.

Germany sits uncomfortably in this schema. While clearly a strong state in political terms, with authoritarian traditions, she was also a relatively early industrializer. The German case hence falls into the middle ground, with the industrial leadership functions of the state being performed by finance capital and the emergence of a distinctive form of capitalist 'self-organization' which is as unremarked, in its way, as is state intervention in France. Thus, the functions performed by the organs of the state in France are in Germany performed by the big banks, through industrial organizations, and through modern equivalents of cartelization. Although, even here, strong state theorists might argue that the non-interventionism of the German state is shallow. Shonfield asserted that the prophet of the social market, Ludwig Erhard, 'has never been averse to using the authority of the state, or his own personal position, to mould the decisions of industrial entrepreneurs in the way that he or the Government wanted'.[26] Similarly, Katzenstein maintains that 'even today . . . there are traces in the West German policy network which resemble the Japanese model more than the Anglo-Saxon one'.[27]

It would be wrong to give the impression that the strong state–weak state orthodoxy is entirely dominant. In an important, recent comparative study Zysman offers an alternative interpretation which rejects the influence of (industrial) culture in favour of 'the structure of the national financial system (which) will be an autonomous influence on the political relations between business and government'. He boldy argues that 'selective credit allocation is the single discretion necessary to all state-led industrial strategies',[28] and, on this basis, identifies three types of financial system and three models of industrial change. The first is 'state-led', where a credit-based, price administered financial system allows bureaucrats to intervene pervasively and invisibly in industrial activities. France and Japan are the examples. The second is 'company-led', where extensive and efficient capital markets allow companies autonomy and deny officials any effective avenues of influence. Here we have the United States. The third model is typical of West Germany (and, more particularly, Sweden), where adjustment is 'tripartite-bargained' in a financial system marked by institution-led or bank-dominated capital markets.[29] Britain, he says, is marked by a failure to make a choice. The financial system would appear to foster a company-led approach but attempts have been made to move to a state-led approach.

Zysman rejects the strong/weak state argument as too aggregate, and criticizes Katzenstein's synthesis as similarly too generalized, but also as static and as incapable of analysing how market dynamics affect the objectives and strategies of actors.[30] He also takes an important position on the historicism of the strong/weak state position, arguing that to assert continuity is inadequate; the mechanisms of continuity need to be explained. Thus, in the French case, 'the interventionist state was not the product of some ingrained national character, of an ideology of *étatisme*, or of an historical tradition of close involvement in the economy. . . . it represented an explicit political victory that shifted the relative positions of business leadership and state bureaucrats.'[31] In other words, a core of bureaucratic planners captured the levers of the financial system in the immediate post-war period to construct a distinctive state-fostered development strategy. Exactly the same position is argued for the UK. Neo-liberalism is seen as a post-war political creation arising out of a failure to recognize the importance of financial instruments for control of the economy.

It might be thought that Zysman has taken an otherwise valid insight a little too far. To differentiate systems of industrial adjustment on the basis of what is essentially a set of policy instruments is a difficult task and one could reasonably inquire into the historical origins of the financial systems themselves and question the ability of any government, or even a reconstructed post-war state, to entirely redesign capital and financial markets. Nevertheless, the argument is stimulating and provides a counterpoint to the strong/weak state typology.

Weaknesses in the Prevailing Theories of Industrial Adaptation

In this section we will illustrate why the prevailing comparative theories of industrial adaptation are of limited utility in conducting research on government–industry relations. In the process, we highlight and comment on some of the findings reported in earlier chapters, and identify some of the specific directions in which the development of new theory might be expected to go. In particular, we take a simplified model of the strong/weak state argument and, by indicating its shortcomings, indicate also why the researchers working within the ESRC initiative have rejected the approach as positively misleading. It is not only possible, it is probable, that the strong/weak state model outlined above is over-simplified. Nevertheless, it serves to illustrate the major theme of this section which is the fact of theoretical disjuncture, although, towards the end of this section, we also affirm some elements of the model's contextual merit.

In several important, areas, the analysis of the role of the state in society proves misleading in informing detailed research into GIR. To take three, rather eclectic, but individually important, sets of examples. The research findings report, first, several cases in which the direction of influence runs counter to what orthodox theory would suggest. Secondly, they identify a variety of informal relationships which operate by reference to their own, possibly selfish, logic and do not necessarily operate as instruments of either government or industry. Thirdly, they emphasize the ubiquitousness of intra-bureaucratic conflict, which, therefore, calls into question any theory that posits a monolithic or consistent bureaucratic influence on GIR.

Unexpected directions of influence

In several of the chapters, the main argument reveals an unorthodox interpretation of the direction of influence within that particular sector or in detected policy networks. In the case of France, Cawson, Holmes, and Stevens find a position rather different from the usual expectations of *dirigiste* control and state-leadership. Instead, they identify a variety of possible sets of power relations. In consumer electronics, for instance, the relationship is one in which Thomson dominates the state agencies and can be described as 'bargained corporatism' verging on 'agency capture' (of the Industry Ministry). In this sector it could almost be said that 'the state acts as Thomson's champion'. In such cases of sector-domination by technological national champions, it appears that the state does not 'lead', it follows.

The opposite phenomenon is analysed by Macmillan and Turner in their examination of the UK pharmaceutical industry. Here one might expect that the behaviour traditionally associated with a regulatory, liberal state would lead to minimalist, non-interventionist, arms-length relationships with the industry. In fact, the pharmaceuticals industry appears to offer an exception to most generalizations about British government–industry relations. Historically, it has had close, informal and very beneficial dealings with state agencies. The limited list episode has partially exploded that previous cosy pattern of relationships in one policy network, but again in an unpredictable fashion. It may be the case that the absence of consultation, and the dogmatic nature of the introduction of the limited list, is more typical of government–industry relations in Britain, but the effect was to disrupt assertively drug-markets at the level of the individual firm. The limited list was proactive, radical, and had, an allegedly quite deliberate, differential impact on drug firms. As such, it constituted a decidedly illiberal deployment of the more usually latent power of the British state.

The same experience of unorthodox influence is evident in the West German chemical industry. The conventional wisdom about the importance of house-banks and the influence of supervisory boards is challenged by Grant, Paterson, and Whitston, who argue that, in this sector, dominated by large international firms, 'the sheer size of the three dominating German chemical firms means that they do not have "house banks" in the conventional sense' (p. 51). While they note 'a sense of organic unity' (p. 37) in the German case, they are dubious about explaining it in terms of strong and weak states. In relation to the chemical industry, the German state is not interventionist, and, as they point out, both the extent and mechanisms for industrial self-organization vary markedly from sector to sector.

In pursuit of the same theme, Vogel argues explicitly that the weak state portrayal of the United States is exaggerated. On the contrary, he argues, America has always pursued activist industrial policies and has had considerable success in 'picking winners' (p. 92). American government, contrary to received wisdom, provides leadership and initiative and 'the DoD has displayed far more initiative in its dealings with industry than MITI' (p. 104).

Here, we are no doubt experiencing the familiar academic dialectic of debunking orthodoxies. It is always convenient to advance an argument by critical contrast with existing theories, but we are persuaded that these instances are not mere cases of academic vandalism. It seems more accurate to suggest that orthodox theory provides an opening hypothesis, but simply proves insufficiently subtle to explore relationships of great complexity and variation *within* as well as between countries.

The importance of informal relations

A second area which research findings, not unexpectedly, reveal
as important is the question of informal relations within the
government–industry relationship. In its way, interpretation of informal
relationships is one of the most difficult of research tasks. Not only are
researchers' judgements subjective, they are themselves frequently based
upon subjective verbal interpretations by participants. An example is
given by Wakiyama who notes that a drawback in the operation of
Japanese 'administrative guidance' is that guidance 'is often conveyed to
the company executives concerned orally . . . without clarifying whether
such guidance reflects MITI's official position' (p. 225). Definitive
empirical investigation of this type of relationship is, in practice,
virtually impossible. Nevertheless, some indication of the workings of
informal policy networks does emerge from the various chapters. In the
UK foundries industry, for instance, Appleby and Bessant document
the profusion of trade and research associations, which have made, on the
whole, a poor job of articulating an industry viewpoint and have failed to
mobilize constructive responses to adaptation. One reason for representational fragmentation appears to be the parochialism and defensiveness of
the directors and employees of trade associations. With one or two notable exceptions, there has been a tendency to put personal independence,
and the secure familiarity of dealing with an industrial sub-sector, ahead
of the need to construct an industry-wide, longer-term strategy. Here,
informal relations and individual preferences have produced apparently
dysfunctional relationships.

A more general and influential set of informal relationships emerges
from the 'legal culture' within which government and industry in the
FRG operates. At a very generalized level, the importance of legality and
legal problem-solving is widely noted in the Federal Republic; the
practical effects of legalism are analysed far less often. Hancher and
Reute, however, produce just such examples. They outline the
importance of legal culture and legal training which facilitates mutual
understanding and good communications, and hence opens up the policy
process 'to create a plurality of policy participants' (p. 175). But, in the
pharmaceuticals industry, the more open policy process allows industry a
'court of appeal' on adverse decisions. When new licenses for drugs are
refused, industry can object under rules of administrative law, and is very
often successful (p. 167). This produces a markedly 'industry friendly'
regulatory regime which appears to be facilitated partly by the simple

availability of legal remedies, but also by the informal relationships and understandings which surround a common concern with legal process.

Similarly, in France, the *grands corps* fraternities operate largely as sets of informal relationships. Here also, a perverse internal logic comes into operation. As outlined above, Cawson *et al.* argue that the direction of influence in the French government–industry relationship is, in some cases, the reverse of state domination. An important supporting mechanism is that the direction of influence within the *grands corps* can be reversed. Far from the state 'colonizing' the commanding heights of finance and industry, the *corps* members on detachment can use their contacts within the state apparatus to forward their personal or organizational interests. Thus, Cawson *et al.* report the view that 'a Civil Servant . . . may be influenced in his approach towards an enterprise by the fact that senior members of his *corps*, upon whom his career may depend, are to be found within that enterprise' (p. 15).

A final example of the importance of informal relations can be drawn from the internationalization of the chemical industry. In their chapter in this collection, and elsewhere,[32] Grant *et al.* stress that the internationalization of the industry has modified national characteristics (such as the role of the house-banks and incorporation of the trade unions in the FRG). The market in industrial chemicals is, to a large extent, a unified European one. Inter-company relationships, consequently, need to take place at a European level, and dealings with the EEC and other international authorities assume a new importance. Opportunities thus exist for resolving problems at a supranational level, and if, for instance, informal cartelization took place, it would be at such a level. Dealings with national governments become less important; or, alternatively, national level government–industry relations will tend to be conducted as a subset of a larger network, and the opportunity for bilateral government–industry accommodation and agreement must be substantially reduced.

In these examples, therefore, we have a series of cases where government–industry relations are mediated through quite distinct personalized or informal sets of relationships, whose primary rationale is neither to exert influence on government nor vice versa. The main motivating force is, rather, to secure common benefits for the participating individuals, whether they are in government, in industry, or in both. The practical effects of such informal contacts on the conduct and outcomes of government–industry relations cannot, therefore, be hypothesized in terms of 'strong' and 'weak' states. The strong/weak perspective implies that relationships are operating as formal channels of deployment of, or resistance to, state influence. In fact, concepts of organizational sociology are more applicable, since they throw light on the informal motivations and behaviour of individuals and groups.

Intra-governmental disputes

A third theme which has recurred in research findings, and the discussion of them, is the ubiquitous nature of intra-governmental and intra-bureaucratic conflict. Again, this is hardly unexpected, but the importance and ramifications of governmental fragmentation require emphasis and pose their own analytical problems. It is clearly necessary to 'unpack' the concept of bureaucracy and to develop some clearer ideas about the dynamics of disputes within the machinery of the state.

Bureaucratic pluralism in the United States is a familiar phenomenon and Irwin's account of the telecommunications domain conflicts between defence, justice, federal, and state regulatory agencies might raise few eyebrows. In the Japanese case, however, it might be thought more surprising to find open and intense conflict between MITI and the MPT (Ministry of Posts & Telecommunications) over the sponsorship and regulation of NTT (Nippon Telephone & Telegraph) and its attendant supplier industries. The regulatory task and responsibility for the privatization process was eventually entrusted to the MPT, which has a more nationalist stand over public procurement. But any lingering myths about MITI's infallibility are put into question by the evidence that it is not only challenged by industry, but also from within the state machine, from other ministries and especially, as Boyd points out, from the Ministry of Finance (p. 71).

The curiosities of inter-departmental conflict are illustrated, also, by the experience of the British pharmaceutical industry. In telecommunications, the battle is waged over expansion of areas of responsibility and, perjoratively, the aim is empire building. In the British drugs example, the reverse seems to be the case. The DHSS, which at present sponsors the industry, is anxious to simplify its customer relationship by passing sponsorship of the industry to the DTI. For their part, DTI officials are leery of taking responsibility for the industry, without influence over the drugs procurement budget, and resist the aquisition of this new responsibility. Conventional theories of bureaucratic aggrandisement would have little to offer here.

Two further standard examples of government fragmentation find confirmation from preceding chapters. The French Industry Ministry is said to be regarded with suspicion, within the administration, as too sympathetic to industry. Cawson *et al.* confirm this view in relation to consumer electronics, and confirm also that not only does the Finance Ministry have its own clear financial objectives for the industry, but that, in the case of disagreements, Thomson and the Industry Ministry would decide a joint position and defend it against Finance. It is also widely remarked that there exists in the FRG a longstanding disagreement between the liberal, FDP dominated Economics Ministry and the interventionist, previously SPD dominated, Research Ministry. Similarly there are federal/*Land* and inter-*Land* variations occasioned by *Land* support for regionally imporant industries or individual firms, such as foundries and the big three chemical companies. The relationship of Hoechst to its 'home' state of Hesse provides an interesting example. Grant, Paterson, and Whitston emphasize the conflict between the company and the environmental movement as embodied in Hesse's 'Green' Environment Minister (p. 47). The company is clearly experiencing a less supportive home base, and, indeed, an increasingly important cleavage is also emerging at the federal level, between the Environment Ministry and the Economics Ministry, in relation to both chemicals and foundries. The Environment Ministry is decidedly critical, and responds with greater sympathy to the views of environmental pressure groups.

When it comes, therefore, to interpreting the role of government agencies within the GIR, the guidance offered by the strong/weak dichotomy is no more than a first, and often inaccurate, approximation. The bureacracy is clearly differentiated by function and by department, but in its attitudes, its ideologies (or 'culture'), and its adherence to traditional behaviour it also varies from department to department and possibly from case to case. In order to understand the operation of a fragmented bureaucracy within the GIR, we need a more fine-grained analytical schema.

National and Sectoral Comparisons

To some extent, the theoretical disjuncture, referred to above, reflects differing levels of analysis. Research which is concerned with government and industry at the sectoral or even firm level will, almost by definition, be ill-served by an analytical framework which is orientated towards international comparison. It remains an open but important question whether government–industry relationships may vary more significantly or consistently between sectors than between nations. That certain sector-specific characteristics do recur consistently across a range of national settings is clear. Whether such sectoral characteristics are more significant than variations in national characteristics is an empirically unresolved question.

In two respects international comparision of the strong/weak state variety continues to offer an important element of context, which more detailed inter-sectoral comparison could usefully recognize. The first of these is the pervasive contrast between 'rhetoric' and 'reality', and centres on the paradoxical effect of party politics and party ideology on policy-making. The second is the issue of national conceptions of the legitimacy of state intervention, and hence the willingness of businessmen to accept the authority of the state.

In Europe and, to a lesser extent, in Japan and the United States, the motive force behind innovation in government–industry relations appears to be party-political. European political parties typically embody ideologies of political economy and of class interests, which are, of course, generalized and cross-sectoral. Much of the public debate about industrial policy is, therefore, about the freedom of private enterprise within a capitalist economy, and the extent to which the state should involve itself in production, in regulating production, or in supporting privately owned industry. Since European government is party government, policy towards industry is typically expressed in robust terms which lean towards conservative, market, or socialist, planning models of the proper use of state power. The ideological bases of party industrial policy are often deeply felt within parties and act as potent symbols, mobilizing both party loyalists and voters. The 'rhetoric' of party and governmental policy is one of the most visible expressions of government–industry relations and can be at odds with traditional 'industry cultures'. Thus, Labour Party policies in Britain, especially from 1974–6, Giscardian policies in France, and even declared LDP policies in Japan 'sound' anti-liberal, anti-statist, and anti-corporatist, respectively. There is, however, a distinction to be made between rhetoric and reality. If rhetoric refers to the policy pronouncements of politicians and ministers then it is a commonplace that such pronouncements often diverge from the reality of actual policy and administrative practice. The 'reality' of GIR reflects the interpenetration of government and industry, the importance of bureaucracy, and the observable pre-ponderance of administrative continuity.

Such is the size and scope of modern government that routinized involvement with industry is inescapable. Examples are legion and range from defence (Westland in Britain, SDI in the USA), through training and research sponsorship, to public procurement (of computers, ICL; or of gas turbines, Northern Engineering). In such a climate, it is inevitable that government makes concessions to industrial priorities, and that cor-porations take note of, and try to influence, government policy. There is, thus, a degree of convergence, in that government activity and transac-tions constitute a practical relationship with industry, regardless of ideology or tradition. These inescapable relationships are, of course, mediated through the bureaucracy.

Like nature, bureaucracy abhors a vacuum. Where the policies of government are overly rhetorical, as arguably they are in Britain,[33] they offer little guidance for the practical conduct of relations with industry. To fill the vacuum, administrators will develop and adapt a pragmatic relationship. Highly rhetorical policies, therefore, transfer responsibility to the bureaucracy, simply because they are, in themselves (and in the short term), non-operable. The government–industry relationship is, therefore, heavily influenced by bureaucratic culture and politics. If strong/weak state biases exist, they are perpetuated particularly by unreformed, unreconstructed bureaucracies. The outcome of an element of bureaucratic dominance, confirmed by several recent studies, is con-siderable continuity in the real world of government and industry. Even when the complexion of government changes radically, as with the elec-tions which brought in Mitterrand and Thatcher, and which confirmed Kohl's Chancellorship, in fact, the practical working out of programmes of activity show relatively little change. As British writers, such as Grant, Rose, and Gamble, have recently emphasized, 'when the rhetoric is stripped away the continuity of policies in most areas is what is striking'.[34] Thus, industrial support and subsidy continued throughout the first Thatcher government; subsidies actually increased in the FRG under the Kohl government; and nationalization in France under Mitterrand did little to socialize industry or to reduce managerial autonomy.

This is important in its implications. It suggests that patterns of government–industry relations are most resistant to political reform and to policy initiatives. It could be argued, on the one hand, that continuity confirms the importance of history and tradition, which are embedded in bureaucratic dominance of the government–industry relationship and in the nationwide 'industrial culture' of which Dyson speaks. On the other hand, it could be argued that politics and policies do make a difference in certain sectors, where governmental priorities are particularly clear and ministers persevere in their objectives. It would be difficult to deny that party rhetoric has been translated into reality in the British coal industry, following the 1984–5 miners' strike; or in the British telecommunications industry, following the privatization of BT. An alternative approach might, therefore, be to consider continuity as a product of inter-organizational networks, dominated by self-interested, élite 'coalitions', who resist change, but whose resistance can be overcome by persistent political initiative.

It would seem that the paradox of rhetoric and reality—namely that the more extreme the rhetoric the less change there is in reality—which has been noted increasingly in studies of industrial policy,[35] must be understood in terms of industrial culture, but *also* in terms of concrete and contemporary inter-organizational alliances, within given sectors, or over particular policies. While strong/weak state explanations are in danger of denying *any* role to party, network analysis can accomodate both the undeniable administrative continuity, and the equally undeniable occasions when continuity breaks down. At the same time, analysis at the sectoral level must recognize the institutionalized strength of administrative continuity. It is this continuity, with its connotations of 'industrial culture', which clearly resists the reformist initiatives of party government, and must provide a contextual element in a disaggregated sectoral analysis.

A second and indispensable element contributed by 'industrial culture' explanations of comparative government–industry relations concerns the legitimacy of state intervention. Industrial and, to a certain extent, macro-economic policy relies on the unconstrained, voluntary compliance of a multiplicity of actors within the market sector of the economy. Virtually all the other main areas of state activity, from law and order and social security to education and housing, are able to call upon mandatory legislation and administrative hierarchies in order to achieve (however imperfectly) their goals. Such uncomplicated mechanisms are not, however, available in the field of industrial policy, and are not the dominant element in the government–industry relationship. By definition, in a capitalist economy, decisions about products, prices, and investment are freely taken by autonomous actors in response to market signals. Government cannot, for ideological and technical reasons, systematically transgress that market logic, and hence, as Lindblom has incisively reaffirmed, business and businessmen are accorded a place of peculiar privilege within society.[36]

What this means is that government must ultimately rely on co-operative relations in its dealings with industry. It may have been over-emphasized, but it is no accident that commentators on Japan have put so much stress on 'consensus' between industrialists and officials; or that observers of the German economy have remarked upon the continuing philosophy of 'national economy', originated by Friedrich List. As with Weber's analysis of patterns of dominance within society, so any analysis of government relations with industry must confront the questions of the authority of the state. The strong state–weak state argument at least offers an explanation of why Japanese businessmen accept government inter-vention, and why American (and British) businessmen reject it. Thus, Vogel's outstanding analysis of 'why American businessmen distrust their state'[37] draws on the historical evolution of a philosophical position. As will be apparent from his chapter in this collection, Vogel has modified his position, while others, such as Blank, would argue that, in the British case, an industrial consensus for greater state leadership had evolved by the early sixties but was destroyed by mistaken policy choices.[38] Nevertheless, explanations of the willingness of business, or sections of industry, to accept the authority of the state must be con-structed at a national societal level. Such important features of the environment within which GIR operates cannot be induced from sectoral level analysis alone. They form an indispensible element in sectoral level 'rules of the game' and, in this area, industrial culture may be a valid con-cept to employ.

From State to Network

In the above sections we have sketched out a political science approach to comparative government–industry relations and we have illustrated its shortcomings using examples from earlier chapters. The strong/weak state model can also be expressed in terms of industrial culture, using that term in a specialized sense to denote attitudes to state intervention. This approach has not been adopted in earlier chapters and, indeed, at several points it is quite explicitly criticized as misleading. In order to develop systematic and empirically grounded comparative research, and to incorporate the sparse existing literature, we need a more sensitive and adaptable body of concepts. At the same time, the editors would reserve judgement on the eventual utility of some version of industrial culture as an explanatory concept. This substantial body of authoritative historical analysis may well be productively reintegrated into a multidimensional model of comparative analysis, at a later stage in the broader research project. In the analytical framework developed below, the concept of industrial culture re-emerges as one of the 'rules of the game', expressed as 'legitimacy of state action'. Thus, we would argue that industrial culture creates a background and represents one source of bias. It must be conceded at this stage, however, that such elegant and magisterial generalizations about strong states, weak states, and industrial culture prove lacking in explaining how the game is played and why these particular 'rules' are at times blatantly breached.

As outlined in Chapter 1, the research initiative incorporated a research framework in the form of a model of 'power dependence'. This offered, and continues to offer, a fruitful way of making sense of complexity and of organizing the empirical detail of government–industry relations. At the same time, it consists broadly of a set of hypotheses, concepts, and examples, which require adaptation to the peculiarities of government–industry relations. The framework has not readily been operationalized, partly because one of the basic conceptual tools, the concept of 'network', has been vaguely defined and elaborated. We go on, at this point, to illustrate the robustness and utility of power dependence within defined networks, as a conceptual tool, which can be used to interpret research findings.

Policy Community and Policy Network

The processes of public policy-making in Western liberal democracies have become more complex with the expansion of the scope of public policy, and the concomitant increase in the specialization and professionalisation of the functions of government. Organized interests have become not only more numerous and more influential: in many policy areas they are now more integrated into the policy process; so much so that neo-pluralist analysis of government–group relations has been challenged as inadequate to explain the phenomena of incorporation and self-regulation.

The existence of various types of policy sub-systems centred upon the functionally differentiated tasks of modern governments is not, of course, a recent phenomenon. 'Iron triangles' composed of interest groups, government agencies, and Congressional committees were identified in several policy areas in the US as early as the 1950s; Redford and James Q. Wilson were writing about the politics of function and 'sub-system' politics a decade later;[39] Wolfe, Lowi, and others described the growth of 'sponsored pluralism' and the 'franchise state'.[40] The transformation of iron triangles into issue networks was detected first by Heclo in 1978,[41] while, more recently, the revival of interest in corporatism has drawn attention to national tripartite bargaining between government and associational groups of capital and labour, and, at the sectoral level, meso-corporatist arrangements.[42]

While the relevance of the concepts of community and network to the study of these and other types of policy sub-systems seems obvious enough, there have, in fact, been very few sustained attempts to employ them analytically. Heclo and Wildavsky's pioneering study of the community life of expenditure controllers in the 'Whitehall village', and Richardson and Jordan's claim that policy communities were now the dominant feature of policy-making in Britain, elicited little immediate response from policy analysts.[43] More recently, Hayward and Hunter have drawn attention to the existence of several separate sub-communities within the national health community, some organized around clients (children, mentally ill and handicapped, and the elderly, for example); others, around policy issues, like abortion, alcoholism, and reorganization.[44]

Policy community is, of course, an integral component of Rhodes' power-dependence framework, and his own work on the national community of local authority associations is a convincing demonstration of the explanatory power of the concept.[45] He uses it explicitly to explain policy-making. He is, however, more concerned with the influence of the national community of local authority associations on a range of policy areas and issues, and much less concerned with the comparison of several policy communities operating in different policy areas in different countries. In undertaking the comparative study of networks which he urges, we depart in one important material respect from his conceptual schema. We have found it useful to make a categorical distinction between community and network. Whereas he defines, and uses, policy community as a type of policy network, we shall argue that the two are conceptually different and that the terms should be used to refer to different phenomena. We begin, therefore, with a reconstruction of those concepts.

Policy community

Community is not the same as network, although they are frequently used synonomously in the literature. One meaning of 'community' (OED) is 'common character; quality in common, commonness, agreement, identity'. Community is also used in the sense of a separate religious or civilian sect: 'a body of people organized into a political, municipal or social unit. Often applied to those members of a civil community who have certain circumstances of nativity, religion or pursuit, common to them, but not shared by those among whom they live'. This latter meaning of community, as a political or social unity, a group within the wider population, appears in one of the earliest formulations of the concept, in F. G. Bailey's *Strategems and Spoils*.[47] W. J. M. Mackenzie picked up and used his concept of 'caste community', vertically interdependent through different levels of the Indian state, to develop concepts of 'policy arena or community', giving as examples the policy arenas of health service and agriculture, which he rightly saw not as an example of pressure-group lobbying, but clientelistic politics in a discrete policy arena.[48] At roughly the same time, Helco and Wildavsky were using the concept of 'community' to distinguish the 'caste' of expenditure controllers in the large Whitehall population.[49] Both Wildavsky and Mackenzie use the market and market-place behaviour as an idiom or analogy for structuring political sub-systems; and both borrow from 'transactional theory'. Here, the connection leads back to the development of resource-exchange and inter-governmental analysis, and the work of Benson and Deil Wright in the US and Theonig in France, from all of whom (and others) Rhodes has drawn, in the development of his power-dependent framework.

The concept of community, in the sense of political or social unity, qualities in common, agreement, identity, was thereafter employed frequently in writing about policy-making and the policy process, although its use was mainly as a metaphor for a policy sub-system, rather than as a tool of analysis. Repeatedly in the literature we find references to an 'education policy community', a 'transport policy community', a 'health services policy community', and so on.[50] This designation is helpful only at a very simple level of categorization to distinguish one broad policy sub-system from another.

The use of community in this very broad sense is of very little help in the analysis of the policy process. This is obvious enough once we begin to 'unpack' the term 'industry', bearing in mind the definition of community given above. Industry is an abstraction, convenient shorthand for a variety of different activities, manufacturing, service, construction, and so on. Within these broad categories, activities can be further divided according to product, service, technology, market, employment. At the most general level, the term 'industrial policy community' should encompass all those who own, manage, finance, and work in those industrial units, together with those whose interests are affected by the activities of those units—consumers and clients, for example—and those individuals whose organizations have a direct interest in, or responsibility for, the activities of those units and their consumers and clients, that is to say, governmental and quasi-governmental agencies of all kinds, at the supra-national, national, and sub-national levels. This 'population' of potential actors can be extended still further by the inclusion of those organizations which have, or take, an interest in the activities of the industrial units, such as Parliament, political parties, the media, analysts. While this large population of actors and potential actors share a common interest in industrial policy, and may contribute to the policy process on a regular or irregular basis, it is suggested that it would be better to reserve the term 'community' for a more disaggregated policy sub-system. The actors and potential actors comprising the population described above could be distinguished from those in other policy areas by adopting the term 'universe'. We could then refer to the existence of an industrial policy universe, an educational policy universe, and so on. Some of their memberships would, of course, overlap.

We now need to unwrap further the concept of policy area, before we can employ the concept of policy community. The disaggregation of industry takes us first to manufacturing, service, and so on, and then to sector. This disaggregation is not without problems of definition, as Cawson, Grant, and others have pointed out.[51] In the UK, the Standard Industrial Classification is not a wholly reliable guide to the identification of parts of industry which have 'common qualities' of product or service or technology or size of unit. There have always been 'boundary' problems, to which are now added the newer ones posed by the new hi-tech industries and new technologies, which do not fit easily or wholly into the old categories: telecommunications, computer hardware and software, genetic engineering, biotechnology. There are also problems of compatability between one country and other. However, for our purposes, this is not an insuperable difficulty because, it is argued, the level of the 'sector' is too broad for the purpose of analysing and comparing structures of dependent relationships. It is true that a policy community may well be found at the sectoral level. For example, from the industrial policy universe it will be possible to identify those actors and potential actors who share a common interest in the activities of the chemical industry, or in pharmaceuticals, or telecommunications. We may then speak of a chemical industry policy community. And it is sometimes the case that policy is made which affects the interests of the whole of the chemical industry policy community. More often, however, it is made and carried out at the sub-sectoral level. It is here that we find smaller, self-contained policy communities whose members share an interest in a part of the chemical industry, or a part of pharmaceuticals. The membership of each policy community is defined by the commonality of product or products, service or range of services, a technology or range of technologies, a market, size of 'batch', and so on. We refer to this common characteristic as the *policy focus*.

Policy network

We can now move from policy community to policy network. Policy community identifies those actors and potential actors drawn from the policy universe who share a common policy focus. Network is the linking process within a policy community or between two or more communities. The origins of policy network can be traced to the work of sociologists and social anthropologists with social network analysis. Until the 1970s, like 'community', 'network' was used mainly as an image or rhetorical device. Since then, social network analysis has developed to the point where it has its own journal and international society.

Scott and Griff define social network analysis as more than a method, metaphor, or set of concepts: 'it is a broad perspective on the analysis of social relations', whose basic principle is that 'agents are significantly connected to others, each of whom has similar connections to further agents.'[52] The analysis and understanding of a network is concerned with the 'features of the network as a whole'. The properties of the network are not reducible to those of individual actors. The network is the *outcome* of their combined actions.

These defining characteristics of social network are a useful starting-point for the analysis of the structures of dependent relationships in policy sub-systems. We have suggested that policy community can be used to identify those actors and potential actors, drawn from the policy universe, who share a common policy focus. It is now argued that those actors will 'transact' with each other, and (in our terms) exchange resources. Network is the linking process, the outcome of those exchanges, within a policy community or between a number of policy communities. A policy network is 'a complex of organisations connected to each other by resource dependencies and distinguished from other complexes by breaks in the structure of resource dependencies'.[53] A policy network may evolve or be constituted around a discrete policy issue or problem, a set of related issues (e.g. export promotion, health and safety), or around a policy process, such as budgeting or auditing or planning. The members of a network may be drawn from one policy community or several.

It is not necessary, for our purposes, to conduct social network analysis, or to establish mathematically the network position of individual actors, or the structural features of the network as a whole; we do not need to measure the cohesiveness of a network by 'connectivity' and 'density'. The utility of the concept of network for our purposes is that it helps to identify the existence of policy networks, and to characterize them in terms which will permit a useful and valid comparison between sectors and countries.

We can now summarize the different concepts:

(i) *Policy area or function* refers to discrete areas of government activity (industry, education, transport, housing, etc.) or functions of government (expenditure control, audit, establishments);

(ii) *Policy universe* refers to all actors or potential actors with a direct or indirect interest in a policy area or function (e.g. industrial policy universe);

(iii) *Policy community* refers to a group of actors or potential actors drawn from the policy universe whose community membership is defined by a common *policy focus*;

(iv) *Policy focus* is identified by such qualities as product, service, technology, market, size of firm, 'batch';

(v) *Policy network* describes the general properties of the processes by which members of one or more policy communities interact in a structure of dependent relationships;

(vi) *Policy issues* and *policy functions* provide the occasion for a policy network.

In Table 12.2 we show the relationships between policy levels and policy actors, and provide some examples of policy communities and policy networks in the chemicals industry in the UK.

From this it will be clear that we have used policy community and

Table 12.2 Policy Community and Policy Network

Policy Level		Policy Actors
Policy area	Industry, Education, Transport, Health, etc.	Policy universe
Policy sector	Chemicals, Telecommunications, Foundries, etc.	
Policy sub-sector (focus)	Basic chemicals, Pharmaceuticals, Agri-chemicals, Paints, Soaps & Toiletries	Policy communities
Policy issue	e.g. Health & Safety, R. & D., 'Over-capacity' → e.g. Drug Licensing, Company Profits, 'Limited List'	Policy networks

policy network to describe different phenomena. In so doing we depart significantly from Rhodes' definition and use of policy community as one type of policy network, one characterized by a high level of integration. Because we find his analysis generally so persuasive, we need to make explicit our reasons from departing from it in this respect. By using policy community to refer to groups of actors who share a common interest or identity, by virtue of their product or service or manufacturing process or technology or market, we are better able to make distinctions, not only between those groups of actors whose differences are obvious enough at the sectoral level, but also between groups of actors *within* those broad sectoral categories. Policy community thus defined provides us with a useful means of categorizing different types of groups of actors at the policy sector level—for example, chemicals or foundries—and at the policy sub-sectoral level—for example, agri-chemicals, paints, pharmaceuticals, soap and toiletries. By distinguishing community from network we are able to explore, and account for, the number and different types of policy communities and policy networks. It also enables us to accommodate, within the analysis, policy communities which generate no easily identifiable policy network, as seems to be the case with the UK foundries industry.[54]

The distinction we made between community and network has three further advantages. First, it enables us to identify those members of a policy community who are excluded from a policy network. Secondly, because all policy issues, problems, and processes are not necessarily handled by one policy network, we are able to compare the membership of networks drawn from the same policy community. Thirdly, it admits of the possibility that the members of a policy network may be drawn from different policy communities, within the same policy area (e.g., basic chemicals and agri-chemicals), or even from different policy areas (e.g. industry and education).

In comparing and classifying policy networks, we follow Rhodes, who suggests that their structures will vary along five key dimensions: the interests of the members of the network, the membership, the extent of members' interdependence, the extent to which the network is isolated from other networks, and the variations in the distribution of resources between the members. The structures of policy networks can then be compared according to the level of their integration. On a simple 'high-low' scale, those which are highly integrated are characterized by the stability of the relationships of their members, the continuity of a highly restrictive membership, the interdependence within the network, based on the members' shared responsibility for the delivery of a service, and the insulation from other networks. Those network structures which are weakly integrated tend to have a much larger number of members with a limited degree of organizational interdependence; they are loose, atomistic, and often inchoate structures.

The level of integration is also influenced by the role played by 'professionals' within the network. Where that role is a pre-eminent and dominating one, Rhodes uses the term 'professionalised network' to distinguish it from other types. His examples include the medical profession in the UK National Health Service, water engineers in the water service, and highway engineers in road transport policy. We would argue that these are examples of policy communities, each of which may have one or more policy networks, handling separately an issue or range of issues. Thus, the National Health Service is not one policy network, but a policy community with several policy networks for, for example, the family doctor service, and for mental health, hospital, and maternity services. Whether or not these networks are professionalized will depend on the extent to which the medical profession, or parts of it, has a dominant role in each.

A rather different kind of professionalized network was identified by Heclo and Wildavsky in their account of the community of expenditure controllers in Whitehall. They describe and characterize the community in terms of 'kinship', 'culture', and 'shared values'. We would argue that the characteristics attributed to the community of expenditure controllers are those associated with professionals. Their pre-eminent and dominant role in the structure of dependent relationships is an example of a professionalized policy network. Similar professionalized networks might be found elsewhere in Whitehall, in the audit policy community, and in the community of personnel managers, for example.

Similar characteristics of kinship, culture, and shared values may be found in other examples of networks dominated by professionals. But, as Rhodes and Dunleavy have pointed out, the influence of professionals is not limited to their institutionalization in policy networks.[55] Ideological influence can exert a major effect on policy-making. Although they are here discussing the relationships between national and sub-national units of government, what they say has relevance for policy networks generally. A 'national level ideology'—a united 'view of the world' based on common ideas, values, and knowledge—may not only set the parameters to the policy-making in the networks of policy communities, but also serve as a means to the integration of those networks. We would expect, therefore, that policy networks dominated by professionals, through their institutionalization and ideological influence, will have a high level of integration.

At this stage in the research programme, the empirical data enables us to do no more than indicate broadly how the concepts of community and network might be used to analyse and compare different industrial policy sectors. For example, we can distinguish at least five policy communities in the UK chemicals industry, each with a different policy focus. Besides a core policy community, organized around the production of basic industrial chemicals, there are separate policy communities for pharmaceuticals, agri-chemicals, paints, and soap and toiletries preparations. In the UK foundries industry, there is a still larger number of policy communities, reflecting sharp differences in product, technology, and market. The companies which comprise the industry have very little in common, apart from the process or technique of metal casting. By contrast, the West German foundries industry is much more cohesive, integrated, and organizationally tightly structured. There is one policy community for the whole industry.

The members of these and other policy communities are joined in several different structures of dependent relationships—policy networks. Some are highly integrated like those in the pharmaceuticals industry, which handle, in separate networks, the policy issues of drug-licensing, price regulation, and cost-containment; others, as in the foundries industry, are weakly integrated. In those policy networks with a high level of integration, memberships tend to be exclusive, closed rather than open, and continous. Some members of the policy community will be excluded. The evidence, so far, suggests that access to a policy network is normally controlled by the dominant government agency, although the exclusion of certain categories of participants may be the condition of another's participation. In the policy sectors we have studied, trade unions are rarely represented; Parliament and its committees, and non-industrial interest groups are invariably excluded. The absence of stable policy networks in the UK foundries industry is partly the result of the number, fragmentation, and competition of the representative associations which comprise the several policy communities. There are six major trade associations, four research associations, and nine trade unions. By comparison, the West German foundries industry has two trade associations, which work closely together, one research association, and one trade union. The two Larzard schemes for the rationalization of the UK foundries industry are interesting examples of attempts to constitute policy networks by restricting the membership to a handful of companies and one trade association. However, a similar attempt to restructure the automative sector of the industry, by constituting a policy network with a restricted membership centred upon a break-away trade association, was unsuccessful.

Policy networks also vary with the type and substance of the policy issue. The issues of drug-licensing and drug-costs are handled by two separate networks in the UK, although some members are common to both. In the chemical industry, there are separate networks for health and safety issues, and for R. & D. The scope of the policy agenda of a network is a critical factor. While government agencies have greater resources with which to influence the agenda of policy issues—the threat of coercive action, for example—the evolution and the continued stable existence of a network is determined, to a great extent, by the skill with which other key members are able to manipulate and control the agenda of policy issues. What is kept off the agenda may be as important as what is handled by the network. The ABPI, historically with a monopoly representation of manufacturers' interests, has been conspicuously successful in its control of the policy agenda by deflecting attention away from the controversial and divisive issue of the therapeutic efficacy of drugs and towards the less contentious issue of clinical trials. The mode and manner of the articulation of an issue is also important in agenda-control. The issue of the regulation of the prices of individual drugs has been kept off the agenda by the articulation of that issue as one of regulating the level of company profits through return on investment, rather than the prices of products. In West Germany, cost-cutting proposals have been kept off the agenda, delayed, or marginalized, less by the manipulative skills of the pharmaceutical industry or its representative associations, than by fragmentation of the health-care community, and the exploitation of its political resources by a key governmental player, the FDP.

Policy networks can also be distinguished by the degree of their insulation from each other. Different parts of the same governmental agency may belong to separate networks; a trade association or professional organization may be a member of one network within the community but not another. Policy networks differ, also, in the extent of the stability of the structures of dependent relationships. As patterns of social networks are 'constantly subject to the possibility of structural transformation', policy networks will change over time. In periods of 'policy turbulence' they will be subject to short-term 'catastrophic discontinuities', such as that initiated by the issue of the 'limited list' or the revocation of drug-licences without consultation.

Policy network: 'rules of the game'

It is a premiss of the framework for the analysis of sectoral policies that the relationships between actors in structures of dependent relationships are predicated upon the acceptance of 'rules of the game'. These rules set limits to the process of exchange (the interactions). To understand how and why a policy network operates, it is necessary to understand the 'unwritten constitution', which guides the behaviour of the actors towards each other and influences the strategic deployment of their resources. Some of the rules can be distinguished by what members say or write or believe the rules to be. Other rules can be inferred from their conduct to each other. In his study of the national community of local government associations, Rhodes lists eleven rules of the game, among them: pragmatism, consensus, fairness, accommodation, secrecy, trust, the 'depoliticization of issues', and the 'right to govern' of the central government.[56] Some of these are common to other studies of networks and to our own sector studies.[57]

One important rule of the game is mutuality. Members of networks accept and expect that mutual advantages and benefits will result from their participation in the network. 'By deliberate mutual adjustments in their expectations and successive iterations of their exchanges, these privileged actors may avoid the temptation to exploit momentary positional advantages to the maximum and the fate of landing in the worst possible outcome in which all lose.'[58] Policy issues are handled within the policy network, on the basis of trust and a respect for confidence. Undertakings given by members of the network, or commitments entered into informally are customarily honoured. The social memory of the network exercises a self-discipline. Secondly, there is not only a willingness to consult informally, but an expectation of consultation. On this basis, and that of a respect for confidence, members of a network are prepared to exchange ideas or discuss future policies, or make available to each other information which would be regarded as sensitive or even damaging in the public domain. The importance of this rule is most obviously demonstrated when it has been broken: when, for example, the DHSS introduces the limited list without prior consultation. Thirdly, there is an emphasis on informality. This is, perhaps, more characteristic of the UK policy sectors studied so far, and may reflect a difference in legal and administrative culture. In a different legal tradition—in West Germany, for example—the conduct of a policy network may be much more formally determined. Fourthly, there are rules about the articulation of policy issues in an acceptable mode and language. Fifthly, there are rules about the use of legal remedy. For example, compare the policy networks for handling the licensing of drugs in the UK and West Germany. In the former, pharmaceutical companies eschew legal challenge in the courts, while in West Germany the legal and administrative culture encourages an adversarialist approach, and legal challenge to the licensing authority is customary, and part of the process by which policy is shaped and implemented. There are also rules about the legitimacy of state action: what members of a network consider acceptable or unacceptable use of the legitimate authority possessed by governmental agencies. Thus, a network may be constituted on the basis of the mutual acceptance of tacit limits to the use of constitutional coercive authority. Its use in an unacceptable way may provoke a 'catastrophic discontinuity'. For example, while members of the UK policy network for handling the issue of company profits in the pharmaceutical industry could not deny the government's constitutional authority to regulate the prices of drugs, the rule of the game governing the behaviour of the members of the network to each other was that the DHSS did not attempt to do this. There was a 'reluctance to exercise legal controls at the level of the individual firm or product as long as industry's overall performance seemed reasonable.'[59]

As Rhodes notes in his study of inter-governmental relations, such rules of the game set only approximate limits to the discretionary behaviour of the participants in policy networks.[60] Rules are not immutable; some may be discarded and replaced by others. Further research at the sectoral level should reveal the existence or absence of such rules; how they have evolved and are evolving; to what extent they are observed, and in what circumstances and why they are broken or discarded. It may also tell us whether rules of the game are affected by changes in government, and different political ideologies.

We have argued that empirical investigation at the sectoral and sub-sectoral levels of industry reveals not one but a variety of policy sub-systems. By using the concepts of policy community and policy network, these policy sub-systems can be described, classified, and compared. Thus, we can identify policy communities, at the sectoral and sub-sectoral levels, which vary in size, composition, interests (policy focus), and homogeneity. Some are small, exclusive, and tightly knit; in others, the membership is large, inclusive, and fragmented. Some, but not all, policy communities have clearly identifiable policy networks, whose characteristics can be described and compared. With the accumulation of more empirical data, we shall be able to make more extensive comparisons of types of network according to their degree of interdependence, both sectorally and cross-nationally.

More tentatively, it may prove possible, subsequently, to extend the scope of analysis by attempting to compare the modes of interaction of different policy sub-systems. Any such attempt would have to accommodate the dynamic element in policy-making, and provide for the likelihood that interactions in the structures of dependent relationships will change over time, and vary between one policy issue and another. Moreover, the process of policy-making subsumes a variety of activities, for example, those of policy initiation, articulation, and legitimation, as well as those through which policy is carried out, monitored, evaluated, and reviewed. The policy issue on the agenda of a policy sub-system may entail one or several of those activities.

Some of the factors which shape the mode of interaction within policy sub-systems include the rules of the game and, within the context of those rules, the strategies employed by the key members in their exchanges with each other (for example, direction, consultation, bargaining, confrontation). Other factors are the homogeneity, integration, and professionalization of networks. Analysis of the principal strategies employed by key participants, of the rules of the game, as well as the level of integration of policy networks, may help to explain how and why policy issues are handled and determined in one way rather than another, in different policy sectors and in different countries. It might then prove possible to construct from the data a typology of modes of interaction which incorporated classical and neoclassical pluralist explanations, at one end of a spectrum of government-group relations, through neo- and meso-corporatist, to *étatisme* at the other.

At this stage, however, perhaps the most we can do is to re-emphasize the breadth and complexity of government–industry relations and the paucity of detailed work which could provide the raw material for model building and typology construction. The discussion in this chapter of international, inter-sectoral, and inter-network comparison of government–industry relationships indicates some possible areas for future theoretical development. We believe the network analysis within a framework of power-dependence has much to offer. We are also satisfied that work now underway will explore the potential of these theoretical possibilities over the next three years. The jury is still out and, although we are assured of a verdict, it will still be some time in coming.

Comparison for What?

The opening paragraphs of this chapter placed the study of government–industry relations in the context of wider questions of political economy. It was also pointed out that the research reflected in this book is primarily concerned with an examination of processes; at this stage we are not offering judgements about the outcomes and the effectiveness of the various configurations of government–industry relations. We should, however, underscore the fact that evaluation of government–industry relations is important and is, potentially, a highly normative undertaking. Government–industry relations is ultimately concerned with the size and distribution of economic benefits within society, and has profound implications for social policies. Judgements on such issues are inevitably value-orientated, as are conclusions about the control and accountability of industry itself. On the whole, normative issues have been skirted round in earlier chapters. There is, however, an implied normative orientation which should be emphasized, if only to allow for the consideration of alternative perspectives.

There is a tendency—it may also be a danger—of assuming that given patterns of government–industry relations are desirable if they appear to contibute towards industrial growth. If they facilitate industrial adaptation, or promote international competitiveness, then such relationships are typically regarded as functional, effective, and 'good'. This orientation is almost inescapable in comparative government–industry relations, where much of the momentum behind comparison is to reveal the 'secrets' of more successful industrial states, especially West Germany and Japan. Hence, the chapters by Grant, Paterson, and Whitston, by Appleby and Bessant, and by Boyd each share a more-or-less submerged theme of seeking to explain the apparent success of West Germany and Japan. Other academic writers are frequently less circumspect. The concept of 'corporatism', in particular, seems to invite judgements on desirable organizational forms. Hence Streeck argues that 'economies or industries with a corporatist system of interest intermediation can be expected to be more efficient',[61] and Atkinson and Coleman declare that 'corporatism is the arrangement most conducive to the successful pursuit of industrial policy'.[62] We would feel far more hesitant in coming to such assertive conclusions.

While accepting the importance of industrial growth, we would resist the tendency to sanctify it as an exclusive subject for study or criterion for evaluation. Government–industry relations must be evaluated in terms, also, of the distribution of economic benefits, the imposition of social costs, the nature of production as well as the quantity, and in terms, also, of more intangible qualities, such as political tolerance, industrial accountability, and regime stability. Our emphasis has been on the simple identification of government–industry relationships, how they work, what goals they define and pursue, and how effective the relationships are in achieving their own self-defined objectives. It would, however, be difficult, and undesirable, to avoid evaluating government–industry relations by reference to more narrow criteria—such as the degree of industrial democracy, or the tendency to create social externalities, like pollution—or in relation to wider criteria—such as the extent of unemployment or the impact of new technology on social relations. The study of comparative government–industry relations should be capable of embracing both narrower and wider normative evaluations. Indeed, our expectation is that, as understanding and conceptualization of government–industry relations increases in sophistication, such evaluations will be facilitated. We anticipate that explanations which identify the dynamics and mechanics of the relationships will come to displace those present explanations which stress the simple domination of individual actors, and which attach overwhelming explanatory weight to single processes, institutions, or ideologies. A better understanding of government–industry relationships should lead to an analysis of the dynamics of the relationship and hence identify the opportunities for, and resistance to, reform. This should allow those who are dissatisfied with present relationships to assess the possibilities for change. That, at least, is our hope.

Notes

1. A. Smith, *The Wealth of Nations* (Harmondsworth: Penguin, 1970: first publ. 1776), p. 446.
2. J. Schumpeter, *Capitalism, Socialism and Democracy*, 3rd edn. (London: Allen & Unwin, 1950).
3. C. Lindblom, *Politics and Markets: The World's Political-Economic Systems* (New York: Basic Books, 1977).

4. See, D. Steel, 'Review Article: Government and Industry in Britain', *British Journal of Political Science* 12 (1983), pp. 449–503; S. Young, *An Annotated Bibliography on Relations Between Government and Industry in Britain 1960–82*, 2 vols. (London: ESRC, 1984); R. Boyd, *Government Industry Relations in Japan: A Review of the Literature* (London: ESRC, 1986); S. Wilks, 'Review Article: Government–Industry Relations', *Policy and Politics* Autumn (1986).

5. There are, of course, significant earlier studies in this area, our argument is simply that there has been no sustained focus. See, for instance, J. Grove, *Government and Industry in Britain* (London: Longman, 1962); or D. Hague, W. Mackenzie, and A. Barker (eds.), *Public Policy and Private Interests: The Institutions of Compromise* (London: Macmillan, 1975).

6. For surveys see L. Panitch, 'Recent theorisation of corporatism: reflections on a growth industry', *British Journal of Sociology* 31 (1980), pp. 159–87; and the chapters by Grant and by Schmitter in W. Grant (ed.), *The Political Economy of Corporatism* (London: Macmillan, 1985). For more empirically orientated collections see, G. Lehmbruch and P. Schmitter (eds.), *Patterns of Corporatist Policy Making* (London: Sage, 1982); A. Cawson (ed.), *Organised Interests and the State: Studies in Meso-Corporatism* (London: Sage, 1985); Streeck and P. Schmitter (eds.), *Private Interest Government: Beyond Market and State* (London: Sage, 1985).

7. See, for instance, OECD, *Transparency for Positive Adjustment: Identifying and Evaluating Government Intervention* (Paris: OECD, 1983); the growth in American interest is equally striking, see W. Hudson, 'The Feasibility of a Comprehensive US Industrial Policy', *Political Science Quarterly* 100 (1985), pp. 461–78; C. Barfield and W. Schambra (eds.), *The Politics of Industrial Policy* (Washington DC: American Enterprise Institute, 1986).

8. There is also, of course, the work inspired by O'Conner, and writers of the Frankfurt school, such as Offe and Habermas. But these analyses of the resilience of the capitalist system are considerably broader than our immediate concern. See, for instance, J. Thompson and D. Held (eds.), *Habermas: Critical Debates* (London: Macmillan, 1982).

9. For two collections which offer generalized support, see P. Katzenstein (ed.), *Between Power and Plenty: Foreign Economic Policies of Advanced Industrial States* (Cambridge Mass. Harvard University Press, 1978); and K. Dyson and S. Wilks (eds.), *Industrial Crisis: A Comparative Study of the State and Industry* paperback edition (Oxford: Basil Blackwell, 1985).

10. An excellent scare-mongering example in this vein is M. Wolf, *The Japanese Conspiracy* (Sevenoaks: New English Library, 1984); a more academic study that also leans dangerously towards caricature is G. Wilson, *Business and Politics: A Comparative Introduction* (London: Macmillan, 1985).

11. K. Dyson, 'The Cultural, Ideological and Structural Context' in K. Dyson and S. Wilks (eds.), op. cit. (n. 9), p. 31.

12. For a full development of this distinction, see K. Dyson, *The State Tradition*

in West Europe (Oxford: Martin Robertson, 1980). See also P. Birnbaum, 'The State Versus Corporatism', *Politics and Society* 11 (1982), pp. 477–501; and B. Badie and P. Birnbaum, *The Sociology of the State* (Chicago: University of Chicago Press, 1983).

13. K. Dyson, 'The Cultural, Ideological and Structural Context' in op. cit. (n. 9), p. 31.

14. A. Gerschenkron, *Economic Backwardness in Historical Perspective* (Cambridge, Mass.: Harvard University Press, 1962); J. Armstrong, *The European Administrative Elite* (Princeton, NJ: Princeton University Press, 1973); C. Trebilcock, *The Industrialisation of the Continental Powers 1780–1914* (London: Longman, 1981).

15. K. Dyson, 'The Cultural, Ideological and Structural Context' in op. cit. (n. 9), p. 42.

16. B. Chapman, *British Government Observed* (London: Allen & Unwin, 1963), p. 61.

17. A. Shonfield, *Modern Capitalism* (London: OUP, 1965).

18. A. Gamble, *Britain in Decline*, 2nd edn. (London: Macmillan, 1985); see also T. Nairn, 'The Twilight of the British State', *New Left Review* 15 (1977), and P. Anderson, *Lineages of the Absolutist State* (London: New Left Books, 1974), Chapter 5.

19. A. Gamble, op. cit. (n. 18), p. 85.

20. A theme taken up very directly in P. Birnbaum, op. cit. (n. 12), especially pp. 495–6.

21. P. Katzenstein (ed.), op. cit. (n. 9).

22. P. Katzenstein, 'Introduction: Domestic and International Forces and Strategies of Foreign Economic Policy' in P. Katzenstein (ed.), ibid., p. 17.

23. P. Katzenstein, 'Conclusion: Domestic Structures and Strategies of Foreign Economic Policy', in ibid., p. 323.

24. Loc. cit.

25. S. Krasner, 'United States Commercial and Monetary Policy', in ibid., pp. 57, 60–61.

26. A. Shonfield, op. cit. (n. 17), p. 293.

27. P. Katzenstein, 'Conclusion . . .', op. cit. (n. 9), p. 329.

28. J. Zysman, *Goverments, Markets and Growth: Financial Systems and the Politics of Industrial Change* (Oxford: Martin Robertson, 1983), pp. 56 and 76.

29. Ibid., pp. 91–4.

30. Ibid., pp. 295–9 and pp. 347–9, n. 23.

31. Ibid, p. 105.

32. W. Grant, 'The Overcapacity Problem in the European Petrochemicals Industry', unpublished working paper, 1985.

33. See S. Wilks, *Industrial Policy and the Motor Industry*, (Manchester: University Press, 1984), Chapter 3; S. Wilks 'Conservative Industrial Policy 1979–83' in P. Jackson (ed.), *Implementing Government Policy Initia-*

tives: The Thatcher Administration 1979–83 (London: RIPA, 1985) and S.
Wilks, 'Has the State Abandoned British Industry?', *Parliamentary Affairs*
39 (January 1986), pp. 312–46.

34. A. Gamble and S. Walkland *The British Party System and Economic Policy
1945–83* (Oxford: Clarendon Press, 1984), p. 176. See also W. Grant, *The
Political Economy of Industrial Policy* (London: Butterworths, 1982),
pp. 8–9; R. Rose, *Do Parties Make a Difference?*, 2nd edn. (London;
Macmillan, 1984).

35. See S. Wilks, *Industrial Policy*, and S. Wilks, 'Conservative Industrial
Policy . . .', both cited in n. 33.

36. C. Lindblom, op. cit. (n. 3), p. 175.

37. D. Vogel, 'Why Businessmen Distrust Their State: The Political Consciousness of American Corporate Executives', *British Journal of Political
Science* 8: 1 (1978).

38. S. Blank, 'Britain: The Politics of Foreign Economic Policy, The Domestic
Economy, and the Problem of Pluralist Stagnation', in P. Katzenstein (ed.),
op. cit. (n. 9).

39. E. Redford *Democracy in the Administrative State*, (Oxford: OUP, 1969);
James Q. Wilson, *City Politics and Public Policy* (New York: John Wiley,
1968).

40. A. Wolfe, *The Limits of Legitimacy* (New York: The Free Press, 1977);
T. Lowi, *The End of Liberalism*, 2nd edn. (New York: W. W. Norton,
1979).

41. H. Heclo, 'Issue Networks and the Executive Establishment' in A. King
(ed.), *The New American Political System* (Washington: American Enterprise Inc., 1978).

42. A. Cawson (ed.), op. cit. (n. 6).

43. H. Heclo and A. Wildavsky, *The Private Government of Public Money*
(London: Macmillan, 1974); J. J. Richardson and A. G. Jordan, *Governing
Under Pressure* (Oxford: Martin Robertson, 1979).

44. S. Hayward & A. Hunter, 'Consultative Processes in Health Policy in the
United Kingdom: A View from the Centre', *Public Administration* 69
(1982), pp. 143–62.

45. R. A. W. Rhodes, *The National World of Local Government* (London:
Macmillan, 1986).

46. R. A. W. Rhodes, 'Power-Dependence, Policy Communities and Inter-
Governmental Networks', *Public Administration Bulletin* 49 (1985),
pp. 4–31. This has a very full list of references to the literature on
community and network.

47. F. G. Bailey, *Strategems and Spoils* (Oxford: Blackwell, 1969).

48. W. J. M. Mackenzie, *Power, Violence and Decision* (Harmondsworth:
Penguin, 1976).

49. There are, of course, many other elements and diverse strands contributing
to the conceptualization in sociology and political science of social and poli-

tical communities, most notably the work of Banfield in the US, and Stacey and Mitchell in the UK.

50. See for example, L. J. Sharpe, 'Central Co-ordination and the Policy Network', *Political Studies* XXXIII (1985).

51. A. Cawson (ed.), op. cit. (n. 6); W. Grant (ed.), op. cit. (n. 6).

52 J. Scott and C. Griff. *Directors of Industry: The British Corporate Network 1904–1976* (Oxford: Polity Press, 1984).

53. J. K. Benson, 'Networks and Policy Sectors: A Framework for Extending Interorganisational Analysis' in D. Rogers and D. Whitten (eds.), *Interorganisational Coordination* (Ames Iowa: Iowa State University Press, 1982).

54. In a formal sense, a social network exists if the actors merely have knowledge of each other. Strictly speaking, therefore, a policy community implies a policy network, however apparently tenuous it appears to be. To insist too rigorously on this risks the conflation of the two terms, and the loss of some useful practical advantages to which we allude.

55. R. A. W. Rhodes, 'Power-Dependence, Policy Community and Inter-Governmental Networks', op. cit. (n. 46); P. Dunleavy, 'Professions and Policy Change: Notes Towards a Model of Ideological Corporation', *Public Administration Bulletin* 36 (1981), pp. 3–16.

56. R. A. W. Rhodes, *The National World Of Local Government*, op. cit. (n. 45).

57. Richardson and Jordan, op. cit. (n. 43); Heclo and Wildavsky, op. cit. (n. 43); A. L. Lijphart, *The Politics of Accommodation: Pluralism and Democracy in the Networks* (California: University Press, 1968).

58. P. C. Schmitter, 'Neo-Corporatism and the State' in W. Grant (ed.), *The Political Economy of Corporatism*, op. cit. (n. 6).

59. L. Hancher and M. Ruete, 'Legal Administrative Culture as Policy Determinants', paper presented at ESRC Conference on Government–Industry Relations, Trinity Hall, Cambridge, December 1985, p. 22.

60. R. A. W. Rhodes, *The National World of Local Government*, op. cit. (n. 45).

61. W. Streeck, *Industrial Relations in West Germany* (London: Heinemann, 1984), p. 149.

62. M. Atkinson and W. Coleman 'Corporatism and Industrial Policy' in A. Cawson (ed.), op. cit. (n. 6), p. 23.